A Popular History of Ireland
from the Earliest
Period to the Emancipation of the Catholics

In Two Volumes

Volume II

Thomas D'Arcy McGee

Contents

BOOK VIII. THE ERA OF THE REFORMATION. 7
CHAPTER IV. 7
CHAPTER V. 16
CHAPTER VI. 23
CHAPTER VII. 29
CHAPTER VIII. 37
CHAPTER IX. 46
CHAPTER X. 54
CHAPTER XI. 65
CHAPTER XII. 71
BOOK IX. FROM THE ACCESSION OF JAMES I ....
   TILL THE DEATH OF CROMWELL. 77
CHAPTER I. 77
CHAPTER II. 87
CHAPTER III. 96
CHAPTER IV. 104
CHAPTER V. 113
CHAPTER VI. 121
CHAPTER VII. 127
CHAPTER VIII. 133
CHAPTER IX. 140
CHAPTER X. 147
CHAPTER XI. 151
CHAPTER XII. 156
BOOK X. FROM THE RESTORATION OF CHARLES II. ....
   TO THE ACCESSION OF GEORGE I. 161
CHAPTER I. 161
CHAPTER II. 167
CHAPTER III. 171
CHAPTER IV. 177
CHAPTER V. 182
CHAPTER VI. 186
CHAPTER VII. 191
CHAPTER VIII. 197
CHAPTER IX. 200
CHAPTER X. 205
CHAPTER XI. 212
CHAPTER XII. 217
BOOK XI. FROM THE ACCESSION OF GEORGE I. ....
   TO THE LEGISLATIVE UNION OF GREAT BRITAIN AND IRELAND. 220

CHAPTER I. 220
CHAPTER II. 226
CHAPTER III. 231
CHAPTER IV. 237
CHAPTER V. 243
CHAPTER VI. 247
CHAPTER VII. 251
CHAPTER VIII. 256
CHAPTER IX. 261
CHAPTER X. 269
CHAPTER XI. 276
CHAPTER XII. 283
CHAPTER XIII. 291
CHAPTER XIV. 296
CHAPTER XV. 302
CHAPTER XVI. 311
CHAPTER XVII. 323
CHAPTER XVIII. 333
CHAPTER XIX. 345
BOOK XII. FROM THE UNION OF GREAT BRITAIN ....
   AND IRELAND TO THE EMANCIPATION OF THE CATHOLICS. 352
CHAPTER I. 352
CHAPTER II. 359
CHAPTER III. 365
CHAPTER IV. 375
CHAPTER V. 382
CHAPTER VI. 387
CHAPTER VII. 391
CHAPTER VIII. 397

A POPULAR HISTORY
OF IRELAND

FROM THE EARLIEST

PERIOD TO THE EMANCIPATION OF THE CATHOLICS

BY

Thomas D'Arcy McGee

HISTORY OF IRELAND
BOOK VIII.

THE ERA OF THE REFORMATION.
(Continued from Volume I)

CHAPTER IV.

SIR HENRY SIDNEY'S DEPUTYSHIP--PARLIAMENT OF 1569-- THE SECOND "GERALDINE LEAGUE"--SIR JAMES FITZ-MAURICE.

Sir Henry Sidney, in writing to his court, had always reported John O'Neil as "the only strong man in Ireland." Before his rout at Lough Swilly, he could commonly call into the field 4,000 foot and 1,000 horse; and his two years' revolt cost Elizabeth, in money, about 150,000 pounds sterling "over and above the cess laid on the country"--besides "3,500 of her Majesty's soldiers" slain in battle. The removal of such a leader in the very prime of life was therefore a cause of much congratulation to Sidney and his royal mistress, and as no other "strong man" was likely soon to arise, the Deputy now turned with renewed ardour to the task of establishing the Queen's supremacy, in things spiritual as well as temporal. With this view he urged that separate governments, with large though subordinate military as well as civil powers, should be created for Munster and Connaught--with competent Presidents, who should reside in the former Province at Limerick, and in the latter, at Athlone. In accordance with this scheme--which continued to be acted upon for nearly a century--Sir Edward Fitton was appointed first President of Connaught, and Sir John Perrott, the Queen's illegitimate brother, President of Munster. Leinster and Ulster were reserved as the special charge of the Lord Deputy.

About the time of O'Neil's death Sidney made an official progress through the South and West, which he describes as wofully wasted by war, both town and country. The earldom of the loyal Ormond was far from being well ordered; and the other great nobles were even less favourably reported; the Earl of Desmond could neither rule nor be ruled; the Earl of Clancarty "wanted force and credit;" the Earl of Thomond had neither wit to govern "nor grace to learn of others;" the Earl of Clanrickarde was well intentioned, but controlled wholly by his wife. Many districts had but "one-twentieth" of their ancient population; Galway was in a state of perpetual defence. Athenry had but four respectable householders left, and these presented him with the rusty keys of their once famous town, which they confessed themselves unable to defend, impoverished as they were by the extortions of their lords. All this to the eye of the able Englishman had been the result of that "cowardly policy, or lack of policy," whose sole maxims had been to play off the great lords against each other and to retard the growth of population, least "through their quiet might follow" future dangers to the English interest. His own policy was based on very different principles. He proposed to make the highest heads bow to the supremacy of the royal sword--to punish with exemplary rigour every sign of insubordination, especially in the great--and, at the same time, to encourage with ample rewards, adventurers, and enterprises of all kinds. He proposed to himself precisely the part Lord Stafford acted sixty years later, and he entered on it with a will which would have won the admiration of that unbending despot. He prided himself on the number of military executions which marked his progress. "Down they go in every corner," he writes, "and down they shall go, God willing!" He seized the Earl of Desmond in his own town of Kilmallock; he took the sons of Clanrickarde, in Connaught, and carried them prisoners to Dublin. Elizabeth became alarmed at these extreme measures, and Sidney obtained leave to explain his new policy in person to her Majesty. Accordingly in October he sailed for England, taking with him the Earl and his brother John of Desmond, who had been invited to Dublin, and were detained as prisoners of State; Hugh O'Neil, as yet known by no other title than

Baron of Dungannon; the O'Conor Sligo, and other chiefs and noblemen. He seems to have carried his policy triumphantly with the Queen, and from henceforth for many a long year "the dulce ways" and "politic drifts" recommended by the great Cardinal Statesman of Henry VIII. were to give way to that remorseless struggle in which the only alternative offered to the Irish was--uniformity or extermination. Of this policy, Sir Henry Sidney may, it seems to me, be fairly considered the author; Stafford, and even Cromwell were but finishers of his work. One cannot repress a sigh that so ferocious a design as the extermination of a whole people should be associated in any degree with the illustrious name of Sidney.

The triumphant Deputy arrived at Carrickfergus in September, 1568, from England. Here he received the "submission," as it is called, of Tirlogh, the new O'Neil, and turned his steps southwards in full assurance that this chief of Tyrone was not another "strong man" like the last. A new Privy Council was sworn in on his arrival at Dublin, with royal instructions "to concur with" the Deputy, and 20,000 pounds a year in addition to the whole of the cess levied in the country were guaranteed to enable him to carry out his great scheme of the "reduction." A Parliament was next summoned for the 17th of January, 1569, the first assembly of that nature which had been convened since Lord Sussex's rupture with *his* Parliament nine years before.

The acts of this Parliament, of the 11th of Elizabeth, are much more voluminous than those of the 2nd of the same reign. The constitution of the houses is also of interest, as the earlier records of every form of government must always be. Three sessions were held in the first year, one in 1570, and one in 1571. After its dissolution, no Parliament sat in Ireland for fourteen years--so unstable was the system at that time, and so dependent upon accidental causes for its exercise. The first sittings of Sidney's Parliament were as stormy as those of Sussex. It was found that many members presented themselves pretending to represent towns not incorporated, and others, officers of election, had returned themselves. Others, again, were non-resident Englishmen, dependent on the Deputy who had never seen the places for which they claimed to sit. The disputed elections of all classes being referred to the judges, they decided that non-residence did not disqualify the latter class; but that those who had returned themselves, and those chosen for non-corporate towns, were inadmissible. This double decision did not give the new House of Commons quite the desired complexion, though Stanihurst, Recorder of Dublin, the Court candidate, was chosen Speaker. The opposition was led by Sir Christopher Barnewall, an able and intrepid man, to whose firmness it was mainly due that a more sweeping proscription was not enacted, under form of law, at this period. The native Englishmen in the House were extremely unpopular out of doors, and Hooker, one of their number, who sat for the deserted borough of Athenry, had to be escorted to his lodgings by a strong guard, for fear of the Dublin mob. The chief acts of the first session were a subsidy, for ten years, of 13 shillings 4 pence for every ploughland granted to the Queen; an act suspending Poyning's act for the continuance of *that* Parliament; an act for the attainder of John O'Neil; an act appropriating to her Majesty the lands of the Knight of the Valley; an act authorizing the Lord Deputy to present to vacant benefices in Munster and Connaught for ten years; an act abolishing the title of "Captain," or *ruler* of counties or districts, unless by special warrant under the great seal; an act for reversing the attainder of the Earl of Kildare. In the sittings of 1570 and '71, the chief acts were for the erection of free schools, for the preservation of the public records, for establishing an uniform measure in the sale of corn, and for the attainder of the White Knight, deceased. Though undoubtedly most of these statutes strengthened Sidney's hands and favoured his policy, they did not go the lengths which in his official correspondence he advocated. For the last seven years of his connection with Irish affairs, he was accordingly disposed to dispense with the unmanageable machinery of a Parliament. Orders in council were much more easily procured than acts of legislation, even when every care had been taken to pack the House of Commons with the dependents of the executive.

The meeting of Parliament in 1569 was nearly coincident with the formal excommunication of Elizabeth by Pope Pius V. Though pretending to despise the bull, the Queen was weak enough to seek its revocation, through the interposition of the Emperor Maximilian. The high tone of the enthusiastic Pontiff irritated her deeply, and perhaps the additional severities which she now directed against her Catholic subjects, may be, in part, traced to the effects of the excommunication. In Ireland, the work of reformation, by means of civil disabilities and executive patronage, was continued with earnestness. In 1564, all Popish priests and friars were prohibited from meeting in Dublin, or even coming within the city gates. Two years later, *The Book of Articles*, copied from the English Articles, was published, by order of "the Commissioners for Causes Ecclesiastical." The articles are twelve in number:--1. The Trinity in Unity; 2. The Sufficiency of the Scriptures to Salvation; 3. The Orthodoxy of Particular Churches; 4. The Necessity of Holy Orders; 5. The Queen's Supremacy; 6. Denial of the Pope's authority "to be more than other Bishops have;" 7. The Conformity of the Book of Common Prayer to the Scriptures; 8. The Ministration of Baptism does not depend on the Ceremonial; 9. Condemns "Private Masses," and denies that the Mass can be a propitiatory Sacrifice for the Dead; 10. Asserts the Propriety of Communion in Both Kinds; 11. Utterly disallows Images, Relics and Pilgrimages; 12. Requires a General Subscription to the foregoing Articles. With this creed, the Irish Establishment started into existence, at the command and, of course, with all the aid of the civil power. The Bishops of Meath and Kildare, the nearest to Dublin, for resisting it were banished their sees; the former to die an exile in Spain, the latter to find refuge and protection with the Earl of Desmond. Several Prelates were tolerated in their sees, on condition of observing a species of neutrality; but all vacancies, if within the reach of the English power, were filled as they occurred by nominees of the crown. Those who actively and energetically resisted the new doctrines were marked out for vengeance, and we shall see in the next decade how Ireland's martyr age began.

The honour and danger of organizing resistance to the progress of the new religion now devolved upon the noble family of the Geraldines of Munster, of whose principal members we must, therefore, give some account. The fifteenth Earl, who had concurred in the act of Henry's election, died in the year of Elizabeth's accession (1558), leaving three sons, Gerald the sixteenth Earl, John, and James. He had also an elder son by a first wife, from whom he had been divorced on the ground of consanguinity. This son disputed the succession unsuccessfully, retired to Spain, and there died. Earl Gerald, though one of the Peers who sat in the Parliament of the second year of Elizabeth, was one of those who strenuously opposed the policy of Sussex, and still more strenuously, as may be supposed, the more extreme policy of Sidney. His reputation, however, as a leader, suffered severely by the combat of Affane, in which he was taken prisoner by Thomas, the tenth Earl of Ormond, with whom he was at feud on a question of boundaries. By order of the Queen, the Lord Deputy was appointed arbitrator in this case, and though the decision was in favour of Ormond, Desmond submitted, came to Dublin, and was reconciled with his enemy in the chapter house of St. Patrick's. A year or two later, Gerald turned his arms against the ancient rivals of his house--the McCarthys of Muskerry and Duhallow--but was again taken prisoner, and after six months' detention, held to ransom by the Lord of Muskerry. After his release, the old feud with Ormond broke out anew--a most impolitic quarrel, as that Earl was not only personally a favourite with the Queen, but was also nearly connected with her in blood through the Boleyns. In 1567, as before related, Desmond was seized by surprise in his town of Kilmallock by Sidney's order, and the following autumn conveyed to London on a charge of treason and lodged in the Tower. This was the third prison he had lodged in within three years, and by far the most hopeless of the three. His brother, Sir John of Desmond, through the representations of Ormond, was the same year arrested and consigned to the same ominous dungeon, from which suspected noblemen seldom emerged, except when the hurdle waited for them at the gate.

This double capture aroused the indignation of all the tribes of Desmond, and led to the formidable combination which, in reference to the previous confederacy in the reign of Henry, may be called "the second Geraldine League." The Earl of Clancarty, and such of the O'Briens, McCarthys, and Butlers, as had resolved to resist the complete revolution in property, religion, and law, which Sidney meditated, united together to avenge the wrongs of those noblemen, their neighbours, so treacherously arrested and so cruelly confined. Sir James, son of Sir Maurice Fitzgerald of Kerry, commonly called James Fitz-Maurice, cousin-germain to the imprisoned noblemen, was chosen leader of the insurrection. He was, according to the testimony of an enemy, Hooker, member for Athenry, "a deep dissembler, passing subtile, and able to compass any matter he took in hand; courteous, valiant, expert in martial affairs." To this we may add that he had already reached a mature age; was deeply and sincerely devoted to his religion; and, according to the eulogist of the rival house of Ormond, one whom nothing could deject or bow down, a scorner of luxury and ease, insensible to danger, impervious to the elements, preferring, after a hard day's fighting, the bare earth to a luxurious couch.

One of the first steps of the League was to despatch an embassy for assistance to the King of Spain and the Pope. The Archbishop of Cashel, the Bishop of Emly, and James, the youngest brother of Desmond, were appointed on this mission, of which

Sidney was no sooner apprised than he proclaimed the confederates traitors, and at once prepared for A campaign in Munster. The first blow was struck by the taking of Clogrennan Castle, which belonged to Sir Edmond Butler, one of the adherents of the League. The attack was led by Sir Peter Carew, an English adventurer, who had lately appeared at Dublin to claim the original grant made to Robert Fitzstephen of the moiety of the kingdom of Cork, and who at present commanded the garrison of Kilkenny. The accomplished soldier of fortune anticipated the Deputy's movements by this blow at the confederated Butlers, who retaliated by an abortive attack on Kilkenny, and a successful foray into Wexford, in which they took the Castle of Enniscorthy. Sidney, taking the field in person, marched through Waterford and Dungarvan against Desmond's strongholds in the vicinity of Youghal. After a week's siege he took Castlemartyr, and continued his route through Barrymore to Cork, where he established his head-quarters. From Cork, upon receiving the submission of some timid members of the League, he continued his route to Limerick, where Sir Edmond Butler and his brothers were induced to come in by their chief the Earl of Ormond. From Limerick he penetrated Clare, took the Castles of Clonoon and Ballyvaughan; he next halted some time at Galway, and returned to Dublin by Athlone. Overawed by the activity of the Deputy, many others of the confederates followed the example of the Butlers. The Earl of Clancarty sued for pardon and delivered up his eldest son as a hostage for his good faith; the Earl of Thomond--more suspected than compromised--yielded all his castles, with the sole exception of Ibrackan. But the next year, mortified at the insignificance to which he had reduced himself, he sought refuge in France, from which he only returned when the intercession of the English ambassador, Norris, had obtained him full indemnity for the past. Sir James Fitzmaurice, thus deserted by his confederates, had need of all that unyielding firmness of character for which he had obtained credit. Castle after castle belonging to his cousins and himself was taken by the powerful siege trains of President Perrott; Castlemaine, the last stronghold which commanded an outlet by sea, surrendered after a three months' siege, gallantly maintained. The unyielding leader had now, therefore, no alternative but to retire into the impregnable passes of the Galtees, where he established his head-quarters. This mountain range, towering from two to three thousand feet over the plain of Ormond, stretches from north-west to south-east, some twenty miles, descending with many a gentle undulation towards the

Funcheon and the Blackwater in the earldom of Desmond. Of all its valleys Aharlow was the fairest and most secluded. Well wooded, and well watered, with outlets and intricacies known only to the native population, it seemed as if designed for a nursery of insurrection. It now became to the patriots of the South what the valley of Glenmalure had long been for those of Leinster--a fortress dedicated by Nature to the defence of freedom. In this fastness Fitzmaurice continued to maintain himself, until a prospect of new combinations opened to him in the West.

The sons of the Earl of Clanrickarde, though released from the custody of Sidney, receiving intimation that they were to be arrested at a court which Fitton, President of Connaught, had summoned at Galway, flew to arms and opened negotiations with Fitzmaurice. The latter, withdrawing from Aharlow, promptly joined them in Galway, and during the campaign which followed, aided them with his iron energy and sagacious counsel. They took and demolished the works of Athenry, and, in part, those of the Court of Athlone. Their successes induced the Deputy to liberate Clanrickarde himself, who had been detained a prisoner in Dublin, from the outbreak of his sons. On his return--their main object being attained--they submitted as promptly as they had revolted, and this hope also being quenched, Fitzmaurice found his way back again, with a handful of Scottish retainers, to the shelter of Aharlow. Sir John Perrott, having by this time no further sieges to prosecute, drew his toils closer and closer round the Geraldine's retreat. For a whole year, the fidelity of his adherents and the natural strength of the place enabled him to baffle all the President's efforts. But his faithful Scottish guards being at length surprised and cut off almost to a man, Fitzmaurice, with his son, his kinsman, the Seneschal of Imokilly, and the son of Richard Burke, surrendered to the President at Kilmallock, suing on his knees for the Queen's pardon, which was, from motives of policy, granted.

On this conclusion of the contest in Munster, the Earl of Desmond and his brother, Sir John, were released from the Tower, and transferred to Dublin, where they were treated as prisoners on parole. The Mayor of the city, who was answerable for their custody, having taken them upon a hunting party in the open country, the brothers put spurs to their horses and escaped into Munster (1574). They were stigmatized as having broken their parole, but they asserted that it was intended on that party to waylay and murder them, and that their only safety was in flight.

Large rewards were offered for their capture, alive or dead, but the necessities of both parties compelled a truce during the remainder of Sidney's official career--which terminated in his resignation--about four years after the escape of the Desmonds from Dublin. Thus were new elements of combination, at the moment least expected, thrown, into the hands of the Munster Catholics.

CHAPTER V.

THE "UNDERTAKERS" IN ULSTER AND LEINSTER--DEFEAT AND DEATH OF SIR JAMES FITZMAURICE.

Queen Elizabeth, when writing to Lord Sussex of a rumoured rising by O'Neil, desired him to assure her lieges at Dublin, that if O'Neil did rise, "it would be for their advantage; for there will be estates for them who want." The Sidney policy of treating Ireland as a discovered country, whose inhabitants had no right to the soil, except such as the discoverers graciously conceded to them--begat a new order of men, unknown to the history of other civilized states, which order we must now be at some pains to introduce to the reader.

These "Undertakers," as they were called, differed widely from the Norman invaders of a former age. The Norman generally espoused the cause of some native chief, and took his pay in land; what he got by the sword he held by the sword. But the Undertaker was usually a man of peace--a courtier like Sir Christopher Hatton--a politician like Sir Walter Raleigh--a poet like Edmund Spencer, or a spy and forger like Richard Boyle, first Earl of Cork. He came, in the wake of war, with his elastic "letters patent," or, if he served in the field, it was mainly with a view to the subsequent confiscations. He was adroit at finding flaws in ancient titles, skilled in all the feudal quibbles of fine and recovery, and ready to employ the secret dagger where hard swearing and fabricated documents might fail to make good his title. Sometimes men of higher mark and more generous dispositions, allured by the temptations of the social revolution, would enter on the same pursuits, but they generally miscarried from want of what was then cleverly called "subtlety," but which plain people could not easily distinguish from lying and perjury. What greatly assisted them in then: designs was the fact that feudal tenures had never been general in Ireland, so that by an easy process of reasoning they could prove nineteen-twentieths of all existing titles "defective," according to their notions of the laws of property.

Sir Peter Carew, already mentioned, was one of the earliest of the Undertakers. He had been bred up as page to the Prince of Orange, and had visited the Courts of France, Germany, and Constantinople. He claimed, by virtue of his descent from Robert Fitzstephen, the barony of Idrone, in Carlow, and one half the kingdom of Desmond. Sir Henry Sidney had admitted these pretensions, partly as a menace against the Kavanaghs and Geraldines, and Sir Peter established himself at Leighlin, where he kept great house, with one hundred servants, over one hundred kerne, forty horse, a stall in his stable, a seat at his board for all comers. He took an active part in all military operations, and fell fighting gallantly on a memorable day to be hereafter mentioned.

After the attainder of John the Proud in 1569, Sir Thomas Smith, Secretary to the Queen, obtained a grant of the district of the Ards of Down, for his illegitimate son, who accordingly entered on the task of its plantation. But the O'Neils of Clandeboy, the owners of the soil, attacked the young Undertaker, who met a grave where he had come to found a lordship. A higher name was equally unfortunate in the same field of adventure. Walter Devereux, Earl of Essex (father of the Essex still more unfortunate), obtained in 1573 a grant of one moiety of Farney and Clandeboy, and having mortgaged his English estates to the Queen for 10,000 pounds, associated with himself many other adventurers. On the 16th of August, he set sail from Liverpool, accompanied by the Lords Dacre and Rich, Sir Henry Knollys, the three sons of Lord Norris, and a multitude of the common people. But as he had left one powerful enemy at court in Leicester--so he found a second at Dublin, in the acting deputy, Fitzwilliam. Though gratified with the title of President of Ulster and afterwards that of Marshal of Ireland, he found his schemes constantly counteracted by orders from Dublin or from England. He was frequently ordered off from his head-quarters at Newry, on expeditions into Munster, until those who had followed his banner became disheartened and mutinous. The O'Neils and the Antrim Scots harassed his colony and increased his troubles. He attempted by treachery to retrieve his fortunes. Having invited the alliance of Con O'Donnell, he seized that chief and sent him prisoner to Dublin. Subsequently his chief opponent, Brian, lord of Clandeboy, paid him an amicable visit, accompanied by his wife, brother, and household. As they were seated at table on the fourth day of then--stay, the soldiers of Essex burst into the banquet hall, put them all, "women, youths and maidens," to the sword. Brian and his wife were saved from the slaughter only to undergo at Dublin the death and mutilation inflicted upon traitors. Yet the ambitious schemes of Walter of Essex did not prosper the more of all these crimes. He died at Dublin, two years afterwards (1576), in the 36th year of his age, as was generally believed from poison administered by the orders of the arch-poisoner, Leicester, who immediately upon his death married his widow.

It is apparent that the interest of the Undertakers could not be to establish peace in Ireland so long as war might be profitably waged. The new "English interest" thus created was often hostile to the soundest rules of policy and always opposed to the dictates of right and justice; but the double desire to conquer and to convert--to anglicize and Protestantize--blinded many to the lawless means by which they were worked out. The massacre of 400 persons of the chief families of Leix and Offally, which took place at Mullaghmast in 1577, is an evidence of how the royal troops were used to promote the ends of the Undertakers. To Mullaghmast, one of the ancient raths of Leinster, situated about five miles from Athy in Kildare, the O'Moores, O'Kellys, Lalors, and other Irish tribes were invited by the local commander of the Queen's troops, Francis Cosby. The Bowens, Hartpoles, Pigotts, Hovendons, and other adventurers who had grants or designs upon the neighbouring territory were invited to meet them. One of the Lalors, perceiving that none of those who entered the rath before him emerged again, caused his friends to fall back while he himself advanced alone. At the very entrance he beheld the dead bodies of some of his slaughtered kinsmen; drawing his sword, he fought his way back to his friends, who barely escaped with their lives to Dysart. Four hundred victims, including 180 of the name of O'Moore, are said to have fallen in this deliberate butchery. Rory O'Moore, the chief of his name, avenged this massacre by many a daring deed. In rapid succession he surprised Naas, Athy, and Leighlin. From the rapidity with which his blows were struck in Kildare, Carlow, and Kilkenny, he appeared to be ubiquitous. He was the true type of a guerilla leader, yet merciful as brave. While Naas was burning, he sat coolly at the market cross enjoying the spectacle, but he suffered no lives to be taken. Having captured Cosby, he did not, as might be expected, put him to death. His confidence in his own prowess and resources amounted to rashness, and finally caused his death. Coming forth from a wood to parley with a party of the Queen's troops led by his neighbour, the Lord of Ossory, a common soldier ran him through the body with a sword. This was on the last day of June, 1578--a day mournful through all the midland districts for the loss of their best and bravest captain.

While these events occupied the minds and tongues of men in the North and East, a brief respite from the horrors of war was permitted to the province of Munster. The Earl of Desmond, only too happy to be tolerated in the possession of his 570,000 acres, was eager enough to testify his allegiance by any sort of service. His brothers, though less compliant, followed his example for the moment, and no danger was to be apprehended in that quarter, except from the indomitable James Fitzmaurice, self-exiled on the continent. No higher tribute could be paid to the character of that heroic man than the closeness with which all his movements were watched by English spies, specially set upon his track. They followed him to the French court, to St. Malo's (where he resided for some time with his family), to Madrid, whence he sent his two sons to the famous University of Alcala, and from Madrid to Rome. The honourable reception he received at the hands of the French and Spanish Sovereigns was duly reported; yet both being at peace with England, his plans elicited no open encouragement from either. At Rome, however, he obtained some material and much moral support. Here he found many zealous advocates among the English and Irish refugees--among them the celebrated Saunders, Alien, sometimes called Cardinal Alien, and O'Mulrian, Bishop of Killaloe. A force of about 1,000 men was enlisted at the expense of Pope Gregory XIII., in the Papal States, and placed under an experienced captain, Hercules Pisano. They were shipped at Civita Vecchia by a squadron under the command of Thomas Stukely, an English adventurer, who had served both for and against the Irish Catholics, but had joined Fitzmaurice in Spain and accompanied him to Rome. On the strength of some remote or pretended relationship to the McMurroghs, Stukely obtained from the Pope the titles of Marquis of Leinster and Baron of Idrone and Ross; at Fitzmaurice's urgent request--so it is stated--he was named Vice-Admiral of the fleet. The whole expedition was fitted out at the expense of the Pope, but it was secretly agreed that it should be supported, after landing in Ireland, at the charge of

Philip II. Fitzmaurice, travelling overland to Spain, was to unite there with another party of adventurers, and to form a junction with Stukely and Pisano on the coast of Kerry. So with the Papal benediction gladdening his heart, and a most earnest exhortation from the Holy Father to the Catholics of Ireland to follow his banner, this noblest of all the Catholic Geraldines departed from Rome, to try again the hazard of war in his own country.

This was in the spring of the year 1579. Sir Henry Sidney, after many years' direction of the government, had been recalled at his own request; Sir William Drury was acting as Lord Justice; and Sir Nicholas Malby as President of Munster. Expectation of the return of Fitzmaurice, at the head of a liberating expedition, began to be rife throughout the south and west, and the coasts were watched with the utmost vigilance. In the month of June, three persons having landed in disguise from a Spanish ship, at Dingle, were seized by government spies, and carried before the Earl of Desmond. On examination, one of them proved to be O'Haly, Bishop of Mayo, and another a friar named O'Rourke; the third is not named. By the timid, temporizing Desmond, they were forwarded to Kilmallock to Drury, who put them to every conceivable torture, in order to extract intelligence of Fitzmaurice's movements. After their thighs had been broken with hammers, they were hanged on a tree, and their bodies used as targets by the brutal soldiery. Fitzmaurice, with his friends, having survived shipwreck on the coast of Galicia, entered the same harbour (Dingle) on the 17th of July. But no tidings had yet reached Munster of Stukely and Pisano; and his cousin, the Earl, sent him neither sign of friendship nor promise of co-operation. He therefore brought his vessels round to the small harbour of Smerwick, and commenced fortifying the almost isolated rock of *Oilen-an-oir*--or golden island, so called from the shipwreck at that point of one of Martin Forbisher's vessels, laden with golden quartz, some years before. Here he was joined by John and James of Desmond, and by a band of 200 of the O'Flaherties of Galway, the only allies who presented themselves. These latter, on finding the expected Munster rising already dead, and the much-talked-of Spanish auxiliary force so mere a handful, soon withdrew in their own galleys, upon which an English ship and pinnace, sweeping round from Kinsale, carried off the Spanish vessels in sight of the powerless little fort. These desperate circumstances inspired desperate councils, and it was decided by the cousins to endeavour to gain the great wood of Kilmore, near Charleville--in the neighbourhood of Sir James' old retreat among the Galtee Mountains. In this march they were closely pursued by the Earl of Desmond, either in earnest or in sham, and were obliged to separate into three small bands, the brothers of the Earl retiring respectively to the fastnesses of Lymnamore and Glenfesk, while Fitzmaurice, with "a dozen horsemen and a few kerne," made a desperate push to reach the western side of the Shannon, where he hoped, perhaps, for better opportunity and a warmer reception. This proved for him a fatal adventure. Jaded after a long day's ride he was compelled to seize some horses from the plough, in the barony of Clanwilliam, in order to remount his men. These horses were the property of his relative, Sir William Burke, who, with his neighbour, Mac-I-Brien of Ara, pursued the fugitives to within six miles of Limerick, where Fitzmaurice, having turned to remonstrate with his pursuers, was fired at and mortally wounded. He did not instantly fall. Dashing into the midst of his assailants he cleft down the two sons of Burke, whose followers immediately turned and fled. Then alighting from his saddle, the wounded chief received the last solemn rites of religion from the hands of Dr. Allen. His body was decapitated by one of his followers, that the noble head might not be subjected to indignity; but the trunk being but hastily buried was soon afterwards discovered, carried to Kilmallock, and there hung up for a target and a show. This tragical occurrence took place near the present site of "Barrington's bridge," on the little river Mulkern, county of Limerick, on the 18th day of August, 1579. In honour of his part in the transaction William Burke was created Baron of Castleconnell, awarded a pension of 100 marks per annum, and received from Elizabeth an autograph letter of condolence on the loss of his sons: it is added by some writers that he died of joy on the receipt of so many favours. Such was the fate of the glorious hopes of Sir James Fitzmaurice. So ended in a squabble with churls about cattle, on the banks of an insignificant stream, a career which had drawn the attention of Europe, and had inspired with apprehension the lion-hearted Queen.

As to the expedition under Stukely, its end was even more romantic. His squadron having put into the Tagus, he found the King of Portugal, Don Sebastian, on the eve of sailing against the Moors, and from some promise of after aid was induced to accompany that chivalrous Prince. On the fatal field of Alcacar, Stukely, Pisano, and the Italians under their command shared the fate of the Portuguese monarch and army. Neither Italy nor Ireland heard of them more.

Gregory XIII. did not abandon the cause. On the receipt of all these ill-tidings he issued another Bull, highly laudatory of the virtues of James Fitzmaurice "of happy memory," and granting the same indulgence to those who would fight under John or James of Desmond, "as that which was imparted to those who fought against the Turks for the recovery of the Holy Land." This remarkable document is dated from Rome, the 13th of May, 1580.

CHAPTER VI.

SEQUEL OF THE SECOND GERALDINE LEAGUE--PLANTATION OF MUNSTER--EARLY CAREER OF HUGH O'NEIL, EARL OF TYRONE--PARLIAMENT OF 1585.

We must continue to read the history of Ireland by the light of foreign affairs, and our chief light at this period is derived from Spain. The death of Don Sebastian concentrated the thoughts of Philip II. on Portugal, which he forcibly annexed to the Spanish crown. The progress of the insurrection in the Netherlands also occupied so large a place in his attention, that his projects against Elizabeth were postponed, year after year, to the bitter disappointment of the Irish leaders. It may seem far-fetched to assert, but it is not the less certainly true, that the fate of Catholic Munster was intimately involved in the change of masters in Portugal, and the fluctuations of war in the Netherlands,

The "Undertakers," who had set their hearts on having the Desmond estates, determined that the Earl and his brothers should not live long in peace, however peaceably they might be disposed. The old trick of forging letters, already alluded to, grew into a common and familiar practice during this and the following reign. Such a letter, purporting to be written by the Earl of Desmond --at that period only too anxious to be allowed to live in peace--was made public at Dublin and London. It was addressed to Sir William Pelham, the temporary Lord Justice, and among other passages contained this patent invention--that he (the Earl and his brethren) "had taken this matter in hand with great authority, both from the Pope's holiness and King Philip, who do undertake to further us in our affairs, as we shall need." It is utterly incredible that any man in Desmond's position could have written such a letter--could have placed in the hands of his enemies a document which must for ever debar him from entering into terms with Elizabeth or her representatives in Ireland. We have no hesitation, therefore, in classing this pretended letter to Pelham with those admitted forgeries which drove the unfortunate Lord Thomas Fitzgerald into premature revolt, in the reign of Henry VIII.

Sir John of Desmond had been nominated by the gallant Fitzmaurice in his last moments as the fittest person to rally the remaining defenders of religion and property in Munster. The Papal standard and benediction were almost all he could bequeath his successor, but the energy of John, aided by some favourable local occurrences, assembled a larger force for the campaign of 1579 than had lately taken the field. Without the open aid of the Earl, he contrived to get together at one time as many as 2,000 men, amongst whom not the least active officer was his younger brother, Sir James, hardly yet of man's age. Drs. Saunders and Allen, with several Spanish officers, accompanied this devoted but undisciplined multitude, sharing all the hardships of the men, and the counsels of the chiefs. Their first camp, and, so to speak, the nursery of their army, was among the inaccessible mountains of Slievelogher in Kerry, where the rudiments of discipline were daily inculcated. When they considered the time ripe for action, they removed their camp to the great wood of Kilmore, near Charleville, from which they might safely assail the line of communication between Cork and Limerick, the main depots of Elizabeth's southern army. Nearly half-way between these cities, and within a few miles of their new encampment, stood the strong town of Kilmallock on the little river Lubach. This famous old Geraldine borough, the focus of several roads, was the habitual stopping place of the Deputies in their progress, as well as of English soldiers on their march. The ancient fortifications, almost obliterated by Fitzmaurice eleven years before, had been replaced by strong walls, lined with earthworks, and crowned by towers. Here Sir William Drury fixed his head-quarters in the spring of 1579, summoning to his aid all the Queen's lieges in Munster. With a force of not less than 1,000 English regulars under his own command, and perhaps twice that number under the banner of the Munster "Undertakers" and others, who obeyed the summons, he made an unsuccessful attempt to beat up the Geraldine quarters at Kilmore. One division of his force, consisting of 300 men by the Irish, and 200 by the English account, was cut to pieces, with their captains, Herbert, Price, and Eustace. The remainder retreated in disorder to their camp at Athneasy, a ford on the

Morning Star River, four miles east of Kilmallock. For nine weeks Drury continued in the field, without gaining any advantage, yet so harassed day and night by his assailants that his health gave way under his anxieties. Despairing of recovery, he was removed by slow stages to Waterford--which would seem to indicate that his communications both with Cork and Limerick were impracticable--but died before reaching the first mentioned city. The chief command in Munster now devolved upon Sir Nicholas Malby, an officer who had seen much foreign service, while the temporary vacancy in the government was filled by the Council at Dublin, whose choice fell on Sir William Pelham, another distinguished military man, lately arrived from England.

Throughout the summer and autumn months the war was maintained, with varying fortune on either side. In the combats of Gortnatibrid and Enagbeg, in Limerick, the final success, according to Irish accounts, was with the Geraldines, though they had the misfortune to lose Cardinal Allen, Sir Thomas Fitzgerald and Sir Thomas Browne. Retiring into winter quarters at Aharlow, they had a third engagement with the garrison of Kilmallock, which attempted, without success, to intercept their march. The campaign of 1580 was, however, destined to be decisive. Sir John of Desmond, being invited to an amicable conference by the Lord Barry, was entrapped by an English force under Captain Zouch, in the woods surrounding Castle Lyons, and put to death on the spot. The young Sir James had previously been captured on a foray into Muskerry, and executed at Cork, so that of the brothers there now remained but Earl Gerald, the next victim of the machinations which had already proved so fatal to his family. Perceiving at length the true designs cherished against him, the Earl took the field in the spring of 1580, and obtained two considerable advantages, one at Pea-field, against the English under Roberts, and a second at Knockgraffon against the Anglo-Irish, under the brothers of the Earl of Ormond, the recusant members of the original league. Both these actions were fought in Tipperary, and raised anew the hopes of the Munster Catholics. An unsuccessful attempt on Adare was the only other military event in which the Earl bore a part; he wintered in Aharlow, where his Christmas was rather that of an outlaw than of the Lord Palatine of Desmond. In Aharlow he had the misfortune to lose the gifted and heroic Nuncio, Dr. Saunders, whose great services, at that period, taken together with those of Cardinal Allen, long endeared the faithful English to the faithful Irish Catholics.

The sequel of the second Geraldine League may be rapidly narrated. In September, 1580, the fort at Smerwick, where Fitzmaurice had landed from Galicia, received a garrison of 800 men, chiefly Spaniards and Italians, under Don Stephen San Joseph. The place was instantly invested by sea and land, under the joint command of the new Lieutenant, Lord Grey de Wilton, and the Earl of Ormond. Among the officers of the besieging force were three especially notable men--Sir Walter Raleigh, the poet Spenser, and Hugh O'Neil, afterwards Earl of Tyrone, but at this time commanding a squadron of cavalry for her Majesty Queen Elizabeth. San Joseph surrendered the place on conditions; that savage outrage ensued, which is known in Irish history as "the massacre of Smerwick." Raleigh and Wingfield appear to have directed the operations by which 800 prisoners of war were cruelly butchered and flung over the rocks. The sea upon that coast is deep and the tides swift; but it has not proved deep enough to hide that horrid crime, or to wash the stains of such wanton bloodshed from the memory of its authors!

For four years longer the Geraldine League flickered in the South. Proclamations offering pardon to all concerned, except Earl Gerald and a few of his most devoted adherents, had their effect. Deserted at home, and cut off from foreign assistance, the condition of Desmond grew more and more intolerable. On one occasion he narrowly escaped capture by rushing with his Countess into a river, and remaining concealed up to the chin in water. His dangers can hardly be paralleled by those of Bruce after the battle of Falkirk, or by the more familiar adventures of Charles Edward. At length, on the night of the 11th of November, 1584, he was surprised with only two followers in a lonesome valley about five miles distant from Tralee, among the mountains of Kerry. The spot is still remembered, and the name of "the Earl's road" transports the fancy of the traveller to that tragical scene. Cowering over the embers of a half-extinct fire in a miserable hovel, the lord of a country, which in time of peace had yielded an annual rental of "40,000 golden pieces," was despatched by the hands of common soldiers, without pity, or time, or hesitation. A few followers watching their *creaghts* or herds, farther up the valley, found his bleeding trunk flung out upon the highway; the head was transported over seas, to rot upon the spikes of London Tower.

The extirpation of the Munster Geraldines, in the right line, according to the theory of the "Undertakers" and the Court of England in general, vested in the Queen the 570,000 acres belonging to the late Earl. Proclamation was accordingly made throughout England, inviting "younger brothers of good families" to undertake the plantation of Desmond--each planter to obtain a certain scope of land, on condition of settling thereupon so many families--"none of the native Irish to be admitted." Under these conditions, Sir Christopher Hatton took up 10,000 acres in Waterford; Sir Walter Raleigh 12,000 acres, partly in Waterford and partly in Cork; Sir William Harbart, or Herbert, 13,000 acres in Kerry; Sir Edward Denny 6,000 in the same county; Sir Warham, St. Leger, and Sir Thomas Norris, 6,000 acres each in Cork; Sir William Courtney 10,000 acres in Limerick; Sir Edward Fitton 11,500 acres in Tipperary and Waterford, and Edmund Spenser a modest 3,000 acres in Cork, on the beautiful Blackwater. The other notable Undertakers were the Hides, Butchers, Wirths, Berklys, Trenchards, Thorntons, Bourchers, Billingsleys, &c., &c. Some of these grants, especially Raleigh's, fell in the next reign into the ravening maw of Richard Boyle, the so-called "*great* Earl of Cork"--probably the most pious hypocrite to be found in the long roll of the "Munster Undertakers."

Before closing the present chapter, we must present to the reader, in a formal manner, the personage whose career is to occupy the chief remaining part of the present Book--Hugh O'Neil, best known by the title of Earl of Tyrone. We have seen him in the camp of the enemies of his country, learning the art of war on the shores of Dingle Bay--a witness to the horrors perpetrated at Smerwick. We may find him later in the same war--in 1584--serving under Perrott and Norris, along the Foyle and the Bann, for the expulsion of the Antrim Scots. The following year, for these and other good services, he received the patent of the Earldom originally conferred on his grandfather, Con O'Neil, but suffered to sink into abeyance by the less politic "John the Proud," in the days when he made his peace with the Queen. The next year he obtained from his clansmen the still higher title of O'Neil, and thus he contrived to combine, in his own person, every principle of authority likely to ensure him following and obedience, whether among the clansmen of Tyrone, or the townsmen upon its borders.

O'Neil's last official act of co-operation with the Dublin government may be considered his participation in the Parliament convoked by Sir John Perrott in 1585, and prorogued till the following year. It is remarkable of this Parliament, the third and last of Elizabeth's long reign, that it was utterly barren of ecclesiastical legislation, if we except "an act against sorcery and witchcraft" from that category. The attainder of the late Earl of Desmond, and the living Viscount of Baltinglass, in arms with the O'Byrnes in Glenmalure, are the only measures of consequence to be found among the Irish statutes of the 27th and 28th of Elizabeth. But though not remarkable for its legislation, the Parliament of 1585 is conspicuously so for its composition. Within its walls with the peers, knights, and burgesses of the anglicized counties, sat almost all the native chiefs of Ulster, Connaught, and Munster. The Leinster chiefs recently in arms, in alliance with the Earl of Desmond, generally absented themselves, with the exception of Feagh, son of Hugh, the senior of the O'Byrnes, and one of the noblest spirits of his race and age. He appears not to have had a seat in either House; but attended, on his own business, under the protection of his powerful friends and sureties.

CHAPTER VII.

BATTLE OF GLENMALURE--SIR JOHN PERROTT'S ADMINISTRATION-- THE SPANISH ARMADA--LORD DEPUTY FITZWILLIAM--ESCAPE OF HUGH ROE O'DONNELL FROM DUBLIN CASTLE--THE ULSTER CONFEDERACY FORMED.

In pursuing to its close the war in Munster, we were obliged to omit the mention of an affair of considerable importance, which somewhat consoled the Catholics for the massacre at Smerwick and the defeat of the Desmonds. We have already observed that what Aharlow was to the southern insurgents, the deep, secluded valley of Glenmalure was to the oppressed of Leinster. It afforded, at this period, refuge to a nobleman whose memory has been most improperly allowed to fall into oblivion. This was James Eustace, Viscount Baltinglass, who had suffered imprisonment in the Castle for refusing to pay an illegal tax of a few pounds, who was afterwards made the object of a special, vindictive enactment, known as "the Statute of Baltinglass," and was in the summer of 1580, on his keeping, surrounded by armed friends and retainers. His friend, Sir Walter Fitzgerald, son-in-law to the chief of Glenmalure, and many of the clansmen of Leix, Offally and Idrone, repaired to him at Slieveroe, near the modern village of Blessington, from which they proceeded to form a junction with the followers of the dauntless Feagh McHugh O'Byrne of Ballincor. Lord Grey, of Wilton, on reaching Dublin in August of that year, obtained information of this gathering, and determined to strike a decisive blow in Wicklow, before proceeding to the South. All the chief captains in the Queen's service--the Malbys, Dudleys, Cosbys, Carews, Moors--had repaired to meet him at Dublin, and now marched, under his command, into the neighbouring highlands. The Catholics, they knew, were concentrated in the valley, on one of the slopes of which Lord Grey constructed a strong camp, and then, having selected the fittest troops for the service, gave orders to attack the Irish camp. Sir William Stanley, one of the officers in command, well describes the upshot, in a letter to Secretary Walshingham: "When we entered the glen," he writes, "we were forced to slide, sometimes three or four fathoms, ere we could stay our feet; it was in depth, where we entered, at least a mile, full of stones, rocks, logs and wood; in the bottom thereof a river full of loose stones, which we were driven to Cross divers times * * * before we were half through the glen, which is four miles in length, the enemy charged us very hotly * * * it was the hottest piece of service that ever I saw, for the time, in any place." As might have been expected, the assailants were repulsed with heavy loss; among the slain were Sir Peter Carew, Colonel Francis Cosby of Mullaghmast memory, Colonel Moor, and other distinguished officers. The full extent of the defeat was concealed from Elizabeth, as well as it could be, in the official despatches; but before the end of August private letters, such as we have quoted, conveyed the painful intelligence to the court. The action was fought on the 25th day of August.

Lord Grey's deputyship, though it lasted only two years, included the three decisive campaigns in the South, already described. At the period of his recall--or leave of absence--the summer of 1582, that "most populous and plentiful country," to use the forcible language of his eloquent Secretary, Edmund Spenser, was reduced to "a heap of carcasses and ashes." The war had been truly a war of extermination; nor did Munster recover her due proportion of the population of the island for nearly two centuries afterwards.

The appointment of Sir John Perrott dates from 1583, though he did not enter on the duties of Lord Deputy till the following year. Like most of the public men of that age, he was both soldier and statesman. In temper he resembled his reputed father, Henry VIII.; for he was impatient of contradiction and control; fond of expense and magnificence, with a high opinion of his own abilities for diplomacy and legislation. The Parliament of 1585-6, as it was attended by almost every notable man in the kingdom, was one of his boasts, though no one seems to have benefited by it much, except Hugh O'Neil, whose title of Earl of Tyrone was then formally recognized. Subordinate to Perrott, the office of Governor of Connaught was held by Sir Richard Bingham--founder of the fortunes of the present Earls of Lucan-- and that of President of Munster, by Sir Thomas Norris, one of four brothers, all employed in the Queen's service, and all destined to lose their lives in that employment.

The most important events which marked the four years' administration of Perrott were the pacification of Thomond and Connaught, the capture of Hugh Roe O'Donnell, and the wreck of a large part of the Spanish Armada, on the northern and western coasts. The royal commission issued for the first-mentioned purpose exemplifies, in a striking manner, the exigencies of Elizabeth's policy at that moment. The persons entrusted with its execution were Sir Richard Bingham, the Earls of Thomond and Clanrickarde; Sir Turlogh O'Brien, Sir Richard Bourke (the McWilliam), O'Conor Sligo, Sir Brian O'Ruarc, and Sir Murrogh O'Flaherty. The chief duties of this singular commission were, to fix a money rental for all lands, free and unfree, in Clare and Connaught; to assess the taxation fairly due to the crown also in money; and to substitute generally the English law of succession for the ancient customs of Tanistry and gavelkind. In Clare, from fortuitous causes, the settlement they arrived at was never wholly reversed; in Connaught, the inhuman severity of Bingham rendered it odious from the first, and the successes of Hugh Roe O'Donnell, a few years later, were hailed by the people of that province as a heaven-sent deliverance.

The treacherous capture of this youthful chieftain was one of the skilful devices on which Sir John Perrott most prided himself. Although a mere lad, the mysterious language of ancient prophecy, which seemed to point him out for greatness, give him consequence in the eyes of both friends and foes. Through his heroic mother, a daughter of the Lord of the Isles, he would naturally find allies in that warlike race. His precocious prowess and talents began to be noised abroad, and stimulated Perrott to the employment of an elaborate artifice, which, however, proved quite successful. A ship, commanded by one Bermingham, was sent round to Donegal, under pretence of being direct from Spain. She carried some casks of Spanish wine, and had a crew of 50 armed men. This ship dropped anchor off Rathmullen Castle on Lough Swilly, in which neighbourhood the young O'Donnell--then barely fifteen--was staying with his foster-father, McSweeny, and several companions of his own age. The unsuspecting youths were courteously invited on board the pretended Spanish ship, where, while they were being entertained in the cabin, the hatches were fastened down, the cable slipped, the sails spread to the wind, and the vessel put to sea. The threats and promises of the astonished clansmen as they gathered to the shore were answered by the mockery of the crew, who safely delivered their prize in Dublin, to the great delight of the Lord Deputy and his Council. Five weary years of fetters and privation the young captives were doomed to pass in the dungeons of the Castle before they breathed again the air of their native North.

But now every ship that reached the English or Irish ports brought tidings more and more positive of the immense armada which King Philip was preparing to launch from the Tagus against England. The piratical exploits of Hawkins and Drake against the Spanish settlements in America, the barbarous execution of Mary, Queen of Scots, and the open alliance of Elizabeth with the Dutch insurgents, all acted as stimulants to the habitual slowness of the Spanish sovereign. Another event, though of minor importance, added intensity to the national quarrel. Sir William Stanley, whose account of the battle of Glenmalure we lately quoted, went over to Philip with 1,300 English troops, whom he commanded as Governor of Daventer, and was taken into the counsels of the Spanish sovereign. The fleet for the invasion of England was on a scale commensurate with the design. One hundred and thirty-five vessels of war, manned by 8,000 sailors, and carrying 19,000 soldiers, sailed from the Tagus, and after encountering a severe storm off Cape Finesterre, re-assembled at Corunna. The flower of Spanish bravery embarked in this fleet, named somewhat presumptuously "the invincible armada." The sons of Sir James Fitzmaurice, educated at Alcala, Thomas, son of Sir John of Desmond, with several other Irish exiles, laymen, and ecclesiastics, were also on board. The fate of the expedition is well known. A series of disasters befell it on the coasts of France and Belgium, and finally, towards the middle of August, a terrific storm swept the Spaniards northward through the British channel, scattering ships and men helpless and lifeless on the coasts of Scotland, and even as far north as Norway. On the Irish shore nineteen great vessels were sunk or stranded. In Lough Foyle, one galleon, manned by 1,100 men, came ashore, and some of the survivors, it is alleged, were given up by O'Donnell to the Lord Deputy, in the vain hope of obtaining in return the liberation of his son. Sir John O'Doherty in Innishowen, Sir Brian O'Ruarc at Dromahaire, and Hugh O'Neil at Dungannon, hospitably entertained and protected several hundreds who had escaped with their lives. On the iron-bound coast of Connaught, over 2,000 men perished. In Galway harbour, 70 prisoners were taken by the Queen's garrison, and executed on St. Augustine's hill. In the Shannon, the crew of a disabled vessel set her on fire, and escaped to another in the offing. On the coasts of Cork and Kerry nearly one thousand men were lost or cast away. In all, according to a state paper of the time, above 6,000 of the Spaniards were either drowned, killed, or captured, on the north, west, and southern coasts. A more calamitous reverse could not have befallen Spain or Ireland in the era of the Reformation.

It is worthy of remark that at the very moment the fear of the armada was most intensely felt in England--the beginning of July--Sir John Perrott was recalled from the government. His high and imperious temper, not less than his reliance on the native chiefs, rather than on the courtiers of Dublin Castle, had made him many enemies. He was succeeded by a Lord Deputy of a different character--Sir William Fitzwilliam--who had filled the same office, for a short period, seventeen years before. The administration of this nobleman was protracted till the year 1594, and is chiefly memorable in connection with the formation of the Ulster Confederacy, under the leadership of O'Neil and O'Donnell.

Fitzwilliam, whose master passion was avarice, had no sooner been sworn into the government than he issued a commission to search for treasure, which the shipwrecked Spaniards were supposed to have saved. "In hopes to finger some of it," he at once marched into the territory of O'Ruarc and O'Doherty; O'Ruarc fled to Scotland, was given up by order of James VI., and subsequently executed at London; O'Doherty and Sir John O'Gallagher, "two of the most loyal subjects in Ulster," were seized and confined in the Castle. An outrage of a still more monstrous kind was perpetrated soon after on the newly elected chieftain of Oriel, Hugh McMahon. Though he had engaged Fitzwilliam by a bribe of 600 cows to recognize his succession, he was seized by order of the Deputy, tried by a jury of common soldiers, on a trumped up charge of "treason," and executed at his own door. Sir Harry Bagnal who, as Marshal of Ireland, had his head-quarters at Newry, next to Fitzwilliam himself, profited most by the consequent partition and settlement of McMahon's vast estates. Emboldened by the impunity which attended such high-handed proceedings, and instigated by the Marshal, Fitzwilliam began to practise, against the ablest as well as the most powerful of all the Northern chiefs, who had hitherto been known only as a courtier and soldier of the Queen. This was Hugh

O'Neil, Earl of Tyrone, another of Sir Henry Sidney's "strong men," with the additional advantage of being familiar from his youth with the character of the men he was now to encounter.

O'Neil, in the full prime of life, really desired to live in peace with Elizabeth, provided he might be allowed to govern Ulster with all the authority attached to his name. Bred up in England, he well knew the immense resources of that kingdom, and the indomitable character of its queen. A patriot of Ulster rather than of Ireland, he had served against the Desmonds, and had been a looker on at Smerwick. To suppress rivals of his own clan, to check O'Donnell's encroachments, and to preserve an interest at the English Court, were the objects of his earlier ambition. In pursuing these objects he did not hesitate to employ English troops in Ulster, nor to accompany the Queen and her Deputy to the service of the Church of England. If, however, he really believed that he could long continue to play the Celtic Prince north of the Boyne, and the English Earl at Dublin or London, he was soon undeceived when the fear of the Spanish Armada ceased to weigh on the Councils of Elizabeth.

A natural son of John the Proud, called from the circumstances of his birth "Hugh of the fetters," communicated to Fitzwilliam the fact of Tyrone having sheltered the shipwrecked Spaniards, and employed them in opening up a correspondence with King Philip. This so exasperated the Earl, that, having seized the unfortunate Hugh of the fetters, he caused him to be hanged as a common felon--a high-handed proceeding which his enemies were expert in turning to account. To protect himself from the consequent danger, he went to England in May, 1590, without obtaining the license of the Lord Deputy, as by law required. On arriving in London he was imprisoned, but, in the course of a month, obtained his liberty, after signing articles, in which he agreed to drop the Celtic title of O'Neil; to allow the erection of gaols in his country; that he should execute no man without a commission from the Lord Deputy, except in cases of martial law; that he should keep his troop of horsemen in the Queen's pay, ready for the Queen's service, and that Tyrone should be regularly reduced to shire-ground. For the performance of these articles, which he confirmed on reaching Dublin, he was to place sureties in the hands of certain merchants of that city, or gentlemen of the Pale, enjoying the confidence of the Crown. On such hard conditions his earldom was confirmed to him, and he was apparently taken into all his former favour. But we may date the conception of his latter and more national policy from the period of this journey, and the brief imprisonment he had undergone in London.

The "profound dissembling mind" which English historians, his cotemporaries, attribute to O'Neil, was now brought into daily exercise. When he discovered money to be the master passion of the Lord Deputy, he procured his connivance at the escape of Hugh Roe O'Donnell from Dublin Castle. On a dark night in the depth of winter the youthful chief, with several of his companions, succeeded in escaping to the hills in the neighbourhood of Powerscourt; but, exhausted and bewildered, they were again taken, and returned to their dungeons. Two years later, the heir of Tyrconnell was more fortunate. In Christmas week, 1592, he again escaped, through a sewer of the Castle, with Henry and Art O'Neil, sons of John the Proud. In the street they found O'Hagan, the confidential agent of Tyrone, waiting to guide them to the fastness of Glenmalure. Through the deep snows of the Dublin and Wicklow highlands the prisoners and their guide plodded their way. After a weary tramp they at length sunk down overwhelmed with fatigue. In this condition they were found insensible by a party despatched by Feagh O'Byrne; Art O'Neil, on being raised up, fell backward and expired; O'Donnell was so severely frost-bitten that he did not recover for many months the free use of his limbs. With his remaining companion he was nursed in the recesses of Glenmalure, until he became able to sit a horse, when he set out for home. Although the utmost vigilance was exercised by all the warders of the Pale, he crossed the Liffey and the Boyne undiscovered, rode boldly through the streets of Dundalk, and found an enthusiastic welcome, first from Tyrone in Dungannon, and soon after from the aged chief, his father, in the Castle of Ballyshannon. Early in the following year, the elder O'Donnell resigned the chieftaincy in favour of his popular son, who was, on the 3rd of May, duly proclaimed the O'Donnell, from the ancient mound of Kilmacrenan.

The Ulster Confederacy, of which, for ten years, O'Neil and O'Donnell were the joint and inseparable leaders, was now imminent. Tyrone, by carrying off, the year previous to O'Donnell's escape, the beautiful sister of Marshal Bagnal, whom he married, had still further inflamed the hatred borne to him by that officer. Bagnal complained bitterly of the abduction to the Queen, charging, among other things, that O'Neil had a divorced wife still alive. A challenge was in consequence sent him by his new brother-in-law, but the cartel was not accepted. Every day's events were hastening a general alliance between the secondary chieftains of the Province and the two leading spirits. The O'Ruarc and Maguire were attacked by Bingham, and successfully defended themselves until the Lord Deputy and the Marshal also marched against them, summoning O'Neil to their aid. The latter, feeling that the time was not yet ripe, temporized with Fitzwilliam during the campaign of 1593, and though in the field at the head of his horsemen, nominally for the Queen, he seems to have rather employed his opportunities to promote that Northern Union which he had so much at heart.

CHAPTER VIII.

THE ULSTER CONFEDERACY--FEAGH MAC HUGH O'BYRNE--CAMPAIGN OF 1595--NEGOTIATIONS, ENGLISH AND SPANISH--BATTLE OF THE YELLOW FORD--ITS CONSEQUENCES.

In the summer of 1594 the cruel and mercenary Fitzwilliam was succeeded by Sir William Russell, who had served the Queen, both in Ireland "and in divers other places beyond sea, in martial affairs." In lieu of the arbitrary exaction of county cess--so grossly abused by his predecessor--the shires of the Pale were to pay for the future into the Treasury of Dublin a composition of 2,100 pounds per annum, out of which the fixed sum of 1,000 pounds was allowed as the Deputy's wages. Russell's administration lasted till May, 1597. In that month he was succeeded by Thomas, Lord Borough, who died in August following of the wounds received in an expedition against Tyrone; after which the administration remained in the hands of the Justices till the appointment of the Earl of Essex.

On the arrival of Russell, Tyrone for the last time ventured to appear within the walls of Dublin. His influence in the city, and even at the Council table, must have been considerable to enable him to enter the gates of the Castle with so much confidence. He came to explain his wrongs against the previous Deputy, to defend himself against Bagnal's charges, and to discover, if possible, the instructions of Russell. If in one respect he was gratified by a personal triumph over his brother-in-law, in another he had cause for serious alarm, on learning that Sir John Norris, brother of the President of Munster, a commander of the highest reputation, was to be sent over under the title of Lord General, with 2,000 veterans who served in Brittany, and 1,000 of a new levy. He further learned that his own arrest had been discussed at the Council, and, leaving Dublin precipitately, he hastened to his home at Dungannon. All men's minds were now naturally filled with wars and rumours of wars.

The first blow was struck at "the firebrand of the mountains," as he was called at Court, Feagh Mac Hugh O'Byrne. The truce made with him expired in 1594, and his application for his renewal was not honoured with an answer. On the contrary, his sureties at Dublin, Geoffrey, son of Hugh, and his own son, James, were committed to close custody in the Castle. His son-in-law, Sir Walter Fitzgerald, had been driven by ill-usage, and his friendship for Lord Baltinglass, to the shelter of Glenmalure, and this was, of course, made a ground of charge against its chief. During the last months of 1594, Mynce, Sheriff of Carlow, informed the Lord Deputy of warlike preparations in the Glen, and that Brian Oge O'Rourke had actually passed to and fro through Dublin city and county, as confidential agent between Feagh Mac Hugh and Tyrone. In January following, under cover of a hunting party among the hills, the Deputy, by a night march on Glenmalure, succeeded in surprising O'Byrne's house at Ballincor, and had almost taken the aged chieftain prisoner. In the flight, Rose O'Toole, his wife, was wounded in the breast, and a priest detected hiding in a thicket was shot dead. Feagh retired to Dromceat, or the Cat's-back Mountain --one of the best positions in the Glen--while a strong force was quartered in his former mansion to observe his movements. In April, his son-in-law, Fitzgerald, was taken prisoner, near Baltinglass, in a retreat where he was laid up severely wounded; in May, a party under the Deputy's command scoured the mountains and seized the Lady Rose, who was attainted of treason, and, like Fitzgerald, barbarously given up to the halter and the quartering knife. Two foster-brothers of the chief were, at the same time and in the same manner, put to death, and a large reward was offered for his own apprehension, alive or dead.

Hugh O'Neil announced his resort to arms by a vigorous protest against the onslaught made on his friend O'Byrne. Without waiting for, or expecting any answer, he surprised the fort erected on the Blackwater which commanded the highway into his own territory. This fort, which was situated between Armagh and Dungannon, about five miles distant from either, served, before the fortification of Charlemont, as the main English stronghold in that part of Ulster. The river Blackwater on which it stood, from its source on the borders of Monaghan to its outlet in Lough Neagh, watered a fertile valley, which now became the principal theatre of war; for Hugh O'Neil, and afterwards for his celebrated nephew, it proved to be a theatre of victory. General Norris, on reaching Ireland, at once marched northward to recover the fort lately taken. O'Neil, having demolished the works, retreated before him; considering Dungannon also unfit to stand a regular siege, he dismantled the town, burnt his own castle to the ground, having first secured every portable article of value. Norris contented himself with reconnoitring the Earl's entrenched camp at some distance from Dungannon, and returned to Newry, where he established his head-quarters.

The campaign in another quarter was attended with even better success for the Confederates. Hugh Roe O'Donnell, no longer withheld by the more politic O'Neil, displayed in action all the fiery energy of his nature. Under his banner he united almost all the tribes of Ulster not enlisted with O'Neil; while six hundred Scots, led by MacLeod of Ara, obeyed his commands. He first descended on the plains of Annally-O'Farrell (the present county of Longford), driving the English settlers before him: he next visited the undertaker's tenants in Connaught, ejecting them from Boyle and Ballymoate, and pursuing them to the gates of Tuam. On his return, the important town and castle of Sligo, the property of O'Conor, then in England, submitted to him. Sir Richard Bingham endeavoured to recover it, but was beaten off with loss. O'Donnell, finding it cheaper to demolish than defend it, broke down the castle and returned in triumph across the Erne.

General Norris, having arranged his plan of campaign at Newry, attempted to victual Armagh, besieged by O'Neil, but was repulsed by that leader after a severe struggle. He, however, succeeded in throwing supplies into Monaghan, where a strong garrison was quartered, and to which O'Neil and O'Donnell proceeded to lay siege. While lying before Monaghan they received overtures of peace from the Lord Deputy, who continually disagreed with Sir John Norris as to the conduct of the war, and lost no opportunity of thwarting his plans. He did not now blush to address, as Earl of Tyrone, the man he had lately proclaimed a traitor at Dublin, by the title of the son of a blacksmith. The Irish leaders at the outset refused to meet the Commissioners--Chief Justice Gardiner and Sir Henry Wallop, Treasurer-at-War--in Dundalk, so the latter were compelled to wait on them in the camp before Monaghan. The terms demanded by O'Neil and O'Donnell, including entire freedom of religious worship, were reserved by the Commissioners for the consideration of the Council, with whose sanction, a few weeks afterwards, all the Ulster chiefs, except "the Queen's O'Reilly," were formally tried before a jury at Dublin, and condemned as traitors.

Monaghan was thrice taken and retaken in this campaign. It was on the second return of General Norris from that town he found himself unexpectedly in presence of O'Neil's army, advantageously posted on the left bank of the little stream which waters the village of Clontibret. Norris made two attempts to force the passage, but without success. Sir Thomas Norris, and the general himself, were wounded; Seagrave, a gigantic Meathian cavalry officer, was slain in a hand to hand encounter with O'Neil; the English retreated hastily on Newry, and Monaghan was again surrendered to the Irish. This brilliant combat at Clontibret closed the campaign of 1595. General Norris, who, like Sir John Moore, two centuries later, commanded the respect, and frankly acknowledged the wrongs of the people against whom he fought, employed the winter months in endeavouring to effect a reconciliation between O'Neil and the Queen's Government. He had conceived a warm and chivalrous regard for his opponent; for he could not deny that he had been driven to take up arms in self-defence. At his instance a royal commission to treat with the Earl was issued, and the latter cheerfully gave them a meeting in an open field without the walls of Dundalk. The same terms which he had proposed before Monaghan were repeated in his *ultimatum*, and the Commissioners agreed to give him a positive answer by the 2nd day of April. On that day they attended at Dundalk, but O'Neil did not appear. The Commissioners delayed an entire fortnight, addressing him in the interim an urgent remonstrance to come in and conclude their negotiation. On the 17th of the month they received his reasons for breaking off the treaty--the principal of which was, that the truce had been repeatedly broken through by the English garrisons--and so the campaign of 1596 was to be fought with renewed animosity on both sides.

Early in May the Lord Deputy made another descent on Ballincor, which Feagh Mac Hugh had recovered in the autumn to lose again in the spring. Though worn with years and infirm of body, the Wicklow chieftain held his devoted bands well together, and kept the garrison of Dublin constantly on the defensive. In the new chieftain of the O'Moores he found at this moment a young and active coadjutor. In an affair at Stradbally Bridge, O'Moore obtained a considerable victory, leaving among the slain Alexander and Francis Cosby, grandsons of the commander in the massacre at Mullaghmast.

The arrival of three Spanish frigates with arms and ammunition in Donegal Bay was welcome news to the Northern Catholics. They were delivered to O'Donnell, who was incessantly in the field, while O'Neil was again undergoing the forms of diplomacy with a new royal commission at Dundalk. He himself disclaimed any correspondence with the King of Spain, but did not deny that such negotiations might be maintained by others. It is alleged that, while many of the chiefs had signed a formal invitation to the Spanish King to assume their crown, O'Neil had not gone beyond verbal assurances of co-operation with them. However this may be, he resolved that the entire season should not be wasted in words, so he attacked the strong garrison left in Armagh, and recovered the primatial city. According to the Irish practice, he dismantled the fortress, which, however, was again reconstructed by the English before the end of the war. Some other skirmishes, of which we have no very clear account, and which we may set down as of no decisive character, terminated the campaign.

In May, 1597, Lord Borough, who had distinguished himself in the Netherlands, replaced Russell as Lord Deputy, and assumed the command-in-chief, in place of Sir John Norris. Simultaneously with his arrival Feagh Mac Hugh O'Byrne, was surprised in Glenmalure by a detachment from Dublin, and slain; he died as he had lived, a hero and a free man. O'Neil, who was warmly attached to the Wicklow chief, immediately despatched such succour as he could spare to Feagh's sons, and promised to continue to them the friendship he had always entertained for their father. Against Tyrone the new Lord Deputy now endeavoured to combine all the military resources at his disposal. Towards the end of July, Sir Conyers Clifford was ordered to muster the available force of Connaught at Boyle, and to march into Sligo and Donegal. A thousand men of the Anglo-Irish were assembled at Mullingar, under the command of young Barnewell of Trimbleston, who was instructed to effect a junction with the main force upon the borders of Ulster. The Lord Deputy, marching in force from Drogheda, penetrated, unopposed, the valley of the Blackwater, and entered Armagh. From Armagh he moved to the relief of the Blackwater fort, besieged by O'Neil. At a place called Drumfliuch, where Battleford Bridge now stands, Tyrone contrived to draw his enemies into an engagement on very disadvantageous ground. The result was a severe defeat to the new Deputy, who, a few days afterwards, died of his wounds at Newry, as his second in command, the Earl of Kildare, did at Drogheda. Sir Francis Vaughan, Sir Thomas Waller, and other distinguished officers, fell in the same action, but the fort, the main prize of the combatants, remained in English hands till the following year. O'Donnell, with equal success, held Ballyshannon, compelled Sir Conyers Clifford to raise the siege with the loss of the Earl of Thomond, and a large part of his following. Simultaneously, Captain Richard Tyrrell of West-Meath--one of O'Neil's favourite officers--having laid an ambuscade for young Barnewell at the pass in West-Meath which now bears his name, the Meathian regiment were sabred to a man. Mullingar and Maryborough were taken and sacked, and in the North, Sir John Chichester, Governor of Carrickfergus, was cut off with his troop by MacDonald of the Glens.

These successes synchronize exactly with the expectation of a second Spanish Armada, which filled Elizabeth with her old apprehensions. Philip was persuaded again to tempt the fortune of the seas, and towards the end of October his fleet, under the Adelantado of Castille, appeared off the Scilly Islands, with a view to secure the Isle of Wight, or some other station, from which to operate an invasion the ensuing spring. Extraordinary means were taken for defence; the English troops in France were recalled, new levies raised, and the Queen's favourite, the young Earl of Essex, appointed to command the fleet, with Raleigh and Lord Thomas Howard as Vice-Admirals. But the elements again fought for the northern island; a storm, which swept the channel for weeks, drove the English ships into their ports, but scattered those of Spain over the Bay of Biscay. In this second expedition sailed Florence Conroy, and other Irish exiles, who had maintained for years a close correspondence with the Catholic leaders. Their presence in the fleet, the existence of the correspondence, and the progress of the revolt itself, will sufficiently account for the apparent vacillations of English policy in Ulster in the last months of 1597. Shortly before Christmas, Ormond, now Lord Lieutenant, accompanied by the Earl of Thomond, attended only by their personal followers, visited Dungannon, and remained three days in conference with O'Neil and O'Donnell. The Irish chiefs reiterated their old demands: freedom of worship, and the retention of the substantial power attached to their ancient rank. They would admit Sheriffs, if they were chosen from among natives of their counties, but they declined to give hostages out of their own families. These terms were referred to the Queen's consideration, who, after much protocoling to and fro, finally ratified them the following April, and affixed the great seal to O'Neil's pardon. But Tyrone, guided by intelligence received from Spain or England, or both, evaded the royal messenger charged to deliver him that instrument, and as the late truce expired the first week of June, devoted himself anew to military preparations.

In the month of June, 1598, the Council at Dublin were in a state of fearful perplexity. O'Neil, two days after the expiration of the truce, invested the fort on the Blackwater, and seemed resolved to reduce it, if not by force, by famine. O'Donnell, as usual, was operating on the side of Connaught, where he had brought back O'Ruarc, O'Conor Sligo, and McDermot, to the Confederacy, from which they had been for a season estranged. Tyrrell and O'Moore, leading spirits in the midland counties were ravaging Ormond's palatinate of Tipperary almost without opposition. An English reinforcement, debarked at Dungarvan, was attacked on its march towards Dublin, and lost 400 men. In this emergency, before which even the iron nerve of Ormond quailed, the Council took the resolution of ordering one moiety of the Queen's troops under Ormond to march south against Tyrrell and O'Moore; the other under Marshal Bagnal, to proceed northward to the relief of the Blackwater fort. Ormond's campaign was brief and inglorious. After suffering a severe check in Leix, he shut himself up in Kilkenny, where he heard of the disastrous fate of Bagnal's expedition.

On Sunday, the 13th of August, the Marshal reached Newry with some trifling loss from skirmishes on the route. He had with him, by the best accounts, six regiments of infantry, numbering in all about 4,000 men and 350 horse. After resting a day, his whole force marched out of the city in three divisions; the first under the command of the Marshal and Colonel Percy, the cavalry under Sir Calisthenes Brooke and Captains Montague and Fleming; the rear guard under Sir Thomas Wingfield and Colonel Cosby. The Irish, whose numbers, both mounted and afoot, somewhat exceeded the Marshal's force, but who were not so well armed, had taken up a strong position at Ballinaboy ("the Yellow ford"), about two miles north of Armagh. With O'Neil were O'Donnell, Maguire, and McDonnell of Antrim--all approved leaders beloved by their men. O'Neil had neglected no auxiliary means of strengthening the position. In front of his lines he dug deep trenches, covered over with green sods, supported by twigs and branches. The pass leading into this plain was lined by 500 kerne, whose Parthian warfare was proverbial. He had reckoned on the headlong and boastful disposition of his opponent, and the result showed his accurate knowledge of character. Bagnal's first division, veterans from Brittany and Flanders, including 600 curassiers in complete armour, armed with lances nine feet long, dashed into the pass before the second and third divisions had time to come up. The kerne poured in their rapid volleys; many of the English fell; the pass was yielded, and the whole power of Bagnal debouched into the plain. His artillery now thundered upon O'Neil's trenches, and the cavalry, with the plain before them, were ordered to charge; but they soon came upon the concealed pitfalls, horses fell, riders were thrown, and confusion spread among the squadron. Then it was O'Neil in turn gave the signal to charge; himself led on the centre, O'Donnell the left, and Maguire, famous for horsemanship, the Irish horse. The overthrow of the English was complete, and the victory most eventful. The Marshal, 23 superior officers, with about 1,700 of the rank and file fell on the field, while all the artillery baggage and 12 stand of colours were taken: the Irish loss in killed and wounded did not exceed 800 men. "It was a glorious victory for the rebels," says the cotemporary English historian, Camden, "and of special advantage: for hereby they got arms and provisions, and Tyrone's name was cried up all over Ireland as the author of their liberty." It may also be added that it attracted renewed attention to the Irish war at Paris, Madrid, and Rome, where the names of O'Neil and O'Donnell were spoken of by all zealous Catholics with enthusiastic admiration.

The battle was over by noon of the 15th of August; and the only effort to arrest the flight of the survivors was made by "the Queen's O'Reilly," who was slain in the attempt. By one o'clock the remnant of the cavalry under Montague were in full career for Dundalk, closely pressed by the mounted men of O'Hanlon. During the ensuing week the Blackwater fort capitulated; the Protestant garrison of Armagh surrendered; and were allowed to march south, leaving their arms and ammunition behind. The panic spread far and wide; the citizens of Dublin were enrolled to defend their walls; Lord Ormond continued shut up in Kilkenny; O'Moore and Tyrrell, who entered Munster by O'Neil's order, to kindle the elements of resistance, compelled the Lord President to retire from Kilmallock to Cork. O'Donnell established his head-quarters at Ballymoate, a dozen miles south of Sligo, which he had purchased from the chieftain of Corran for 400 pounds and 300 cows. The castle had served for thirteen years as an English stronghold, and was found staunch enough fifty years later to withstand the siege trains of Coote and Ludlow. From this point the Donegal chieftain was enabled to stretch his arm in every direction over lower Connaught. The result was, that before the end of the year 1598, nearly all the inhabitants of Clanrickarde and the surrounding districts were induced, either from policy or conviction, to give in their adhesion to the Northern Confederacy.

CHAPTER IX.

ESSEX'S CAMPAIGN OF 1599--BATTLE OF THE CURLIEU MOUNTAINS--O'NEIL'S NEGOTIATIONS WITH SPAIN-- MOUNTJOY, LORD DEPUTY.

The last favourite of the many who enjoyed the foolish, if not guilty, favours of Elizabeth was Robert Devereux, Earl of Essex, son of that unfortunate nobleman spoken of in a previous chapter as the "undertaker" of Farney and Clandeboy. Born in 1567, the Earl had barely reached the age of manhood when he won the heart of his royal mistress, already verging on threescore. Gifted by nature with a handsome person, undoubted courage, and many generous qualities, he exhibited, in the most important transactions of life, the recklessness of a madman and the levity of a spoiled child; it was apparent to the world that nothing short of the personal fascination which he exercised over the Queen could so long have preserved him from the consequences of his continual caprices and quarrels. Such was the character of the young nobleman, who, as was afterwards said, at the instigation of his enemies, was sent over to restore the ascendancy of the English arms in the revolted provinces. His appointment was to last during the Queen's pleasure; he was provided with an army of 20,000 foot and 2,000 horse; three-fourths of the ordinary annual revenue of England (340,000 pounds out of 450,000 pounds) was placed at his disposal, and the largest administrative powers, civil and military, were conferred on him. A new plan of campaign in Ulster was decided upon at the royal council table, and Sir Samuel Bagnal, brother of the late Marshal, and other experienced officers, were to precede or accompany him to carry it into execution. The main feature of this plan was to get possession by sea and strongly fortify Ballyshannon, Donegal, Derry, and the entrance to the Foyle, so as to operate at once in the rear of the northern chiefs, as well as along the old familiar base of Newry, Monaghan, and Armagh.

Essex, on being sworn into office at Dublin, on the 15th of April, 1599, immediately issued a proclamation offering pardon and restoration of property to such of the Irish as would lay down their arms by a given day, but very few persons responded to this invitation. He next despatched reinforcements to the garrisons of Wicklow and Naas, menaced by the O'Moores and O'Byrnes, and to those of Drogheda, Dundalk, Newry, and Carrickfergus, the only northern strongholds remaining in possession of the Queen. The principal operations, it had been agreed before he left England, were to be directed against Ulster, but with the waywardness which always accompanied him, he disregarded that arrangement, and set forth, at the head of 7,000 men, for the opposite quarter. He was accompanied in this march by the Earls of Clanrickarde and Thomond, Sir Conyers Clifford, Governor of Connaught, and O'Conor of Sligo, the only native chief who remained in the English ranks. In Ormond he received the submission of Lord Mountgarrett, son-in-law to Tyrone, and took the strong castle of Cahir from another of the insurgent Butlers. After a halt at Limerick, he set out against the Geraldines, who the previous year had joined the Northern league, at the instance of Tyrrell and O'Moore. Although the only heir of the Earl of Desmond was a prisoner, or ward of Elizabeth in England, James Fitzgerald, son of Thomas Roe, son of the fifteenth Earl by that marriage which had been pronounced invalid, assumed the title at the suggestion of O'Neil, and was recognized as the Desmond by the greater portion of the relatives of that family. Fitzmaurice, Lord of Lixnaw, the Knight of Glynn, the White Knight, the Lord Roche, Pierce Lacy of Buree and Bruff, the last descendant of Hugh de Lacy and the daughter of Roderick O'Conor, with the McCarthys, O'Donohoes, O'Sullivans, Condons, and other powerful tribes, were all astir to the number, as Carew supposes, of 8,000 men, all emulous of their compatriots in the North. Issuing from Limerick, Essex marched southward to strengthen the stronghold of Askeaton, into which he succeeded, after a severe skirmish by the way, in throwing supplies. Proceeding to victual Adare, he experienced a similar check, losing among others Sir Henry Norris, the third of those brave brothers who had fallen a victim to these Irish wars. In returning to Dublin, by way of Waterford and Kildare, he was assailed by O'Moore at a difficult defile, which, to this day, is known in Irish as "the pass of the plumes" or feathers. The Earl forced a passage with the loss of 500 lives, and so returned with little glory to Dublin.

The next military incident of the year transpired in the West. We have spoken of O'Conor Sligo as the only native chief who followed Essex to the South. He had been lately at the English Court, where he was treated with the highest distinction, in order that he might be used to impede O'Donnell's growing power in lower Connaught. On returning home he was promptly besieged by the Donegal chief in his remaining castle at Coolooney, within five miles of Sligo. Essex, on learning this fact, ordered Sir Conyers Clifford to march to the relief of O'Conor with all the power he could muster. Clifford despatched from Galway, by sea, stores and materials for the refortification of Sligo town, and set out himself at the head of 2,100 men, drafted from both sides of the Shannon, under twenty-five ensigns. He had under him Sir Alexander Radcliffe, Sir Griffin Markham, and other experienced officers. Their rendezvous, as usual, was the old monastic town of Boyle, about a day's march to the south of Sligo. From Boyle, the highway led into the Curlieu mountains, which divide Sligo on the south-east from Roscommon. Here, in the strong pass of Ballaghboy, O'Donnell with the main body of his followers awaited their approach. He had left the remainder, under his cousin and brother-in-law, Nial Garve (or the *rough*), to maintain the siege of Coolooney Castle. O'Ruarc and the men of Breffni joined him during the battle, but their entire force is nowhere stated. It was the eve of the Assumption of the Blessed Virgin, and the first anniversary of the great victory of the Yellow Ford. The night was spent by the Irish in fasting and prayer, the early morning in hearing Mass, and receiving the Holy Communion. The day was far advanced when the head of Clifford's column appeared in the defile, driving in a barricade erected at its entrance. The defenders, according to orders, discharged their javelins and muskets, and fell back farther into the gorge. The English advanced twelve abreast, through a piece of woodland, after which the road crossed a patch of bog. Here the thick of the battle was fought. Sir Alexander Radcliffe, who led the vanguard, fell early in the action, and his division falling back on the centre threw them all into confusion. O'Ruarc arriving with his men at the critical moment completed the rout, and pursued the fugitives to the gates of Boyle. The gallant Clifford, scorning to fly, was found among the slain, and honourably interred by his generous enemies in the monastery of Lough Key. On his head being shown to O'Conor at Coolooney, he at once surrendered to O'Donnell, and entered into the

Northern Confederacy. Theobald Burke, the commander of the vessels sent round from Galway to fortify Sligo, also submitted to O'Donnell, and was permitted to return to the port from which he had lately sailed, with very different intentions.

Essex, whose mind was a prey to apprehension from his enemies in England had demanded reinforcements before he could undertake anything against Ulster. It seems hardly credible that the 15,000 regular troops in the country at his coming should be mostly taken up with garrison duty, yet we cannot otherwise account for their disappearance from the field. He asked for 2,000 fresh troops, and while awaiting their arrival, sent a detachment of 600 men into Wicklow, who were repulsed with loss by Phelim, son of Feagh, the new Chief of the O'Byrnes. Essex was thrown into transports of rage at this new loss. The officers who retreated were tried by court-martial, and, contrary to his usually generous temper, the surviving men were inhumanly decimated.

Early in September, the reinforcement he had asked for arrived with a bitterly reproachful letter from the Queen. He now hastened to make a demonstration against Tyrone, although, from some cause unexplained, he does not seem to have drawn out the whole force at his disposal. From Newry he proceeded northward towards Carrickfergus, with only 1,300 foot and 300 horse. On the high ground to the north of the river Lagan, overlooking Anaghclart Bridge, he found the host of O'Neil encamped, and received a courteous message from their leader, soliciting a personal interview. Essex at first declined, but afterwards accepted the invitation, and at an appointed hour the two commanders rode down to the opposite banks of the river, wholly unattended, the advanced guard of each looking curiously on from the uplands. O'Neil spurred his horse into the stream up to the saddle girth, and thus for an hour, exposed to the generous but impulsive Englishman, the grievances of himself and his compatriots. With all the art, for which he was distinguished, he played upon his knowledge of the Earl's character: he named those enemies of his own whom he also knew to be hostile to Essex, he showed his provocations in the strongest light, and declared his readiness to submit to her Majesty, on condition of obtaining complete liberty of conscience, an act of indemnity to include his allies in all the four Provinces; that the principal officers of state, the judges, and one half the army should in future be Irish by birth. This was, in effect, a demand for national independence, though the Lord Lieutenant may not have seen it in that light. He promised, however, to transmit the propositions to England, and within presence of six principal officers of each side, agreed to a truce till the 1st of May following. Another upbraiding letter from Elizabeth, which awaited him on his return to Dublin, drove Essex to the desperate resolution of presenting himself before her, without permission. The short remainder of his troubled career, his execution in the Tower in February, 1601, and Elizabeth's frantic lamentations, are familiar to readers of English history.

In presenting so comprehensive an ultimatum to Essex, O'Neil was emboldened by the latest intelligence received from Spain. Philip II., the life-long friend of the Catholics, had, indeed, died the previous September, but one of the first acts of his successor, Philip III., was to send envoys into Ireland, assuring its chiefs that he would continue to them the friendship and alliance of his father. Shortly before the conference at Anaghclart, a third Armada, under the Adelantado of Castile, was awaiting orders in the port of Corunna, and England, for the third time in ten years, was placed in a posture of defence. The Spaniards sailed, but soon divided into two squadrons, one of which passed down the British Channel unobserved, and anchored in the waters of the Sluys, while the other sailed for the Canaries to intercept the Hollanders. At the same time, however, most positive assurances were renewed that an auxiliary force might shortly be expected to land in Ireland in aid of the Catholics. The non-arrival of this force during the fortunate campaign of 1599 was not much felt by the Catholics; and was satisfactorily explained by Philip's envoys--but the mere fact of the existence of the Spanish alliance gave additional confidence and influence to the confederates. That fact was placed beyond all question by the arrival of two Spanish ships laden with stores for O'Neil, immediately after the interview with Essex. In the summer or autumn ensuing, Mathew of Oviedo, a Spaniard, consecrated at Rome, Archbishop of Dublin, brought over 22,000 crowns towards the pay of the Irish troops, and a year afterwards, Don Martin de la Cerda was sent to reside as envoy with Tyrone.

The year 1600 was employed by Hugh O'Neil, after the manner of his ancestors, who were candidates for the Kingship of Tara, in a visitation of the Provinces. Having first planted strong garrisons on the southern passes leading into Ulster, he marched at the head of 3,000 men into West-Meath, where he obliged Lord Delvin and Sir Theobald Dillon to join the Confederation. From Meath he marched to Ely, whose chief he punished for a late act of treachery to some Ulster soldiers invited to his assistance. From Ely he turned aside to venerate the relic of the Holy Cross, at Thurles, and being there he granted his protection to the great Monastery built by Donald More O'Brien. At Cashel he was joined by the Geraldine, whom he caused to be recognized as Earl of Desmond. Desmond and his supporters accompanied him through Limerick into Cork, quartering their retainers on the lands of their enemies, but sparing their friends; the Earl of Ormond with a corps of observation moving on a parallel line of march, but carefully avoiding a collision. In the beginning of March the Catholic army halted at Inniscarra, upon the river Lee, about five miles west of Cork. Here O'Neil remained three weeks in camp consolidating the Catholic party in South Munster. During that time he was visited by the chiefs of the ancient Eugenian clans--O'Donohoe, O'Donovan, and O'Mahoney: thither also came two of the most remarkable men of the southern Province, Florence McCarthy, Lord of Carberry, and Donald O'Sullivan, Lord of Bearehaven. McCarthy "like Saul, higher by the head and shoulders than any of his house," had brain in proportion to his brawn; O'Sullivan, as was afterwards shown, was possessed of military virtues of a high order. Florence was inaugurated with O'Neil's sanction as McCarthy More, and although the rival house of Muskerry fiercely resisted his claim to superiority at first, a wiser choice could not have been made had the times tended to confirm it.

While at Inniscarra, O'Neil lost in single combat one of his most accomplished officers, the chief of Fermanagh. Maguire, accompanied only by a Priest and two horsemen, was making observations nearer to the city than the camp, when Sir Warham St. Leger, Marshal of Munster, issued out of Cork with a company of soldiers, probably on a similar mission. Both were in advance of their attendants when they came unexpectedly face to face. Both were famous as horsemen and for the use of their weapons, and neither would retrace his steps. The Irish chief, poising his spear, dashed forward against his opponent, but received a pistol shot which proved mortal the same day. He, however, had strength enough left to drive his spear through the neck of St. Leger, and to effect his escape from the English cavalry. Saint Leger was carried back to Cork where he expired; Maguire, on reaching the camp, had barely time left to make his last confession, when he breathed his last. This untoward event, the necessity of preventing possible dissensions in Fermanagh, and still more, the menacing movements of the new Deputy, lately sworn in at Dublin, obliged O'Neil to return home earlier than he intended. Soon after reaching Dungannon he had the gratification of receiving a most gracious letter from Pope Clement VIII., together with a crown of phoenix feathers, symbolical of the consideration with which he was regarded by the Sovereign Pontiff.

A new Deputy had landed at Howth on the 24th of February, 1600, and was sworn in at Dublin the day following. This was Charles Blount, Lord Mountjoy, afterwards Earl of Devonshire, a nobleman now in his 37th year. He had been the rival, the enemy, and the devoted friend of the unfortunate Essex, whom he equalled in personal gifts, in courage, and in gallantry, but far exceeded in judgment, firmness, and foresight. He was one of a class of soldier-statesmen, peculiar to the second half of Elizabeth's reign, who affected authorship and the patronage of letters as a necessary complement to the manners of a courtier and commander. On the 2nd of April, Mountjoy, still at Dublin, wrote to her Majesty that the army had taken heart since his arrival, that he had no fear of the loss of the country, but was more anxious for Connaught than any other Province. He deplored the capture of Lord Ormond by the O'Moores, but hoped, if God prospered her arms during the summer, either "to bow or to break the crooked humours of these people." The three succeeding years of peace granted to England-- interrupted only by the mad *emeute* of Essex, and the silly intrigues of the King of Scotland--enabled Elizabeth to direct all the energies of the State, which had so immensely increased in wealth during her reign, for the subjugation of the Irish revolt.

The capture of Ormond by the O'Moores took place in the month of April, at a place called Corroneduff, in an interview between the Earl, the President of Munster, and Lord Thomond, on the one part, and the Leinster Chief on the other. Ormond, who stood out from his party, had asked to see the famous Jesuit, Father Archer, then with O'Moore. The Priest advanced leaning on his staff, which, in the heat of a discussion that arose, he raised once or twice in the air. The clansmen, suspecting danger to the Jesuit, rushed forward and dragged the Earl from his horse. Lord Thomond and the President, taking the alarm, plied their spurs, and were but too glad to escape. Ormond remained a prisoner from April to June, during which interval he was received by Archer into the Church, to which he firmly adhered till the day of his death. On his liberation he entered into bonds for 3,000 pounds not to make reprisals, but Mountjoy took vengeance for him. The fair, well-fenced, and well-cultivated land of Leix was cruelly ravaged immediately after Ormond's release--the common soldiers cut down with their swords "corn to the value of 10,000 pounds and upwards," and the brave chief, Owny, son of Rory, having incautiously exposed himself in an attack on Maryborough, was, on the 17th of August, killed by a musket shot.

CHAPTER X.

MOUNTJOY'S ADMINISTRATION--OPERATIONS IN ULSTER AND MUNSTER--CAREW'S "WIT AND CUNNING"--LANDING OF SPANIARDS IN THE SOUTH--BATTLE OF KINSALE--DEATH OF O'DONNELL IN SPAIN.

The twofold operations against Ulster, neglected by Essex, were vigorously pressed forward by the energetic Mountjoy. On the 16th of May, a fleet arrived in Lough Foyle, having on board 4,000 foot and 200 horse, under the command of Sir Henry Dowcra, with abundance of stores, building materials, and ordnance. At the same moment, the Deputy forced the Moira pass, and made a feigned demonstration against Armagh, to draw attention from the fleet in the Foyle. This feint served its purpose; Dowcra was enabled to land and throw up defensive works at Derry, which he made his head-quarters, to fortify Culmore at the entrance to the harbour, where he placed 600 men, under the command of Captain Atford, and to seize the ancient fort of Aileach, at the head of Lough Swilly, where Captain Ellis Flood was stationed with 150 men. The attempt against Ballyshannon was, on a nearer view, found impracticable, and deferred; the Deputy, satisfied that the lodgment had been made upon Lough Foyle, retired to Dublin, after increasing the garrisons at Newry, Carlingford, and Dundalk. The Catholic chieftains immediately turned their attention to the new fort at Deny, appeared suddenly before it with 5,000 men, but failing to draw out its defenders, and being wholly unprovided with a siege train and implements--as they appear to have been throughout-- they withdrew the second day, O'Donnell leaving a party in hopes to starve out the foreigners. This party were under the command of O'Doherty, of Innishowen, and Nial Garve O'Donnell, the most distinguished soldier of his name, after his illustrious cousin and chief. On the 28th of June, a party of the besieged, headed by Sir John Chamberlaine, made a sally from the works, but were driven in with loss, and Chamberlaine killed. On the 29th of July, O'Donnell, who had returned from his annual incursion into Connaught and Thomond, seized the English cavalry horses, and defeated the main force of the besieged, who had issued out to their rescue. From this affair Dowcra was carried back wounded into Deny.

But treason was busy in the Irish camp and country among the discontented members of the neighbouring clans. The election of chiefs for life, always a fruitful source of bickering and envy, supplied the very material upon which "the princely policie" of division, recommended by Bacon to Essex, might be exercised. Dowcra succeeded in the summer in winning over Art O'Neil, son of Turlogh, the early adversary of the great Hugh; before the year was over, by bribes and promises, he seduced Nial Garve, in the absence of his chief in Connaught, and Nial, having once entered on the career of treason, pursued it with all the dogged courage of Ms disposition. Though his wife, sister to Red Hugh, forsook him, though his name was execrated throughout the Province, except by his blindly devoted personal followers, he served the English during the remainder of the war with a zeal and ability to which they acknowledged themselves deeply indebted. By a rapid march, at the head of 1,000 men, supplied by Dowcra, he surprised the town of Lifford, which his new allies promptly fortified with walls of stone, and entrusted to him to defend. Red Hugh, on learning this alarming incident, hastened from the West to invest the place. After sitting before it an entire month, with no other advantage than a sally repulsed, he concluded to go into winter quarters. Arthur O'Neil and Nial Garve had the dignity of knighthood conferred upon them, and were, besides, recognized for the day by the English officials as the future O'Neil and O'Donnell. In like manner, "a Queen's Maguire" had been raised up in Fermanagh, "a Queen's O'Reilly" in Cavan, and other chiefs of smaller districts were provided with occupation enough at their own doors by the "princely policie" of Lord Bacon.

The English interest in Munster during the first year of Mountjoy's administration had recovered much of its lost predominance. The new President, Sir George Carew, afterwards Earl of Totness, was brother to that knightly "undertaker" who claimed the moiety of Desmond, and met his death at Glenmalure. He was a soldier of the new school, who prided himself especially on his "wit and cunning," in the composition of "sham and counterfeit letters." He had an early experience in the Irish wars, first as Governor of Askeaton Castle, and afterwards as Lieutenant General of the Ordnance. Subsequently he was employed in putting England in a state of defence against the Spaniards, and had just returned from an embassy to Poland, when he was ordered to join Mountjoy with the rank of Lord President. He has left us a memoir of his administration, civil and military, edited by his natural son and Secretary, Thomas Stafford--exceedingly interesting to read both as to matter and manner, but the documents embodied in which are about as reliable as the speeches which are read in Livy. Some of them are admitted forgeries; others are at least of doubtful authenticity. After escaping with Lord Thomond from the scene of Ormond's capture, his first act on reaching Cork was to conclude a month's truce with Florence McCarthy. This he did, in order to gain time to perfect a plot for the destruction of O'Neil's other friend, called in derision, by the Anglo-Irish of Munster, the *sugane* (or straw-rope) Earl of Desmond.

This plot, so characteristic of Carew and of the turn which English history was about to take in the next reign, deserves to be particularly mentioned. There was, in the service of the Earl, one Dermid O'Conor, captain of 1,400 hired troops, who was married to lady Margaret Fitzgerald, daughter to the late, and niece to the new-made Earl of Desmond. This lady, naturally interested in the restoration of her young brother, then the Queen's ward or prisoner at London, to the title and estates, was easily drawn into the scheme of seducing her husband from his patron. To justify and cloak the treachery a letter was written by Carew to the *sugane* Earl reminding him of *his* engagement to deliver up O'Conor; this *letter*, as pre-arranged, was intercepted by the latter, who, watching his opportunity, rushed with it open into the Earl's presence, and arrested him, in the name of O'Neil, as a traitor to the Catholic cause! Anxious to finger his reward--1,000 pounds and a royal commission for himself--before giving up his capture, O'Conor imprisoned the Earl in the keep of Castle-Ishin, but the White Knight, the Knight of Glynn, Fitzmaurice of Kerry, and Pierce Lacy, levying rapidly 2,000 men, speedily delivered him from confinement, while his baffled betrayer, crest-fallen and dishonoured, was compelled to quit the Province. The year following he was attacked while marching through Galway, and remorselessly put to death by Theobald Burke, usually called Theobald of the ships.

Another device employed to destroy the influence of O'Neil's Desmond was the liberation of the young son of the late Earl from the Tower and placing him at the disposal of Carew. The young nobleman, attended by a Captain Price, who was to watch all his movements, landed at Youghal, where he was received by the Lord President, the Clerk of the Council, Mr. Boyle, afterwards Earl of Cork, and Miler Magrath, an apostate ecclesiastic, who had been the Queen's Archbishop of Cashel. By his influence with the warders, Castlemaine, in Kerry, surrendered to the President. On reaching Kilmallock, he was received with such enthusiasm that it required the effort of a guard of soldiers to make way for him through the crowd. According to their custom the people showered down upon him from the windows handfuls of wheat and salt--emblems of plenty and of safety--but the next day, being Sunday, turned all this joy into mourning, not unmingled with anger and shame. The young lord, who had been bred up a Protestant by his keepers, directed his steps to the English Church, to the consternation of the devoted adherents of his house. They clung round him in the street and endeavoured to dissuade him from proceeding, but he continued his course, and on his return was met with hootings and reproaches by those who had hailed him with acclamations the day before. Deserted by the people, and no longer useful to the President, he was recalled to London, where he resumed his quarters in the Tower, and shortly afterwards died. The capture of the strong castle of Glynn from the knight of that name, and the surrender of Carrigafoyle by O'Conor of Kerry, were the other English successes which marked the campaign of 1600 in Munster. On the other hand, O'Donnell had twice exercised his severe supremacy over southern Connaught, burning the Earl of Thomond's new town of Ennis, and sweeping the vales and plains of Clare, and of Clanrickarde, of the animal wealth of their recreant Earls, now actively enlisted against the national confederacy.

    The eventful campaign of 1601 was fought out in almost every quarter of the kingdom. To hold the coast line, and prevent the advantages being obtained, which the possession of Derry, and other harbours on Lough Foyle gave them, were the tasks of O'Donnell; while to defend the southern frontier was the peculiar charge of O'Neil. They thus fought, as it were, back to back against the opposite lines of attack. The death of O'Doherty, early in this year, threw the succession to Innishowen into confusion, and while O'Donnell was personally endeavouring to settle conflicting claims, Nial Garve seized on the famous Franciscan monastery which stood at the head of the bay, within sight of the towers of Donegal Castle. Hugh Roe immediately invested the place, which his relative as stoutly defended. Three months, from the end of June till the end of September, the siege was strictly maintained, the garrison being regularly supplied with stores and ammunition from sea. On the night of the 29th of September an explosion of gunpowder occurred, and soon the monastery was wrapped in flames. This was the moment chosen for the final attack. The glare of the burning Abbey reflected over the beautiful bay, the darkness of night all round, the shouts of the assailants, and the shrieks of the fugitives driven by the flames upon the spears of their enemies, must have formed a scene of horrors such as even war rarely combines. Hundreds of the besieged were slain, but Nial Garve himself, with the remainder, covered by the fire of an English ship in the harbour, escaped along the strand to the neighbouring monastery of Magherabeg, which he quickly put into a state of defence. All that was left to O'Donnell of that monastery, the burial place of his ancestors, and the chief school of his kinsmen, was a skeleton of stone, standing amid rubbish and ashes. It was never re-inhabited by the Franciscans. A group of huts upon the shore served them for shelter, and the ruined chapel for a place of worship, while they were still left in the land.

While Hugh Roe was investing Donegal Abbey the war had not paused on the southern frontier. We have said that Mountjoy had made a second and a third demonstration against Armagh the previous year; in one of these journeys he raised a strong fort at the northern outlet of the Moira pass, which he called Mount Norris, in honour of his late master in the art of war. This work, strongly built and manned, gave him the free *entree* of the field of battle whenever he chose to take it. In June of this year he was in the valley of the Blackwater, menaced O'Neil's castle of Benburb, and left Sir Charles Danvers with 750 foot and 100 horse in possession of Armagh. He further proclaimed a reward of 2,000 pounds for the capture of Tyrone alive, or 1,000 pounds for his head. But no Irishman was found to entertain the thought of that bribe. An English assassin was furnished with passports by Danvers, and actually drew his sword on the Earl in his own tent, but he was seized, disarmed, and on the ground of insanity was permitted to escape. Later in the summer Mountjoy was again on the Blackwater, where he laid the foundation of Charlemont, called after himself, and placed 350 men in the works under the command of Captain Williams, the brave defender of the old fort in the same neighbourhood.

There were thus quartered in Ulster at this period the 4,000 foot and 400 horse under Dowcra, chiefly on the Foyle, with whatever companies of Kerne adhered to Arthur O'Neil and Nial Garve; with Chichester in Carrickfergus there were 850 foot and 150 horse; with Danvers in Armagh, 750 foot and 100 horse; in Mount Norris, under Sir Samuel Bagnal, 600 foot and 50 horse; in and about Downpatrick, lately taken by the Deputy, under Moryson, 300 foot; in Newry, under Stafford, 400 foot and 50 horse; in Charlemont, with Williams, 300 foot and 50 horse; or, in all, of English regulars in Ulster alone, 7,000 foot and 800 horse. The position of the garrisons on the map will show how firm a grasp Mountjoy had taken of the Northern Province.

The last scene of this great struggle was now about to shift to the opposite quarter of the kingdom. The long-looked for Spanish fleet was known to have left the Tagus--had been seen off the Scilly Islands. On the 23rd of September the Council, presided over by Mountjoy, was assembled in Kilkenny Castle: there were present Carew, Ormond, Sir Richard Wingfield, Marshal of the Queen's troops, uncle to Carew, and founder of the family of Powerscourt; also Chief Justice Gardiner, and other members less known. While they were still sitting a message arrived from Cork that the Spanish fleet was off that harbour, and soon another that they had anchored in Kinsale, and taken possession of the town without opposition. The course of the Council was promptly taken. Couriers were at once despatched to call in the garrisons far and near which could possibly be dispensed with for service in Munster. Letters were despatched to England for reinforcements, and a winter campaign in the South was decided on.

The Spanish auxiliary force, when it sailed from the Tagus, consisted originally of 6,000 men in fifteen armed vessels and thirty transports. When they reached Kinsale, after suffering severely at sea, and parting company with several of their comrades, the soldiers were reduced to 3,400 men--a number inferior to Dowcra's force on the Foyle. The General, Don Jaun del Aguila, was a brave, but testy, passionate and suspicious officer. He has been severely censured by some Irish writers for landing in the extreme South, within fourteen miles of the English arsenal and head-quarters at Cork, and for his general conduct as a commander. However vulnerable he may be on the general charge, he does not seem fairly to blame for the choice of the point of debarkation. He landed in the old Geraldine country, unaware, of course, of the events of the last few weeks, in which the *sugane* Earl, and Florence McCarthy, had been entrapped by Carew's "wit and cunning," and shipped for London, from which they never returned. Even the northern chiefs, up to this period, evidently thought their cause much stronger in the South, and Munster much farther restored to vigour and courage than it really was. To the bitter disappointment and disgust of the Spaniards, only O'Sullivan Beare, O'Driscoll, and O'Conor of Kerry, declared openly for them; while they could hear daily of chiefs they had been taught to count as friends, either as prisoners or allies of the English. On the 17th of October--three weeks from their first arrival--they were arrested in Kinsale by a mixed army of English and Anglo-Irish, 15,000 strong, under the command of the Deputy and President, of whom above 5,000 had freshly arrived at Cork from England. With Mountjoy were the Earls of Thomond and Clanrickarde, more zealous than the English themselves for the triumph of England. The harbour was blockaded by ten ships of war, under Sir Richard Leviston, and the forts at the entrance, Rincorran and Castlenepark, being taken by cannonade, the investment on all sides was complete. Don Juan's messengers found O'Neil and O'Donnell busily engaged on their own frontiers, but both instantly resolved to muster all their strength for a winter campaign in Munster. O'Donnell *rendezvoused* at Ballymote, from which he set out, at the head of 2,500 men, of Tyrconnell and Connaught, on the 2nd day of November. O'Neil, with McDonnell of Antrim, McGennis of Down, McMahon of Monaghan, and others, his suffragans, marched at the head of between 3,000 and 4,000 men, through West-Meath towards Ormond. Holy Cross was their appointed place of meeting, where they expected to be joined by such of the neighbouring Catholics as were eager to strike a blow for liberty of worship. O'Donnell reached the neighbourhood first, and encamped in a strongly defensible position, "plashed on every quarter" for greater security. Mountjoy, anxious to engage him before O'Neil should come up, detached a numerically superior force, under Carew, for that purpose: but O'Donnell, evacuating his quarters by night, marched over the mountain of Slieve Felim, casting away much of his heavy baggage, and before calling halt was 32 *Irish* miles distant from his late encampment. After this extraordinary mountain march, equal to 40 of our present miles, he made a detour to the westward, descended on Castlehaven, in Cork, and formed a junction with 700 Spaniards, who had just arrived to join Del Aguila. A portion of these veterans were detailed to the forts of Castlehaven, Baltimore, and Dunboy, commanding three of the best havens in Munster; the remainder joined O'Donnell's division.

During the whole of November the siege of Kinsale was pressed with the utmost vigour by Mountjoy. The place mounted but three or four effective guns, while 20 great pieces of ordnance were continually playing on the walls. On the 1st of December a breach was found practicable, and an assault made by a party of 2,000 English was bravely repulsed by the Spaniards. The English fleet, ordered round to Castlehaven on the 3rd, were becalmed, and suffered some damage from a battery, manned by Spanish gunners, on the shore. The lines were advanced closer towards the town, and the bombardment became more effective. But the English ranks were considerably thinned by disease and desertion, so that on the last day of December, when the united Irish force took up their position at Belgoley, a mile to the north of their lines, the Lord Deputy's effective force did not, it is thought, exceed 10,000 men. The Catholic army has generally been estimated at 6,000 native foot and 500 horse; to these are to be added 300 Spaniards, under Don Alphonso Ocampo, who joined O'Donnell at Castlehaven.

The prospect for the besiegers was becoming exceedingly critical, but the Spaniards in Kinsale were far from being satisfied with their position. They had been fully three months within walls, in a region wholly unknown to them before their allies appeared. They neither understood nor made allowance for the immense difficulties of a winter campaign in a country trenched with innumerable swollen streams, thick with woods, which, at that season, gave no shelter, and where camping out at nights was enough to chill the hottest blood. They only felt their own inconveniences: they were cut off from escape by sea by a powerful English fleet, and Carew was already practising indirectly on their commander his "wit and cunning," in the fabrication of rumours, and the forging of letters. Don Juan wrote urgent appeals to the northern chiefs to attack the English lines without another day's delay, and a council of war, the third day after their arrival at Belgoley, decided that the attack should be made on the morrow. This decision was come to on the motion of O'Donnell, contrary to the judgment of the more circumspect and far-seeing O'Neil. Overruled, the latter acquiesced in the decision, and cheerfully prepared to discharge his duty.

A story is told by Carew that information was obtained of the intended attack from McMahon, in return for a bottle of *aquavitae* presented to him by the President. This tale is wholly unworthy of belief, told of a chief of the first rank, encamped in the midst of a friendly country. It is also said--and it seems credible enough--that an intercepted letter of Don Juan's gave the English in good time this valuable piece of information. On the night of the 2nd of January, new style (24th of December, O.S.--in use among the English), the Irish army left their camp in three divisions, the vanguard led by Tyrrell, the centre by O'Neil, and the rear by O'Donnell. The night was stormy and dark, with continuous peals and flashes of thunder and lightning. The guides lost their way, and the march, which, even by the most circuitous route, ought not to have exceeded four or five miles, was protracted through the entire night. At dawn of day, O'Neil, with whom were O'Sullivan and Ocampo, came in sight of the English lines, and, to his infinite surprise, found the men under arms, the cavalry in troop posted in advance of their quarters. O'Donnell's division was still to come up, and the veteran Earl now found himself in the same dilemma into which Bagnal had fallen at the Yellow Ford. His embarrassment was perceived from the English camp; the cavalry were at once ordered to advance. For an hour O'Neil maintained his ground alone; at the end of that time he was forced to retire. Of Ocampo's 300 Spaniards, 40 survivors were, with their gallant leader, taken prisoners; O'Donnell at length arrived, and drove back a wing of the English cavalry; Tyrrell's horsemen also held their ground tenaciously. But the rout of the centre proved irremediable. Fully 1,200 of the Irish were left dead on the field, and every prisoner taken was instantly executed. On the English side fell Sir Richard Graeme; Captains Danvers and Godolphin, with several others, were wounded; their total loss they stated at 200, and the Anglo-Irish, of whom they seldom made count in their reports, must have lost in proportion. The Earls of Thomond and Clanrickarde were actively engaged with their followers, and their loss could hardly have been less than that of the English regulars. On the night following their defeat, the Irish leaders held council together at Innishanon, on the river Bandon, where it was agreed that O'Donnell should instantly take shipping for Spain to lay the true state of the contest before Philip III.; that O'Sullivan should endeavour to hold the Castle of Dunboy, as commanding a most important harbour; that Rory O'Donnell, second brother of Hugh Roe, should act as Chieftain of Tyrconnell, and that O'Neil should return into Ulster to make the best defence in his power. The loss in men was not irreparable; the loss in arms, colours, and reputation, was more painful to bear, and far more difficult to retrieve.

On the 12th of January, nine days after the battle, Don Juan surrendered the town, and agreed to give up at the same time Dunboy, Baltimore, and Castlehaven. He had lost 1,000 men out of his 3,000 during a ten weeks' siege, and was heartily sick of Irish warfare. On his return to Spain he was degraded from his rank, for his too great intimacy with Carew, and confined a prisoner in his own house. He is said to have died of a broken heart occasioned by these indignities.

O'Donnell sailed from Castlehaven in a Spanish ship, on the 6th of January, three clays after the battle, and arrived at Corunna on the 14th. He was received with all the honours due to a crown prince by the Conde de Caracena, Governor of Galicia. Among other objects, he visited the remains of the tower of Betanzos, from which, according to Bardic legends, the sons of Milesius had sailed to seek for the Isle of Destiny among the waves of the west. On the 27th he set out for the Court, accompanied as far as Santa Lucia by the governor, who presented him with 1,000 ducats towards his expenses. At Compostella the Archbishop offered him his own palace, which O'Donnell respectfully declined: he afterwards celebrated a Solemn High Mass for the Irish chief's intention, entertained him magnificently at dinner, and presented him, as the governor had done, with 1,000 ducats. At Zamora he received from Philip III. a most cordial reception, and was assured that in a very short time a more powerful armament than Don Juan's should sail with him from Corunna. He returned to that port, from which he could every day look out across the western waves that lay between him and home, and where he could be kept constantly informed of what was passing in Ireland. Spring was over and gone, and summer, too, had passed away, but still the exigencies of Spanish policy delayed the promised expedition. At length O'Donnell set out on a second visit to the Spanish Court, then at Valladolid, but he reached no further than Simancas, when, fevered in mind and body, he expired on the 10th of September, 1602, in the 29th year of his age. He was attended in his last moments by two Franciscan Fathers who accompanied him, Florence, afterwards Archbishop of Tuam, and Maurice Donlevy, of his own Abbey of Donegal. His body was interred with regal honours in the Cathedral of Valladolid, where a monument was erected to his memory by the King of Spain.

Thus closed the career of one of the brightest and purest characters in any history. His youth, his early captivity, his princely generosity, his daring courage, his sincere piety won the hearts of all who came in contact with him. He was the sword as O'Neil was the brain of the Ulster Confederacy; the Ulysses and Achilles of the war, they fought side by side, without jealousy or envy, for almost as long a period as their prototypes had spent in besieging Troy.

CHAPTER XI.

THE CONQUEST OF MUNSTER--DEATH OF ELIZABETH, AND SUBMISSION OF O'NEIL--"THE ARTICLES OF MELLIFONT."

The days of Queen Elizabeth were now literally numbered. The death of Essex, the intrigues of the King of Scotland, and the successes of Tyrone, preyed upon her spirits. The Irish chief was seldom out of her mind, and, as she often predicted, she was not to live to receive his submission. She was accustomed to send for her godson, Harrington, who had served in Ireland, to ask him questions concerning Tyrone; the French ambassador considered Tyrone's war one of the causes that totally destroyed her peace of mind in her latter days. She received the news of the victory of Kinsale with pleasure, but, even then, she was not destined to receive the submission of Tyrone.

The events of the year, so inauspiciously begun for the Irish arms, continued of the same disastrous character. Castlehaven was surrendered by its Spanish guard, according to Del Aguila's agreement. Baltimore, after a momentary resistance, was also given up, but O'Sullivan, who considered the Spanish capitulation nothing short of treason, threw a body of native troops, probably drawn from Tyrrell's men, into Dunboy, under Captain Richard Mageoghegan, and Taylor, an Englishman, connected by marriage with Tyrrell. Another party of the same troops took possession of Clear Island, but were obliged to abandon it as untenable. The entire strength of the Dunboy garrison amounted to 143 men; towards the end of April --the last of the Spaniards having sailed in March-- Carew left Cork at the head of 3,000 men to besiege Dunboy. Sir Charles Wilmot moved on the same point from Kerry, with a force of 1,000 men, to join Carew. In the pass near Mangerton Wilmot was encountered by Donald O'Sullivan and Tyrrell, at the head of then remaining followers, but forced a passage and united with his superior on the shores of Berehaven. On the 1st of June the English landed on Bear Island, and on the 6th opened their cannonade. They were 4,000 men, with every military equipment necessary, against 143. After eleven days' bombardment the place was shattered to pieces; the garrison offered to surrender, if allowed to retain their arms, but their messenger was hanged, and an instant assault ordered. Over fifty of this band of Christian Spartans had fallen in the defence, thirty attempted to escape in boats, or by swimming, but were killed to a man while in the water. The remainder retreated with Mageoghegan, who was severely wounded, to a cellar approached by a narrow stair, where the command was assumed by Taylor. All day the assault had been carried on till night closed upon the scene of carnage. Placing a strong guard on the approach to the crypt, Carew returned to the charge with the returning light. Cannon were first discharged into the narrow chamber which held the last defenders of Dunboy, and then a body of the assailants rushing in, despatched the wounded Mageoghegan with their swords, having found him, candle in hand, dragging himself towards the gunpowder. Taylor and fifty-seven others were led out to execution; of all the heroic band, not a soul escaped alive.

The remaining fragments of Dunboy were blown into the air by Carew on the 22nd of June. Dursey Castle, another island fortress of O'Sullivan's, had fallen even earlier; so that no roof remained to the lord of Berehaven. Still he held his men well together in the glens of Kerry, during the months of Summer, but the ill-news from Spain in September threw a gloom over those mountains deeper than was ever cast by equinoctial storm. Tyrrell was obliged to separate from him in the Autumn, probably from the difficulty of providing for so many mouths, and O'Sullivan himself prepared to bid a sad farewell to the land of his inheritance. On the last day of December he left Glengariffe, with 400 fighting men, and 600 women, children, and servants, to seek a refuge in the distant north. After a retreat almost unparalleled, the survivors of this exodus succeeded in reaching the friendly roof of O'Ruarc, at Dromahaire, not far from Sligo. Their entire march, from the extreme south to the almost extreme north-west of the island, a distance, as they travelled it, of not less than 200 miles, was one scene of warfare and suffering. They were compelled to kill their horses, on reaching the Shannon, in order to make boats of the hides, to ferry them to the western bank. At Aughrim they were attacked by a superior force under Lord Clanrickarde's brother, and Captain Henry Malby, but they fought with the courage of despair, routed the enemy, slaying Malby, and other officers. Of the ten hundred who left the shores of Glengariffe, but 35 souls reached the Leitrim chieftain's mansion. Among these were the chief himself, with Dermid, father of the historian, who at the date of this march had reached the age of seventy. The conquest of Munster, at least, was now complete. In the ensuing January, Owen McEgan, Bishop of Ross, was slain in the midst of a guerilla party, in the mountains of Carberry, and Ms chaplain, being taken, was hanged with the other prisoners. The policy of extermination recommended by Carew was zealously carried out by strong detachments under Wilmot, Harvey, and Flower; Mr. Boyle and the other "Undertakers" zealously assisting as volunteers.

Mountjoy, after transacting some civil business at Dublin, proceeded in person to the north, while Dowcra, marching out of Derry, pressed O'Neil from the north and north-east. In June, Mountjoy was at Charlemont, which he placed under the custody of Captain Toby Caufield, the founder of an illustrious title taken from that fort. He advanced on Dungannon, but discovered it from the distance, as Norris had once before done, in flames, kindled by the hand of its straitened proprietor. On Lough Neagh he erected a new fort called Mountjoy, so that his communications on the south now stretched from that great lake round to Omagh, while those of Dowcra, at Augher, Donegal, and Lifford, nearly completed the circle. Almost the only outlet from this chain of posts was into the mountains of O'Cane's country, the north-east angle of the present county of Derry. The extensive tract so enclosed and guarded had still some natural advantages for carrying on a defensive war. The primitive woods were standing in masses at no great distance from each other; the nearly parallel vales of Faughan, Moyala, and the river Roe, with the intermediate leagues of moor and mountain, were favourable to the movements of native forces familiar with every ford and footpath. There was also, while this central tract was held, a possibility of communication with other unbroken tribes, such as those of Clandeboy and the Antrim glens on the east, and Breffni O'Ruarc on the west. Never did the genius of Hugh O'Neil shine out brighter than in these last defensive operations. In July, Mountjoy writes apologetically to the Council, that "notwithstanding her Majesty's great forces, O'Neil doth still live." He bitterly complains of his consummate caution, his "pestilent judgment to spread and to nourish his own infection," and of the reverence entertained for his person by the native population. Early in August, Mountjoy had arranged what he hoped might prove the finishing stroke in the struggle. Dowcra from Derry, Chichester from Carrickfergus, Danvers from Armagh, and all who could be spared from Mountjoy, Charlemont, and Mount Norris, were gathered under his command, to the number of 8,000 men, for a foray into the interior of Tyrone. Inisloghlin, on the borders of Down and Antrim, which contained a great quantity of valuables, belonging to O'Neil, was captured. Magherlowney and Tulloghoge were next taken. At the latter place stood the ancient stone chair on which the O'Neils were inaugurated time out of mind; it was now broken into atoms by Mountjoy's orders. But the most effective warfare was made on the growing crops. The 8,000 men spread themselves over the fertile fields along the valleys of the Bann and the Roe, destroying the standing grain with fire, where it would burn, or with the *praca*, a peculiar kind of harrow, tearing it up by the roots. The horsemen trampled crops into the earth which had generously nourished them; the infantry shore them down with their sabres, and the sword, though in a very different sense from that of Holy Scripture, was, indeed, converted into a sickle. The harvest month never shone upon such fields in any Christian land. In September, Mountjoy reported to Cecil, "that between Tulloghoge and Toome there lay unburied a thousand dead," and that since his arrival on the Blackwater--a period of a couple of months--"there were about 3,000 starved in Tyrone." In O'Cane's country, the misery of his clansmen drove the chief to surrender to Dowcra, and the news of Hugh Roe's death having reached Donegal, his brother repaired to Athlone, and made his submission to Mountjoy, early in December. O'Neil, unable to maintain himself on the river, Roe, retired with 600 foot and 60 horse, to Glencancean, near Lough Neagh, the most secure of his fastnesses. His brother Cormac McMahon, and Art O'Neil, of Clandeboy, shared with him the wintry hardships of that last asylum, while Tyrone, Clandeboy, and Monaghan, were given up to horrors, surpassing any that had been known or dreamt of in former wars. Moryson, secretary to Mountjoy, in his account of this campaign, observes, "that no spectacle was more frequent in the ditches of towns, and especially in wasted countries, than to see multitudes of these poor people dead, with their mouths all coloured green, by eating nettles, docks, and all things they could rend above ground."

The new year, opening without hope, it began to be rumoured that O'Neil was disposed to surrender on honourable terms. Mountjoy and the English Council long urged the aged Queen to grant such terms, but without effect. Her pride as a sovereign had been too deeply wounded by the revolted Earl to allow her easily to forgive or forget his offences. Her advisers urged that Spain had followed her own course towards the Netherlands, in Ireland; that the war consumed three-fourths of her annual revenue, and had obliged her to keep up an Irish army of 20,000 men for several years past. At length she yielded her reluctant consent, and Mountjoy was authorized to treat with the arch-rebel upon honourable terms. The agents employed by the Lord Deputy in this negotiation were Sir William Godolphin and Sir Garrett Moore, of Mellifont, ancestor of the Marquis of Drogheda--the latter, a warm personal friend, though no partizan of O'Neil's. They found him in his retreat near Lough Neagh early in March, and obtained his promise to give the Deputy an early meeting at Mellifont. Elizabeth's serious illness, concealed from O'Neil, though well known to Mountjoy, hastened the negotiations. On the 27th of March he had intelligence of her decease at London on the 24th, but carefully concealed it till the 5th of April following. On the 31st of March, he received Tyrone's submission at Moore's residence, the ancient Cistercian Abbey, and not until a week later did O'Neil learn that he had made his peace with a dead sovereign.

The honourable terms on which this memorable religious war was concluded were these: O'Neil abjured all foreign allegiance, especially that of the King of Spain; renounced the title of O'Neil; agreed to give up his correspondence with the Spaniards, and to recall his son, Henry, who was a page at the Spanish Court, and to live in peace with the sons of John the Proud. Mountjoy granted him an amnesty for himself and his allies; agreed that he should be restored to his estates as he had held them before the war, and that the Catholics should have the free exercise of their religion. That the restoration of his ordinary chieftain rights, which did not conflict with the royal prerogative, was also included, we have the best possible evidence: Sir Henry Dowcra having complained to Lord Mountjoy that O'Neil quartered men on O'Cane, who had surrendered to himself, Mountjoy made answer--"My Lord of Tyrone is taken in with promise to be restored, as well to all his lands as to his honour and dignity, and O'Cane's country is his, and must be obedient to his commands." That the article concerning religion was understood by the Catholics to concede full freedom of worship, is evident from subsequent events. In Dublin, sixteen of the principal citizens suffered fine and imprisonment for refusing to comply with the act of uniformity; in Kilkenny the Catholics took possession of the Black Abbey, which had been converted into a lay fee; in Waterford they did the same by St. Patrick's Church, where a Dominican preacher was reported to have said, among other imprudent things, that "Jesabel was dead"-- alluding to the late Queen. In Cork, Limerick, and Cashel, the cross was carried publicly in procession, the old Churches restored to their ancient rites, and enthusiastic proclamation made of the public restoration of religion. These events having obliged the Lord Deputy to make a progress through the towns and cities, he was met at Waterford by a vast procession, headed by religious in the habits of their order, who boldly declared to him "that the citizens of Waterford could not, in conscience, obey any prince that persecuted the Catholic religion." When such was the spirit of the town populations, we are not surprised to learn that, in the rural districts, almost exclusively Catholic, the people entered upon the use of many of their old Churches, and repaired several Abbeys--among the number, Buttevant, Kilcrea, and Timoleague in Cork; Quin Abbey in Clare; Kilconnell in Galway; Rosnariell in Mayo, and Multifarnham in West-Meath. So confident were they that the days of persecution were past, that King James prefaces his proclamation of July, 1605, with the statement--"Whereas we have been informed that our subjects in the kingdom of Ireland, since the death of our beloved sister, have been deceived by a false rumour, to wit, that we would allow them liberty of conscience," and so forth. How cruelly they were then undeceived belongs to the history of the next reign; here we need only remark that the Articles of Limerick were not more shamefully violated by the statute 6th and 7th, William III., than the Articles of Mellifont were violated by this Proclamation of the third year of James I.

CHAPTER XII.

STATE OF RELIGION AND LEARNING DURING THE REIGN OF ELIZABETH.

During the greater part of the reign of Elizabeth, the means relied upon for the propagation of the reformed doctrines were more exclusively those of force and coercion than even in the time of Edward VI. Thus, when Sir William Drury was Deputy, in 1578, he bound several citizens of Kilkenny, under a penalty of 40 pounds each, to attend the English Church service, and authorized the Anglican Bishop "to make a rate for the repair of the Church, and to distrain for the payment of it"--the first mention of Church rates we remember to have met with. Drury's method of proceeding may be further inferred from the fact, that of the thirty-six executions ordered by him in the same city, "one was a blackamoor and two were witches, who were condemned by the law of nature, for there was no positive law against witchcraft [in Ireland] in those days." That defect was soon supplied, however, by the statute 27th of Elizabeth, "against witchcraft and sorcery." Sir John Perrott, successor to Drury, trod in the same path, as we judge from the charge of severity against recusants, upon which, among other articles, he was recalled from the government. Towards the end of the sixteenth century, however, it began to be discovered by the wisest observers that violent methods were worse than useless with the Irish. Edmund Spenser urged that "religion should not be forcibly impressed into them with terror and sharp penalties, as now is the manner, but rather delivered and intimated with mildness and gentleness." Lord Bacon, in his "Considerations touching the Queen's Service in Ireland," addressed to Secretary Cecil, recommends "the recovery of the hearts of the people," as the first step towards their conversion. With this view he suggested "a toleration of religion (for a time not definite), except it be in some principal towns and cities," as a measure "warrantable in religion, and in policy of absolute necessity." The philosophic Chancellor farther suggested, as a means to this desired end, the preparation of "versions of Bibles and Catechisms, and other works of instruction in the Irish language." In accordance with these views of conversion, the University of Trinity College was established by a royal charter, in the month of January, 1593. The Mayor and Corporation of Dublin had granted the ancient monastery of All Hallows as a site for the buildings; some contributions were received from the Protestant gentry, large grants of confiscated Abbey and other lands, which afterwards yielded a princely revenue, were bestowed upon it, and the Lord Treasurer Burleigh graciously accepted the office of its Chancellor. The first Provost was Archbishop Loftus, and of the first three students entered, one was the afterwards illustrious James Usher. The commanders and officers engaged at Kinsale presented it with the sum of 1,800 pounds for the purchase of a library; and at the subsequent confiscations in Munster and Ulster, the College came in for a large portion of the forfeited lands.

Although the Council in England generally recommended the adoption of persuasive arts and a limited toleration, those who bore the sword usually took care that they should not bear it in vain. A High Commission Court, armed with ample powers to enforce the Act of Uniformity, had been established at Dublin in 1593; but its members were ordered to proceed cautiously after the Ulster Confederacy became formidable, and their powers lay dormant in the last two or three years of the century. Essex and Mountjoy were both fully convinced of the wisdom of Bacon's views; the former showed a partial toleration, connived at the celebration of the Holy Sacrifice, even in the capital, and liberated some priests from prison. Mountjoy, in answer to the command of the English Council "to deal moderately in the great matter of religion," replied by letter that he had already advised "such as dealt in it for a time to hold a restrained hand therein." "The other course," he adds, "might have overthrown the means of our own end of a reformation of religion." This conditional toleration--such as it was--excited the indignation of the more zealous Reformers, whose favourite preacher, the youthful Usher, did not hesitate to denounce it from the pulpit of Christ Church, as an unhallowed compromise with antichrist. In 1601, Usher, then but 21 years of age, preached his well-known sermon from the text of the forty days, in which Ezekiel "was to bear the iniquity of the house of Judah--a day for a year." "From this year," cried the youthful zealot, "will I reckon the sin of Ireland, that those whom you now embrace shall be your ruin, and you shall bear their iniquity." When the northern insurrection of 1641 took place, this rhetorical menace was exalted, after the fact, into the dignity of a prophecy fulfilled. After the victory of Kinsale, however, the Ultra Protestant party had less cause to complain of the temporizing of the civil power; the pecuniary mulct of twelve pence for each absence from the English service was again enforced at least in Dublin, and several priests, then in prison, were, on various pretences, put to death. Among those who suffered in the capital was the learned Jesuit, Henry Fitzsimons, son of a Mayor of the city, the author of ***Brittanomachia***, with whom, while in the Castle, Usher commenced a controversy, which was never finished. But the terms agreed upon at Mellifont, between Mountjoy and Tyrone, again suspended for a short interval the sword of persecution.

Notwithstanding its manifold losses by exile and the scaffold, the ancient Church was enabled, through the abundance of vocations, and the zeal of the ordained, to keep up a still powerful organization. Philip O'Sullivan states, under the next reign that the government had ascertained through its spies, the names of 1,160 priests, secular and regular, still in the country. There must have been between 300 and 400 others detained abroad, either as Professors in the Irish Colleges in Spain, France, and Flanders, or as ecclesiastics, awaiting major orders. Of the regulars at home, 120 were Franciscans, and about 50 Jesuits. There are said to have been but four Fathers of the Order of St. Dominick remaining at the time of Elizabeth's death. The reproach of Cambrensis had long been taken away, since every Diocese might now point to its martyrs. Of these we recall among the Hierarchy the names of O'Hely, Bishop of Killala, executed at Kilmallock hi 1578; O'Hurley, Archbishop of Cashel, burned at the stake in Dublin in 1582; Creagh, Archbishop of Armagh, who died a prisoner in the Tower in 1585; Archbishop McGauran, his successor, slain in the act of ministering to the wounded in the engagement at Tulsk, in Roscommon, in 1593; McEgan, Bishop of Ross, who met his death under precisely similar circumstances in Carberry in 1603. Yet through all these losses the episcopal succession was maintained unbroken. In the early part of the next reign O'Sullivan gives the names of the four Archbishops, Peter Lombard of Armagh, Edward McGauran of Dublin,

David O'Carny of Cashel, and Florence Conroy of Tuam. On the other hand, the last trying half century had furnished, so far as we can learn, no instance of apostacy among the Bishops, and but half a dozen at most from all orders of the clergy. We read that Owen O'Conor, an apostate, was advanced by letters patent to Killala in 1591; that Maurice O'Brien of Ara was, in 1570, by the same authority, elevated to the See of Killaloe, which he resigned in 1612; that Miler Magrath, in early life a Franciscan friar, was promoted by the Queen to the Sees of Clogher, Killala, Anchory and Lismore successively. He finally settled in the See of Cashel, in which he died, having secretly returned to the religion of his ancestors. For the rest, "the Queen's Bishops" were chiefly chosen out of England, though some few natives of the Pale, or of the walled towns, educated at Oxford, may be found in the list.

Of the state of learning in those troubled times the brief story is easily told. The Bardic Order still flourished and was held in honour by all ranks of the native population. The national adversity brought out in them, as in others, many noble traits of character. The Harper, O'Dugan, was the last companion that clung to the last of the Desmonds; the Bard of Tyrconnell, Owen Ward, accompanied the Ulster chiefs in their exile, and poured out his Gaelic dirge above their Roman graves. Although the Bardic compositions continued to be chiefly personal, relating to the inauguration, journeys, exploits, or death of some favourite chief, a large number of devotional poems on the passion of our Lord and the glories of the Blessed Virgin are known to be of this age. The first forerunners of what was destined to be a numerous progeny, the controversial ode or ballad, appeared in Elizabeth's reign, in the form of comparisons between the old and new religions, lamentations over the ruin of religious houses, and the apostacy of such persons as Miler Magrath and the son of the Earl of Desmond. The talents of many of the authors are admitted by Spenser, a competent judge, but the tendency of their writings, he complains, was to foster the love of lawlessness and rebellion rather than of virtue and loyalty. He recommended them for correction to the mercies of the Provost Marshal, whom he would have "to walk the country with half a dozen or half a score of horsemen," in quest of the treasonable poets.

As this was the age of the general diffusion of printing, we may observe that the casting of Irish type for the use of Trinity College, by order of Queen Elizabeth, is commonly dated from the year 1591; but as the College was not opened for two years later, the true date must be anticipated. John Kearney, Treasurer of St. Patrick's Church, who died about the year 1600, published a Protestant Catechism from the College Press, which, says O'Reilly, "was the first book ever printed in Irish types." In the year 1593, Florence Conroy translated from the Spanish into Irish a catechism entitled "Christian Instruction," which, he states in the preface, he had no opportunity of sending into Ireland "until the year of the age of our Lord 1598." Whether it was then printed we are not informed, but there does not seem to have been any Irish type in Catholic hands before the foundation of the Irish College at Louvain in 1616.

The merit of first giving to the press, in the native language of the country, a version of the Sacred Scriptures, belongs clearly to Trinity College. Nicholas Walsh, Bishop of Ossory, who died in 1585, had commenced, with the assistance of John Kearney, to translate the Greek Testament into Gaelic. He had also the assistance of Dr. Nehemiah Donnellan, and Dr. William Daniel, or O'Daniel, both of whom subsequently filled the See of Tuam. This translation, dedicated to King James, and published by O'Daniel in 1603, is still reprinted by the Bible Societies. The first Protestant translation of the Old Testament, made under Bishop Bedel's eye, and with such revision of particular passages as his imperfect knowledge of the language enabled him to suggest, though completed in the reign of Charles I., was not published before the year 1680. It was Bedel, also, who caused the English liturgy to be recited in Irish, in his Cathedral, as early as 1630. Ireland and her affairs naturally attracted, during Elizabeth's reign, the attention of English writers. Of these it is enough to mention the Poet Spenser, Secretary to Lord Grey de Wilton, Fynes Moryson, Secretary to Lord Mountjoy, and the Jesuit Father, Campian. Campian, early distinguished at Oxford, was employed as Cambrensis had been four centuries earlier, and as Plowden was two centuries later, to write down everything Irish. He crossed the Channel in 1570, and composed two books rapidly, without accurate or full information as to the condition or history of the country. The nearer view of Catholic suffering and Catholic constancy exercised a powerful influence on this accomplished scholar; he became a convert and a Jesuit. For members of that order there was but one exit out of life, under the law of England: he suffered death at Tyburn in 1581. Richard Stanihurst, son of the Recorder of Dublin, and uncle of Archbishop Usher, went through precisely the same experiences as his friend Campian, except that he died, a quarter of a century later, Chaplain to the Archdukes at Brussels, instead of expiring at the stake. His English hexameters are among the curiosities of literature, but his contributions to the history of his country, especially his allusions to events and characters in and about his own time, are not without their use. Stanihurst wrote his historical tracts, as did Lombard the Catholic and Usher the Protestant Primate, O'Sullivan, White, O'Meara, and almost all the Irish writers of that age, without exception, in the Latin language. The first Latin book printed in Ireland is thought to be O'Meara's poem in praise of Thomas, Earl of Ormond and Ossory, published in 1615. The earliest English books printed in Ireland are unknown to me; the collection of Anglo-Irish statutes, ordered to be published while Sir Henry Sidney was Deputy, was the most important undertaking of that class in the reign of Elizabeth. As to institutions of learning, if we except Trinity College, which increased rapidly in numbers and reputation under the patronage of the Crown, and the College of Saint Nicholas, at Galway--protected by its remote situation on the brink of the Atlantic--there was no famous seat of learning left in the island. In the next reign 1,300 scholars are stated to have attended that western "school of humanity," when the Ecclesiastical Commissioners despotically ordered it to be closed, because the learned Principal, John Lynch, "would not confirm to the religion established." But the greater number of the children of Catholics, who still retained property enough to educate them, were sent beyond seas, a fact with which King James, soon after his accession, reproached the deputation of that body. A proclamation issued by Lord Deputy Chichester, in 1610, alludes to the same custom, and commands all noblemen, merchants, and others, whose children are abroad for educational purposes, to recall them within one year from the date thereof; and in case they refuse to return, all parents, friends, &c., sending them money, directly or indirectly, will be punished as severely as the law permits. It was mainly to guard against this danger that "the School of Wards" was established by Elizabeth, and enlarged by James I., in which the great Duke of Ormond, Sir Phelim O'Neil, Murrogh, Lord Inchiquin, and other sons of noble families, were educated for the next generation. Early in the reign of James there were not less than 300 of these Irish children in the Tower, or at the Lambeth School,--and it is humiliating to find the great name of Sir Edward Coke among those who gloried in the success of this unnatural substitution of the State for the Parent in the work of education.

BOOK IX.
FROM THE ACCESSION OF JAMES I. TILL THE DEATH OF CROMWELL.

CHAPTER I.

JAMES I.--FLIGHT OF THE EARLS--CONFISCATION OF ULSTER-- PENAL LAWS--PARLIAMENTARY OPPOSITION.

James the Sixth of Scotland was in his 37th year when he ascended the throne under the title of "James the First, King of Great Britain and Ireland." His accession naturally excited the most hopeful expectations of good government in the breasts of the Irish Catholics. He was son of Mary Queen of Scots, whom they looked upon as a martyr to her religion, and grandson of that gallant King James who styled himself "Defender of the Faith," and "*Dominus Hiberniae*" in introducing the first Jesuits to the Ulster Princes. His ancestors had always been in alliance with the Irish, and the antiquaries of that nation loved to trace their descent from the Scoto-Irish chiefs who first colonized Argyle, and were for ages crowned at Scone. He himself was known to have assisted the late Catholic struggle as effectually, though less openly than the King of Spain, and it is certain that he had employed Catholic agents, like Lord Home and Sir James Lindsay, to excite an interest in his succession among the Catholics, both in the British Islands and on the Continent.

The first acts of the new sovereign were calculated to confirm the expectations of Catholic liberty thus entertained. He was anxious to make an immediate and lasting peace with Spain; refused to receive a special embassy from the Hollanders; his ambassador at Paris was known to be on terms of intimacy with the Pope's Nuncio; and although personally he assumed the tone of an Anglican Churchman, on crossing the border he had invited leading Catholics to his Court, and conferred the honour of Knighthood on some of their number. The imprudent demonstrations in the Irish towns were easily quieted, and no immediate notice was taken of their leaders. In May, 1603, Mountjoy, on whom James had conferred the higher rank of Lord Lieutenant, leaving Carew as Lord Deputy, proceeded to England, accompanied by O'Neil, Roderick O'Donnell, Maguire, and other Irish gentlemen. The veteran Tyrone, now past threescore, though hooted by the London rabble, was graciously received in that court, with which he had been familiar forty years before. He was at once confirmed in his title, the Earldom of Tyrconnell was created for O'Donnell, and the Lordship of Enniskillen for Maguire. Mountjoy, created Earl of Devonshire, retained the title of Lord Lieutenant, with permission to reside in England, and was rewarded by the appointment of Master of the Ordnance and Warden of the New Forest, with an ample pension from the Crown to him and his heirs for ever, the grant of the county of Lecale (Down), and the estate of Kingston Hall, in Dorsetshire, He survived but three short years to enjoy all these riches and honours; at the age of 44, wasted with dissipation and domestic troubles, he passed to his final account.

The necessity of conciliating the Catholic party in England, of maintaining peace in Ireland, and prosecuting the Spanish negotiations, not less, perhaps, than his own original bias, led James to deal favourably with the Catholics at first. But having attempted to enforce the new Anglican Canons, adopted in 1604, against the Puritans, that party retaliated by raising against him the cry of favouring the Papists. This cry alarmed the King, who had always before his eyes the fear of Presbyterianism, and he accordingly made a speech in the Star Chamber, declaring his utter detestation of Popery, and published a proclamation banishing all Catholic missionaries from the country. All magistrates were instructed to enforce the penal laws with rigour, and an elaborate spy system for the discovery of concealed recusants was set on foot. This reign of treachery and terror drove a few desperate men into the gunpowder plot of the following year, and rendered it difficult, if not impossible, for the King to return to the policy of toleration, with which, to do him justice, he seems to have set out from Scotland.

Carew, President of Munster during the late war, became Deputy to Mountjoy on his departure for England. He was succeeded in October, 1604, by Sir Arthur Chichester, who, with the exception of occasional absences at Court, continued in office for a period of eleven years. This nobleman, a native of England, furnishes, in many points, a parallel to his cotemporary and friend, Robert Boyle, Earl of Cork. The object of his life was to found and to endow the Donegal peerage out of the spoils of Ulster, as richly as Boyle endowed his earldom out of the confiscation of Munster. Both were Puritans rather than Churchmen, in their religious opinions; Chichester, a pupil of the celebrated Cartwright, and a favourer all his life of the congregational clergy in Ulster. But they carried their repugnance to the interference of the civil magistrate in matters of conscience so discreetly as to satisfy the high church notions both of James and Elizabeth. For the violence they were thus compelled to exercise against themselves, they seem to have found relief in bitter and continuous persecution of others. Boyle, as the leading spirit in the government of Munster, as Lord Treasurer, and occasionally as Lord Justice, had ample opportunities, during his long career of forty years, to indulge at once his avarice and his bigotry; and no situation was ever more favourable than Chichester's for a proconsul, eager to enrich himself at the expense of a subjugated Province.

In the projected work of the reduction of the whole country to the laws and customs of England, it is instructive to observe that a Parliament was not called in the first place. The reformers proceeded by proclamations, letters patent, and orders in council, not by legislation. The whole island was divided into 32 counties and 6 judicial circuits, all of which were visited by Justices in the second or third year of this reign, and afterwards semi-annually. On the Northern Circuit Sir Edward Pelham and Sir John Davis were accompanied by the Deputy in person, with a numerous retinue. In some places the towns were so wasted by the late war, pestilence, and famine, that the Viceregal party were obliged to camp out in the fields, and to carry with them their own provisions. The Courts were held in ruined castles and deserted monasteries; Irish interpreters were at every step found necessary; sheriffs were installed in Tyrone and Tyrconnell for the first time; all lawyers appearing in court and all justices of the peace were tendered the oath of supremacy--the refusal of which necessarily excluded Catholics both from the bench and the bar. An enormous amount of litigation as to the law of real property was created by a judgment of the Court of King's Bench at Dublin, in 1605, by which the ancient Irish customs, of tanistry and gavelkind, were declared null and void, and the entire Feudal system, with its rights of primogeniture, hereditary succession, entail, and vassalage, was held to exist in as full force in England. Very evidently this decision was not less a violation of the articles of Mellifont than was the King's proclamation against freedom of conscience issued about the same tune.

Sir John Davis, who has left us two very interesting tracts on Irish affairs, speaking of the new legal regulations of which he was one of the principal superintendents, observes that the old-fashioned allowances to be found so often in the Pipe-Rolls, *pro guidagio et spiagio*, into the interior, may well be spared thereafter, since "the under sheriffs and bailiffs errant are better guides and spies in time of peace than they were found in tune of war." He adds, what we may very well believe, that the Earl of Tyrone complained he had so many eyes upon him, that he could not drink a cup of sack without the government being advertised of it within a few hours afterwards. This system of social *espionage*, so repugnant to all the habits of the Celtic family, was not the only mode of annoyance resorted to against the veteran chief. Every former dependent who could be induced to dispute his claims as a landlord, under the new relations established by the late decision, was sure of a judgment in his favour. Disputes about boundaries with O'Cane, about the commutation of chieftain-rents into tenantry, about church lands claimed by Montgomery, Protestant Bishop of Derry, were almost invariably decided against him. Harassed by these proceedings, and all uncertain of the future, O'Neil listened willingly to the treacherous suggestion of St. Lawrence and Lord Howth, that the leading Catholics of the Pale, and those of Ulster, should endeavour to form another confederation. The execution of Father Garnet, Provincial of the Jesuits in England, the heavy fines inflicted on Lords Stourton, Mordaunt, and Montague, and the new oath of allegiance, framed by Archbishop Abbott, and sanctioned by the English Parliament--all events of the year 1606--were calculated to inspire the Irish Catholics with desperate councils. A dutiful remonstrance against the Act of Uniformity the previous year had been signed by the principal Anglo-Irish Catholics for transmission to the King, but their delegates were seized and imprisoned in the Castle, while their principal agent, Sir Patrick Barnwell, was sent to London and confined in the Tower. A meeting, at Lord Howth's suggestion, was held about Christmas, 1606, at the Castle of Maynooth, then in possession of the dowager Countess of Kildare, one of whose daughters was married to Christopher Nugent, Baron of Delvin, and her granddaughter to Rory, Earl of Tyrconnell. There were present O'Neil, O'Donnell, and O'Cane, on the one part, and Lords Delvin and Howth on the other. The precise result of this conference, disguised under the pretext of a Christmas party, was never made known, but the fact that it had been held, and that the parties present had entertained the project of another confederacy for the defence of the Catholic religion, was mysteriously communicated in an anonymous letter, directed to Sir William Usher, Clerk of the Council, which was dropped in the Council Chamber of Dublin Castle, in March, 1607. This letter, it is now generally believed, was written by Lord Howth, who was thought to have been employed by Secretary Cecil, to entrap the northern Earls, in order to betray them. In May, O'Neil and O'Donnell were cited to attend the Lord Deputy in Dublin, but the charges were for the time kept in abeyance, and they were ordered to appear in London before the feast of Michaelmas. Early in September O'Neil was with Chichester at Slane, in Meath, when he received a letter from Maguire, who had been out of the country, conveying information on which he immediately acted. Taking leave of the Lord Deputy as if to prepare for his journey to London, he made some stay with his old friend, Sir Garrett Moore, at Mellifont, on parting from whose family he tenderly bade farewell to the children and even the servants, and was observed to shed tears. At Dungannon he remained two days, and on the shore of Lough Swilly he joined O'Donnell and others of his connexions. The French ship, in which Maguire had returned, awaited them off Rathmullen, and there they took shipping for France. With O'Neil, in that sorrowful company, were his last countess, Catherine, daughter of Magenniss, his three sons, Hugh, John, and Brian; his nephew, Art, son of Cormac, Rory O'Donnell, Caffar, his brother, Nuala, his sister, who had forsaken her husband Nial *Garve*, when he forsook his country; the lady Rose O'Doherty, wife of Caffar, and afterwards of Owen Roe O'Neil; Maguire, Owen MacWard, chief bard of Tyrconnell, and several others. "Woe to the heart that meditated, woe to the mind that conceived, woe to the council that decided on the project of that voyage!" exclaimed the Annalists of Donegal, in the next age. Evidently it was the judgment of their immediate successors that the flight of the Earls was a rash and irremediable step for them; but the information on which they acted, if not long since destroyed, has, as yet, never been made public. We can pronounce no judgment as to the wisdom of their conduct, from the incomplete statements at present in our possession.

There remained now few barriers to the wholesale confiscation of Ulster, so long sought by "the Undertakers," and these were rapidly removed. Sir Cahir O'Doherty, chief of Innishowen, although he had earned his Knighthood while a mere lad, fighting by the side of Dowcra, in an altercation with Sir George Paulett, Governor of Derry, was taunted with conniving at the escape of the Earls, and Paulett in his passion struck him in the face. The youthful chief--he was scarcely one and twenty--was driven almost to madness by this outrage. On the night of the 3rd of May, by a successful stratagem, he got possession of Culmore fort, at the month of Lough Foyle, and before morning dawned had surprised Derry; Paulett, his insulter, he slew with his own hand, most of the garrison were slaughtered, and the town reduced to ashes. Nial *Garve* O'Donnell, who had been cast off by his old protectors, was charged with sending him supplies and men, and for three months he kept the field, hoping that every gale might bring him assistance from abroad. But those same summer months and foreign climes had already proved fatal to many of the exiles, whose co-operation he invoked. In July, Rory O'Donnell expired at Rome, in August, Maguire died at Genoa, on his way to Spain, and in September, Caffar O'Donnell was laid in the same grave with his brother, on St. Peter's hill. O'Neil survived his comrades, as he had done his fortunes, and like another Belisarius, blind and old, and a pensioner on the bounty of strangers, he lived on, eight weary years, in Rome. O'Doherty, enclosed in his native peninsula, between the forces of the Marshal Wingfield and Sir Oliver Lambert, Governor of Connaught, fell by a chance shot, at the rock of Doon, in Kilmacrenan. The superfluous traitor, Nial Garve, was, with his sons, sent to London, and imprisoned in the Tower for life. In those dungeons, Cormac, brother of Hugh O'Neil, and O'Cane also languished out their days, victims to the careless or vindictive temper of King James. Sir Arthur Chichester received, soon after these events, a grant of the entire barony of Innishowen, and subsequently a grant of the borough of Dungannon, with 1,300 acres adjoining; Wingfield obtained the district of Fercullan near Dublin, with the title of Viscount Powerscourt; Lambert was soon after made Earl of Cavan, and enriched with the lands of Carig, and other estates in that county.

To justify at once the measures he proposed, as well as to divert from the exiles the sympathies of Europe, King James issued a proclamation bearing date the 5th of November, 1608, giving to the world the English version of the flight of the Earls. The whole of Ulster was then surveyed in a cursory manner by a staff over which presided Sir William Parsons as Surveyor-General. The surveys being completed early in 1609, a royal commission was issued to Chichester, Lambert, St. John, Ridgeway, Moore, Davis, and Parsons, with the Archbishop of Armagh, and the Bishop of Derry, to inquire into the portions forfeited. Before these Commissioners Juries were sworn on each particular case, and these Juries duly found that, in consequence of "the rebellion" of O'Neil, O'Donnell, and O'Doherty, the entire six counties of Ulster, enumerated by baronies and parishes, were forfeited to the Crown. By direction from England the Irish Privy Council submitted a scheme for planting these counties "with colonies of civil men well affected in religion," which scheme, with several modifications suggested by the English Privy Council, was finally promulgated by the royal legislator under the title of "Orders and Conditions for the Planters." According to the division thus ordered, upwards of 43,000 acres were claimed and conceded to the Primate and the Protestant Bishops of Ulster; in Tyrone, Derry, and Armagh, Trinity College got 30,000 acres, with six advowsons in each county. The various trading guilds of the city of London--such as the drapers, vintners, cordwainers, drysalters--obtained in the gross 209,800 acres, including the city of Derry, which they rebuilt and fortified, adding **London** to its ancient name. The grants to individuals were divided into three classes-- 2,000, 1,500, and 1,000 acres each. Among the conditions on which these grants were given was this--"that they should not suffer any labourer, that would not take the oath of supremacy," to dwell upon their lands. But this despotic condition--equivalent to sentence of death on tens of thousands of the native peasantry--was fortunately found impracticable in the execution. Land was little worth without hands to till it; labourers enough could not be obtained from England and Scotland, and the Hamiltons, Stewarts, Folliots, Chichesters, and Lamberts, having, from sheer necessity, to choose between Irish cultivators and letting their new estates lie waste and unprofitable, it is needless to say what choice they made.

The spirit of religious persecution was exhibited not only in the means taken to exterminate the peasantry, to destroy the northern chiefs, and to intimidate the Catholics of "the Pale" by abuse of law, but by many cruel executions. The Prior of the famous retreat of Lough Derg was one of the victims of this persecution; a Priest named O'Loughrane, who had accidentally sailed in the same ship with the Earls to France, was taken prisoner on his return, hanged and quartered. Conor O'Devany, Bishop of Down and Conor, an octogenarian, suffered martyrdom with heroic constancy at Dublin, in 1611. Two years before, John, Lord Burke of Brittas, was executed in like manner on a charge of having participated in the Catholic demonstrations which took place at Limerick on the accession of King James. The edict of 1610 in relation to Catholic children educated abroad has been quoted in a previous chapter, *apropos* of education, but the scheme submitted by Knox, Bishop of Raphoe, to Chichester in 1611 went even beyond that edict. In this project it was proposed that whoever should be found to harbour a Priest should forfeit all his possessions to the Crown--that quarterly returns should be made out by counties of all who refused to take the oath of supremacy, or to attend the English Church service--that no Papist should be permitted to exercise the function of a schoolmaster; and, moreover, that all churches injured during the late war should be repaired at the expense of the Papist inhabitants for the use of the Anglican congregation.

Very unexpectedly to the nation at large, after a lapse of 27 years, during which no Parliament had been held, writs were issued for the attendance of both Houses, at Dublin, on the 18th of May, 1613. The work of confiscation and plantation had gone on for several years without the sanction of the legislature, and men were at a loss to conceive for what purpose elections were now ordered, unless to invent new penal laws, or to impose fresh burdens on the country. With all the efforts which had been made to introduce civil men, well affected in religion, it was certain that the Catholics would return a large majority of the House of Commons, not only in the chief towns, but from the fifteen old, and seventeen new counties, lately created. To counterbalance this majority, over forty boroughs, returning two members each, were created, by royal charter, in places thinly or not at all inhabited, or where towns were merely projected on the estates of leading "Undertakers." Against the issue of writs returnable by these fictitious corporations, the Lords Gormanstown, Slane, Killeen, Trimbleston, Dunsany, and Howth, signed an humble remonstrance to the King, concluding with a prayer for the relaxation of the penal laws affecting religion. The King, whose notions of prerogative were extravagantly high, was highly incensed at this petition of the Catholic peers of Leinster, and Chichester proceeded with his full approbation to pack the Parliament. At the elections, however, many "recusant lawyers" and other Catholic candidates were returned, so that when the day of meeting arrived, 101 Catholic representatives assembled at Dublin, some accompanied by bands of from 100 to 200 armed followers. The supporters of the government claimed 125 votes, and six were found to be absent, making the whole number of the House of Commons 232. The Upper House consisted of 50 Peers, of whom there were 25 Protestant Bishops, so that the Deputy was certain of a majority in that chamber, on all points of ecclesiastical legislation, at least. Although, with the facts before us, we cannot agree with Sir John Davis that King James I. gave Ireland her "first free Parliament," it is impossible not to entertain a high sense of admiration for the constitutional firmness of the recusant or Catholic party in that assembly. At the very outset they successfully resisted the proposition to meet in the Castle, surrounded by the Deputy's guards, as a silent menace. They next contended that before proceeding to the election of Speaker the Council should submit to the Judges the decision of the alleged invalid elections. A tumultous and protracted debate was had on this point. The Castle party argued that they should first elect a Speaker and then proceed to try the elections; the Catholics contended that there were persons present whose votes would determine the Speakership, but who had no more title in law than the horseboys at the door. This was the preliminary trial of strength. The candidate of the Castle for the Speakership was Sir John Davis; of the Catholics, Sir John Everard, who had resigned his seat on the bench rather than take the oath of supremacy framed by Archbishop Abbott. The Castle party having gone into the lobby to be counted, the Catholics placed Sir John Everard in the Chair. On their return the government supporters placed Sir John Davis in Everard's lap, and a scene of violent disorder ensued. The House broke up in confusion; the recusants in a body declared their intention not to be present at its deliberations, and the Lord Deputy, finding them resolute, suddenly prorogued the session. Both parties sent deputies to England to lay their complaints at the foot of the throne. The Catholic spokesmen, Talbot and Lutrell, were received with a storm of reproaches, and committed, the former to the Tower, the other to the Fleet Prison. They were, however, released after a brief confinement, and a Commission was issued to inquire into the alleged electoral frauds. By the advice of Everard and others of their leaders, a compromise was effected with the Castle party; members returned for boroughs incorporated after the writs were issued were declared excluded, the contestation of seats on other grounds of irregularity were withdrawn, and the House accordingly proceeded to the business for which they were called together. The chief acts of the sessions of 1614, '15, and '16, beside the grant of four entire subsidies to the Crown, were an act joyfully recognizing the King's title; acts repealing statutes of Elizabeth and Henry VIII., as to distinctions of race; an act repealing the 3 and 4 of Philip and Mary, against "bringing Scots into Ireland," and the acts of attainder against O'Neil, O'Donnell, and O'Doherty. The recusant minority have been heavily censured by our recent historians for consenting to these attainders. Though the censure may be in part deserved, it is, nevertheless, clear that they had not the power to prevent their passage, even if they had been unanimous in their opposition; but they had influence enough, fortunately, to oblige the government to withdraw a sweeping penal law which it was intended to propose. An Act of oblivion and amnesty was also passed, which was of some advantage. On the whole, both for the constitutional principles which they upheld, and the religious proscription which they resisted, the recusant minority in the Irish Parliament of James I. deserve to be held in honour by all who value religious and civil liberty.

CHAPTER II.

LAST YEARS OF JAMES--CONFISCATION OF THE MIDLAND COUNTIES--ACCESSION OF CHARLES I.--GRIEVANCES AND "GRACES"--ADMINISTRATION OF LORD STRAFFORD.

From the dissolution of James's only Irish Parliament in October, 1615, until the tenth of Charles I.--an interval of twenty years--the government of the country was again exclusively regulated by arbitrary proclamations and orders in Council. Chichester, after the unusually long term of eleven years, had leave to retire in 1816; he was succeeded by the Lord Grandison, who held the office of Lord Deputy for six years, and he, in turn, by Henry Carey, Viscount Falkland, who governed from 1622 till 1629--seven years. Nothing could well be more fluctuating than the policy pursued at different periods by these Viceroys and their advisers; violent attempts at coercion alternated with the meanest devices to extort money from the oppressed; general declarations against recusants were repeated with increased vehemence, while particular treaties for a local and conditional toleration were notoriously progressing; in a word, the administration of affairs exhibited all the worst vices and weaknesses of a despotism, without any of the steadiness or magnanimity of a really paternal government. Some of the edicts issued deserve particular notice, as characterizing the administrations of Grandison and Falkland.

The municipal authorities of Waterford, having invariably refused to take the oath of supremacy, were, by an order in Council, deprived of their ancient charter, which was withheld from them for nine years. The ten shilling tax on recusants for non-attendance at the Anglican service was rigorously enforced in other cities, and was almost invariably levied with costs, which not seldom swelled the ten shillings to ten pounds. A new instrument of oppression was also, in Lord Grandison's time, invented--"the Commission for the Discovery of Defective Titles." At the head of this Commission was placed Sir William Parsons, the Surveyor-General, who had come into the kingdom in a menial situation, and had, through a long half century of guile and cruelty, contributed as much to the destruction of its inhabitants, by the perversion of law, as any armed conqueror could have done by the edge of the sword. Ulster being already applotted, and Munster undergoing the manipulation of the new Earl of Cork, there remained as a field for the Parsons Commission only the Midland Counties and Connaught. Of these they made the most in the shortest space of time. A horde of clerkly spies were employed under the name of "Discoverers," to ransack old Irish tenures in the archives of Dublin and London, with such good success, that in a very short time 66,000 acres in Wicklow, and 385,000 acres in Leitrim, Longford, the Meaths, and King's and Queen's Counties, were "found by inquisition to be vested in the Crown." The means employed by the Commissioners, in some cases, to elicit such evidence as they required, were of the most revolting description. In the Wicklow case, courts-martial were held, before which unwilling witnesses were tried on the charge of treason, and some actually put to death. Archer, one of the number, had his flesh burned with red hot iron, and was placed on a gridiron over a charcoal fire, till he offered to testify anything that was necessary. Yet on evidence so obtained whole baronies and counties were declared forfeited to the Crown.

The recusants, though suffering under every sort of injustice, and kept in a state of continual apprehension --a condition worse even than the actual horrors they endured--counted many educated and wealthy persons in their ranks, besides mustering fully ninety per cent, of the whole population. They were, therefore, far from being politically powerless. The recall of Lord Grandison from the government was attributed to their direct or indirect influence upon the King. When James Usher, then Bishop of Meath, preached before his successor from the text "He beareth not the sword in vain," they were sufficiently formidable to compel him publicly to apologise for his violent allusions to their body. Perhaps, however, we should mainly see in the comparative toleration, extended by Lord Falkland, an effect of the diplomacy then going on, for the marriage of Prince Charles to the Infanta of Spain. When, in 1623, Pope Gregory XV. granted a dispensation for this marriage, James solemnly swore to, a private article of the marriage treaty, by which he bound himself to suspend the execution of the Penal laws, to procure their repeal in Parliament, and to grant a toleration of Catholic worship in private houses. But the Spanish match was unexpectedly broken off, immediately after his decease (June, 1625), whereupon Charles married Henrietta Maria, daughter of Henry IV. of France.

The new monarch inherited from his father three kingdoms heaving in the throes of disaffection and rebellion. In England the most formidable of the malcontents were the Puritans, who reckoned many of the first nobility, and the ablest members of the House of Commons among their chiefs; the restoration of episcopacy, and the declaration by the subservient Parliament of Scotland, that no General Assembly should be called without the King's sanction, had laid the sure foundations of a religious insurrection in the North; while the events, which we have already described, filled the minds of all orders of men in Ireland with agitation and alarm. The marriage of Charles with Henrietta Maria gave a ray of assurance to the co-religionists of the young Queen, for they had not then discovered that it was ever the habit of the Stuarts "to sacrifice their friends to the fear of their enemies." While he was yet celebrating his nuptials at Whitehall, surrounded by Catholic guests, the House of Commons presented Charles "a pious petition," praying him to put into force the laws against recusants; a prayer which he was compelled by motives of policy to answer in the affirmative. The magistrates of England received orders accordingly, and when the King of France remonstrated against this flagrant breach of one of the articles of the marriage treaty (the same included in the terms of the Spanish match), Charles answered that he had never looked on the promised toleration as anything but an artifice to secure the Papal dispensation. But the King's compliance failed to satisfy the Puritan party in the House of Commons, and that same year began their contest with the Crown, which ended only on the scaffold before Whitehall in 1648. Of their twenty-three years' struggle, except in so far as it enters directly into our narrative, we shall have little to say, beyond reminding the reader, from time to time, that though it occasionally lulled down it was never wholly allayed on either side.

Irish affairs, in the long continued suspension of the functions of Parliament, were administered in general by the Privy Council, and in detail by three special courts, all established in defiance of ancient constitutional usage. These were the Court of Castle Chamber, modelled on the English Star Chamber, and the Ecclesiastical High Commissioners Court, both dating from 1563; and the Court of Wards and Liveries, originally founded by Henry VIII., but lately remodelled by James. The Castle Chamber was composed of certain selected members of the Privy Council acting in secret with absolute power; the High Commission Court was constituted under James and Charles, of the principal Archbishops and Bishops, with the Lord Deputy, Chancellor, Chief Justice, Master of the Rolls, Master of the Wards, and some others, laymen and jurists. They were armed with unlimited power "to visit, reform, redress, order, correct and amend, all such errors, heresies, schisms, abuses, offences, contempts and enormities," as came under the head of spiritual or ecclesiastical jurisdiction. They were, in effect, the Castle Chamber, acting as a spiritual tribunal of last resort; and were provided with their own officers, Registers and Receivers of Fines, Pursuivants, Criers and Gaolers. The Court of Wards exercised a jurisdiction, if possible, more repugnant to our first notions of liberty than that of the High Commission Court. It retained its original power "to bargain and sell the custody, wardship and marriage," of all the heirs of such persons of condition as died in the King's homage; but their powers, by royal letters patent of the year 1617, were to be exercised by a Master of Wards, with an Attorney and Surveyor, all nominated by the Crown. The Court was entitled to farm all the property of its Wards during nonage, for the benefit of the Crown, "taking one year's rent from heirs male, and two from heirs female," for charges of stewardship. The first master, Sir William Parsons, was appointed in 1622, and confirmed at the beginning of the next reign, with a salary of 300 pounds per annum, and the right to rank next to the Chief Justice of the King's Bench at the Privy Council. By this appointment the minor heirs of all the Catholic proprietors were placed, both as to person and property, at the absolute disposal of one of the most intense anti-Catholic bigots that ever appeared on the scene of Irish affairs.

In addition to these civil grievances an order had lately been issued to increase the army in Ireland by 5,000 men, and means of subsistence had to be found for that additional force, within the kingdom. In reply to the murmurs of the inhabitants, they were assured by Lord Falkland that the King was their friend, and that any just and temperate representation of their grievances would secure his careful and instant attention. So encouraged, the leading Catholics convoked a General Assembly of their nobility and gentry, "with several Protestants of rank," at Dublin, in the year 1628, in order to present a dutiful statement of their complaints to the King. The minutes of this important Assembly, it is to be feared, are for ever lost to us. We only know that it included a large number of landed proprietors, of whom the Catholics were still a very numerous section. "The entire proceedings of this Assembly," says Dr. Taylor, "were marked by wisdom and moderation. They drew up a number of articles, in the nature of a Bill of Rights, to which they humbly solicited the royal assent, and promised that, on their being granted, they would raise a voluntary assessment of 100,000 pounds for the use of the Crown. The principal articles in these 'graces,' as they were called, were provisions for the security of property, the due administration of justice, the prevention of military exactions, the freedom of trade, the better regulation of the clergy, and the restraining of the tyranny of the ecclesiastical courts. Finally, they provided that the Scots, who had been planted in Ulster, should be seemed in their possessions, and a general pardon granted for all offences." Agents were chosen to repair to England with this petition, and the Assembly, hoping for the best results, adjourned. But the ultra Protestant party had taken the alarm, and convoked a Synod at Dublin to counteract the General Assembly. This Synod vehemently protested against selling truth "as a slave," and "establishing for a price idolatry in its stead." They laid it down as a dogma of *their* faith that "to grant Papists a toleration, or to consent that they may freely exercise their religion and profess their faith and doctrines, was a grievous sin;" wherefore they prayed God "to make those in authority zealous, resolute, and courageous against all Popery, superstition, and idolatry." This declaration of the extreme Protestants, including not only Usher, and the principal Bishops, but Chichester, Boyle, Parsons, and the most successful "Undertakers," all deeply imbued with Puritan notions, naturally found among their English brethren advocates and defenders. The King, who had lately, for the third time, renewed with France the articles of his marriage treaty, was placed in a most difficult position. He desired to save his own honour, he sorely needed the money of the Catholics, but he trembled before the compact, well organized fanaticism of the Puritans. In his distress he had recourse to a councillor, who, since the assassination of Buckingham, his first favourite, divided with Laud the royal confidence. This was Thomas, Lord Wentworth, better known by his subsequent title of Earl of Strafford, a statesman born to be the wonder and the bane of three kingdoms. Strafford (for such for clearness we must call him) boldly advised the King to grant "the graces" as his own personal act, to pocket the proposed subsidy, but to contrive that the promised concessions he was to make should never go into effect. This infamous deception was effected in this wise: the King signed, with his own hand, a schedule of fifty-one "graces," and received from the Irish agents in London bonds for 120,000 pounds, (equal to ten times the amount at present), to be paid in three annual instalments of 40,000 pounds. He also agreed that Parliament should be immediately called in Ireland, to confirm these concessions, while at the same time he secretly instructed Lord Falkland to see that the writs of election were informally prepared, so that no Parliament could be held. This was accordingly done; the agents of the General Assembly paid their first instalment; the subscribers held the King's autograph; the writs were issued, but on being returned, were found to be technically incorrect, and so the legal confirmation of the graces was indefinitely postponed, under one pretext or another. As evidence of the national demands at this period, we should add, that beside the redress of minor grievances, the articles signed by the King provided that the recusants should be allowed to practise in the courts of law; to sue the livery of their lands out of the Court of Wards, on taking an oath of civil allegiance in lieu of the oath of supremacy; that the claims of the Crown to the forfeiture of estates, under the plea of defects of title, should not be held to extend beyond sixty years anterior to 1628; that the "Undertakers" should have time allowed them to fulfil the conditions of their leases; that the proprietors of Connaught should be allowed to make a new enrollment of their estates, and that a Parliament should be held. A royal proclamation announced these concessions, as existing in the royal intention, but, as we have already related, such promises proved to be worth no more than the paper on which they were written.

In 1629 Lord Falkland, to disarm the Puritan outcry against him, had leave to withdraw, and for four years --an unusually long interregnum--the government was left in the hands of Robert Boyle, now Earl of Cork, and Adam Loftus, Viscount Ely, one of the well dowered offspring of Queen Elizabeth's Archbishop of Dublin. Ely held the office of Lord Chancellor, and Cork that of Lord High Treasurer; as Justices, they now combined in their own persons almost all the power and patronage of the kingdom. Both affected a Puritan austerity and enthusiasm, which barely cloaked a rapacity and bigotry unequalled in any former administration. In Dublin, on Saint Stephen's Day, 1629, the Protestant Archbishop, Bulkley, and the Mayor of the city, entered the Carmelite Chapel, at the head of a file of soldiers, dispersed the congregation, desecrated the altar, and arrested the officiating friars. The persecution was then taken up and repeated wherever the executive power was strong enough to defy the popular indignation. A Catholic seminary lately established in the capital was confiscated, and turned over to Trinity College as a training school. Fifteen religious houses, chiefly belonging to the Franciscan Order, which had hitherto escaped from the remoteness of their situation, were, by an order of the English Council, confiscated to the Crown, and their novices compelled to emigrate in order to complete their studies abroad. A reprimand from the King somewhat stayed the fury of the Justices, whose supreme power ended with Stafford's appointment in 1633.

The advent of Stafford was characteristic of his whole course. The King sent over another letter concerning recusants, declaring that the laws against them, at the suggestion of the Lords Justices, should be put strictly in force. The Justices proved unwilling to enter this letter on the Council book, and it was accordingly withheld till Stafford's arrival, but the threat had the desired effect of drawing "a voluntary contribution" of 20,000 pounds out of the alarmed Catholics. Equipped partly with this money Stafford arrived in Dublin in July, 1633, and entered at once on the policy, which he himself designated by the one emphatic word--"THOROUGH." He took up his abode in the Castle, surrounded by a Body Guard, a force hitherto unknown at the Irish Court; he summoned only a select number of the Privy Council, and, having kept them waiting for hours, condescended to address them in a speech full of arrogance and menace. He declared his intention of maintaining and augmenting the army; advised them to amend their grants forthwith; told them frankly he had called them to Council, more out of courtesy than necessity, and ended by requiring from them a year's subsidy in advance. As this last request was accompanied by a positive promise to obtain the King's consent to the assembling of Parliament, it was at once granted; and soon after writs were issued for the meeting of both Houses in July following.

When this long-prayed-for Parliament at last met, the Lord Deputy took good care that it should be little else than a tribunal to register his edicts. A great many officers of the army had been chosen as Burgesses, while the Sheriffs of counties were employed to secure the election of members favourable to the demands of the Crown. In the Parliament of 1613 the recusants were, admitting all the returns to be correct, nearly one-half; but in that of 1634 they could not have exceeded one-third. The Lord Deputy nominated their Speaker, whom they did not dare to reject, and treated them invariably with the supreme contempt which no one knows so well how to exhibit towards a popular assembly as an apostate liberal. "Surely," he said in his speech from the throne, "so great a meanness cannot enter your hearts, as once to suspect his Majesty's gracious regard of you, and performance with you, once you affix yourselves upon his grace." His object in this appeal was the sordid and commonplace one--to obtain more money without rendering value for it. He accordingly carried through four whole subsidies of 50,000 pounds sterling each in the session of 1634; and two additional subsidies of the same amount at the opening of the next session. The Parliament, having thus answered his purpose, was summarily dissolved in April, 1635, and for four years more no other was called. During both sessions he had contrived, according to his agreement with the King, to postpone indefinitely the act which was to have confirmed "the graces," guaranteed in 1628. He even contrived to get a report of a Committee of the House of Commons, and the opinions of some of the Judges, against legislating on the subject at all, which report gave King Charles "a great deal of contentment."

With sufficient funds in hand for the ordinary expenses of the government, Strafford applied himself earnestly to the self-elected task of making his royal master "as absolute as any King in Christendom" on the Irish side of the channel. The plantation of Connaught, delayed by the late King's death, and abandoned among the new King's graces, was resumed as a main engine of obtaining more money. The proprietary of that Province had, in the thirteenth year of the late reign, paid 3,000 pounds into the Record Office at Dublin, for the registration of their deeds, but the entries not being made by the clerk employed, the title to every estate in the five western counties was now called in question. The "Commissioners to Inquire into Defective Titles" were let loose upon the devoted Province, with Sir William Parsons at their head, and the King's title to the whole of Mayo, Sligo and Roscommon, was found by packed, bribed, or intimidated juries; the grand jury of Galway having refused to find a similar verdict, were summoned to the Court of Castle Chamber, sentenced to pay a fine of 4,000 pounds each to the Crown, and the Sheriff that empanelled them, a fine of 1,000 pounds. The lawyers who pleaded for the actual proprietors were stripped of their gowns, the sheriff died in prison, and the work of spoliation proceeded. The young Earl of Ormond was glad to compound for a portion of his estates; the Earl of Kildare was committed to prison for refusing a similar composition; the Earl of Cork was compelled to pay a heavy fine for his intrusion into lands originally granted to the Church; the O'Byrnes of Wicklow commuted for 15,000 pounds, and the London Companies, for their Derry estates, paid no less than 70,000 pounds: a forced contribution for which those frugal citizens never forgave the thorough-going Deputy. By these means, and others less violent, such as bounties to the linen trade, he raised the annual revenue of the kingdom to 80,000 pounds a year, and was enabled to embody for the King's service an army of 10,000 foot and 1,000 horse.

These arbitrary measures were entirely in consonance with the wishes of Charles. In a visit to England in 1636, the King assured Strafford personally of his cordial approbation of all he had done, encouraged him to proceed fearlessly in the same course, and conferred on him the higher rank of Lord Lieutenant. Three years later, on the first rumour of a Scottish invasion of England, Strafford was enabled to remit his master 30,000 pounds from the Irish Treasury, and to tender the services of the Anglo-Irish army, as he thought they could be safely dispensed with by the country in which they had been thus far recruited and maintained.

CHAPTER III.

LORD STRAFFORD'S IMPEACHMENT AND EXECUTION--PARLIAMENT OF 1639-'41--THE INSURRECTION OF 1641--THE IRISH ABROAD.

The tragic end of the despot, whose administration we have sketched, was now rapidly approaching. When he deserted the popular ranks in the English House of Commons for a Peerage and the government of Ireland, the fearless Pym prophetically remarked, "Though you have left us, I will not leave you while your head is on your shoulders." Yet, although conscious of having left able and vigilant enemies behind him in England, Strafford proceeded in his Irish administration as if he scorned to conciliate the feelings or interests of any order of men. By the highest nobility, as well as the humblest of the mechanic class, his will was to be received as law; so that neither in Church, nor in State, might any man express even the most guarded doubt as to its infallibility. Lord Mountnorris, for example, having dropped a casual, and altogether innocent remark at the Chancellor's table on the private habits of the Deputy, was brought to trial by court martial on a charge of mutiny, and sentenced to military execution. Though he was not actually put to death, he underwent a long and rigorous imprisonment, and at length was liberated without apology or satisfaction. If they were not so fully authenticated, the particulars of this outrageous case would hardly be credible.

The examples of resistance to arbitrary power, which for some years had been shown by both England and Scotland, were not thrown away upon the still worse used Irish. During the seven years of Strafford's iron rule, Hampden had resisted the collection of ship money, Cromwell had begun to figure in the House of Commons, the Solemn League and Covenant was established in Scotland, and the Scots had twice entered England in arms to seal with their blood, if need were, their opposition to an episcopal establishment of religion. It was in 1640, upon the occasion of their second invasion, that Strafford was recalled from Ireland to assume command of the royal forces in the North of England. After a single indecisive campaign, the King entertained the overtures of the Covenanters, and the memorable Long Parliament having met in November, one of its first acts was the impeachment of Strafford for high crimes and misdemeanors. The chief articles against him related to his administration of Irish affairs, and were sustained by delegates from the Irish House of Commons, sent over for that purpose: the whole of the trial deserves to be closely examined by every one interested in the constitutional history of England and Ireland.

A third Parliament, known as the 14th, 15th and 16th Charles I., met at Dublin on the 20th March, 1639, was prorogued till June, and adjourned till October. Yielding the point so successfully resisted in 1613, its sittings were held in the Castle, surrounded by the viceregal guard. With one exception, the acts passed in its first session were of little importance, relating only to the allotment of glebe lands and the payment of twentieths. The exception, which followed the voting of four entire subsidies to the King, was an Act ordaining "that this Parliament shall not determine by his Majesty's assent to this and other Bills." A similar statute had been passed in 1635, but was wholly disregarded by Strafford, who no doubt meant to take precisely the same course in the present instance. The members of this Assembly have been severely condemned by modern writers for passing a high eulogium upon Strafford in their first session and reversing it after his fall. But this censure is not well founded. The eulogium was introduced by the Castle party in the Lords, as part of the preamble to the Supply Bill, which, on being returned to the Commons, could only be rejected *in toto*, not amended--a proceeding in the last degree revolutionary. But those who dissented from that ingenious device, at the next session of the House, took care to have their protest entered on the journals and a copy of it despatched to the King. This second proceeding took place in February, 1640, and as the Lord Lieutenant was not arraigned till the month of November following, the usual denunciations of the Irish members are altogether undeserved. At no period of his fortune was the Earl more formidable as an enemy than at the very moment the Protest against "his manner of government" was ordered "to be entered among the Ordinances" of the Commons of Ireland. Nor did this Parliament confine itself to mere protestations against the abuses of executive power. At the very opening of the second session, on the 20th of January, they appointed a committee to wait on the King in England, with instructions to solicit a bill in explanation of Poyning's law, another enabling them to originate bills in Committee of their own House, a right taken away by that law, and to ask the King's consent to the regulation of the courts of law, the collecting of the revenue, and the quartering of soldiers by statute instead of by Orders in Council. On the 16th of February the House submitted a set of queries to the Judges, the nature of which may be inferred from the first question, viz.: "Whether the subjects of this Kingdom be a free people, and to be governed only by the common law of England, and statutes passed in this Kingdom ?" When the answers received were deemed insufficient, the House itself, turning the queries into the form of resolutions, proceeded to vote on them, one by one, affirming in every point the rights, the liberties, and the privileges of their constituents.

The impeachment and attainder of Strafford occupied the great part of March and April, 1641, and throughout those months the delegates from Ireland assisted at the pleadings in Westminster Hall and the debates in the English Parliament. The Houses at Dublin were themselves occupied in a similar manner. Towards the end of February articles of impeachment were drawn up against the Lord Chancellor, Bolton, Dr. Bramhall, Bishop of Derry, Chief-Justice Lowther, and Sir George Radcliffe, for conspiring with Strafford to subvert the constitution, and laws, and to introduce an arbitrary and tyrannical government. In March, the King's letter for the continuance of Parliament was laid before the Commons, and on the 3rd of April, his further letter, declaring that all his Majesty's subjects of Ireland "shall, from henceforth, enjoy the benefit of the said graces [of 1628] according to the true intent thereof." By the end of May the Judges, not under impeachment, sent in their answers to the Queries of the Commons, which answers were voted insufficient, and Mr. Patrick Darcy, Member for Navan, was appointed to serve as Proculator at a Conference with the Lords, held on the 9th of June, "in the dining-room of the Castle," in order to set forth the insufficiency of such replies. The learned and elaborate argument of Darcy was ordered to be printed by the House; and on the 26th day of July, previous to their prorogation, they resolved unanimously, that the subjects of Ireland "were a free people, to be governed only by the common law of England, and statutes made and established in the kingdom of Ireland, and according to the lawful custom used in the same." This was the last act of this memorable session; the great northern insurrection in October having, of course, prevented subsequent sessions from being held. Constitutional agitators in modern times have been apt to select their examples of a wise and patriotic parliamentary conduct from the opposition to the Act of Union and the famous struggles of the last century; but whoever has looked into such records as remain to us of the 15th and 16th of Charles First, and the debates on the impeachment of Lord Chancellor Bolton, will, in my opinion, be prepared to admit, that at no period whatever was constitutional law more ably expounded in Ireland than in the sessions of 1640 and 1641; and that not only the principles of Swift and of Molyneux had a triumph in 1782, but the older doctrines also of Sir Ralph Kelly, Audley Mervin, and Patrick Darcy.

Strafford's Deputy, Sir Christopher Wandesford, having died before the close of 1640, the King appointed Robert, Lord Dillon, a liberal Protestant, and Sir William Parsons, Lords Justices. But the pressure of Puritan influence in England compelled him in a short time to remove Dillon and substitute Sir John Borlace, Master of the Ordnance --a mere soldier-- in point of fanaticism a fitting colleague for Parsons. The prorogation of Parliament soon gave these administrators opportunities to exhibit the spirit in which they proposed to carry on the government. When at a public entertainment in the capital, Parsons openly declared that in twelve months more no Catholics should be seen in Ireland, it was naturally inferred that the Lord Justice spoke not merely for himself but for the growing party of the English Puritans and Scottish Covenanters. The latter had repeatedly avowed that they never would lay down their arms until they had wrought the extirpation of Popery, and Mr. Pym, the Puritan leader in England, had openly declared that his party intended not to leave a priest in Ireland. The infatuation of the unfortunate Charles in entrusting at such a moment the supreme power, civil and military, to two of the devoted partizans of his deadliest enemies, could not fail to arouse the fears of all who felt themselves obnoxious to the fanatical party, either by race or by religion.

The aspirations of the chief men among the old Irish for entire freedom of worship, their hopes of recovering at least a portion of their estates, the example of the Scots, who had successfully upheld both their Church and nation against all attempts at English supremacy, the dangers that pressed, and the fears that overhung them, drove many of the very first abilities and noblest characters into the conspiracy which exploded with such terrific energy on the 23rd of October, 1641. The project, though matured on Irish soil, was first conceived among the exiled Catholics, who were to be found at that day in all the schools and camps of Spain, Italy, France and the Netherlands. Philip III. had an Irish legion, under the command of Henry O'Neil, son of Tyrone, which, after his death was transferred to his brother John. In this legion, Owen Roe O'Neil, nephew of Tyrone, learned the art of war, and rose to the rank of Lieutenant-Colonel. The number of Irish serving abroad had steadily increased after 1628, when a license of enlistment was granted by King James. An English emissary, evidently well-informed, was enabled to report, about the year 1630, that there were in the service of the Archduchess Isabella, in the Spanish Netherlands alone, "100 Irish officers able to command companies, and 20 fit to be colonels." The names of many others are given as men of noted courage, good engineers, and "well-beloved" captains, both Milesians and Anglo-Irish, residing at Lisbon, Florence, Milan and Naples. The emissary adds that they had long been providing arms for an attempt upon Ireland, "and had in readiness 5,000 or 6,000 arms laid up in Antwerp for that purpose, *bought out of the deduction of their monthly pay*." After the death of the Archduchess, in 1633, an attempt was made by the Franco-Dutch, under Prince Maurice and Marshal Chatillon, to separate the Belgian Provinces from Spain. In the sanguinary battle at Avien victory declared for the French, and on their junction with Prince Maurice, town after town surrendered to their arms. The first successful stand against them was made at Louvain, defended by 4,000 Belgians, Walloons, Spaniards and Irish; the Irish, 1,000 strong, under the command of Colonel Preston, of the Gormanstown family, greatly distinguished themselves. The siege was raised on the 4th of July, 1635, and Belgium was saved for that time to Philip IV. At the capture of Breda, in 1637, the Irish were again honourably conspicuous, and yet more so in the successful defence of Arras, the capital of Artois, three years later. Not yet strengthened by the citadel of Vauban, this ancient Burgundian city, famous for its cathedral and its manufactures, dear to the Spaniards as one of the conquests of Charles V., was a vital point in the campaign of 1640. Besieged by the French, under Marshal Millerie, it held out for several weeks under the command of Colonel Owen Roe O'Neil. The King of France lying at Amiens, within convenient distance, took care that the besiegers wanted for nothing; while the Prince-Cardinal, Ferdinand, the successor of the Archduchess in the government, marched to its relief at the head of his main force with the Imperialists, under Launboy, and the troops of the Duke of Lorrain, commanded by that Prince in person. In an attack on the French lines the Allies were beaten off with loss, and the brave commander was left again unsuccoured in the face of his powerful assailant. Subsequently Don Philip de Silva, General of the Horse to the Prince Cardinal, was despatched to its relief, but failed to effect anything; a failure for which he was court-martialed, but acquitted. The defenders, after exhausting every resource, finally surrendered the place on honourable terms, and marched out covered with glory. These stirring events, chronicled in prose and verse at home, rekindled the martial ardour which had slumbered since the disastrous day of Kinsale.

In the ecclesiastics who shared their banishment, the military exiles had a voluntary diplomatic *corps* who lost no opportunity of advancing the common cause. At Rome, their chief agent was Father Luke Wadding, founder of Saint Isidore's, one of the most eminent theologians and scholars of his age. Through the friendship of Gregory XV. and Urban VIII., many Catholic princes became deeply interested in the religious wars which the Irish of the previous ages had so bravely waged, and which their descendants were now so anxious to renew. Cardinal Richelieu--who wielded a power greater than that of Kings--had favourably entertained a project of invasion submitted to him by the son of Hugh O'Neil, a chief who, while living, was naturally regarded by the exiles as their future leader.

To prepare the country for such an invasion (if the return of men to their own country can be called by that name), it was necessary to find an agent with talents for organization, and an undoubted title to credibility and confidence. This agent was fortunately found in the person of Rory or Roger O'Moore, the representative of the ancient chiefs of Leix, who had grown up at the Spanish Court as the friend and companion of the O'Neils. O'Moore was then in the prime of life, of handsome person, and most seductive manners; his knowledge of character was profound; his zeal for the Catholic cause, intense; his personal probity, honour, and courage, undoubted. The precise date of O'Moore's arrival in Ireland is not given in any of the cotemporary accounts, but he seems to have been resident in the country some time previous to his appearance in public life, as he is familiarly spoken of by his English cotemporaries as "Mr. Roger Moore of Ballynagh." During the Parliamentary session of 1640, he took lodgings in Dublin, where he succeeded in enlisting in his plans Conor Maguire, Lord Enniskillen, Philip O'Reilly, one of the members for the county of Cavan, Costelloe McMahon, and Thorlogh O'Neil, all persons of great influence in Ulster. During the ensuing assizes in the Northern Province he visited several country towns, where in the crowd of suitors and defendants he could, without attracting special notice, meet and converse with those he desired to gain over. On this tour he received the important accession of Sir Phelim O'Neil of Kinnaird, in Tyrone, Sir Con Magennis of Down, Colonel Hugh McMahon of Monaghan, and Dr. Heber McMahon, Administrator of Clogher. Sir Phelim O'Neil, the most considerable man of his name tolerated in Ulster, was looked upon as the greatest acquisition, and at his castle of Kinnaird his associates from the neighbouring counties, under a variety of pretexts, contrived frequently to meet. From Ulster, the indefatigable O'Moore carried the threads of the conspiracy into Connaught with equal success, finding both among the nobility and clergy many adherents. In Leinster, among the Anglo-Irish, he experienced the greatest timidity and indifference, but an unforeseen circumstance threw into his hands a powerful lever, to move that province. This was the permission granted by the King to the native regiments, embodied by Strafford, to enter into the Spanish service, if they so desired. His English Parliament made no demur to the arrangement, which would rid the island of some thousands of disciplined Catholics, but several of their officers, under the inspiration of O'Moore, kept their companies together, delaying their departure from month to month. Among these were Sir James Dillon, Colonel Plunkett, Colonel Byrne, and Captain Fox, who, with O'Moore, formed the first directing body of the Confederates in Leinster.

In May, 1641, Captain Neil O'Neil arrived from the Netherlands with an urgent request from John, Earl of Tyrone, to all his clansmen to prepare for a general insurrection. He also brought them the cheering news that Cardinal Richelieu--then at the summit of his greatness --had promised the exiles arms, money, and means of transport. He was sent back, almost immediately, with the reply of Sir Phelim, O'Moore and their friends, that they would be prepared to take the field a few days before or after the festival of All Hallows--the 1st of November. The death of Earl John, the last surviving son of the illustrious Tyrone, shortly afterwards, though it grieved the Confederates, wrought no change in their plans. In his cousin-germain, the distinguished defender of Arras, they reposed equal confidence, and their confidence could not have been more worthily bestowed.

CHAPTER IV.

THE INSURRECTION OF 1641.

The plan agreed upon by the Confederates included four main features. I. A rising after the harvest was gathered in, and a campaign during the winter months, when supplies from England were most difficult to be obtained by their enemies. II. A simultaneous attack on one and the same day or night on all the fortresses within reach of their friends. III. To surprise the Castle of Dublin, which was said to contain arms for 12,000 men. IV. Aid in officers, munitions, and money from abroad. All the details of this project were carried successfully into effect, except the seizure of Dublin Castle--the most difficult as it would have been the most decisive blow to strike.

Towards the end of August, a meeting of those who could most conveniently attend was held in Dublin. There were present O'Moore and Maguire, of the civilians, and Colonels Plunkett, Byrne, and McMahon of the army. At this meeting the last week of October, or first of November, was fixed upon as the time to rise; subsequently Saturday, the 23rd of the first named month, a market day in the capital was selected. The northern movements were to be arranged with Sir Phelim O'Neil, while McMahon, Plunkett, and Byrne, with 200 picked men, were to surprise the Castle guard--consisting of only a few pensioners and 40 halbediers--turn the guns upon the city to intimidate the Puritan party, and thus make sure of Dublin; O'Moore, Lord Maguire, and other civilians, were to be in town, in order to direct the next steps to be taken. As the day approached, the arrangements went on with perfect secrecy but with perfect success. On the 22nd of October half the chosen band were in waiting, and the remainder were expected in during the night. Some hundreds of persons, in and about Dublin, and many thousands throughout the country, must have been in possession of that momentous secret, yet it was by the mere accident of trusting a drunken dependent out of sight, that the first knowledge of the plot was conveyed to the Lords Justices on the very eve of its execution.

Owen O'Connolly, the informant on this occasion, was one of those ruffling squires or henchmen, who accompanied gentlemen of fortune in that age, to take part in their quarrels, and carry their confidential messages. That he was not an ordinary domestic servant, we may learn from the fact of his carrying a sword, after the custom of the class to which we have assigned him. At this period he was in the service of Sir John Clotworthy, one of the most violent of the Puritan Undertakers, and had conformed to the established religion. Through what recklessness, or ignorance of his true character, he came to be invited by Colonel Hugh McMahon to his lodgings, and there, on the evening of the 22nd, entrusted with a knowledge of next day's plans, we have now no means of deciding. O'Connolly's information, as tendered to the Justices, states that on hearing of the proposed attack on the Castle, he pretended an occasion to withdraw, leaving his sword in McMahon's room to avoid suspicion, and that after jumping over fences and palings, he made his way from the north side of the city to Sir William Parsons at the Castle. Parsons at first discredited the tale, which O'Connolly (who was in liquor) told in a confused and rambling manner, but he finally decided to consult his colleague, Borlase, by whom some of the Council were summoned, the witness's deposition taken down, orders issued to double the guard, and officers despatched, who arrested McMahon at his lodgings. When McMahon came to be examined before the Council, it was already the morning of the 23rd; he boldly avowed his own part in the plot, and declared that what was that day to be done was now beyond the power of man to prevent. He was committed close prisoner to the Castle where he had hoped to command, and search was made for the other leaders in town. Maguire was captured the next morning, and shared McMahon's captivity; but O'Moore, Plunkett, and Byrne succeeded in escaping out of the city. O'Connolly was amply rewarded in lands and money; and we hear of him once afterwards, with the title of Colonel, in the Parliamentary army.

As McMahon had declared to the Justices, the rising was now beyond the power of man to prevent. In Ulster, by stratagem, surprise, or force, the forts of Charlemont and Mountjoy, and the town of Dungannon, were seized on the night of the 22nd by Sir Phelim O'Neil or his lieutenants; on the next day Sir Conor Magennis took the town of Newry, the McMahons possessed themselves of Carrickmacross and Castleblaney, the O'Hanlons Tandragee, while Philip O'Reilly and Roger Maguire razed Cavan and Fermanagh. A proclamation of the northern leaders appeared the same day, dated from Dungannon, setting forth their "true intent and meaning" to be, not hostility to his Majesty the King, "nor to any of his subjects, neither English nor Scotch; but only for the defence and liberty of ourselves and the Irish natives of this kingdom." A more elaborate manifesto appeared shortly afterwards from the pen of Rory O'Moore, in which the oppressions of the Catholics for conscience' sake were detailed, the King's intended "graces" acknowledged, and their frustration by the malice of the Puritan party exhibited: it also endeavoured to show that a common danger threatened the Protestants of the Episcopal Church with Roman Catholics, and asserted in the strongest terms the devotion of the Catholics to the Crown. In the same politic and tolerant spirit, Sir Conor Magennis wrote from Newry on the 25th to the officers commanding at Down. "We are," he wrote, "for our lives and liberties. We desire no blood to be shed, but if you mean to shed our blood, be sure we shall be as ready as you for that purpose." This threat of retaliation, so customary in all wars, was made on the third day of the rising, and refers wholly to future contingencies; the monstrous fictions which were afterwards circulated of a wholesale massacre committed on the 23rd were not as yet invented, nor does any public document or private letter, written in Ireland in the last week of October, or during the first days of November, so much as allude to those tales of blood and horror, afterwards so industriously circulated, and so greedily swallowed.

Fully aroused from their lethargy by McMahon's declaration, the Lords Justices acted with considerable vigour. Dublin was declared to be in a state of siege; courts martial were established; arms were distributed to the Protestant citizens, and some Catholics; and all strangers were ordered to quit the city under pain of death. Sir Francis Willoughby, Governor of Galway, who arrived on the night of the 22nd, was entrusted with the command of the Castle, Sir Charles Coote was appointed Military Governor of the city, and the Earl, afterwards Duke of Ormond, was summoned from Carrick-on-Suir to take command of the army. As Coote played a very conspicuous part in the opening scenes of this war, and Ormond till its close, it may be well to describe them both, more particularly, to the reader.

Sir Charles Coote, one of the first Baronets of Ireland, like Parsons, Boyle, Chichester, and other Englishmen, had come over to Ireland during the war against Tyrone, in quest of fortune. His first employments were in Connaught, where he filled the offices of Provost-Marshal and Vice-Governor in the reign of James I. His success as an Undertaker entitles him to rank with the fortunate adventurers we have mentioned; in Roscommon, Sligo, Leitrim, Queen's, and other counties, his possessions and privileges raised him to the rank of the richest subjects of his time. In 1640 he was a colonel of foot, with the estates of a Prince and the habits of a Provost-Marshal. His reputation for ferocious cruelty has survived the remembrance even of his successful plunder of other people's property; before the campaigns of Cromwell there was no better synonym for wanton cruelty than the name of Sir Charles Coote.

James Butler, Earl, Marquis, and Duke of Ormond deservedly ranks amongst the principal statesmen of his time. During a public career of more than half a century his conduct in many eminent offices of trust was distinguished by supreme ability, life-long firmness and consistency. As a courtier of the House of Stuart, it was impossible that he should have served and satisfied both Charleses without participating in many indefensible acts of government, and originating some of them. Yet judged, not from the Irish but the Imperial point of view, not by an abstract standard but by the public morality of his age, he will be found fairly deserving of the title of "the great Duke" bestowed on him during his lifetime. When summoned by the Lords Justices to their assistance in 1641, he was in the thirty-first year of his age, and had so far only distinguished himself in political life as the friend of the late Lord Strafford. He had, however, the good fortune to restore in his own person the estates of his family, notwithstanding that they were granted in great part to others by King James; his attachment to the cause of King Charles was very naturally augmented by the fact that the partiality of that Prince and his ill-fated favourite had enabled him to retrieve both the hereditary wealth and the high political influence which formerly belonged to the Ormond Butlers. Such an ally was indispensable to the Lords Justices in the first panic of the insurrection; but it was evident to near observers that Ormond, a loyalist and a churchman, could not long act in concert with such devoted Puritans as Parsons, Borlase, and Coote.

The military position of the several parties--there were at least three--when

Ormond arrived at Dublin, in the first week of November, may be thus stated: I. In Munster and Connaught there was but a single troop of royal horse, each, left as a guard with the respective Presidents, St. Leger and Willoughby; in Kilkenny, Dublin, and other of the midland counties, the gentry, Protestant and Catholic, were relied on to raise volunteers for their own defence; in Dublin there had been got together 1,500 old troops; six new regiments of foot were embodied; and thirteen volunteer companies of 100 each. In the Castle were arms and ammunition for 12,000 men, with a fine train of field artillery, provided by Stafford for his campaign in the north of England. Ormond, as Lieutenant-General, had thus at his disposal, in one fortnight after the insurrection broke out, from 8,000 to 10,000 well appointed men; his advice was to take the field at once against the northern leaders before the other Provinces became equally inflamed. But his judgment was overruled by the Justices, who would only consent, while awaiting their cue from the Long Parliament, to throw reinforcements into Drogheda, which thus became their outpost towards the north. II. In Ulster there still remained in the possession of "the Undertakers" Enniskillen, Deny, the Castles of Killeagh and Crohan in Cavan, Lisburn, Belfast, and the stronghold of Carrickfergus, garrisoned by the regiments of Colonel Chichester and Lord Conway. King Charles, who was at Edinburgh endeavouring to conciliate the Scottish Parliament when news of the Irish rising reached him, procured the instant despatch of 1,500 men to Ulster, and authorized Lords Chichester, Ardes and Clandeboy, to raise new regiments from among their own tenants. The force thus embodied--which may be called from its prevailing element the *Scottish* army--cannot have numbered less than 5,000 foot, and the proportionate number of horse. III. The Irish in the field by the first of November are stated in round numbers at 30,000 men in the northern counties alone; but the whole number supplied with arms and ammunition could not have reached one-third of that nominal total. Before the surprise of Charlemont and Mountjoy forts, Sir Phelim O'Neil had but a barrel or two of gunpowder; the stores of those forts, with 70 barrels taken at Newry by Magennis, and all the arms captured in the simultaneous attack, which at the outside could not well exceed 4,000 or 5,000 stand--constituted their entire equipment. One of Ormond's chief reasons for an immediate campaign in the North was to prevent them having time to get "pikes made"--which shows their deficiency even in that weapon. Besides this defect there was one, if possible, still more serious. Sir Phelim was a civilian, bred to the profession of the law; Rory O'Moore, also, had never seen service; and although Colonel Owen O'Neil and others had promised to join them "at fourteen days' notice," a variety of accidents prevented the arrival of any officer of distinction during the brief remainder of that year. Sir Phelim, however, boldly assumed the title of "Lord General of the Catholic Army in Ulster," and the still more popular title with the Gaelic speaking population of "The O'Neil."

The projected winter campaign, after the first week's successes, did not turn out favourably for the northern Insurgents. The beginning of November was marked by the barbarous slaughter committed by the Scottish garrison of Carrickfergus in the Island Magee. Three thousand persons are said to have been driven into the fathomless north sea, over the cliffs of that island, or to have perished by the sword. The ordinary inhabitants could not have exceeded one-tenth as many, but the presence of so large a number may be accounted for by the supposition that they had fled from the mainland across the peninsula, which is left dry at low water, and were pursued to their last refuge by the infuriated Covenanters. From this date forward until the accession of Owen Roe O'Neil to the command, the northern war assumed a ferocity of character foreign to the nature of O'Moore, O'Reilly and Magenis. That Sir Phelim permitted, if he did not sometimes in his gusts of stormy passion instigate, those acts of cruelty, which have stained his otherwise honourable conduct, is too true; but he stood alone among his confederates in that crime, and that crime stands alone in his character. Brave to rashness and disinterested to excess, few rebel chiefs ever made a more heroic end out of a more deplorable beginning.

The Irish Parliament, which was to have met on the 16th of November, was indefinitely prorogued by the Lords Justices, who preferred to act only with their chosen quorum of Privy Counsellors. The Catholic Lords of the Pale, who at first had arms granted for their retainers out of the public stores, were now summoned to surrender them by a given day; an insult not to be forgiven. Lords Dillon and Taafe, then deputies to the King, were seized at Ware by the English Puritans, their papers taken from them, and themselves imprisoned. O'Moore, whose clansmen had recovered Dunamase and other strongholds in his ancient patrimony, was still indefatigable in his propaganda among the Anglo-Irish. By his advice Sir Phelim marched to besiege Drogheda, at the head of his tumultuous bands. On the way southward he made an unsuccessful attack upon Lisburn, where he lost heavily; on the 24th of November he took possession of Mellifont Abbey, from whose gate the aged Tyrone had departed in tears, twenty-five years before. From Mellifont he proceeded to invest Drogheda; Colonel Plunkett, with the title of General, being the sole experienced officer as yet engaged in his ranks. A strongly walled town as Drogheda was, well manned, and easily accessible from the sea, cannot be carried without guns and engineers by any amount of physical courage. Whenever the Catholics were fairly matched in the open field, they were generally successful, as at Julianstown, during this siege, where one of their detachments cut off five out of six companies marching from Dublin to reinforce the town; but though the investment was complete, the vigilant governor, Sir Henry Tichburne, successfully repulsed the assailants. O'Moore, who lay between Ardee and Dundalk with a reserve of 2,000 men, found time during the siege to continue his natural career, that of a diplomatist. The Puritan party, from the Lord Justice downwards, were, indeed, every day hastening that union of Catholics of all origins which the founder of the Confederacy so ardently desired to bring about. Their avowed maxim was that the more men rebelled, the more estates there would be to confiscate. In Munster, their chief instruments were the aged Earl of Cork, still insatiable as ever for other men's possessions, and the President St. Leger; in Leinster, Sir Charles Coote. Lord Cork prepared 1,100 indictments against men of property in his Province, which he sent to the Speaker of the Long Parliament, with an urgent request that they might be returned to him, with authority to proceed against the parties named, as outlaws. In Leinster, 4,000 similar indictments were found in the course of two days by the free use of the rack with witnesses. Sir John Read, an officer of the King's Bedchamber, and Mr. Barnwall, of Kilbrue, a gentleman of threescore and six, were among those who underwent the torture. When these were the proceedings of the tribunals in peaceable cities, we may imagine what must have been the excesses of the soldiery in the open county. In the South, Sir William St. Leger directed a series of murderous raids upon the peasantry of Cork, which at length produced their natural effect. Lord Muskerry and other leading recusants, who had offered their services to maintain the peace of the Province, were driven by an insulting refusal to combine for their own protection. The 1,100 indictments of Lord Cork soon swelled their ranks, and the capture of the ancient city of Cashel by Philip O'Dwyer announced the insurrection of the South. Waterford soon after opened its gates to Colonel Edmund Butler; Wexford declared for the Catholic cause, and Kilkenny surrendered to Lord Mountgarret. In Wicklow, Coote's troopers committed murders such as had not been equalled since the days of the Pagan Northmen. Little children were carried aloft writhing on the pikes of these barbarians, whose worthy commander confessed that "he liked such frolics." Neither age nor sex was spared, and an ecclesiastic was especially certain of instant death. Fathers Higgins and White of Naas, in Kildare, were given up by Coote to these "lambs," though each had been granted a safe conduct by his superior officer, Lord Ormond. And these murders were taking place at the very tune when the Franciscans and Jesuits of Cashel were protecting Dr. Pullen, the Protestant Chancellor of that Cathedral and other Protestant prisoners; while also the Castle of Cloughouter, in Cavan, the residence of Bishop Bedell, was crowded with Protestant fugitives, all of whom were carefully guarded by the chivalrous Philip O'Reilly.

At length the Catholic Lords of the Pale began to feel the general glow of an outraged people, too long submissive under every species of provocation. The Lords Justices having summoned them to attend in Dublin on the 8th of December, they met at Swords, at the safe distance of seven miles, and sent by letter their reasons for not trusting themselves in the capital. To the allegations in this letter the Justices replied by proclamation, denying most of them, and repeating their summons to Lords Fingal, Gormanstown, Slane, Dunsany, Netterville, Louth, and Trimleston, to attend in Dublin on the 17th. But before the 17th came, as if to ensure the defeat of then own summons, Coote was let loose upon the flourishing villages of Fingal, and the flames kindled by his men might easily be discovered from the round tower of Swords. On the 17th, the summoned Lords, with several of the neighbouring gentry, met by appointment on the hill of Crofty, in the neighbouring county of Meath; while they were engaged in discussing the best course to be taken, a party of armed men on horseback, accompanied by a guard of musketeers, was seen approaching. They proved to be O'Moore, O'Reilly, Costelloe McMahon, brother of the prisoner, Colonel Byrne, and Captain Fox. Lord Gormanstown, advancing in front of his friends, demanded of the new-comers "why they came armed into the Pale?" To which O'Moore made answer "that the ground of their coming thither was for the freedom and liberty of their consciences, the maintenance of his Majesty's prerogative, in which they understood he was abridged, and the making the subjects of this kingdom as free as those of England." Lord Gormanstown, after consulting a few moments with his friends, replied: "Seeing these be your true ends, we will likewise join with you." The leaders then embraced, amid the acclamations of their followers, and the general conditions of then: union having been unanimously agreed upon, a warrant was drawn out authorizing the Sheriff of Meath to summon the gentry of the county to a final meeting at the Hill of Tara on the 24th of December.

CHAPTER V.

THE CATHOLIC CONFEDERATION--ITS CIVIL GOVERNMENT AND MILITARY ESTABLISHMENT.

How a tumultuous insurrection grew into a national organization, with a senate, executive, treasury, army, ships, and diplomacy, we are now to describe. It may, however, be assumed throughout the narrative, that the success of the new Confederacy was quite as much to be attributed to the perverse policy of its enemies as to the counsels of its best leaders. The rising in the midland and Munster counties, and the formal adhesion of the Lords of the Pale, were two of the principal steps towards the end. A third was taken by the Bishops of the Province of Armagh, assembled in Provincial Synod at Kells, on the 22nd of March, 1642, where, with the exception of Dease of Meath, they unanimously pronounced "the war just and lawful." After solemnly condemning all acts of private vengeance, and all those who usurped other men's estates, this provincial meeting invited a national synod to meet at Kilkenny on the 10th day of May following. On that day accordingly, all the Prelates then in the country, with the exception of Bishop Dease, met at Kilkenny. There were present O'Reilly, Archbishop of Armagh; Butler, Archbishop of Cashel; O'Kealy, Archbishop of Tuam; David Rothe, the venerable Bishop of Ossory; the Bishops of Clonfert, Elphin, Waterford, Lismore, Kildare, and Down and Conor; the proctors of Dublin, Limerick, and Killaloe, with sixteen other dignitaries and heads of religious orders--in all, twenty-nine prelates and superiors, or their representatives. The most remarkable attendants were, considering the circumstances of their Province, the prelates of Connaught. Strafford's reign of terror was still painfully remembered west of the Shannon, and the immense family influence of Ulick Burke, then Earl, and afterwards Marquis of Clanrickarde, was exerted to prevent the adhesion of the western population to the Confederacy. But the zeal of the Archbishop of Tuam, and the violence of the Governor of Galway, Sir Francis Willoughby, proved more than a counterpoise for the authority of Clanrickarde and the recollection of Strafford: Connaught, though the last to come into the Confederation, was also the last to abandon it.

The Synod of Kilkenny proceeded with the utmost solemnity and anxiety to consider the circumstances of their own and the neighbouring kingdoms. No equal number of men could have been found in Ireland, at that day, with an equal amount of knowledge of foreign and domestic politics. Many of them had spent years upon the Continent, while the French Huguenots held their one hundred "cautionary towns," and "leagues" and "associations" were the ordinary instruments of popular resistance in the Netherlands and Germany. Nor were the events transpiring in the neighbouring island unknown or unweighed by that grave assembly. The true meaning and intent of the Scottish and English insurrections were by this time apparent to every one. The previous months had been especially fertile in events, calculated to rouse their most serious apprehensions. In March, the King fled from London to York; in April, the gates of Hull were shut in his face by Hotham, its governor; and in May, the Long Parliament voted a levy of 16,000 without the royal authority. The Earl of Warwick had been appointed the Parliamentary commander of the fleet, and the Earl of Essex, their Lord General, with Cromwell as one of his captains. From that hour it was evident the sword alone could decide between Charles and his subjects. In Scotland, too, events were occurring in which Irish Catholics were vitally interested. The contest for the leadership of the Scottish royalists between the Marquises of Hamilton and Montrose had occupied the early months of the year, and given their enemies of the Kirk and the Assembly full time to carry on their correspondence with the English Puritans. In April, all parties in Scotland agreed in despatching a force of 2,500 men, under "the memorable Major Monroe," for the protection of the Scottish settlers in Ulster. On the 15th of that month this officer landed at Carrickfergus, which was "given up to him by agreement," with the royalist Colonel Chichester; the fortress, which was by much the strongest in that quarter, continued for six years the head-quarters of the Scottish general, with whom we shall have occasion to meet again.

The state of Anglo-Irish affairs was for some months one of disorganization and confusion. In January and February the King had been frequently induced to denounce by proclamation his "Irish rebels." He had offered the Parliament to lead their reinforcements in person, had urged the sending of arms and men, and had repeatedly declared that he would never consent to tolerate Popery in that country. He had failed to satisfy his enemies, by these profuse professions had dishonoured himself, and disgusted many who were far from being hostile to his person or family. Parsons and Borlase were still continued in the government, and Coote was entrusted by them, on all possible occasions, with a command distinct from that of Ormond. Having proclaimed the Lords of the Pale rebels for refusing to trust their persons within the walls of Dublin, Coote was employed during January to destroy Swords, their place of rendezvous, and to ravage the estates of their adherents in that neighbourhood. In the same month 1,100 veterans arrived at Dublin under Sir Simon Harcourt; early in February arrived Sir Richard Grenville with 400 horse, and soon after Lieutenant-Colonel George Monk, afterwards Duke of Albemarle, with Lord Leicester's regiment, 1,500 strong. Up to this period Ormond had been restrained by the Justices, who were as timid as they were cruel, to operations within an easy march of Dublin. He had driven the O'Moores and their Allies out of Naas; had reinforced some garrisons in Kildare; he had broken up, though not without much loss, an entrenched camp of the O'Byrnes at Kilsalgen wood, on the borders of Dublin; at last the Justices felt secure enough, at the beginning of March, to allow him to march to the relief of Drogheda. Sir Phelim O'Neil had invested the place for more than three months, had been twice repulsed from its walls, made a last desperate attempt, towards the end of February, but with no better success. After many lives were lost the impetuous lawyer-soldier was obliged to retire, and on the 8th of March, hearing of Ormond's approach at the head of 4,000 fresh troops, he hastily retreated northward. On receiving this report, the Justices recalled Ormond to the capital; Sir Henry Tichburne and Lord Moore were despatched with a strong force, on the rear of the Ulster forces, and drove them out of Ardee and Dundalk--the latter after a sharp action. The march of Ormond into Meath had, however, been productive of offers of submission from many of the gentry of the Pale, who attended the meetings at Crofty and Tara. Lord Dunsany and Sir John Netterville actually surrendered on the Earl's guarantee, and were sent to Dublin; Lords Gormanstown, Netterville, and Slane, offered by letter to follow their example; but the two former were, on reaching the city, thrust into the dungeons of the Castle, by order of the Justices; and the proposals of the latter were rejected with contumely. About the same time the Long Parliament passed an act declaring 2,500,000 acres of the property of Irish recusants forfeited to the State, and guaranteeing to all English "adventurers" contributing to the expenses of the war, and all soldiers serving in it, grants of land in proportion to their service and contribution. This act, and a letter from Lord Essex, the Parliamentarian Commander-in-Chief, recommending the transportation of captured recusants to the West Indian Colonies, effectually put a stop to these negotiations. In Ulster, by the end of April, there were 19,000 troops, regulars and volunteers, in the garrison or in the field. Newry was taken by Monroe and Chichester, where 80 men and women and 2 priests were put to death. Magennis was obliged to abandon Down, and McMahon Monaghan; Sir Philem was driven to burn Armagh and Dungannon, and to take his last stand at Charlemont. In a severe action with Sir Robert and Sir William Stewart, he had displayed his usual courage with better than his usual fortune, which, perhaps, we may attribute to the presence with him of Sir Alexander McDonnell, brother to Lord Antrim, the famous ***Colkitto*** of the Irish and Scottish wars. But the severest defeat which the Confederates had was in the heart of Leinster, at the hamlet of Kilrush, within four miles of Athy. Lord Ormond, returning from a second reinforcement of Naas and other Kildare forts, at the head, by English account, of 4,000 men, found on the 13th of April the Catholics of the midland counties, under Lords Mountgarrett, Ikerrin, and Dunboyne, Sir Morgan Cavenagh, Rory O'Moore, and Hugh O'Byrne, drawn up, by his report, 8,000 strong, to dispute his passage. With Ormond were the Lord Dillon, Lord Brabazon, Sir Richard Grenville, Sir Charles Coote, and Sir T. Lucas. The combat was short but murderous. The Confederates left 700 men, including Sir Morgan Cavenagh, and some other officers, dead on the field; the remainder retreated in disorder, and Ormond, with an inconsiderable diminution of numbers, returned in triumph to Dublin. For this victory the Long Parliament, in a moment of enthusiasm, voted the Lieutenant-General a jewel worth 500 pounds. If any satisfaction could be derived from such an incident, the violent death of their most ruthless enemy, Sir Charles Coote, might have afforded the Catholics some consolation. That merciless saberer, after the combat at Kilrush, had been employed in reinforcing Birr, and relieving the Castle of Geashill, which the Lady Letitia of Offally held against the neighbouring tribe of O'Dempsey. On his return from this service he made a foray against a Catholic force, which had mustered in the neighbourhood of Trim; here, on the night of the 7th of May, heading a sally of his troop, he fell by a musket shot--not without suspicion of being fired from his own ranks. His son and namesake, who imitated him in all things, was ennobled at the restoration by the title of the Earl of Mountrath. In Munster the President St. Leger, though lately reinforced by 1,000 men from England, did not consider himself strong enough for other than occasional forays into the neighbouring county, and little was effected in that Province.

Such was the condition of affairs at home and abroad when the National Synod assembled at Kilkenny. As the most popular tribunal invested with the highest moral power in the kingdom, it was their arduous task to establish order and authority among the chaotic elements of the revolution. By the admission of those most opposed to them they conducted their deliberations for nearly three weeks with equal prudence and energy. They first, on the motion of the venerable Bishop Rothe, framed an oath of association to be publicly taken by all their adherents, by the first part of which they were bound to bear "true faith and allegiance" to King Charles and his lawful successors, "to maintain the fundamental laws of Ireland, the free exercise of the Roman Catholic faith and religion." By the second part of this oath all Confederate Catholics --for so they were to be called--as solemnly bound themselves never to accept or submit to any peace "without the consent and approbation of the general assembly of the said Confederate Catholics." They then proceeded to make certain constitutions, declaring the war just and lawful; condemning emulations and distinctions founded on distinctions of race, such as "new" and "old Irish;" ordaining an elective council for each Province; and a Supreme or National Council for the whole kingdom; condemning as excommunicate all who should, having taken the oath, violate it, or who should be guilty of murder, violence to persons, or plunder under pretence of the war. Although the attendance of the lay leaders of the movement at Kilkenny was far from general, the exigencies of the case compelled them, to nominate, with the concurrence of the Bishops, the first Supreme Council of which Lord Mountgarrett was chosen President, and Mr. Richard Belling, an accomplished writer and lawyer, Secretary. By this body a General Assembly of the entire Nation was summoned to meet at the same city, on the

23rd of October following--the anniversary of the Ulster rising, commonly called by the English party "Lord Maguire's day." The choice of such an occasion by men of Mountgarrett's and Selling's moderation and judgment, six months after the date of the alleged "massacre," would form another proof, if any were now needed, that none of the alleged atrocities were yet associated with the memory of that particular day.

The events of the five months, which intervened between the adjournment of the National Synod at the end of May, and the meeting of the General Assembly on the 23rd of October, may best be summed up under the head of the respective provinces. I. The oath of Confederation was taken with enthusiasm in Munster, a Provincial Council elected, and General Barry chosen Commander-in-Chief. Barry made an attempt upon Cork, which was repulsed, but a few days later the not less important city of Limerick opened its gates to the Confederates, and on the 21st of June the citadel was breached and surrendered by Courtenay, the Governor. On the 2nd of July St. Leger died at Cork (it was said of vexation for the loss of Limerick), and the command devolved on his son-in-law, Lord Inchiquin, a pupil of the school of Wards, and a soldier of the school of Sir Charles Coote. With Inchiquin was associated the Earl of Barrymore for the civil administration, but on Barrymore's death in September both powers remained for twelve months in the hands of the survivor. The gain of Limerick was followed by the taking of Loughgar and Askeaton, but was counterbalanced by the defeat of Liscarroll, when the Irish loss was 800 men, with several colours; Inchiquin reported only 20 killed, including the young lord Kinalmeaky, one of the five sons whom the Earl of Cork gave to this war. II. In Connaught, Lord Clanrickarde was still enabled to avert a general outbreak. In vain the western Prelates besought him in a pathetic remonstrance to place himself at the head of its injured inhabitants, and take the command of the Province. He continued to play a middle part between the President, Lord Ranelagh, Sir Charles Coote the younger, and Willoughby, Governor of Galway, until the popular impatience burst all control. The chief of the O'Flahertys seized Clanrickarde's castle, of Aughrenure, and the young men of Galway, with a skill and decision quite equal to that of the Derry apprentices of an after day, seized an English ship containing arms and supplies, lying in the bay, marched to the Church of Saint Nicholas, took the Confederate oath, and shut Willoughby up in the citadel. Clanrickarde hastened to extinguish this spark of resistance, and induced the townsmen to capitulate on his personal guarantee. But Willoughby, on the arrival of reinforcements, under the fanatical Lord Forbes, at once set the truce made by Clanrickarde at defiance, burned the suburbs, sacked the Churches, and during August and September, exercised a reign of terror in the town. About the same time local risings took place in Sligo, Mayo, and Roscommon, at first with such success that the President of the Province, Lord Ranelagh, shut himself up in the castle of Athlone, where he was closely besieged. III. In Leinster, no military movement of much importance was made, in consequence of the jealousy the Justices entertained of Ormond, and the emptiness of the treasury. In June, the Long Parliament remitted over the paltry sum of 11,500 pounds to the Justices, and 2,000 of the troops, which had all but mutinied for their pay, were despatched under Ormond to the relief of Athlone. Commissioners arrived during the summer, appointed by the Parliament to report on the affairs of Ireland, to whom the Justices submitted a penal code worthy of the brain of Draco or Domitian; Ormond was raised to the rank of Marquis, by the King; while the army he commanded grew more and more divided, by intrigues emanating from the castle and beyond the channel. Before the month of October, James Touchet, Earl of Castlehaven, an adventurous nobleman, possessed of large estates both in Ireland and England, effected his escape from Dublin Castle, where he had been imprisoned on suspicion by Parsons and Borlase, and joined the Confederation at Kilkenny. In September, Colonel Thomas Preston, the brave defender of Louvain, uncle to Lord Gormanstown, landed at Wexford, with three frigates and several transports, containing a few siege guns, field pieces, and other stores, 500 officers, and a number of engineers. IV. In Ulster, where the first blow was struck, and the first hopes were excited, the prospect had become suddenly overclouded. Monroe took Dunluce from Lord Antrim by the same stratagem by which Sir Phelim took Charlemont--inviting himself as a guest, and arresting his host at his own table. A want of cordial co-operation between the Scotch commander and "the Undertakers" alone prevented them extinguishing, in one vigorous campaign, the northern insurrection. So weak and disorganized were now the thousands who had risen at a bound one short year before, that the garrisons of Enniskillen, Deny, Newry, and Drogheda, scoured almost unopposed the neighbouring counties. The troops of Cole, Hamilton, the Stewarts, Chichesters, and Conways, found little opposition, and gave no quarter. Sir William Cole, among his claims of service rendered to the State, enumerated "7,000 of the rebels famished to death," within a circuit of a few miles from Enniskillen. The disheartened and disorganized natives were seriously deliberating a wholesale emigration to the Scottish highlands, when a word of magic effect was whispered from the sea coast to the interior. On the 6th of July, Colonel Owen Roe O'Neil arrived off Donegal with a single ship, a single company of veterans, 100 officers, and a considerable quantity of ammunition. He landed at Doe Castle, and was escorted by his kinsman, Sir Phelim, to the fort of Charlemont. A general meeting of the northern clans was quickly called at Clones, in Monaghan, and there, on an early day after his arrival, Owen O'Neil was elected "General-in-Chief of the Catholic Army" of the North, Sir Phelim resigning in his favour, and taking instead the barren title of "President of Ulster." At the same moment Lord Lieven arrived from Scotland with the remainder of the 10,000 voted by the Parliament of that kingdom. He had known O'Neil abroad, had a high opinion of his abilities, and wrote to express his surprise "that a man of his reputation should be engaged in so bad a cause;" to which O'Neil replied that "he had a better right to come to the relief of his own country than his lordship had to march into England against his lawful King." Lieven, before returning home, urged Monroe to act with promptitude, for that he might expect a severe lesson if the new commander once succeeded in collecting an army. But Monroe proved deaf to this advice, and while the Scottish and English forces in the Province would have amounted, if united, to 20,000 foot and 1,000 horse, they gave O'Neil time enough to embody, officer, drill, and arm (at least provisionally), a force not to be despised by even twice their numbers.

CHAPTER VI.

THE CONFEDERATE WAR--CAMPAIGN OF 1643--THE CESSATION.

The city of Kilkenny, which had become the capital of the Confederacy, was favourably placed for the direction of the war in Leinster and Munster. Nearly equidistant from Dublin, Cork, and Limerick, a meeting place for most of the southern and south-western roads, important in itself both as a place of trade, and as the residence of the Duke of Ormond and the Bishop of Ossory, a better choice could not, perhaps, have been made, so far as regarded the ancient southern "Half-Kingdom." But it seems rather surprising that the difficulty of directing the war in the North and North-West, from a point so far south, did not occur to the statesmen of the Confederacy. In the defective communications of those days, especially during a war, partaking even partially of the character of civil strife, it was hard, if not impossible to expect, that a supervision could be exercised over a general or an army on the Erne or the Bann, which might be quite possible and proper on the Suir or the Shannon. A similar necessity in England necessitated the creation of the Presidency of the North, with its council and head-quarters in the city of York; nor need we be surprised to find that, from the first, the Confederate movements combined themselves into two groups--the northern and the southern-- those which revolved round the centre of Kilkenny, and those which took their law from the head-quarters of Owen O'Neil, at Belturbet, or wherever else his camp happened to be situated.

The General Assembly met, according to agreement, on the 23rd of October, 1642, at Kilkenny. Eleven-bishops and fourteen lay lords represented the Irish peerage; two hundred and twenty-six commoners, the large majority of the constituencies. Both bodies sat in the same chamber, divided only by a raised dais. The celebrated lawyer, Patrick Darcy, a member of the Commons' House, was chosen as chancellor, and everything was conducted with the gravity and deliberation befitting so venerable an Assembly, and so great an occasion. The business most pressing, and most delicate, was felt to be the consideration of a form of supreme executive government. The committee on this subject, who reported after the interval of a week, was composed of Lords Gormanstown and Castlehaven, Sir Phelim O'Neil, Sir Richard Belling, and Mr. Darcy. A "Supreme Council" of six members for each province was recommended, approved, and elected. The Archbishops of Armagh, Dublin, and Tuam, the Bishops of Down and of Clonfert, the Lords Gormanstown, Mountgarrett, Roche, and Mayo, with fifteen of the most eminent commoners, composed this council. It was provided that the vote of two-thirds should be necessary to any act affecting the basis of the Confederacy, but a quorum of nine was sufficient for the transaction of ordinary business. A guard of honour of 500 foot and 200 horse was allowed for their greater security. The venerable Mountgarrett, the head of the Catholic Butlers, (son-in-law of the illustrious Tyrone, who, in the last years of Elizabeth, had devoted his youthful sword to the same good cause,) was elected president of this, council; and Sir Richard Belling, a lawyer, and a man of letters, the continuator of Sir Philip Sydney's *Arcadia*, was appointed secretary.

The first act of this Supreme Council was to appoint General O'Neil as Commander-in-Chief in Ulster; General Preston, in Leinster; General Barry, in Munster; and Sir John Burke as Lieutenant-General in Connaught; the supreme command in the West being held over for Clanrickarde, who, it was still hoped, might be led or driven into the Confederacy. We shall endeavour to indicate in turn the operations of these commanders, thus chosen or confirmed; leaving the civil and diplomatic business transacted by the General Assembly, or delegated to the Supreme Council, for future mention.

Contrary to the custom of that age, the Confederate troops were not withdrawn into winter quarters. In November, General Preston, at the head of 6,000 foot and 600 horse, encountered Monk at Tymahoe and Ballinakil, with some loss; but before the close of December he had reduced Birr, Banagher, Burris, and Fort Falkland, and found himself master of King's county, from the Shannon to the Barrow. In February, however, he sustained a serious check at Rathconnell, in endeavouring to intercept the retreat of the English troops from Connaught, under the command of Lord Ranelagh, and the younger Coote; and in March, equal ill success attended his attempt to intercept Ormond, in his retreat from the unsuccessful siege of the town of Ross. Lord Castlehaven, who was Preston's second in command, attributes both these reverses to the impetuosity of the general, whose imprudence seems to have been almost as great as his activity was conspicuous. In April and May, Preston and Castlehaven took several strongholds in Carlow, Kildare, and West-Meath, and the General Assembly, which met for its second session, on the 20th of May, 1643, at Kilkenny, had, on the whole, good grounds to be satisfied with the success of the war in Leinster.

In the Southern Province, considerable military successes might also be claimed by the Confederates. The Munster troops, under Purcell, the second in command, a capable soldier, who had learned the art of war in the armies of the German Empire, relieved Ross, when besieged by Ormond; General Barry had successfully repulsed an attack on his head-quarters, the famous old Desmond town of Killmallock. In June, Barry, Purcell, and Castlehaven drove the enemy before them across the Funcheon, and at Kilworth brought their main body, under Sir Charles Vavasour, to action. Vavasour's force was badly beaten, himself captured, with his cannon and colours, and many of his officers and men. Inchiquin, who had endeavoured to form a junction with Vavasour, escaped to one of the few remaining garrisons open to him--probably Youghal.

In Connaught, the surrender of Galway, on the 20th of June, eclipsed all the previous successes, and they were not a few, of Lieutenant-General Burke. From the day Lord Ranelagh and the younger Coote deserted the Western province, the Confederate cause had rapidly advanced. The surrender of "the second fort in the Kingdom"--a sea-port in that age, not unworthy to be ranked with Cadiz and Bristol, for its commercial wealth and reputation--was a military event of the first importance. An English fleet appeared three days after the surrender of Willoughby, in Galway harbour; but nine long years elapsed before the Confederate colours were lowered from the towers of the Connaught citadel.

In the North, O'Neil, who, without injustice to any of his contemporaries, may certainly be said to have made, during his seven years' command, the highest European reputation among the Confederate generals, gathered his recruits into a rugged district, which forms a sort of natural camp in the north-west corner of the island. The mountain plateau of Leitrim, which sends its spurs downwards to the Atlantic, towards Lough Erne, and into Longford, accessible only by four or five lines of road, leading over narrow bridges and through deep defiles, was the nursery selected by this cautious leader, in which to collect and organize his forces. In the beginning of May--seven months after the date of his commission, and ten from his solitary landing at Doe Castle--we find him a long march from his mountain fortress in Leitrim, at Charlemont, which he had strengthened and garrisoned, and now saved from a surprise attempted by Monroe, from Carrickfergus. Having effected that immediate object, he again retired towards the Leitrim highlands, fighting by the way a smart cavalry action at Clonish, with a superior force, under Colonels Stewart, Balfour, and Mervyn. In this affair O'Neil was only too happy to have carried off his troop with credit; but a fortnight brought him consolation for Clonish in the brilliant affair of Portlester. He had descended in force from his hills and taken possession of the greater part of the ancient Meath. General Monk and Lord Moore were despatched against him, but reinforced by a considerable body of Meathian Confederates, under Sir James Dillon, he resolved to risk his first regular engagement in the field. Taking advantage of the situation of the ground, about five miles from Trim, he threw up some field works, placed sixty men in Portlester mill, and patiently awaited the advance of the enemy. Their assault was overconfident, their rout complete. Lord Moore, and a large portion of the assailants were slain, and Monk fled back to Dublin. O'Neil, gathering fresh strength from these movements, abandoned his mountain stronghold, and established his head-quarters on the river Erne between Lough Oughter (memorable in his life and death) and the upper waters of Lough Erne. At this point stood the town of Belturbet, which, in "the Plantation" of James I., had been turned over exclusively to British settlers, whose "cagework" houses, and four acres of garden ground each, had elicited the approval of the surveyor Pynnar, twenty years before. The surrounding country was covered with the fortified castles and loop-holed lawns of the chief **_Undertakers_**--but few were found of sufficient strength to resist the arms of O'Neil. At Belturbet, he was within a few days' march of the vital points of four other counties, and in case of the worst, within the same distance of his protective fastness. Here, towards the end of September, busied with present duties and future projects, he heard, for the first time, with astonishment and grief, that the requisite majority of "the Supreme Council" had concluded, on the 13th of that month, a twelve-months' truce with Ormond, thus putting in peril all the advantages already acquired by the bravery of the Confederate troops, and the skill of their generals.

The war had lasted nearly two years, and this was the first time the Catholics had consented to negotiate. The moment chosen was a critical one for all the three Kingdoms, and the interests involved were complicated in the extreme. The Anglo-Irish, who formed the majority of the Supreme Council, connected by blood and language with England, had entered into the war, purely as one of religious liberty. Nationally, they had, apart from the civil disabilities imposed on religious grounds, no antipathy, no interest, hostile to the general body of English loyalists, represented in Ireland by the King's lieutenant, Ormond. On his side, that nobleman gave all his thoughts to, and governed all his actions by the exigencies of the royal cause, throughout the three Kingdoms. When Charles seemed strong in England, Ormond rated the Catholics at a low figure; but when reverses increased he estimated their alliance more highly. After the drawn battle of Edgehill, fought on the very day of the first meeting of the General Assembly at Kilkenny, the King had established his head-quarters at Oxford, in the heart of four or five of the most loyal counties in England. Here he at first negotiated with the Parliament, but finally the sword was again invoked, and while the King proclaimed the Parliament rebels, "the solemn league and covenant" was entered into, at first separately, and afterwards jointly, by the Puritans of England and Presbyterians of Scotland. The military events during that year, and in the first half of the next, were upon the whole not unfavourable to the royal cause. The great battle of Marston Moor, (July 2nd, 1644,) which "extinguished the hopes of the Royalists in the Northern counties," was the first Parliamentary victory of national importance. It was won mainly by the energy and obstinacy of Lieutenant-General Cromwell, from that day forth the foremost English figure in the Civil War. From his court at Oxford, where he had seen the utter failure of endeavouring to conciliate his English and Scottish enemies, the King had instructed Ormond--lately created a Marquis--to treat with the Irish Catholics, and to obtain from them men and money. The overtures thus made were brought to maturity in September; the Cessation was to last twelve months; each party was to remain in possession of its own quarters, as they were held at the date of the treaty; the forces of each were to unite to punish any infraction of the terms agreed on; the agents of the Confederates, during the cessation, were to have free access and safe conduct to the King; and for these advantages, the Supreme Council were to present his Majesty immediately with 15,000 pounds in money, and provisions to the value of 15,000 pounds more.

Such was "the truce of Castlemartin," condemned by O'Neil, by the Papal Nuncio, Scarampi, and by the great majority of the old Irish, lay and clerical; still more violently denounced by the Puritan Parliament as favouring Popery, and negotiated by Popish agents; beneficial to Ormond and the Undertakers, as relieving Dublin, freeing the channel from Irish privateers, and securing them in the garrisons throughout the Kingdom which they still held; in one sense advantageous to Charles, from the immediate supplies it afforded, and the favourable impression it created of his liberality, at the courts of his Catholic allies; but on the other hand disadvantageous to him in England and Scotland, from the pretexts it furnished his enemies, of renewing the cry of his connivance with Popery, a cry neither easily answered, nor, of itself, liable quickly to wear out.

CHAPTER VII.

THE CESSATION AND ITS CONSEQUENCES.

While the Confederate delegates, reverently uncovered, and Ormond, in hat and plume, as representing royalty, were signing "the cessation" at Castlemartin, the memorable Monroe, with all his men, were taking the covenant, on their knees, in the church of Carrickfergus, at the hands of the informer O'Connolly, now a colonel in the Parliamentary army, and high in the confidence of its chiefs. Soon after this ceremony, Monroe, appointed by the English Parliament Commander-in-Chief of all their forces in Ulster, united under his immediate leadership, of Scots, English, and Undertakers, not less than 10,000 men. With this force he marched southward as far as Newry, which he found an easy prey, and where he put to the sword, after surrender, sixty men, eighteen women, and two ecclesiastics. In vain the Confederates entreated Ormond to lead them against the common enemy in the North; pursuing always a line of policy of his own, in which their interest had a very slender part, that astute politician neither took the field, nor consented that they should do so of themselves. But the Supreme Council, roused by the remonstrances of the clergy, ordered Lord Castlehaven, with the title of Commander-in-Chief, to march against Monroe. This was virtually superseding O'Neil in his own province, and that it was so felt, even by its authors, is plain from their giving him simultaneously the command in Connaught. O'Neil, never greater than in acts of self-denial and self-sacrifice, stifled his profound chagrin, and cheerfully offered to serve under the English Earl, placed over his head. But the northern movements were, for many months, languid and uneventful; both parties seemed uncertain of their true policy; both, from day to day, awaited breathlessly for tidings from Kilkenny, Dublin, London, Oxford, or

Edinburgh, to learn what new forms the general contest was to take, in order to guide their own conduct by the shifting phases of that intricate diplomacy.

Among the first consequences of the cessation were the debarkation at Mostyn, in Scotland, of 3,000 well provided Irish troops, under ***Colkitto*** (the left-handed,) Alexander McDonnell, brother of Lord Antrim. Following the banner of Montrose, these regiments performed great things at Saint Johnstown, at Aberdeen, at Inverlochy, all which have been eloquently recorded by the historians of that period. "Their reputation," says a cautious writer, "more than their number, unnerved the prowess of their enemies. No force ventured to oppose them in the field; and as they advanced, every fort was abandoned or surrendered." A less agreeable result of "the cessation," for the court at Oxford, was the retirement from the royal army of the Earl of Newcastle, and most of his officers, on learning that such favourable conditions had been made with Irish Papists. To others of his supporters--as the Earl of Shrewsbury--Charles was forced to assume a tone of apology for that truce, pleading the hard necessities which compelled him: the truth seems to be, that there were not a few then at Oxford, who, like Lord Spencer, would gladly have been on the other side--or at all events in a position of neutrality--provided they could have found "a salve for their honour," as gentlemen and cavaliers.

The year 1644 opened for the Irish with two events of great significance--the appointment of Ormond as Viceroy, in January, and the execution at Tyburn, by order of the English Parliament, of Lord Maguire, a prisoner in the Tower since October, 1641. Maguire died with a courage and composure worthy of his illustrious name, and his profoundly religious character. His long absence had not effaced his memory from the hearts of his devoted clansmen of Fermanagh, and many a prayer was breathed, and many a vow of vengeance muttered among them, for what they must naturally have regarded as the cold-blooded judicial murder of their chief.

Two Irish deputations--one Catholic, the other Protestant --proceeded this year to the King, at Oxford, with the approval of Ormond, who took care to be represented by confidential agents of his own. The Catholics found a zealous auxiliary in the queen, Henrietta Maria, who, as a co-religionist, felt with them, and, as a Frenchwoman, was free from insular prejudices against them. The Irish Protestants found a scarcely less influential advocate in the venerable Archbishop Usher, whose presence and countenance, as the most puritanical of his prelates, was most essential to the policy of Charles. The King heard both parties graciously--censured some of the demands of both as extravagant, and beyond his power to concede--admitted others to be reasonable and worthy of consideration--refused to confirm the churches they had seized to the Catholics--but was willing to allow them their "seminaries of education"--would not consent to enforce the penal laws on the demand of the Protestants --but declared that neither should the Undertakers be disturbed in their possessions or offices. In short, he pathetically exhorted both parties to consider his case as well as their own; promised them to call together the Irish Parliament at the earliest possible period; and so got rid of both deputations, leaving Ormond master of the position for some time longer.

The agents and friends of the Irish Catholics on the Continent were greatly embarrassed, and not a little disheartened by the cessation. At Paris, at Brussels, at Madrid, but above all at Rome, it was regretted, blamed, or denounced, according to the temper or the insight of the discontented. His Catholic Majesty had some time before remitted a contribution of 20,000 dollars to the Confederate Treasury; one of Richelieu's last acts was to invite Con, son of Hugh O'Neil, to the French Court, and to permit the shipment of some pieces of ordnance to Ireland; from Rome, the celebrated Franciscan, Father Luke Wadding, had remitted 26,000 dollars, and the Nuncio Scarampi had brought further donations. The facility, therefore, with which the cessation had been agreed upon, against the views of the agents of the Catholic powers at Kilkenny, without any apparently sufficient cause, had certainly a tendency to check and chill the enthusiasm of those Catholic Princes who had been taught to look on the insurrection of the Irish as a species of Crusade. Remonstrances, warm, eloquent, and passionate, were poured in upon the most influential members of the Supreme Council, from those who had either by delegation, or from their own free will, befriended them abroad. These remonstrances reached that powerful body at Waterford, at Limerick, or at Galway, whither they had gone on an official visitation, to hear complaints, settle controversies, and provide for the better collection of the assessments imposed on each Province.

An incident which occurred in Ulster, soon startled the Supreme Council from their pacific occupations. General Monroe, having proclaimed that all Protestants within his command should take "the solemn league and covenant," three thousand of that religion, still loyalists, met at Belfast, to deliberate on their answer. Monroe, however, apprised of their intentions, marched rapidly from Carrickfergus, entered the town under cover of night, and drove out the loyal Protestants at the point of the sword. The fugitives threw themselves into Lisburn, and Monroe appointed Colonel Hume as Governor of Belfast, for the Parliaments of Scotland and England. Castlehaven, with O'Neil still second in command, was now despatched northward against the army of the Covenant. Monroe, who had advanced to the borders of Meath as if to meet them, contented himself with gathering in great herds of cattle; as they advanced, he slowly fell back before them through Louth and Armagh, to his original head-quarters; Castlehaven then returned with the main body of the Confederate troops to Kilkenny, and O'Neil, depressed, but not dismayed, carried his contingent to their former position at Belturbet.

In Munster, a new Parliamentary party had time to form its combinations under the shelter of the cessation. The Earl of Inchiquin, who had lately failed to obtain the Presidency of Munster from the King at Oxford, and the Lord Broghill, son of the great Southern Undertaker--the first Earl of Cork,--were at the head of this movement. Under pretence that the quarters allotted them by the cessation had been violated, they contrived to seize upon Cork, Youghal, and Kinsale. At Cork, they publicly executed Father Mathews, a Friar, and proceeding from violence to violence, they drove from the three places all the Catholic inhabitants. They then forwarded a petition to the King, beseeching him to declare the Catholics "rebels," and declaring their own determination to "die a thousand deaths sooner than condescend to any peace with them." At the same time they entered into or avowed their correspondence with the English Parliament, which naturally enough encouraged and assisted them. The Supreme Council met these demonstrations with more stringent instructions to General Purcell, now their chief in command, (Barry having retired on account of advanced age,) to observe the cessation, and to punish severely every infraction of it. At the same time they permitted or directed Purcell to enter into a trace with Inchiquin till the following April; and then they rested on their arms, in religious fidelity to the engagements they had signed at Castlemartin.

The twelve-months' truce was fast drawing to a close, when the battle of Marston Moor stimulated Ormond to effect a renewal of the treaty. Accordingly, at his request, Lord Muskerry, and five other commissioners, left Kilkenny on the last day of August for Dublin. Between them and the Viceroy, the cessation was prolonged till the first of December following; and when that day came, it was further protracted, as would appear, for three months, by which time, (March, 1645,) Ormond informed them that he had powers from the King to treat for a permanent settlement.

During the six months that the original cessation was thus protracted by the policy of Ormond, the Supreme Council sent abroad new agents, "to know what they had to trust to, and what succours they might really depend on from abroad." Father Hugh Bourke was sent to Spain, and Sir Richard Belling to Rome, where Innocent X, had recently succeeded to that generous friend of the Catholic Irish. Urban VIII. The voyage of these agents was not free from hazard, for, whereas, before the cessation, the privateers commissioned by the Council, sheltered and supplied in the Irish harbours, had kept the southern coast clear of hostile shipping, now that they had been withdrawn under the truce, the parliamentary cruisers had the channel all to themselves. Waterford and Wexford--the two chief Catholic ports in that quarter-- instead of seeing their waters crowded with prizes, now began to tremble for their own safety. The strong fort of Duncannon, on the Wexford side of Waterford harbour, was corruptly surrendered by Lord Esmond, to Inchiquin and the Puritans. After a ten-weeks' siege, however, and the expenditure of 19,000 pounds of powder, the Confederates retook the fort, in spite of all the efforts made for its relief. Esmond, old and blind, escaped by a timely death the penalty due to his treason. Following up this success, Castlehaven rapidly invested other southern strongholds in possession of the same party, Cappoquin, Lismore, Mallow, Mitchelstown, Doneraile and Liscarroll surrendered on articles; Rostellan, commanded by Inchiquin's brother, was stormed and taken; Boghill was closely besieged in Youghal, but, being relieved from sea, successfully defended himself. In another quarter, the Parliament was equally active. To compensate for the loss of Galway, they had instructed the younger Coote, on whom they had conferred the Presidency of Connaught, to withdraw the regiment of Sir Frederick Hamilton, and 400 other troops, from the command of Monroe, and with these, Sir Robert Stewart's forces, and such others as he could himself raise, to invest Sligo. Against the force thus collected, Sligo could not hope to contend, and soon, from that town, as from a rallying and resting place, 2,000 horsemen were daily launched upon the adjoining country.

Lord Clanrickarde, the royal president of the province, as unpopular as trimmers usually are in times of crisis, was unable to make head against this new danger. But the Confederates, under Sir James Dillon, and Dr. O'Kelly, the heroic Archbishop of Tuam, moved by the pitiful appeals of the Sligo people, boldly endeavoured to recover the town. They succeeded in entering the walls, but were subsequently repulsed and routed. The Archbishop was captured and tortured to death; some of the noblest families of the province and of Meath had also to mourn their chiefs; and several valuable papers, found or pretended to be found in the Archbishop's carriage, were eagerly given to the press of London by the Parliament of England. This tragedy at Sligo occurred on Sunday, October 26th, 1645.

CHAPTER VIII.

GLAMORGAN'S TREATY--THE NEW NUNCIO RINUCCINI-- O'NEIL'S POSITION--THE BATTLE OF BENBURB.

Ormond had amused the Confederates with negotiations for a permanent peace and settlement, from spring till midsummer, when Charles, dissatisfied with these endless delays, despatched to Ireland a more hopeful ambassador. This was Herbert, Earl of Glamorgan, one of the few Catholics remaining among the English nobility; son and heir to the Marquis of Worcester, and son-in-law to Henry O'Brien, Earl of Thomond. Of a family devoutly attached to the royal cause, to which it is said they had contributed not less than 200,000 pounds, Glamorgan's religion, his rank, his Irish connections, the intimate confidence of the King which he was known to possess, all marked out his embassy as one of the utmost importance.

The story of this mission has been perplexed and darkened by many controversies. But the general verdict of historians seems now to be, that Charles I., whose many good qualities as a man and a ruler are cheerfully admitted on all hands, was yet utterly deficient in downright good faith; that duplicity was his besetting sin; and that Glamorgan's embassy is one, but only one, of the strongest evidences of that ingrained duplicity.

It may help to the clearer understanding of the negotiations conducted by Glamorgan in Ireland, if we give in the first place the exact dates of the first transactions. The Earl arrived at Dublin about the 1st of August, and, after an interview with Ormond, proceeded to Kilkenny. On the 28th of that month, preliminary articles were agreed to and signed by the Earl on behalf of the King, and by Lords Mountgarrett and Muskerry on behalf of the Confederates. It was necessary, it seems, to get the concurrence of the Viceroy to these terms, and accordingly the negotiators on both sides repaired to Dublin. Here, Ormond contrived to detain them ten long weeks in discussions on the articles relating to religion; it was the 12th of November when they returned to Kilkenny, with a much modified treaty. On the next day, the 13th, the new Papal Nuncio, a prelate who, by his rank, his eloquence, and his imprudence, was destined to exercise a powerful influence on the Catholic councils, made his public entry into that city.

This personage was John Baptist Rinuccini, Archbishop of Fermo, in the Marches of Ancona, which see he had preferred to the more exalted dignity of Florence. By birth a Tuscan, the new Nuncio had distinguished himself from boyhood by his passionate attachment to his studies. At Bologna, at Perugia, and at Rome, his intense application brought him early honours, and early physical debility. His health, partially restored in the seclusion of his native valley of the Arno, enabled him to return again to Rome. Enjoying the confidence of Gregory XV. and Uban VIII., he was named successively, Clerk of the Chamber, Secretary of the Congregation of Rites, and Archbishop of Fermo. This was the prelate chosen by the new Pope, Innocent X., for the nunciature in Ireland: a man of noble birth, in the fifty-third year of his age, of uncertain bodily health, of great learning, especially as a canonist, of a fiery Italian temperament,--"regular and even austere in his life, and far from any taint of avarice or corruption,"--such was the admission of his enemies.

Leaving Italy in May, accompanied by the Dean of Fermo, who has left us a valuable record of the embassy, his other household officers, several Italian noblemen, and Sir Richard Belling, the special agent at Rome, the Nuncio, by way of Genoa and Marseilles, reached Paris. In France he was detained nearly five months, in a fruitless attempt to come to some definite arrangement as to the conduct of the Catholic war, through Queen Henrietta Maria, then resident with the young Prince of Wales--afterwards Charles II.--at the French court. The Queen, like most persons of her rank, overwhelmed with adversity, was often unreasonably suspicious and exacting. Her sharp woman's tongue did not spare those on whom her anger fell, and there were not wanting those, who, apprehensive of the effect in England of her negotiating directly with a papal minister, did their utmost to delay or to break off their correspondence. A nice point of court etiquette further embarrassed the business. The Nuncio could not uncover his head before the Queen, and Henrietta would not receive him otherwise than uncovered. After three months lost in Paris, he was obliged to proceed on his journey, contenting himself with an exchange of complimentary messages with the Queen, whom even the crushing blow of Naseby could not induce to waive a point of etiquette with a Priest.

On reaching Rochelle, where he intended to take shipping, a further delay of six weeks took place, as was supposed by the machinations of Cardinal Mazarin. Finally, the Nuncio succeeded in purchasing a frigate of 26 guns, the *San Pietro*, on which he embarked with all his Italian suite, Sir Richard Belling, and several Franco-Irish officers. He had also on board a considerable sum in Spanish gold, (including another contribution of 36,000 dollars from Father Wadding,) 2,000 muskets, 2,000 cartouch belts, 4,000 swords, 2,000 pike heads, 400 brace of pistols, 20,000 pounds of powder, with match, shot, and other stores. Weighing from St. Martin's in the Isle of Rhe, the *San Pietro* doubled the Land's End, and stood over towards the Irish coast. The third day out they were chased for several hours by two Parliamentary cruisers, but escaped under cover of the night; on the fourth morning, being the 21st of October, they found themselves safely embayed in the waters of Kenmare, on the coast of Kerry.

The first intelligence which reached the Nuncio on landing, was the negotiation of Glamorgan, of which he had already heard, while waiting a ship at Rochelle. The next was the surrender by the Earl of Thomond, of his noble old castle of Bunratty, commanding the Shannon within six miles of Limerick, to the Puritans. This surrender had, however, determined the resolution of the city of Limerick, which hitherto had taken no part in the war, to open its gates to the Confederates. The loss of Bunratty was more than compensated by the gaining of one of the finest and strongest towns in Munster, and to Limerick accordingly the Nuncio paid the compliment of his first visit. Here he received the mitre of the diocese in dutiful submission from the hands of the Bishop, on entering the Cathedral; and here he celebrated a solemn requiem mass for the repose of the soul of the Archbishop of Tuam, lately slain before Sligo. Prom Limerick, borne along on his litter, such was the feebleness of his health, he advanced by slow stages to Kilkenny, escorted by a guard of honour, despatched on that duty, by the Supreme Council.

The pomp and splendour of his public entry into the Catholic capital was a striking spectacle. The previous night he slept at a village three miles from the city, for which he set out early on the morning of the 13th of November, escorted by his guard, and a vast multitude of the people. Five delegates from the Supreme Council accompanied him. A band of fifty students mounted on horseback met him on the way, and their leader, crowned with laurel, recited some congratulatory Latin verses. At the city gate he left the litter and mounted a horse richly housed; here the procession of the clergy and the city guilds awaited him; at the Market Cross, a Latin oration was delivered in his honour, to which he graciously replied in the same language. From the Cross he was escorted to the Cathedral, at the door of which he was received by the aged Bishop, Dr. David Rothe. At the high altar he intonated the *Te Deum*, and gave the multitude the apostolic benediction. Then he was conducted to his lodgings, where he was soon waited upon by Lord Muskerry and General Preston, who brought him to Kilkenny Castle, where, in the great gallery, which elicited even a Florentine's admiration, he was received in stately formality by the President of the Council--Lord Mountgarrett. Another Latin oration on the nature of his embassy was delivered by the Nuncio, responded to by Heber, Bishop of Clogher, and so the ceremony of reception ended.

The Nuncio brought from Paris a new subject of difficulty, in the form of a memorial from the English Catholics at Rome, praying that they might be included in the terms of any peace which might be made by their Irish co-religionists with the King. Nothing could be more natural than that the members of the same persecuted church should make common cause, but nothing could be more impolitic than some of the demands made in the English memorial. They wished it to be stipulated with Charles, that he would allow a distinct military organization to the English and Irish Catholics in his service, under Catholic general officers, subject only to the King's commands, meaning thereby, if they meant what they said, independence of all parliamentary and ministerial control. Yet several of the stipulations of this memorial were, after many modifications and discussions, adopted by Glamorgan into his original articles, and under the treaty thus ratified, the Confederates bound themselves to despatch 10,000 men, fully armed and equipped, to the relief of Chester and the general succour of the King in England. Towards the close of December, the English Earl, with two Commissioners from the Supreme Council, set forth for Dublin, to obtain the Viceroy's sanction to the amended treaty. But in Dublin a singular counterplot in this perplexed drama awaited them. On St.

Stephen's day, while at dinner, Glamorgan was arrested by Ormond, on a charge of having exceeded his instructions, and confined a close prisoner in the castle. The gates of the city were closed, and every means taken to give *eclat* to this extraordinary proceeding. The Confederate Commissioners were carried to the castle, and told they might congratulate themselves on not sharing the cell prepared for Glamorgan. "Go back," they were told, "to Kilkenny and tell the President of the Council, that the Protestants of England would fling the King's person out at his window, *if they believed it possible* that he lent himself to such an undertaking." The Commissioners accordingly went back and delivered their errand, with a full account of all the circumstances. Fortunately, the General Assembly had been called for an early day in January, 1646, at Kilkenny. When, therefore, they met, their first resolution was to despatch Sir Robert Talbot to the Viceroy, with a letter suspending all negotiations till the Earl of Glamorgan was set at liberty. By the end of January, on the joint bail, for 40,000 pounds, of the Earls of Clanrickarde and Kildare, the English envoy was enlarged, and, to the still further amazement of the simple-minded Catholics, on his arrival at Kilkenny, he justified rather than censured the action of Ormond. To most observers it appeared that these noblemen understood each other only too well.

From January till June, Kilkenny was delivered over to cabals, intrigues, and recriminations. There was an "old Irish party," to which the Nuncio inclined, and an "Anglo-Irish party," headed by Mountgarrett and the majority of the Council. The former stigmatized the latter as Ormondists, and the latter retorted on them with the name of the Nuncio's party. In February came news of a foreign treaty made at Rome between Sir Kenelm Digby and the Pope's Ministers, most favourable to the English and Irish Catholics. On the 28th of March, a final modification of Glamorgan's articles, reduced to thirty in number, was signed by Ormond for the King, and Lord Muskerry and the other Commissioners for the Confederates. These thirty articles conceded, in fact, all the most essential claims of the Irish; they secured them equal rights as to property, in the Army, in the Universities, and at the Bar; they gave them seats in both Houses and on the Bench; they authorized a special commission of Oyer and Terminer, composed wholly of Confederates; they declared that "the independency of the Parliament of Ireland on that of England," should be decided by declaration of both Houses "agreeably to the laws of the

Kingdom of Ireland." In short, this final form of Glamorgan's treaty gave the Irish Catholics, in 1646, all that was subsequently obtained either for the church or the country, in 1782, 1793, or 1829. Though some conditions were omitted, to which Rinuccini and a majority of the Prelates attached importance, Glamorgan's treaty was, upon the whole, a charter upon which a free church and a free people might well have stood, as the fundamental law of their religious and civil liberties.

The treaty, thus concluded at the end of March, was to lie as an *escroll* in the hands of the Marquis of Clanrickarde till the 1st of May, awaiting Sir Kenelm Digby with the Roman protocol. And then, not withstanding the dissuasions of Rinuccini to the contrary, it was to be kept secret from the world, though some of its obligations were expected to be at once fulfilled, on their side, by the Catholics. The Supreme Council, ever eager to exhibit their loyalty, gathered together 6,000 troops for the relief of Chester and the service of the King in England, so soon as both treaties--the Irish and the Roman--should be signed by Charles. While so waiting, they besieged and took Bunratty castle--already referred to--but Sir Kenelm Digby did not arrive with May, and they now learned, to their renewed amazement, that Glamorgan's whole negotiation was disclaimed by the King in England. In the same interval Chester fell, and the King was obliged to throw himself into the hands of the Scottish Parliament, who surrendered him for a price to their English coadjutors. These tidings reached Ireland during May, and, varied with the capture of an occasional fortress, lost or won, occupied all men's minds. But the first days of June were destined to bring with them a victory of national--of European importance--won by Owen O'Neil, in the immediate vicinity of his grand-uncle's famous battle-field of the Yellow Ford.

During these three years of intrigue and negotiation, the position of General O'Neil was hazardous and difficult in the extreme. One campaign he had served under a stranger, as second on his own soil. In the other two he was fettered by the terms of "cessation" to his own quarters; and to add to his embarrassments, his impetuous kinsman Sir Phelim, brave, rash, and ambitious, recently married to a daughter of his ungenerous rival, General Preston, was incited to thwart and obstruct him amongst their mutual clansmen and connections. The only recompense which seems to have been awarded to him, was the confidence of the Nuncio, who, either from that knowledge of character in which the Italians excel, or from bias received from some other source, at once singled him out as the man of his people. What portion of the Nuncio's supplies reached the Northern General we know not, but in the beginning of June, he felt himself in a position to bring on an engagement with Monroe, who, lately reinforced by both Parliaments, had marched out of Carrickfergus into Tyrone, with a view of penetrating as far south as Kilkenny. On the 4th day of June, the two armies encountered at Benburb, on the little river Blackwater, about six miles north of Armagh, and the most signal victory of the war came to recompense the long-enduring patience of O'Neil.

The battle of Benburb has been often and well described. In a naturally strong position--with this leader the choice of ground seems to have been a first consideration --the Irish, for four hours, received and repulsed the various charges of the Puritan horse. Then as the sun began to descend, pouring its rays upon the opposing force, O'Neil led his whole force--five thousand men against eight--to the attack. One terrible onset swept away every trace of resistance. There were counted on the field, 3,243 of the Covenanters, and of the Catholics, but 70 killed and 100 wounded. Lord Ardes, and 21 Scottish officers, 32 standards, 1,500 draught horses, and all the guns and tents, were captured. Monroe fled in panic to Lisburn, and thence to Carrickfergus, where he shut himself up, till he could obtain reinforcements. O'Neil forwarded the captured colours to the Nuncio, at Limerick, by whom they were solemnly placed in the choir of St. Mary's Cathedral, and afterwards, at the request of Pope Innocent, sent to Rome. *Te Deum* was chanted in the Confederate Capital; penitential psalms were sung in the Northern fortress. "The Lord of Hosts," wrote Monroe, "had rubbed shame on our faces, till once we are humbled;" O'Neil emblazoned the cross and keys on his banner with the Red Hand of Ulster, and openly resumed the title originally chosen by his adherents at Clones, "the Catholic Army."

CHAPTER IX.

FROM THE BATTLE OF BENBURB TILL THE LANDING OF CROMWELL AT DUBLIN.

The Nuncio, elated by the great victory of O'Neil, to which he felt he had personally contributed by his seasonable supplies, provoked and irritated by Ormond's intrigues and the King's insincerity, rushed with all the ardour of his character into making the war an uncompromising Catholic crusade. In this line of conduct, he was supported by the Archbishops of Dublin and Cashel, by ten of the Bishops, including the eminent Prelates of Limerick, Killalla, Ferns, and Clogher; the Procurator of Armagh; nine Vicars-general, and the Superiors of the Jesuits, Dominicans, Franciscans, and Augustinians. The peace party, on the other hand, were not without clerical adherents, but they were inconsiderable, as to influence and numbers. They were now become as anxious to publish the Thirty Articles agreed upon at the end of March, as they then were to keep them secret. Accordingly, with Ormond's consent, copies of the treaty were sent early in August to the sheriffs of counties, mayors of cities, and other leading persons, with instructions to proclaim it publicly in due form; upon hearing which, the Nuncio and his supporters of the clergy, secular and regular, assembled in council at Waterford, on the 12th of August, solemnly declared that they gave no consent, and would not, "to any peace," that did not grant "further, surer, and safer considerations for their religion, king, and country," according to the original oath of the Confederacy.

The rupture between the clergy and the laymen of the Council was now complete. The prelates who signed the decree of Waterford, of course, thereby withdrew from the body whose action they condemned. In vain the learned Darcy and the eloquent Plunkett went to and fro between the two bodies: concord and confidence were at an end. The synod decided to address Lord Mountgarrett in future as President of "the *late* Supreme Council." The heralds who attempted to publish the Thirty Articles in Clonmel and Waterford were hooted or stoned; while in Limerick the mayor, endeavouring to protect them, shared this rough usage. Ormond, who was at Kilkenny at the critical moment of the breach, did his utmost to sustain the resolution of those who were stigmatized by his name; while the Nuncio, suspicious of Preston, wrote urgently to O'Neil to lead his army into Leinster, and remove the remnant of the late council from Kilkenny. All that those who held a middle course between the extremes could do, was to advocate an early meeting of the General Assembly; but various exigencies delayed this much-desired meeting, till the 10th day of January, 1647.

The five intervening months were months of triumph for Rinuccini. Lord Digby appeared at Dublin as a special agent from the King, to declare his consent to Glamorgan's original terms; but Ormond still insisted that he had no authority to go beyond the Thirty Articles. Charles himself wrote privately to Rinuccini, promising to confirm everything which Glamorgan had proposed, as soon as he should come into "the Nuncio's hands." Ormond, after a fruitless attempt to convert O'Neil to his views, had marched southward with a guard of 1,500 foot, and 500 horse, to endeavour to conciliate the towns, and to win over the Earl of Inchiquin. In both these objects he failed. He found O'Neil before him in his county palatinate of Tipperary, and the Mayor of Cashel informed him that he dared not allow him into that city, for fear of displeasing the northern general. Finding himself thus unexpectedly within a few miles of "the Catholic Army," 10,000 strong, the Viceroy retreated precipitately through Kilkenny, Carlow, and Kildare, to Dublin. Lord Digby, who had accompanied him, after an unsuccessful attempt to cajole the Synod of Waterford, made the best of his way back to France; the Marquis of Clanrickarde, who had also been of the expedition, shared the flight of Ormond. Towards the middle of September, O'Neil's army, after capturing Roscrea Castle, marched to Kilkenny, and encamped near that city. His forces had now augmented to 12,000 foot, and 1,500 horse; on the 18th of the month, he escorted the Nuncio in triumph into Kilkenny, where the Ormondist members of the old council were committed to close custody in the castle. A new council, of four bishops and eight laymen, was established on the 26th, with the Nuncio as president; Glamorgan succeeded Castlehaven, who had gone over to Ormond, as commander in Munster; while O'Neil and Preston were ordered to unite their forces for the siege of Dublin. The sanguine Italian dreamt of nothing less, for the moment, than the creation of Viceroys, the deliverance of the King, and the complete restoration of the ancient religion.

O'Neil and Preston, by different routes, on which they were delayed in taking several garrisoned posts, united at Lucan in the valley of the Liffey, seven miles west of Dublin, on the 9th of November. Their joint forces are represented at 16,000 foot, and 1,600 horse--of which Preston had about one-third, and O'Neil the remainder. Preston's head-quarters were fixed at Leixlip, and O'Neil's at Newcastle--points equi-distant, and each within two hours' march of the capital. Within the walls of that city there reigned the utmost consternation. Many of the inhabitants fled beyond seas, terrified by the fancied cruelty of the Ulstermen. But Ormond retained all his presence of mind, and readiness of resources. He entered, at first covertly, into arrangements with the Parliamentarians, who sent him a supply of powder; he wrote urgently to Monroe to make a diversion in his favour; he demolished the mills and suburbs which might cover the approaches of the enemy; he employed soldiers, civilians, and even women, upon the fortifications,-- Lady Ormond setting an example to her sex, in rendering her feeble assistance. Clanrickarde, in Preston's tent, was doing the work of stimulating the old antipathy of that general towards O'Neil, which led to conflicting advices in Council, and some irritating personal altercations. To add to the Confederate embarrassment, the winter was the most severe known for many years; from twenty to thirty sentinels being frozen at night at their posts. On the 13th of November, while the plan of the Confederate attack was still undecided, commissioners of the Parliament arrived, with ample stores, in Dublin Bay. On the next day they landed at Ringsend, and entered into negotiations with Ormond; on the 16th the siege was raised, and on the 23rd Ormond broke off the treaty, having unconsciously saved Dublin from the Confederates, by the incorrect reports of supplies being received, which were finally carried northward to Monroe.

The month of January brought the meeting of the General Assembly. The attendance in the great gallery of Ormond Castle was as large, and the circumstances upon the whole as auspicious as could be desired, in the seventh year of such a struggle. The members of the old council, liberated from arrest, were in their places. O'Neil and Preston, publicly reconciled, had signed a solemn engagement to assist and sustain each other. The Nuncio, the Primate of Ireland, and eleven bishops took their seats; the peers of oldest title in the kingdom were present; two hundred and twenty-four members represented the Commons of Ireland, and among the spectators sat the ambassadors of France and Spain, and of King Charles. The main subject of discussion was the sufficiency of the Thirty Articles, and the propriety of the ecclesiastical censure promulgated against those who had signed them. The debate embraced all that may be said on the question of clerical interference in political affairs, on conditional and unconditional allegiance, on the power of the Pontiff speaking *ex cathedra*, and the prerogatives of the temporal sovereign. It was protracted through an entire month, and ended with a compromise, which declared that the Commissioners had acted in good faith in signing the articles, while it justified the Synod of Waterford for having, as judges of the nature and intent of the oath of Confederation, declared them insufficient and unacceptable. A new oath of Confederacy, solemnly binding the associates not to lay down their arms till they had established the free and public exercise of religion as it had existed in the reign of Henry VII., was framed and taken by the entire General Assembly; the Thirty Articles were declared insufficient and unacceptable by all but a minority of twelve votes; a new Supreme Council of twenty-four was chosen, in whom there were not known to be above four or five partisans of Ormond's policy. The church plate throughout the kingdom was ordered to be coined into money, and a formal proposal to co-operate with the Viceroy on the basis of the new oath was made, but instantly rejected; among other grounds, on this, that the Marquis had, at that moment, his son and and other sureties with the Puritans who, in the last resort, he infinitely preferred to the Roman Catholics.

The military events of the year 1647 were much more decisive than its politics. Glamorgan still commanded in Munster, Preston in Leinster, and O'Neil in both Ulster and Connaught. The first was confronted by Inchiquin, at the head of a corps of 5,000 foot and 1,500 horse, equipped and supplied by the English Puritans; the second saw the garrisons of Dundalk, Drogheda, and Dublin, reinforced by fresh regiments of Covenanters, and fed by Parliamentary supplies from the sea; the latter was in the heart of Connaught, organizing and recruiting and attempting all things within his reach, but hampered for money, clothing and ammunition. In Connaught, O'Neil was soon joined by the Nuncio, who, as difficulties thickened, began to lean more and more on the strong arm of the victor of Benburb; in Munster, the army refused to follow the lead of Glamorgan, and clamoured for their old chief, Lord Muskerry; finally, that division of the national troops was committed by the Council to Lord Taafe, a politician of the school of Ormond and Clanrickarde, wholly destitute of military experience. The vigorous Inchiquin had little difficulty in dealing with such an antagonist; Cashel was taken without a blow in its defence, and a slaughter unparalleled till the days of Drogheda and Wexford, deluged its streets and churches. At Knocknos, later in the autumn (Nov. 12th), Taafe was utterly routed; the gallant *Colkitto*, serving under him, lamentably sacrificed after surrendering his sword; and Inchiquin enabled to dictate a cessation covering Munster--far less favourable to Catholics than the truce of Castlemartin --to the Supreme Council. This truce was signed at Dungarvan, on the 20th of May, 1648, and on the 27th the Nuncio published his solemn decree of excommunication against all its aiders and abettors, and himself made the best of his way from Kilkenny to Maryboro', where O'Neil then lay.

The military and political situation of O'Neil, during the latter months of 1647 and the whole of 1648, was one of the most extraordinary in which any general had ever been placed. His late sworn colleague, Preston, was now combined with Inchiquin against him; the royalist Clanrickarde, in the western counties, pressed upon his rear, and captured his garrison in Athlone; the Parliamentary general, Michael Jones, to whom Ormond had finally surrendered Dublin, observed rather than impeded his movements in Leinster; the lay majority of the Supreme Council proclaimed him a traitor--a compliment which he fully returned; the Nuncio threw himself wholly into his hands; finally, at the close of '48, Ormond, returning from France to Ireland, concluded, on the 17th of January, a formal alliance with the lay members, under the title of "Commissioners of Trust," for the King and Kingdom; and Rinuccini, despairing, perhaps, of a cause so distracted, sailed in his own frigate, from Galway, on the 23rd of February. Thus did the actors change their parts, alternately triumphing and fleeing for safety. The verdict of history may condemn the Nuncio, of whom we have now seen the last, for his imperious self-will, and his too ready recourse to ecclesiastical censures; but of his zeal, his probity, and his disinterestedness, there can be, we think, no second opinion.

Under the treaty of 1649--which conceded full civil and religious equality to the Roman Catholics--Ormond was once more placed at the head of the government and in command of the royal troops. A few days after the signing of that treaty, news of the execution of Charles I. having reached Ireland, the Viceroy proclaimed the Prince of Wales by the title of Charles II., at Cork and Youghal. Prince Rupert, whose fleet had entered Kinsale, caused the same ceremony to be gone through in that ancient borough. With Ormond were now cordially united Preston, Inchiquin, Clanrickarde, and Muskerry, on whom the lead of the Supreme Council devolved, in consequence of the advanced age of Lord Mountgarrett, and the remainder of the twelve Commissioners of Trust. The cause of the young Prince, an exile, the son of that Catholic queen from whom they had expected so much, was far from unpopular in the southern half of the island. The Anglican interest was strong and widely diffused through both Leinster and Munster; and, except a resolute prelate, like Dr. French, Bishop of Ferns, or a brave band of townsmen like those of Waterford, Limerick, and Galway, or some remnant of mountain tribes, in Wicklow and Tipperary, the national, or "old Irish policy," had decidedly lost ground from the hour of the Nuncio's departure.

Owen O'Neil and the Bishops still adhered to that national policy. The former made a three-months' truce with General Monck, who had succeeded Monroe in the command of all the Parliamentary troops in his province. The singular spectacle was even exhibited of Monck forwarding supplies to O'Neil, to be used against Inchiquin and Ormond, and O'Neil coining to the rescue of Coote, and raising for him the siege of Londonderry. Inchiquin, in rapid succession, took Drogheda, Trim, Dundalk, Newry, and then rapidly countermarched to join Ormond in besieging Dublin. At Rathmines, near the city, both generals were surprised and defeated by the Parliamentarians under Michael Jones. Between desertions, and killed and wounded, they lost, by their own account, nearly 3,000, and by the Puritan accounts, above 5,000 men. This action was the virtual close of Ormond's military career; he never after made head against the Parliamentary forces in open field. The Catholic cities of Limerick and Galway refused to admit his garrisons; a synod of the Bishops, assembled at Jamestown (in Roscommon), strongly recommended his withdrawal from the kingdom; and Cromwell had arrived, resolved to finish the war in a single campaign. Ormond sailed again for France, before the end of 1649, to return no more until the restoration of the monarchy, on the death of the great Protector.

CHAPTER X.

CROMWELL'S CAMPAIGN---1649-1650.

An actor was now to descend upon the scene, whose character has excited more controversy than that of any other personage of those times. Honoured as a saint, or reprobated as a hypocrite, worshipped for his extraordinary successes, or anathematized for the unworthy artifices by which he rose--who shall deal out, with equal hand, praise and blame to Oliver Cromwell'? Not for the popular writer of Irish history, is that difficult judicial task. Not for us to re-echo cries of hatred which convince not the indifferent, nor correct the errors of the educated or cultivated: the simple, and, as far as possible, the unimpassioned narrative of facts, will constitute the whole of our duty towards the Protector's campaign in Ireland.

Cromwell left London in great state, early in July, "in a coach drawn by six gallant Flanders mares," and made a sort of royal procession across the country to Bristol. From that famous port, where Strongbow confederated with Dermid McMurrogh, and from which Dublin drew its first Anglo-Norman colony, he went on to Milford Haven, at which he embarked, arriving in Dublin on the 15th of August. He entered the city in procession, and addressed the townsfolk from "a convenient place." He had with him two hundred thousand pounds in money, eight regiments of foot, six of horse, and some troops of dragoons; besides the divisions of Jones and Monck, already in the country, and subject to his command. Among the officers were names of memorable interest--Henry Cromwell, second son of the Protector, and future Lord Deputy; Monck, Blake, Jones, Ireton, Ludlow, Hardress Waller, Sankey, and others equally prominent in accomplishing the King's death, or in raising up the English commonwealth.

Cromwell's command in Ireland extends from the middle of August, 1649, to the end of May, 1650, about nine months in all, and is remarkable for the number of sieges of walled towns crowded into that brief period. There was, during the whole time, no great action in the field, like Marston Moor, or Benburb, or Dunbar; it was a campaign of seventeenth century cannon against mediaeval masonry; what else was done, was the supplemental work of mutual bravery on both sides. Drogheda, Dundalk, Newry, and Carlingford fell in September; Arklow, Enniscorthy, and Wexford in October; Ross, one of the first seaports in point of commerce, surrendered the same month; Waterford was attempted and abandoned in November; Dungarvan, Kinsale, Bandon, and Cork were won over by Lord Broghill in December; Fethard, Callan, and Cashel in January and February; Carrick and Kilkenny in March; and Clonmel, early in May. Immediately after this last capitulation, Cromwell was recalled to lead the armies of the Parliament into Scotland: during the nine months he had commanded in Ireland, he had captured five or six county capitals, and a great number of less considerable places. The terror of his siege-trains and Ironsides was spread over the greater part of three Provinces, and his well-reported successes had proved so many steps to the assumption of that sovereign power at which he already aimed.

Of the spirit in which these several sieges were conducted, it is impossible to speak without a shudder. It was, in truth, a spirit of hatred and fanaticism, altogether beyond the control of the revolutionary leader. At Drogheda, the work of slaughter occupied five entire days. Of the brave garrison of 3,000 men, not thirty were spared, and these, "were in hands for the Barbadoes;" old men, women, children and priests, were unsparingly put to the sword. Wexford was basely betrayed by Captain James Stafford, commander of the castle, whose midnight interview with Cromwell, at a petty rivulet without the walls, tradition still recounts with horror and detestation. This port was particularly obnoxious to the Parliament, as from its advantageous position on the Bristol channel, its cruisers greatly annoyed and embarrassed their commerce. "There are," Cromwell writes to Speaker Lenthall, "great quantities of iron, hides, tallow, salt, pipe and barrel staves, which are under commissioners' hands to be secured. We believe there are near a hundred cannon in the fort and elsewhere in and about the town. Here is likewise some very good shipping; here are three vessels, one of them of thirty-four guns, which a week's time would fit for sea; there is another of about twenty guns, very nearly ready likewise." He also reports two other frigates, one on the stocks, which "for her handsomeness' sake" he intended to have finished for the Parliament, and another "most excellent vessel for sailing," taken within the fort, at the harbour's mouth. By the treachery of Captain Stafford, this strong and wealthy town was at the mercy of those "soldiers of the Lord and of Gideon," who had followed Oliver to his Irish wars. The consequences were the same as at Drogheda-- merciless execution on the garrison and the inhabitants.

In the third month of Cromwell's campaign, the report of Owen O'Neil's death went abroad, palsying the Catholic arms. By common consent of friend and foe, he was considered the ablest civil and military leader that had appeared in Ireland during the reigns of the Stuart kings. Whether in native ability he was capable of coping with Cromwell, was for a long time a subject of discussion; but the consciousness of irreparable national loss, perhaps, never struck deeper than amid the crash of that irresistible cannonade of the walled towns and cities of Leinster and Munster. O'Neil had lately, despairing of binding the Scots or the English, distrustful alike of Coote and of Monck, been reconciled to Ormond, and was marching southward to his aid at the head of 6,000 chosen men. Lord Chancellor Clarendon assures us that Ormond had the highest hopes from this junction, and the utmost confidence in O'Neil's abilities. But at a ball at Derry, towards the end of August, he received his death, it is said, in a pair of poisoned russet leather slippers presented to him by one Plunkett; marching southward, borne in a litter, he expired at Clough Oughter Castle, near his old Belturbet camp, on the 6th of November, 1649. His last act was to order one of his nephews--Hugh O'Neil--to form a junction with Ormond in Munster without delay. In the chancel of the Franciscan Abbey of Cavan, now grass-grown and trodden by the hoofs of cattle, his body was interred; his nephew and successor did honour to his memory at Clonmel and Limerick. It was now remembered, even by his enemies, with astonishment and admiration, how for seven long years he had subsisted and kept together an army, the creature of his genius; without a government at his back, without regular supplies, enforcing obedience, establishing discipline, winning great victories, maintaining, even at the worst, a native power in the heart of the kingdom. When the archives of those years are recovered (if they ever are), no name more illustrious for the combination of great qualities will be found preserved there than the name of this last national leader of the illustrious lineage of O'Neil.

The unexpected death of the Ulster general favoured still farther Cromwell's southern movements. The gallant, but impetuous Bishop of Clogher, Heber McMahon, was the only northern leader who could command confidence enough to keep O'Neil's force together, and on him, therefore, the command devolved. O'Ferrall, one of Owen's favourite officers, was despatched to Waterford, and mainly contributed to Cromwell's repulse before that city; Hugh O'Neil covered himself with glory at Clonmel and Limerick; Daniel O'Neil, another nephew of Owen, remained attached to Ormond, and accompanied him to France; but within six months from the loss of their Fabian chief, who knew as well when to strike as to delay, the brave Bishop of Clogher sacrificed the remnant of "the Catholic Army" at the pass of Scariffhollis, in Donegal, and, two days after, his own life by a martyr's death, at Omagh. At the date of Cromwell's departure--when Ireton took command of the southern army--there remained to the Confederates only some remote glens and highlands of the North and West, the cities of Limerick and Galway, with the county of Clare, and some detached districts of the province of Connaught.

The last act of Cromwell's proper campaign was the siege of Clonmel, where he met the stoutest resistance he had anywhere encountered. The Puritans, after effecting a breach, made an attempt to enter, chanting one of their scriptural battle-songs. They were, by their own account, "obliged to give back a while," and finally night settled down upon the scene. The following day, finding the place no longer tenable, the garrison silently withdrew to Waterford, and subsequently to Limerick. The inhabitants demanded a parley, which was granted; and Cromwell takes credit, and deserves it, when we consider the men he had to humour, for having kept conditions with them.

From before Clonmel he returned at once to England, where he was received with royal honours. All London turned out to meet the Conqueror who had wiped out the humiliation of Benburb, and humbled the pride of the detested Papists. He was lodged in the palace of the king, and chosen "Captain-general of all the forces raised, or to be raised, by the authority of the Parliament of England."

CHAPTER XI.

CLOSE OF THE CONFEDERATE WAR.

The tenth year of the contest of which we have endeavoured to follow the most important events, opened upon the remaining Catholic leaders, greatly reduced in numbers and resources, but firm and undismayed. Two chief seaports, and some of the western counties still remained to them; and accordingly we find meetings of the Bishops and other notables during this year (1650), at Limerick, at Loughrea, and finally at Jamestown, in the neighbourhood of Owen O'Neil's nursery of the first "Catholic Army."

The Puritan commander was now Henry Ireton, son-in-law of Cromwell, by a marriage contracted about two years before. The completion of the Protector's policy could have devolved upon few persons more capable of understanding, or more fearless in executing it; and in two eventful campaigns he proved himself the able successor of the Protector. In August following Cromwell's departure, Waterford and Duncannon were taken by Ireton; and there only remained to the Confederates the fortresses of Sligo, Athlone, Limerick, and Galway, with the country included within the irregular quadrangle they describe. The younger Coote making a feint against Sligo, which Clanrickarde hastened to defend, turned suddenly on his steps, and surprised Athlone. Sligo, naturally a place of no great strength after the invention of artillery, soon after fell, so that Galway and Limerick alone were left, at the beginning of 1651, to bear all the brunt of Puritan hostility.

Political events of great interest happened during the two short years of Ireton's command. The Assembly, which met at Jamestown in August, and again at Loughrea in November, 1650, made the retirement of Ormond from the Government a condition of all future efforts in the royal cause, and that nobleman, deeply wounded by this condition, had finally sailed from Galway, in December, leaving to Clanrickarde the title of Lord Deputy, and to Castlehaven the command of the forces which still kept the field. The news from Scotland of the young king's subscription to the covenant, and denunciation of all terms with Irish Papists, came to aid the councils of those, who, like the eloquent French, Bishop of Ferns, demanded a national policy, irrespective of the exigencies of the Stuart family. An embassy was accordingly despatched to Brussels, to offer the title of King-Protector to the Duke of Lorraine, or failing with him, to treat with any "other Catholic prince, state, republic, or person, as they might deem expedient for the preservation of the Catholic religion and nation." A wide latitude, dictated by desperate circumstances. The ambassadors were Bishop French and Hugh Rochfort; the embassy one of the most curious and instructive in our annals.

The Duke expressed himself willing to undertake an expedition to Ireland--to supply arms and money to the Confederates--on the condition of receiving Athlone, Limerick, Athenry and Galway into his custody, with the title of Protector. A considerable sum of money (20,000 pounds) was forwarded at once; four Belgian frigates laden with stores were made ready for sea; the Canon De Henin was sent as envoy to the Confederates, and this last venture looked most promising of success, had not Clanrickarde in Galway, and Charles and Ormond in Paris, taking alarm at the new dignity conferred upon the Duke, countermined the Bishop of Ferns and Mr. Rochfort, and defeated by intrigue and correspondence their hopeful enterprise.

The decisive battle of Worcester, fought on the 3rd of September, 1651, drove Charles II. into that nine years' exile, from which he only returned on the death of Cromwell. It may be considered the last military event of importance in the English civil war. In Ireland the contest was destined to drag out another campaign, before the walls of the two gallant cities, Galway and Limerick.

Limerick was the first object of attack. Ireton, leaving Sankey to administer martial law in Tipperary, struck the Shannon opposite Killaloe, driving Castlehaven before him. Joined by Coote and Reynolds, fresh from the sieges of Athenry and Athlone, he moved upon Limerick by the Connaught bank of the river, while Castlehaven fled to Clanrickarde in Galway, with a guard of forty horse, all that remained intact of the 4,000 men bequeathed him by Ormond. From the side of Munster, Lord Muskerry attempted a diversion in favour of Limerick, but was repulsed at Castleishen, by "the flying camp" of Lord Broghill. The besiegers were thus not only delivered of a danger, but reinforced by native troops--if the "Undertakers" could be properly called so--which made them the most formidable army that had ever surrounded an Irish city. From early summer till the last week of October, the main force of the English and Anglo-Irish, supplied with every species of arm then invented, assailed the walls of Limerick. The plague, which during these months swept with such fearful mortality over the whole kingdom, struck down its defenders, and filled all its streets with desolation and grief. The heroic bishops, O'Brien of Emly, and O'Dwyer of Limerick, exerted themselves to uphold, by religious exhortations, the confidence of the besieged; while Hugh O'Neil and General Purcell maintained the courage of their men. Clanrickarde had offered to charge himself with the command, but the citizens preferred to trust in the skill and determination of the defender of Clonmel, whose very name was a talisman among them. The municipal government, however, composed of the men of property in the city, men whose trade was not war, whose religion was not enthusiastic, formed a third party,--a party in favour of peace at any price. With the Mayor at their head, they openly encouraged the surrender of one of the outworks to the besiegers, and this betrayal, on the 27th of October, compelled the surrender of the entire works. Thus Limerick fell, divided within itself by military, clerical, and municipal factions; thus glory and misfortune combined to consecrate its name in the national veneration, and the general memory of mankind. The Bishop of Emly and General Purcell were executed as traitors; the Bishop of Limerick escaped in the disguise of a common soldier, and died at Brussels; O'Neil's life was saved by a single vote; Sir Geoffrey Gabney, Aldermen Stritch and Fanning, and other leading Confederates, expiated their devotion upon the scaffold.

On the 12th of May following--seven months after the capture of Limerick, Galway fell. Ireton, who survived the former siege but a few days, was succeeded by Ludlow, a sincere republican of the school of Pym and Hampden--if that school can be called, in our modern sense, republican. It was the sad privilege of General Preston, whose name is associated with so many of the darkest, and with some of the brightest incidents of this war, to order the surrender of Galway, as he had two years previously given up Waterford. Thus the last open port, the last considerable town held by the Confederates, yielded to the overwhelming power of numbers and munitions, in the twelfth year of that illustrious war which Ireland waged for her religious and civil liberties, against the forces of the two adjoining kingdoms, sometimes estranged from one another, but always hostile alike to the religious belief and the political independence of the Irish people.

With the fall of Galway, the Confederate war drew rapidly to a close. Colonels Fitzpatrick, O'Dwyer, Grace, and Thorlogh O'Neil, surrendered their posts; Lords Enniskillen and West-Meath followed their example; Lord Muskerry yielded Ross Castle, on Killarney, in June; Clanrickarde laid down his arms at Carrick, in October. The usual terms granted were liberty to transport themselves and followers to the service of any foreign state or prince at peace with the commonwealth; a favoured few were permitted to live and die in peace on their own estates, under the watchful eye of some neighbouring garrison.

The chief actors in the Confederate war not already accounted for, terminated their days under many different circumstances. Mountgarrett and Bishop Rothe died before Galway fell, and were buried in the capital of the Confederacy; Bishop McMahon of Clogher, surrendered to Sir Charles Coote, and was executed like a felon by one he had saved from destruction a year before at Derry; Coote, after the Restoration, became Earl of Mountrath, and Broghill, Earl of Orrery; Clanrickarde died unnoticed on his English estate, under the Protectorate; Inchiquin, after many adventures in foreign lands, turned Catholic in his old age, and this burner of churches bequeathed an annual alms for masses for his soul; Jones, Corbet, Cook, and the fanatical preacher, Hugh Peters, perished on the scaffold with the other regicides executed by order of the English Parliament; Ormond having shared the evils of exile with the King, shared also the splendour of his restoration, became a Duke, and took his place, as if by common consent, at the head of the peerage of the empire; his Irish rental, which before the war was but 7,000 pounds a year, swelled suddenly on the Restoration to 80,000 pounds; Nicholas French, after some sojourn in Spain, where he was coadjutor to the Archbishop of Saint James, returned to Louvain, where he made his first studies, and there spent the evening of his days in the composition of those powerful pamphlets which kept alive the Irish cause at home and on the continent; a Roman patrician did the honours of sepulture to Luke Wadding, and Cromwell interred James Usher in Westminster Abbey; the heroic defender of Clonmel and Limerick, and the gallant, though vacillating Preston, were cordially received in France; while the consistent republican, Ludlow, took refuge as a fugitive in Switzerland.

Sir Phelim O'Neil, the first author of the war, was among the last to suffer the penalties of defeat. For a moment, towards the end, he renewed his sway over the remnant of Owen's soldiers, took Ballyshannon, and two or three other places. Compelled at last to surrender, he was carried to Dublin, and tried on a charge of treason, a committee closeted behind the bench dictating the interrogatories to his judges, and receiving his answers in reply. Condemned to death, as was expected, he was offered his life by the Puritan colonel, Hewson, on the very steps of the scaffold, if he would inculpate the late King Charles in the rising of 1641. This he "stoutly refused to do," and the execution proceeded with all its atrocious details. Whatever may have been the excesses committed under his command by a plundered people, at their first insurrection--and we know that they have been exaggerated beyond all bounds--it must be admitted he died the death of a Christian, a soldier, and a gentleman.

CHAPTER XII.

IRELAND UNDER THE PROTECTORATE--ADMINISTRATION OF HENRY CROMWELL--DEATH OF OLIVER.

The English republic rose from the scaffold of the King, in 1649; its first government was a "Council of State" of forty-one members; under this council, Cromwell held at first the title of Lord General; but, on the 16th December, 1653, he was solemnly installed, in Westminster Hall, as "Lord Protector of the Commonwealth of England, Scotland, and Ireland." He was then in his fifty-fourth year; his reign--if such it may be called--lasted less than five years.

The policy of the Protector towards Ireland is even less defensible than his military severities. For the barbarities of war there may be some apology, the poor one at least that such outrages are inseparable from war itself; but for the cold-blooded, deliberate atrocities of peace, no such defence can be permitted before the tribunal of a free posterity.

The Long Parliament, still dragging out its date, under the shadow of Cromwell's great name, declared in its session of 1652, the rebellion in Ireland "subdued and ended," and proceeded to legislate for that kingdom as a conquered country. On the 12th of August, they passed their Act of Settlement, the authorship of which was attributed to Lord Orrery, in this respect the worthy son of the first Earl of Cork. Under this Act, there were four chief descriptions of persons whose status was thus settled: 1st. All ecclesiastics and royalist proprietors were exempted from pardon of life or estate. 2nd. All royalist commissioned officers were condemned to banishment, and the forfeit of two-thirds of their property, one-third being retained for the support of their wives and children. 3rd. Those who had not been in arms, but could be shown, by a Parliamentary commission, to have manifested "a constant, good affection" to the war, were to forfeit one-third of their estates, and receive "an equivalent" for the remaining two-thirds west of the Shannon. 4th. All husbandmen and others of the inferior sort, "not possessed of lands or goods exceeding the value of 10 pounds," were to have a free pardon, on condition also of transporting themselves across the Shannon.

This last condition of the Cromwellian settlement distinguished it, in our annals, from every other proscription of the native population formerly attempted. The great river of Ireland, rising in the mountains of Leitrim, nearly severs the five western counties from the rest of the kingdom. The province thus set apart, though one of the largest in superficial extent, had also the largest proportion of waste and water, mountain and moorland. The new inhabitants were there to congregate from all the other provinces before the 1st day of May, 1654, under penalty of outlawry and all its consequences; and when there, they were not to appear within two miles of the Shannon or four miles of the sea. A rigorous passport system, to evade which was death without form of trial, completed this settlement, the design of which was to shut up the remaining Catholic inhabitants from all intercourse with mankind, and all communion with the other inhabitants of their own country.

A new survey of the whole kingdom was also ordered, under the direction of Dr. William Petty, the fortunate economist, who founded the house of Lansdowne. By him the surface of the kingdom was estimated at ten millions and a half plantation acres, three of which were deducted for waste and water. Of the remainder, above 5,000,000 were in Catholic hands in 1641; 300,000 were church and college lands; and 2,000,000 were in possession of the Protestant settlers of the reigns of James and Elizabeth. Under the Protectorate, 5,000,000 acres were confiscate; this enormous spoil, two-thirds of the whole island, went to the soldiers and adventurers who had served against the Irish, or had contributed to the military chest, since 1641--except 700,000 acres given in "exchange" to the banished in Clare and Connaught; and 1,200,000 confirmed to "innocent Papists." Such was the complete uprooting of the ancient tenantry or clansmen, from their original holdings, that during the survey, orders of Parliament were issued to bring back individuals from Connaught to point out the boundaries of parishes in Munster. It cannot be imputed among the sins so freely laid to the historical account of the native legislature, that an Irish parliament had any share in sanctioning this universal spoliation. Cromwell anticipated the union of the kingdoms by a hundred and fifty years, when he summoned, in 1653, that assembly over which "Praise-God Barebones" presided; members for Ireland and Scotland sat on the same benches with the commons of England. Oliver's first deputy in the government of Ireland was his son-in-law, Fleetwood, who had married the widow of Ireton; but his real representative was his fourth son, Henry Cromwell, Commander-in-Chief of the army. In 1657, the title of Lord Deputy was transferred from Fleetwood to Henry, who united the supreme civil and military authority in his own person, until the eve of the restoration, of which he became an active partisan. We may thus properly embrace the five years of the Protectorate as the period of Henry Cromwell's administration.

In the absence of a Parliament, the government of Ireland was vested in the Deputy, the Commander-in-Chief, and four commissioners, Ludlow, Corbett, Jones, and Weaver. There was, moreover, a High Court of Justice, which perambulated the kingdom, and exercised an absolute authority over life and property, greater than even Strafford's Court of Castle Chamber had pretended to. Over this court presided Lord Lowther, assisted by Mr. Justice Donnellan, by Cooke, solicitor to the Parliament on the trial of King Charles, and the regicide, Reynolds. By this court, Sir Phelim O'Neil, Viscount Mayo, and Colonels O'Toole and Bagnall, were condemned and executed; by them the mother of Colonel Fitzpatrick was burnt at the stake; and Lords Muskerry and Clanmaliere set at liberty, through some secret influence. The commissioners were not behind the High Court of Justice in executive offices of severity. Children under age, of both sexes, were captured by thousands, and sold as slaves to the tobacco planters of Virginia and the West Indies. Secretary Thurloe informs Henry Cromwell that "the Committee of the Council have authorized 1,000 girls and as many youths, to be taken up for that purpose." Sir William Petty mentions 6,000 Irish boys and girls shipped to the West Indies. Some cotemporary accounts make the total number of children and adults so transported 100,000 souls. To this decimation, we may add 34,000 men of fighting age, who had permission to enter the armies of foreign powers, at peace with the commonwealth. The chief commissioners, sitting at Dublin, had their deputies in a commission of delinquencies, sitting at Athlone, and another of transportation, sitting at Loughrea. Under their superintendence, the distribution made of the soil among the Puritans "was nearly as complete as that of Canaan by the Israelites." Whenever native labourers were found absolutely necessary for the cultivation of the estates of their new masters, they were barely tolerated "as the Gibeonites had been by Joshua." Such Irish gentlemen as had obtained pardons, were obliged to wear a distinctive mark on their dress under pain of death; those of inferior rank were obliged to wear a round black spot on the right cheek under pain of the branding iron and the gallows; if a Puritan lost his life in any district inhabited by Catholics, the whole population were held subject to military execution. For the rest, whenever "Tory" or recusant fell into the hands of these military colonists, or the garrisons which knitted them together, they were assailed with the war cry of the Jews--"That thy feet may be dipped in the blood of thine enemies, and that the tongues of thy dogs may be red with the same." Thus penned in between "the mile line" of the Shannon, and "the four mile-line" of the sea, the remnant of the Irish nation passed seven years of a bondage unequalled in severity by anything which can be found in the annals of Christendom.

The conquest was not only a military but a religious subjugation. The 27th of Elizabeth--the old act of uniformity--was rigorously enforced. The Catholic lawyers were disbarred and silenced; the Catholic schoolmasters were forbidden to teach, under pain of felony. Recusants, surrounded in glens and caves, offering up the holy sacrifice through the ministry of some daring priest, were shot down or smoked out like vermin. The ecclesiastics never, in any instance, were allowed to escape. Among those who suffered death during the short space of the Protectorate, are counted "three bishops and three hundred ecclesiastics." The surviving prelates were in exile, except the bedridden Bishop of Kilmore, who for years had been unable to officiate. So that, now, that ancient hierarchy which in the worst Danish wars had still recruited its ranks as fast as they were broken, seemed on the very eve of extinction. Throughout all the island no episcopal hand remained to bless altars, to ordain priests, or to confirm the faithful. The Irish church as well as the Irish state, touched its lowest point of suffering and endurance in the decade which intervened between the death of Charles I. and the death of Cromwell.

The new population imposed upon the kingdom, soon split up into a multitude of sects. Some of them became Quakers: many adhered to the Anabaptists; others, after the Restoration, conformed to the established church. That deeper tincture of Puritanism which may be traced in the Irish, as compared with the English establishment, took its origin even more from the Cromwellian settlement than from the Calvinistic teachings of Archbishop Usher.

Oliver died in 1658, on his "fortunate day," the 3rd of September, leaving England to experience twenty months of republican intrigue and anarchy. Richard Cromwell-- Lambert--Ludlow--Monck--each played his part in this stormy interval, till, the time being ripe for a restoration, Charles II. landed at Dover on the 23rd of May, 1660 and was carried in triumph to London.

BOOK X.
FROM THE RESTORATION OF CHARLES II. TO THE ACCESSION OF GEORGE I.

CHAPTER I.

REIGN OF CHARLES II.

Hope is dear to the heart of man, and of all her votaries none have been more constant than the Irish. Half a century of the Stuarts had not extinguished their blind partiality for the descendants of the old Scoto-Irish kings. The restoration of that royal house was, therefore, an event which penetrated to the remotest wilds of Connaught, lighting up with cheering expectation the most desolate hovels of the proscribed. To the Puritans settled in Ireland, most of whom, from the mean condition of menial servants, common soldiers and subaltern officers, had become rich proprietors, the same tidings brought apprehension and alarm. But their leaders, the Protestant gentry of an earlier date, wealthy, astute and energetic, uniting all their influence for the common protection, turned this event, which seemed at one time to threaten their ruin, to their advantage and greater security. The chief of these greater leaders was the accomplished Lord Broghill, whom we are to know during this reign under his more famous title of Earl of Orrery.

The position of the Irish as compared with the English Puritans, was essentially different in the eyes of Ormond, Clarendon, and the other counsellors of the king. Though the former represented dissent as against the church, they also represented the English as against the Irish interest, in Ireland. As dissenters they were disliked and ridiculed, but as colonists they could not be disturbed. When national antipathy was placed in one scale and religious animosity in the other, the intensely national feeling of England for the Cromwellians, as Englishmen settled in a hostile country, prevailed over every other consideration. In this, as in all other conjunctures, it has been the singular infelicity of the one island to be subjected to a policy directly opposite to that pursued in the other. While in England it was considered wise and just to break down the Puritans as a party--through the court, the pulpit, and the press; to drive the violent into exile, and to win the lukewarm to conformity; in Ireland it was decided to confirm them in their possessions, to leave the government of the kingdom in their hands, and to strengthen their position by the Acts of Settlement and Explanation. These acts were hailed as "the Magna Charta of Irish Protestantism," but so far as the vast majority of the people were concerned, they were as cruelly unjust as the revocation of the Edict of Nantes, or the edicts which banished the Moors and Jews from the Spanish peninsula.

The struggle for possession of the soil inaugurated by the confiscations of Elizabeth and James was continued against great odds by the Catholic Irish throughout this reign. Though the royal declaration of Breda, which preceded the restoration, had not mentioned them expressly, they still claimed under it not only the "liberty to tender consciences," but that "just satisfaction" to those unfairly deprived of their estates, promised in that declaration. Accordingly, several of the old gentry returned from Connaught, or places abroad, took possession of their old homes, or made their way at once to Dublin or London, to urge their claims to their former estates. To their dismay, they found in Dublin, Coote and Broghill established as Lords Justices, and the new Parliament--the first that sat for twenty years--composed of an overwhelming majority of Undertakers, adventurers, and Puritan representatives of boroughs, from which all the Catholic electors had been long excluded. The Protestant interest, or "ascendancy party," as it now began to be commonly called, counted in the Commons 198 members to 64 Catholics; in the House of Lords, 72 Protestant to 21 Catholic peers. The former elected Sir Audley Mervyn their Speaker, and the able but curiously intricate and quaint discourses of the ancient colleague of Kelly and Darcy in the assertion of Irish legislative independence, shows how different was the spirit of Irish Protestantism in 1661 as compared with 1641. The Lords chose Bramhall, the long-exiled Bishop of Derry, now Archbishop of Armagh, as their Speaker, and attempted to compel their members "to take the sacrament" according to the Anglican ritual. The majority of both Houses, to secure the good-will of Ormond, voted him the sum of 30,000 pounds, and then proceeded to consider "the Bill of Settlement," in relation to landed property. The Catholic bar, which had been apparently restored to its freedom, presented a striking array of talent, from which their co-religionists selected those by whom they desired to be heard at the bar of the House. The venerable Darcy and the accomplished Belling were no longer their oracles of the law; but they had the services of Sir Nicholas Plunkett, an old confederate, of Sir Richard Nagle, author of the famous "Coventry Letter," of Nugent, afterwards Lord Riverston, and other able men. In the House of Lords they had an intrepid ally in the Earl of Kildare, and in England an agent equally intrepid, in Colonel Richard Talbot, afterwards Earl of Tyrconnell. The diplomatic and parliamentary struggle between the two interests, the disinherited and the new proprietory, was too protracted, and the details are too involved for elucidation in every part; but the result tells its own story. In 1675--in the fifteenth year of the restoration--the new settlers possessed above 4,500,000 acres, to about 2,250,000 still retained by the old owners. These relative proportions were exactly the reverse of those existing before the Cromwellian settlement; a single generation had seen this great revolution accomplished in landed property.

The Irish Parliament having sent over to England the heads of their bill, according to the constitutional rule established by Poyning's Act, the Irish Catholics sent over Sir Nicholas Plunkett to obtain modifications of its provisions. But Plunkett was met in England with such an outcry from the mob and the press as to the alleged atrocities of the Confederate war, and his own former negotiations on the continent, that he was unable to effect anything; while Colonel Talbot, for his too warm expostulations with Ormond, was sent to the Tower. An order of Council, forbidding Plunkett the presence, and declaring that "no petition or further address be made from the Roman Catholics of Ireland, as to the Bill of Settlement," closed the controversy, and the Act soon after received the royal assent.

Under this act, a court was established at Dublin, to try the claims of "nocent" and "innocent." Notwithstanding every influence which could be brought to bear on them, the judges, who were Englishmen, declared in their first session, one hundred and sixty-eight innocent to nineteen nocent. Proceeding in this spirit "to the great loss and dissatisfaction of the Protestants," the latter, greatly alarmed, procured the interference of Ormond, now Lord Lieutenant (1662), in effecting a modification of the commission, appointing the court, by which its duration was limited to an early day. The consequence was, that while less than 800 claims were decided on when the fatal day arrived, over 3,000 were left unheard, at least a third of whom were admitted even by their enemies to be innocent. About 500 others had been restored by name in the Act of Settlement itself; but, by the Act of Explanation (1665), "no Papist who had not been adjudged innocent" under the former act could be so adjudged thereafter, "or entitled to claim any lands or settlements." Thus, even the inheritance of hope, and the reversion of expectation, were extinguished for ever for the sons and daughters of the ancient gentry of the kingdom.

The religious liberties of this people, so crippled in property and political power, were equally at the mercy of the mob and of the monarch. To combat the war of calumny waged against them by the Puritan press and pulpit, the leading Catholics resolved to join in an official and authentic declaration of their true principles, as to the spiritual power of the Pope, their allegiance to the prince, and their relations to their fellow subjects of other denominations. With this intention a meeting was held at the house of the Marquis of Clanrickarde, in Dublin, at which Lords Clancarty, Carlingford, Fingal, Castlehaven, and Inchiquin, and the leading commoners of their faith, were present. At this meeting, Father Peter Walsh, a Franciscan, and an old courtier of Ormond's, as "Procurator of all the Clergy of Ireland," secular and regular, produced credentials signed by the surviving bishops or their vicars--including the Primate O'Reilly, the Bishops of Meath, Ardagh, Kilmore, and Ferns. Richard Belling, the secretary to the first Confederate Council, and Envoy to Rome, submitted the celebrated document known as "The Remonstrance," deeply imbued with the spirit of the Gallican church of that day. It was signed by about seventy Catholic peers and commoners, by the Bishop of Kilmore, by Procurator Walsh, and by the townsmen of Wexford--almost the only urban community of Catholics remaining in the country. But the propositions it contained as to the total independency of the temporal on the spiritual power, and the ecclesiastical patronage of princes, were condemned at the Sorbonne, at Louvain, and at Rome. The regular orders, by their several superiors, utterly rejected it; the exiled bishops withdrew their proxies from Father Walsh, and disclaimed his conduct; the Internuncio at Brussels, charged with the affairs of the British Isles, denounced it as contrary to the canons; and the elated Procurator found himself involved in a controversy from which he never afterwards escaped, and with which his memory is still angrily associated.

The conduct of Ormond in relation to this whole business of the Remonstrance, was the least creditable part of his administration. Writhing under the eloquent pamphlets of the exiled Bishop of Ferns, keenly remembering his own personal wrongs against the former generation of bishops, of whom but three or four were yet living, he resolved "to work that division among the Romish clergy," which he had long meditated. With this view, he connived at a meeting of the surviving prelates and the superiors of regular orders, at Dublin, in 1666. To this synod safe conduct was permitted to the Primate O'Reilly, banished to Belgium nine years before; to Peter Talbot, Archbishop of Dublin, John Burke, Archbishop of Tuam, Patrick Plunkett, Bishop of Ardagh, the vicars-general of other prelates, and the superiors of the regulars. This venerable body deliberated anxiously for an entire week, Father Walsh acting as ambassador between them and the Viceroy; at length, in spite of all politic considerations, they unanimously rejected the servile doctrine of the "Remonstrance," substituting instead a declaration of their own dictation. Ormond now cast off all affectation of liberality; Primate O'Reilly was sent back to his banishment, the other prelates and clergy were driven back to their hiding-places, or into exile abroad, and the wise, experienced, high-spirited duke, did not hesitate to avail himself of "the Popish plot" mania, which soon after broke out, to avenge himself upon an order of men whom he could neither break nor bend to his purposes! Of 1,100 secular priests, and 750 regulars, still left, only sixty-nine had signed the Clanrickarde House Remonstrance.

An incident of this same year--1666--illustrates more forcibly than description could do, the malignant feeling which had been excited in England against everything Irish. The importation of Irish cattle had long been considered an English grievance, it was now declared by law "a nuisance." The occasion taken to pass this statute was as ungracious as the act itself was despicable. In consequence of "the great fire," which still glows for us in the immortal verse of Dryden, the Irish had sent over to the distressed, a contribution of 15,000 bullocks. This was considered by the generous recipients a mere pretence to preserve the trade in cattle between the two kingdoms, and accordingly both Houses, after some sharp resistance in the Lords', gravely enacted that the importation of Irish beef into England was "a nuisance," to be abated. From this period most probably dates the famous English sarcasm against Irish bulls.

The act prohibiting the export of cattle from Ireland, and the equally exclusive and unjust Navigation Act-- originally devised by Cromwell--so paralyzed every Irish industry, that the Puritan party became almost as dissatisfied as the Catholics. They maintained a close correspondence with their brethren in England, and began to speculate on the possibilities of another revolution. Ormond, to satisfy their demands, distributed 20,000 stand of arms among them, and reviewed the Leinster Militia, on the Curragh, in 1667. The next year he was recalled, and Lords Robarts, Berkely, and Essex, successively appointed to the government. The first, a Puritan, and almost a regicide, held office but a few months; the second, a cavalier and a friend of toleration, for two years; while Essex, one of those fair-minded but yielding characters, known in the next reign as "Trimmers," petitioned for his own recall and Ormond's restoration, in 1676. The only events which marked these last nine years--from Ormond's removal till his reappointment-- were the surprise of Carrickfergus by a party of unpaid soldiers, and their desperate defence of that ancient stronghold; the embassies to and from the Irish Catholics and the court, of Colonel Richard Talbot; and the establishment of extensive woollen manufactories at Thomastown, Callan, and Kilkenny, under the patronage of Ormond.

CHAPTER II.

REIGN OF CHARLES II. (CONCLUDED.)

For the third time, the aged Ormond, now arrived at the period usually allotted to the life of man, returned to Ireland, with the rank of Viceroy. During the ensuing seven years, he clung to power with all the tenacity of his youth, and all the policy of his prime; they were seven years of extraordinary sectarian panic and excitement--the years of the Cabal, the Popish plot, and the Exclusion Bill, in England--and of fanatical conspiracies and explosions almost as dangerous in Ireland.

The Popish plot mania held possession of the English people much longer than any other moral epidemic of equal virulence. In the month of October, 1678, its alleged existence in Ireland was communicated to Ormond; in July, 1681, its most illustrious victim, Archbishop Plunkett, perished on the scaffold at Tyburn. Within these two points of time what a chronicle of madness, folly, perjury, and cruelty, might be written?

Ormond, too old in statecraft to believe in the existence of these incredible plots, was also too well aware of the dangerous element of fanaticism represented by Titus Oates, and his imitators, to subject himself to suspicion. On the first intelligence of the plot, he instantly issued his proclamation for the arrest of Archbishop Talbot, of Dublin, who had been permitted to return from exile under the rule of Lord Berkely, and had since resided with his brother, Colonel Talbot, at Cartown, near Maynooth. This prelate was of Ormond's own age, and of a family as ancient; while his learning, courage, and morality, made him an ornament to his order. He was seized in his sick bed at Cartown, carried to Dublin in a chair, and confined a close prisoner in the castle, where he died two years later. He was the last distinguished captive destined to end his days in that celebrated state prison, which has since been generally dedicated to the peaceful purposes of reflected royalty.

Colonel Talbot was at the same time arrested, but allowed to retire beyond seas; Lord Mountgarrett, an octogenarian, and in his dotage, was seized, but nothing could be made out against him; a Colonel Peppard was also denounced from England, but no such person was found to exist. So far the first year of the plot had passed over, and proved nothing against the Catholic Irish. But the example of successful villainy in England, of Oates idolized, pensioned, and all-powerful, extended to the sister kingdom, and brought an illustrious victim to the scaffold. This was Oliver Plunkett, a scion of the noble family of Fingal, who had been Archbishop of Armagh, since the death of Dr. O'Reilly, in exile, in 1669. Such had been the prudence and circumspection of Dr. Plunkett, during his perilous administration, that the agents of Lord Shaftesbury, sent over to concoct evidence for the occasion, were afraid to bring him to trial in the vicinage of his arrest, or in his own country. Accordingly, they caused him to be removed from Dublin to London, contrary to the laws and customs of both Kingdoms, which had first been violated towards state prisoners in the case of Lord Maguire, forty years before.

Dr. Plunkett, after ten months' confinement without trial in Ireland, was removed, 1680, and arraigned at London, on the 8th of June, 1681, without having had permission to communicate with his friends or to send for witnesses. The prosecution was conducted by Maynard and Jeffries, in violation of every form of law, and every consideration of justice. A "crown agent," whose name is given as Gorman, was introduced by "a stranger" in court, and volunteered testimony in his favour. The Earl of Essex interceded with the King on his behalf, but Charles answered, almost in the words of Pilate--"I cannot pardon him, because I dare not. His blood be upon your conscience; you could have saved him if you pleased." The Jury, after a quarter of an hour's deliberation, brought in their verdict of guilty, and the brutal Chief-Justice condemned him to be hung, emboweled, and quartered on the 1st day of July, 1681. The venerable martyr, for such he may well be called, bowed his head to the bench, and exclaimed: ***Deo gratias!*** Eight years from the very day of his execution, on the banks of that river beside which he had been seized and dragged from his retreat, the last of the Stuart kings was stricken from his throne, and his dynasty stricken from history! Does not the blood of the innocent cry to

Heaven for vengeance?

The charges against Dr. Plunkett were, that he maintained treasonable correspondence with France and Rome, and the Irish on the continent; that he had organised an insurrection in Louth, Monaghan, Cavan, and Armagh; that he made preparations for the landing of a French force at Carlingford; and that he had held several meetings to raise men for these purposes. Utterly absurd and false as these charges were, they still indicate the troubled apprehensions which filled the dreams of the ascendency party. The fear of French invasion, of new insurrections, of the resumption of estates, haunted them by night and day. Every sign was to them significant of danger, and every rumour of conspiracy was taken for fact. The report of a strange fleet off the Southern coast, which turned out to be English, threw them all into panic; and the Corpus Christi crosses which the peasantry affixed to their doors, were nothing but signs for the Papist destroyer to pass by, and to spare his fellows in the general massacre of Protestants.

Under the pressure of these panics, real or pretended, proclamation after proclamation issued from the Castle. By one of these instruments, Ormond prohibited Catholics from entering the Castle of Dublin, or any other fortress; from holding fairs or markets within the walls of corporate towns, and from carrying arms to such resorts. By another, he declared all relatives of known *Tories*--a Gaelic term for a driver of prey--to be arrested, and banished the kingdom, within fourteen days, unless such Tories were killed, or surrendered, within that time. Where this device failed to reach the destined victims--as in the celebrated case of Count Redmond O'Hanlon--it is to be feared that he did not hesitate to whet the dagger of the assassin, which was still sometimes employed, even in the British Islands, to remove a dangerous antagonist. Count O'Hanlon, a gentleman of ancient lineage, as accomplished as Orrery, or Ossory, was indeed an outlaw to the code then in force; but the stain of his cowardly assassination must for ever blot and rot the princely escutcheon of James, Duke of Ormond.

The violence of religious and social persecution began to subside during the last two or three years of Charles II. Monmouth's banishment, Shaftesbury's imprisonment, the execution of Russell and Sidney on the scaffold, marked the return of the English public mind to political pursuits and objects. Early in 1685, the king was taken mortally ill. In his last moments he received the rites of the Catholic church, from the hands of Father Huddleston, who was said to have saved his life at the battle of Worcester, and who was now even more anxious to save his soul.

 This event took place on the 16th of February. King James was immediately proclaimed successor to his brother. One of his first acts was to recall Ormond from Ireland and to appoint in his place the Earl of Clarendon, son of the historian and statesman of the Restoration. Ormond obeyed, not without regret; he survived his fall about three years. He was interred in Westminster in 1688, three months before the landing of William, and the second banishment of the Stuarts.

CHAPTER III.

THE STATE OF RELIGION AND LEARNING IN IRELAND DURING THE SEVENTEENTH CENTURY.

Before plunging into the troubled torrent of the revolution of 1688, let us cast a glance back on the century, and consider the state of learning and religion during those three generations. If we divide the Irish literature of this century by subjects, we shall find extant a respectable body, both in quantity and quality, of theology, history, law, politics, and poetry. If we divide it by the languages in which that literature was written, we may consider it as Latin, Gaelic, and English.

I. Latin continued throughout Europe, even till this late day, the language of the learned, but especially of theologians, jurists, and historians. In Latin, the great tomes of O'Sullivan, Usher, Colgan, Wadding, and White, were written--volumes which remain as so many monuments of the learning and industry of that age. The chief objects of these illustrious writers were, to restore the ancient ecclesiastical history of Ireland, to rescue the memory of her saints and doctors from oblivion, and to introduce the native annals of the kingdom to the attention of Europe. Though Usher differed in religion, and in his theory of the early connection of the Irish with the Roman Church, from all the rest, yet he stands pre-eminent among them for labour and research. The Waterford Franciscan, Wadding, can only be named with him for inexhaustible patience, various learning, and untiring zeal. Both were honoured of princes and parliaments. The Confederates would have made Wadding a cardinal; King James made Usher an archbishop; one instructed the Westminster Assembly; the other was sent by the King of Spain to maintain the thesis of the Immaculate Conception at Rome, and subsequently was entrusted by the Pope to report upon the propositions of Jansenius. O'Sullivan, Conde de Berehaven, in Spain, and Peter White, have left us each two or three Latin volumes on the history of the country, highly prized by all subsequent writers. But the most indispensable of the legacies left us in this tongue, are Colgan's "Acta Sanctorum"--from January to March--and Dr. John Lynch's "Cambrensis Eversus." Many other works and authors might be mentioned, but these are the great Latinists to whom we are indebted for the most important services rendered to our national history.

II. In the Gaelic literature of the country we count Geoffrey Keating, Duald McFirbis, and "the Four Masters" of Donegal. Few writers have been more rashly judged than Keating. A poet, as well as a historian, he gave a prominence in the early chapters of his history to bardic tales, which English critics have seized upon to damage his reputation for truthfulness and good sense. But these tales he gives as tales--as curious and illustrative--rather than as credible and unquestionable. The purity of his style is greatly extolled by Gaelic critics; and the interest of his narrative, even in a translation, is undoubted. McFirbis, an annalist and genealogist by inheritance, is known to us not only for his profound native lore, and tragic death, but also for the assistance he rendered Sir James Ware, Dr. Lynch, and Roderick O'Flaherty. The master-piece, however, of our Gaelic literature of this age, is the work now called "The Annals of the Four Masters." In the reign of James I., a few Franciscan friars, living partly in Donegal Abbey and partly in St. Anthony's College, at Louvain, undertook to collect and collate all the manuscript remains of Irish antiquity they could gather or borrow, or be allowed to copy. Father Hugh Ward was the head of this group, and by him the lay brother Michael O'Clery, one of the greatest benefactors his country ever saw, was sent from Belgium to Ireland. From 1620 to 1630, O'Clery travelled through the kingdom, buying or transcribing everything he could find relating to the lives of the Irish saints, which he sent to Louvain, where Ward and Colgan undertook to edit and illustrate them. Father Ward died in the early part of the undertaking, but Father Colgan spent twenty years in prosecuting the original design, so far as concerned our ecclesiastical biography.

After collecting these materials, Father O'Clery waited, as he tells us, on "the noble Fergall O'Gara," one of the two knights elected to represent the county of Sligo in the Parliament of 1634, and perceiving the anxiety of O'Gara, "from the cloud which at present hangs over our ancient Milesian race," he proposed to collect the civil and military annals of Erin into one large digest. O'Gara, struck with this proposal, freely supplied the means, and O'Clery and his coadjutors set to work in the Franciscan Convent of Donegal, which still stood, not more than half in ruins.

On the 22nd of January, 1632, they commenced this digest, and on the 10th of August, 1636, it was finished--having occupied them four years, seven months and nineteen days. The MS., dedicated to O'Gara, is authenticated by the superiors of the convent; from that original two editions have recently been printed in both languages.

These annals extend to the year 1616, the time of the compilers. Originally they bore the title of "Annals of the Kingdom of Ireland," but Colgan having quoted them as "The Annals of the Four Masters," that name remains ever since. The "Four Masters" were Brother Michael O'Clery, Conary and Peregrine O'Clery, his brothers, both laymen and natives of Donegal, and Florence Conroy of Roscommon, another hereditary antiquary.

The first edition of the New Testament, in the Gaelic tongue, so far as we are aware, appeared at Dublin, in 1603, in quarto. The translation was the work of a native scholar, O'Cionga (Anglicized King). It was made at the expense and under the supervision of Dr. William O'Donnell, one of the first fellows of Trinity, and published at the cost of the people of Connaught. Dr. O'Donnell, an amiable man, and an enemy of persecution, became subsequently Archbishop of Tuam, in which dignity he died, in 1628. A translation of the Book of Common Prayer, by O'Donnell, appeared early in the century, and towards its close (1685), a translation of the Old Testament, made for Bishop Bedell by the Gaelic scholars of Meath and Cavan, was published at the expense of the famous Robert Boyle. Bedell had also caused to be published Gaelic translations of certain homilies of Saint Leo and Saint John Chrysostom, on the importance of studying the holy Scriptures. The only other Gaelic publications of this period were issued from the Irish colleges at Louvain and Rome. Thence issued the devotional tracts of Conroy, of Gernon, and O'Molloy, and the Irish grammars of O'Clery and Stapleton. The devotional tracts, with their fanciful titles, of "Lamps," and "Mirrors," were smuggled across from Ostend and Dunkirk with other articles of contraband, and did much to keep alive the flame of faith and hope in the hearts of the Gaelic-speaking population.

The bardic order also, though shorn of much of their ancient splendour, and under the Puritan *regime* persecuted as vagrants, still flourished as an estate of the realm. The national tendency to poetic writing was not confined to the hereditary verse-makers, but was illustrated by such men as the martyred Plunkett, and the Bishops of Meath and Kerry--Dr. Thomas Dease, and Dr. John O'Connell. But the great body of Gaelic verse of the first half of this century is known under the name of "The Contentions of the Bards," the subject being the relative dignity, power, and prowess of the North and South. The gauntlet in this poetic warfare, was thrown down by McDaire, the Bard of Donogh O'Brien, fourth Earl of Thomond, and taken up on the part of Ulster by Lewy O'Clery. Reply led to rejoinder, and one epistle to another, until all the chief bards of the four provinces had taken sides. Half a dozen writers, *pro* and *con*, were particularly distinguished; McDaire himself, Turlogh O'Brien, and Art Oge O'Keefe on behalf of the Southerners; O'Clery, O'Donnell, the two McEgans, and Robert McArthur on the side of the North.

An immense mass of devotional Gaelic poetry may be traced to this period. The religious wars, the calamities of the church and of the people, inspired many a priest and layman to seize the harp of David, and pour forth his hopes and griefs in sacred song. The lament of Mac Ward over the Ulster princes buried at Rome, the odes of Dermod Conroy and Flan McNamee, in honour of our Blessed Lady, are of this class. Thus it happened that the bardic order, which in ancient times was the formidable enemy of Christianity, became, through adversity and affliction, its greatest supporter.

III. Our Hiberno-English literature is almost entirely the creation of this century. Except some few remarkable state papers, we have no English writings of any reputation of an earlier period. Now, however, when the language of the empire, formed and enriched by the great minds of Elizabeth's era, began to extend its influence at home and abroad, a school of Hiberno-English writers appeared, both numerous and distinguished. This school was as yet composed mainly of two classes--the dramatic poets, and the pamphleteers. Of the latter were Bishop French, Sir Richard Nagle, Sir Richard Belling, Lord Orrery, Father Peter Walsh, and William Molyneux; of the former, Ludowick Barry, Sir John Denham, the Earl of Roscommon, and Richard Flecknoe,--the Mac Flecknoe of Dryden. It is true there appeared as yet no supreme name like Swift's; but as indicating the gradual extension of the English language into Ireland, the popular pamphlets and pieces written for the stage, are illustrations of our mental life not to be overlooked.

Of the ancient schools of the island, after the final suppression of the college at Galway in 1652, not one remained. A diocesan college at Kilkenny, and the Dublin University, were alone open to the youth of the country. But the University remained exclusively in possession of the Protestant interest, nor did it give to the world during the century, except Usher, Ware and Orrery, any graduate of national, not to say, European reputation. In the bye-ways of the South and West, in the Irish colleges on the continent of Europe--at Paris, Louvain, Lisle, Salamanca, Lisbon, or Rome--the children of the proscribed majority could alone acquire a degree in learning, human or divine. It was as impossible two centuries ago, to speak of Trinity College with respect, as it is in our time, remembering all it has since done, to speak of it without veneration.

Though the Established Church had now completed its century and a half of existence, it was as far from the hearts of the Irish as ever. Though the amiable Bedell and the learned O'Donnell had caused the sacred Scriptures to be translated into the Gaelic tongue, few converts had been made from the Catholic ranks, while the spirit of animosity was inflamed by a sense of the cruel and undeserved disabilities inflicted in the name of religion. The manifold sects introduced under Cromwell gave a keener edge to Catholic contempt for the doctrines of the reformation; and although the restoration of the monarchy threw the extreme sectaries into the shade, it added nothing to the influence of the church, except the fatal gift of political patronage. For the first time, the high dignity of Archbishop of Armagh began to be regarded as the inheritance of the leader of the House of Lords; then Brahmall and Boyle laid the foundation of that primatial power which Boulter and Stone upheld under another dynasty, but which vanished before the first dawn of Parliamentary independence.

In the quarter of a century which elapsed from the restoration to the revolution, the condition of the Catholic clergy and laity was such as we have already described. In 1662, an historian of the Jesuit missionaries in Ireland described the sufferings of ecclesiastics as deplorable; they were forced to fly to the herds of cattle in remote places, to seek a refuge in barns and stables, or to sleep at night in the porticoes of temples, lest they should endanger the safety of the laity. In that same year, Orrery advised Ormond to purge the walled towns of Papists, who were still "three to one Protestant;" in 1672, Sir William Petty computed them at "eight to one" of the entire population.

"So captive Israel multiplied in chains."

The martyrdom of the Archbishop of Dublin, in 1680, and of the Archbishop of Armagh in 1681, were, however, the last of a series of executions for conscience' sake, from the relation of which the historian might well have been excused, if it was not necessary to remind our emancipated posterity at what a price they have been purchased.

CHAPTER IV.

ACCESSION OF JAMES II.--TYRCONNELL'S ADMINISTRATION.

From the accession of King James till his final flight from Ireland, in July, 1690, there elapsed an interval of five years and five months; a period fraught with consequences of the highest interest to this history. The new King was, on his accession, in his fifty-second year; he had served, as Duke of York, with credit both by land and sea, was an avowed Catholic, and married to a Catholic princess, the beautiful and unfortunate Mary of Modena.

Within a month from the proclamation of the King, Ormond quitted the government for the last time, leaving Primate Boyle, and Lord Granard, as Justices. In January, 1686, Lord Clarendon, son of the historian, assumed the government, in which he continued, till the 16th of March, 1687. The day following the national anniversary, Colonel Richard Talbot, Earl of Tyrconnell, a Catholic, and the former agent for the Catholics, was installed as Lord Deputy. Other events, connecting these with each other, had filled with astonishment and apprehension the ascendancy party.

James proceeded openly with what he hoped to make a counter-reformation of England, and to accomplish which he relied on France on the one hand, and Ireland on the other. In both cases he alarmed the fears and wounded the pride of England; but when he proceeded from one illegality to another, when he began to exercise a dispensing power above the laws--to instruct the judges, to menace the parliament, and imprison the bishops--the nobility, the commons, and the army gradually combined against him, and at last invited over the Prince of Orange, as the most capable vindicator of their outraged constitution.

The headlong King had a representative equally rash, in Tyrconnell. He was a man old enough to remember well the uprising of 1641, had lived in intimacy with James as Duke of York, was personally brave, well skilled in intrigue, but vain, loud-spoken, confident, and incapable of a high command in military affairs. The colonelcy of an Irish regiment, the earldom of Tyrconnell, and a seat in the secret council or cabinet of the King, were honours conferred on him during the year of James's accession. When Clarendon was named Lord-Lieutenant at the beginning of 1686, Tyrconnell was sent over with him as Lieutenant-General of the army. At his instigation, a proclamation was issued, that "all classes" of his Majesty's subjects might be allowed to serve in the army; and another, that all arms hitherto given out should be deposited, for greater security, at one of the King's stores provided for the purpose in each town or county. Thus that exclusively Protestant militia, which for twenty years had executed the Act of Settlement and the Act of Uniformity in every quarter of the kingdom, found themselves suddenly disarmed, and a new Catholic army rising on their ruins. The numbers disbanded are nowhere stated; they probably amounted to 10,000 or 15,000 men and very naturally they became warm partisans of the Williamite revolution. The recriminations which arose between the new and the old militia were not confined to the nicknames, Whig and Tory, or to the bandying of sarcasms on each others' origin; swords were not unfrequently drawn, and muskets discharged, even in the streets of Dublin, under the very walls of the Castle.

Through Tyrconnell's influence, a similar revolution had been wrought in the exclusive character of the courts of justice, and the corporations of towns, to that which remodelled the militia. Rice, Daly, and Nugent, were elevated to the bench during Lord Clarendon's time; the Corporation of Dublin having refused to surrender their exclusive charter, were summarily rejected by a *quo warranto*, issued in the exchequer; other towns were similarly treated, or induced to make surrender, and a new series of charters at once granted by James, entitling Catholics to the freedom of the boroughs, and the highest municipal offices. And now, for the first time in that generation, Catholic mayors and sheriffs, escorted by Catholic troops as guards of honour, were seen marching in open day to their own places of worship, to the dismay and astonishment of the ascendancy party. Not that all Protestants were excluded either from town councils, the militia, or the bench, but those only were elected or appointed who concurred in the new arrangements, and were, therefore, pretty certain to forfeit the confidence of their co-religionists in proportion as they deserved that of the Deputy. Topham and Coghill, Masters in Chancery, were deprived of their offices, and the Protestant Chancellor was arbitrarily removed to make way for Baron Rice, a Catholic. The exclusive character of Trinity College was next assailed, and though James did not venture to revoke the charter of Elizabeth, establishing communion with the Church of England as the test of fellowship, the internal administration was in several particulars interfered with, its plate was seized in the King's name under plea of being public property, and the annual parliamentary grant of 388 pounds was discontinued. These arbitrary acts filled the more judicious Catholics with apprehension, but gained the loud applause of the unreasoning multitude. Dr. Macguire, the successor of the martyred Plunkett, who felt in Ulster the rising tide of resistance, was among the signers of a memorial to the King, dutifully remonstrating against the violent proceedings of his Deputy. From Rome also, disapprobation was more than once expressed, but all without avail; neither James nor Talbot could be brought to reason. The Protestants of the eastern and southern towns and counties who could contrive to quit their homes, did so; hundreds fled to Holland to return in the ranks of the Prince of Orange; thousands fled to England, bringing with them their tale of oppression, embellished with all the bitter exaggeration of exiles; ten thousand removed from Leinster into Ulster, soon to recross the Boyne, under very different auspices. Very soon a close correspondence was established between the fugitives in Holland, England, and Ulster, and a powerful lever was thus placed in the hands of the Prince of Orange, to work the downfall of his uncle and father-in-law. But the best allies of William were, after all, the folly and fatuity of James. The importation of Irish troops, by entire battalions, gave the last and sorest wound to the national pride of England, and still further exasperated the hatred and contempt which his majesty's English regiments had begun to feel for their royal master.

Tyrconnell, during the eventful summer months when the revolution was ripening both in Holland and England, had taken, unknown even to James, a step of the gravest importance. To him the first intelligence of the preparations of William were carried by a ship from Amsterdam, and by him they were communicated to the infatuated King, who had laughed at them as too absurd for serious consideration. But the Irish ruler, fully believing his informants, and never deficient in audacity, had at once entered into a secret treaty with Louis XIV. to put Ireland under the protection of France, in the event of the Prince of Orange succeeding to the British throne. No proposition could more entirely suit the exigencies of Louis, of whom William was by far the ablest and most relentless enemy. The correspondence which has come to light in recent times, shows the importance which he attached to Tyrconnell's proposition--an importance still further enhanced by the direct but unsuccessful overture made to the earl by William himself, on landing in England, and before embarking in the actual invasion of Ireland.

William Henry, Prince of Orange, now about to enter on the scene, was in 1688 in the thirty-seventh year of his age. Fearless of danger, patient, silent, impervious to his enemies, rather a soldier than a statesman, indifferent in religion, and personally adverse to persecution for conscience' sake, his great and almost his only public passion was the humiliation of France through the instrumentality of a European coalition. As an anti-Gallican, as the representative of the most illustrious Protestant family in Europe, as allied by blood and marriage to their kings, he was a very fit and proper chief for the English revolutionists; but for the two former of these reasons he was just as naturally antipathetic to the Catholic and Celtic majority of the Irish. His designs had been long gradually maturing, when James's incredible imprudence hastened his movements. Twenty-four ships of war were assembled at Helvoetsluys; 7,000 sailors were put on board; all the veterans of the Netherlands were encamped at Nimeguen, where 6,000 recruits were added to their numbers. On the 5th of November, the anniversary of the gunpowder plot, "the Deliverer," as he was fondly called in England, landed at Torbay; on the 25th of December, James, deserted by his nobles, his army, and even his own unnatural children, arrived, a fugitive and a suppliant, at the court of France.

A few Irish incidents of this critical moment deserve mention. The mania against everything Irish took in England forms the most ludicrous and absurd. Wharton's doggerel refrain of Lillibullero, was heard in every circle outside the court; all London, lighted with torches, and marshalled under arms, awaited during the memorable "Irish night" the advent of the terrible and detested regiments brought over by Tyrconnell; some companies of these troops quartered in the country were fallen upon by ten times their numbers, and cut to pieces. Others, fighting and inquiring their way, forced a passage to Chester or Bristol, and obtained a passage home. They passed at sea, or encountered on the landing-places, multitudes of the Protestant Irish, men, women and children, flying in exactly the opposite direction. Tyrconnell was known to meditate the repeal of the Act of Settlement; the general rumour of a Protestant massacre fixed for the 9th of December, originated no one knew how, was spread about no one knew by whom. In vain the Lord Deputy tried to stay the panic--his assurance of protection, and the still better evidence of their own experience, which proved the Irish Catholics incapable of such a project, could not allay their terrors. They rushed into England by every port, and inflamed still more the hostility which already prevailed against King James.

In Ulster, David Cairnes of Knockmany, the Rev. John Kelso of Enniskillen, a Presbyterian, and Rev. George Walker of Donaghmore, an Anglican minister, were active instruments of the Prince of Orange. On the 7th of December the gates of Derry were shut by "the youthhood" against the Earl of Antrim and his Highlanders. Enniskillen was seized by a similar impulse of the popular will, and an association was quickly formed throughout Ulster in imitation of the English association which had invited over William, under the auspices of Lord Blaney, Sir Arthur Rawdon, Sir Clotworthy Skeffington, and others, "for the maintenance of the Protestant religion and the dependency of Ireland upon England." By these associates, Sligo, Coleraine, and the fort of Culmore, at the mouth of the Foyle, were seized for King William; while the Town Council of Derry, in order to gain time, despatched one ambassador with one set of instructions to Tyrconnell, and another, with a very different set, to "the Committee for Irish Affairs," which sat at Whitehall, under the presidency of the Earl of Shrewsbury.

CHAPTER V.

KING JAMES IN IRELAND--IRISH PARLIAMENT OF 1689.

A few days after his arrival in France, James despatched a messenger to Tyrconnell, with instructions expressing great anxiety as to the state of affairs in Ireland. "I am sure," wrote the fugitive monarch, "you will hold out to the utmost of your power, and I hope this king will so press the Hollanders, that the Prince of Orange will not have men to spare to attack you." All the aid he could obtain from Louis at the moment was 7,000 or 8,000 muskets, which were sent accordingly.

Events succeeded each other during the first half of the year 1689 with revolutionary rapidity. The conventions of England and Scotland, though far from being unanimous, declared by immense majorities, that James had abdicated, and that William and Mary should be offered the crowns of both kingdoms. In February, they were proclaimed as king and queen of "England, France, and Ireland," and in May, the Scottish commissioners brought them the tender of the crown of Scotland. The double heritage of the Stuart kings was thus, after nearly a century of possession, transferred by election to a kindred prince, to the exclusion of the direct descendants of the great champion of "the right divine," who first united under his sceptre the three kingdoms.

James, at the Court of France, was duly informed of all that passed at London and Edinburgh. He knew that he had powerful partizans in both conventions. The first fever of popular excitement once allayed, he marked with exultation the symptoms of reaction. There was much in the circumstances attending his flight to awaken popular sympathy, and to cast a veil over his errors. The pathetic picture drawn of parental suffering by the great dramatist in the character of King *Lear*, seemed realized to the life in the person of King James. Message followed message from the three kingdoms, urging him to return and place himself at the head of his faithful subjects in a war against the usurper. The French king approved of these recommendations, for in fighting James's battle he was fighting his own, and a squadron was prepared at Brest to carry the fugitive back to his dominions. Accompanied by his natural sons, the Duke of Berwick and the Grand Prior Fitzjames, by Lieutenant-Generals de Rosen and de Maumont, Majors-General de Pusignan and de Lery (or Geraldine), about a hundred officers of all ranks, and 1,200 veterans, James sailed from Brest, with a fleet of 33 vessels, and landed at Kinsale on the 12th day of March (*old style*). His reception by the Southern population was enthusiastic in the extreme. From Kinsale to Cork, from Cork to Dublin, his progress was accompanied by Gaelic songs and dances, by Latin orations, loyal addresses, and all the decorations with which a popular favourite can be welcomed. Nothing was remembered by that easily pacified people but his great misfortunes and his steady fidelity to his and their religion. Fifteen chaplains, nearly all Irish, accompanied him, and added to the delight of the populace; while many a long-absent soldier, now came back in the following of the king, to bless the sight of some aged parent or faithful lover. The royal entry into Dublin was the crowning pageant of this delusive restoration. With the tact and taste for such demonstrations hereditary in the citizens, the trades and arts were marshalled before him. Two venerable harpers played on their national instruments near the gate by which he entered; a number of religious in their robes, with a huge cross at their head, chanted as they went; forty young girls, dressed in white, danced the ancient **Rinka**, scattering flowers as they danced. The Earl of Tyrconnell, lately raised to a dukedom, the judges, the mayor and corporation, completed the procession, which marched over newly sanded streets, beneath arches of evergreens and windows hung with "tapestry and cloth of Arras." Arrived at the castle the sword of state was presented to him by the deputy, and the keys of the city by the recorder. At the inner entrance, the primate, Dr. Dominick Macguire, waited in his robes to conduct him to the chapel, lately erected by Tyrconnell, where *Te Deum* was solemnly sung. But of all the incidents of that striking ceremonial, nothing more powerfully impressed the popular imagination than the green flag floating from the main tower of the castle, bearing the significant inscription--"***Now or Never--Now and Forever***."

A fortnight was devoted by James in Dublin to daily and nightly councils and receptions. The chief advisers who formed his court were the Count d'Avaux, Ambassador of France, the Earl of Melfort, principal Secretary of State, the Duke of Tyrconnell, Lieutenant-General Lord Mountcashel, Chief Justice Nugent, and the superior officers of the army, French and Irish. One of the first things resolved upon at Dublin was the appointment of the gallant Viscount Dundee as Lieutenant-General in Scotland--and the despatch to his assistance of an Irish auxiliary force, which served under that renowned chief with as much honour as their predecessors had served under Montrose. Communications were also opened through the Bishop of Chester with the west of England Jacobites, always numerous in Cheshire, Shropshire, and other counties nearest to Ireland. Certain changes were then made in the Privy Council; Chief Justice Keating's attendance was dispensed with as one opposed to the new policy, but his judicial functions were left untouched. Dr. Cartwright, Bishop of Chester, and the French Ambassador were sworn in, and writs were issued convoking the Irish Parliament for the 7th day of May following.

Intermitting, for the present, the military events which marked the early months of the year, we will follow the acts and deliberations of King James's Parliament of 1689. The Houses met, according to summons, at the appointed time, in the building known as "the Inns of Court," within a stone's throw of the castle. There were present 228 Commoners, and 46 members of the Upper House. In the Lords several Protestant noblemen and prelates took their seats, and some Catholic peers of ancient date, whose attainders had been reversed, were seen for the first time in that generation in the front rank of their order. In the Lower House the University and a few other constituencies were represented by Protestants, but the overwhelming majority were Catholics, either of Norman or Milesian origin. The King made a judicious opening speech, declaring his intention to uphold the rights of property, and to establish liberty of conscience alike for Protestant and Catholic. He referred to the distressed state of trade and manufactures, and recommended to the attention of the Houses, those who had been unjustly deprived of their estates under the "Act of Settlement."

Three measures passed by this Parliament entitle its members to be enrolled among the chief assertors of civil and religious liberty. One was the "Act for establishing Liberty of Conscience," followed by the supplemental act that all persons should pay tithes only to the clergy of their own communion. An act abolishing writs of error and appeal into England, established the judicial independence of Ireland; but a still more necessary measure repealing Poyning's Law, was defeated through the personal hostility of the King. An act repealing the Act of Settlement was also passed, under protest from the Protestant Lords, and received the royal sanction. A bill to establish Inns of Court, for the education of Irish law students, was, however, rejected by the King, and lost; an "Act of Attainder," against persons in arms against the Sovereign, whose estates lay in Ireland, was adopted. Whatever may be the bias of historians, it cannot be denied that this Parliament showed a spirit worthy of the representatives of a free people. "Though Papists," says Mr. Grattan, our highest parliamentary authority, "they were not slaves; they wrung a constitution from King James before they accompanied him to the field."

The King, unfortunately, had not abandoned the arbitrary principles of his family, even in his worst adversity. His interference with the discussions on Poyning's Law, and the Inns of Court bill, had shocked some of his most devoted adherents. But he proceeded from obstructive to active despotism. He doubled, by his mere proclamation, the enormous subsidy of 20,000 pounds monthly voted him by the Houses. He established, by the same authority, a bank, and decreed in his own name a bank restriction act. He debased the coinage, and established a fixed scale of prices to be observed by all merchants and traders. In one respect--but in one only--he grossly violated his own professed purpose of establishing liberty of conscience, by endeavouring to force fellows and scholars on the University of Dublin contrary to its statutes. He even went so far as to appoint a provost and librarian without consent of the senate. However we may condemn the exclusiveness of the College, this was not the way to correct it; bigotry on the one hand, will not justify despotism on the other.

More justifiable was the interference of the King for the restoration of rural schools and churches, and the decent maintenance of the clergy and bishops. His appointments to the bench were also, with one or two exceptions, men of the very highest character. "The administration of justice during this brief period," says Dr. Cooke Taylor, "deserves the highest praise. With the exception of Nugent and Fritton, the Irish judges would have been an honour to any bench."

CHAPTER VI.

THE REVOLUTIONARY WAR--CAMPAIGN OF 1689--SIEGES OF DERRY AND ENNISKILLEN.

When Tyrconnell met the King at Cork, he gave his Majesty a plain account of the posture of military affairs. In Ulster, Lieutenant-General Richard Hamilton, at the head of 2,500 regular troops, was holding the rebels in check, from Charlemont to Coleraine; in Munster, Lieutenant-General Justin McCarthy, Lord Mountcashel, had taken Bandon and Castlemartyr; throughout the four provinces, the Catholics, to the number of fifty regiments (probably 30,000 men), had volunteered their services; but for all these volunteers he had only 20,000 old arms of all kinds, not over 1,000 of which were found really valuable. There were besides these, regiments of horse, Tyrconnell's, Russell's, and Galmony's, and one of dragoons, eight small pieces of artillery, but neither stores in the magazines, nor cash in the chest. While at Cork, Tyrconnell, in return for his great exertions, was created a Duke, and General-in-Chief, with De Rosen as second in command.

A week before James reached Dublin, Hamilton had beaten the rebels at Dromore, and driven them in on Coleraine, from before which he wrote urgently for reinforcements. On receipt of this communication, the Council exhibited, for the first time, those radical differences of opinion, amounting almost to factious opposition, which crippled all King James's movements at this period. One party strenuously urged that the King himself should march northward with such troops as could be spared; that his personal appearance before Derry, would immediately occasion the surrender of that city, and that he might in a few weeks, finish in person the campaign of Ulster. Another, at whose head was Tyrconnell, endeavoured to dissuade his Majesty from this course, but he at length decided in favour of the plan of Melfort and his friends. Accordingly, he marched out of Dublin, amid torrents of April rain, on the eighth of that month, intending to form a junction with Hamilton, at Strabane, and thence to advance to Derry. The march was a weary one through a country stripped bare of every sign of life, and desolate beyond description. A week was spent between Dublin and Omagh; at Omagh news of an English fleet on the Foyle caused the King to retrace his steps hastily to Charlemont. At Charlemont, however, intelligence of fresh successes gained by Hamilton and De Rosen, at Cladyford and Strabane, came to restore his confidence; he instantly set forward, despite the tempestuous weather, and the almost impassable roads, and on the eighteenth reached the Irish camp at Johnstown, within four or five miles of Derry.

It was now four months since "the youthhood" of Derry had shut the Watergate against Lord Antrim's regiment, and established within their walls a strange sort of government, including eighteen clergymen and the town democracy. The military command remained with Lieutenant-Colonel Lundy, of Mountjoy's regiment, but the actual government of the town was vested, first, in "Governor" Baker, and afterwards in the Reverend George Walker, rector of Donaghmore, best known to us as **Governor** Walker. The Town Council had despatched Mr. Cairnes, and subsequently Captain Hamilton, founder of the Abercorn peerage, to England for succour, and had openly proclaimed William and Mary as King and Queen. Defensive works were added, where necessary, and on the very day of the affair of Cladyford, 480 barrels of gunpowder were landed from English ships and conveyed within the walls.

As the Royalist forces concentrated towards Derry, the chiefs of the Protestant Association fell back before them, each bringing to its garrison the contribution of his own followers. From the valley of the Bann, over the rugged summits of Carntogher, from the glens of Donegal, and the western sea coast round to Mayo, troops of the fugitives hurried to the strong town of the London traders, as to a city of refuge. Enniskillen alone, resolute in its insular situation, and in a courage akin to that which actuated the defenders of Derry, stood as an outpost of the main object of attack, and delayed the junction of the Royalists under Mountcashel with those under Hamilton and De Rosen. Coleraine was abandoned. Captain Murray, the commander of Culmore, forced his way at the head of 1,500 men into Derry, contrary to the wishes of the vacillating and suspected Lundy, and, from the moment of his arrival, infused his own determined spirit into all ranks of the inhabitants.

Those who had advised King James to present himself in person before the Protestant stronghold, had not acted altogether, upon presumption. It is certain that there were Jacobites, even in Derry. Lundy, the governor, either despairing of its defence, or undecided in his allegiance between James and William, had opened a correspondence with Hamilton and De Rosen. But the true answer of the brave townsmen, when the King advanced too near their walls, was a cannon shot which killed one of his staff, and the cry of "No Surrender" thundered from the walls. James, awakened from his self-complacent dream by this unexpected reception, returned to Dublin, to open his Parliament, leaving General Hamilton to continue the siege. Colonel Lundy, distrusted, overruled, and menaced, escaped over the walls by night, disguised as a common labourer, and the party of Murray, Baker, Walker, and Cairnes, reigned supreme.

The story of the siege of Derry--of the heroic constancy of its defenders--of the atrocities of De Rosen and Galmoy--the clemency of Maumont--the forbearance of Hamilton--the struggles for supremacy among its magnates--the turbulence of the townsfolk--the joyful raising of the siege--all these have worthily employed some of the most eloquent pens in our language. The relief came by the breaking of the boom across the harbour's mouth on the last day of July; the bombardment had commenced on the 21st of April; the gates had been shut on the 7th of December. The actual siege had lasted above three months, and the blockade about three weeks. The destruction of life on both sides has never been definitely stated. The besieged admit a loss of 4,000 men; the besiegers of 6,000. The want of siege guns in the Jacobite camp is admitted by both parties, but, nevertheless, the defence of the place well deserves to be celebrated, as it has been by an imperial historian, "as the most memorable in British annals."

Scarcely inferior in interest and importance to the siege of Derry, was the spirited defence of Enniskillen. That fine old town, once the seat of the noble family of Maguire, is naturally dyked and moated round about, by the waters of Lough Erne. In December, '88, it had closed its gates, and barricaded its causeways to keep out a Jacobite garrison. In March, on Lord Galmoy's approach, all the outlying garrisons, in Fermanagh and Cavan, had destroyed their posts, and gathered into Enniskillen. The cruel and faithless Galmoy, instead of inspiring terror into the united garrison, only increased their determination to die in the breach. So strong in position and numbers did they find themselves, with the absolute command of the lower Lough Erne to bring in their supplies, that in April they sent off a detachment to the relief of Derry, and in the months of May and June, made several successful forays to Ballincarrig, Omagh, and Belturbet. In July, provided with a fresh supply of ammunition from the fleet intended for the relief of Derry, they beat up the Duke of Berwick's quarters at Trellick, but were repulsed with some loss. The Duke being soon after recalled to join De Rosen, the siege of Enniskillen was committed to Lord Mountcashel, under whom, as commander of the cavalry, served Count Anthony Hamilton, author of the witty but licentious "Memoirs of Grammont," and other distinguished officers. Mountcashel's whole force consisted of three regiments of foot, two of dragoons, and some horse; but he expected to be joined by Colonel Sarsfield from Sligo, and Berwick from Derry. The besieged had drawn four regiments of foot from Cavan alone, and were probably twice that number in all; and they had, in Colonels Wolseley and Berry, able and energetic officers. The Enniskilleners did not await the attack within their fortress. At Lisnaskea, under Berry, they repulsed the advanced guard of the Jacobites under Anthony Hamilton; and the same day--the day of the relief of Derry--their whole force were brought into action with Mountcashel's at Newtown-Butler. To the cry of "No Popery," Wolseley led them into an action, the most considerable yet fought. The raw southern levies on the Royalist side, were routed by the hardy Enniskilleners long familiar with the use of arms, and well acquainted with every inch of the ground; 2,000 of them were left on the field; 400 prisoners were taken, among them dangerously, but not mortally wounded, was the Lieutenant-General himself.

    The month of August was a month of general rejoicing for the Williamites of Ulster, De Rosen and Berwick had retreated from Deny; Sarsfield, on his way to join Mountcashel, fell back to Sligo on hearing of his defeat at Newtown-Butler; Culmore, Coleraine, and Ballyshannon, were retaken and well supplied; fugitives returned triumphantly to their homes, in Cavan, Fermanagh, Tyrone, and Armagh. A panic created by false reports spread among his troops at Sligo, compelled Sarsfield to fall still further back to Athlone. Six months after his arrival, with the exception of the forts of Charlemont and Carrickfergus, King James no longer possessed a garrison in that province, which had been bestowed by his grandfather upon the ancestors of those who now unanimously rejected and resisted him.

    The fall of the gallant Dundee in the battle of Killicrankie, five days before the relief of Derry, freed King William from immediate anxiety on the side of Scotland, and enabled him to concentrate his whole disposable force on Ireland. On the 13th of August, an army of eighteen regiments of foot, and four or five of horse, under the Marshal Duke de Schomberg, with Count Solmes as second in command, sailed into Belfast Lough, and took possession of the town. On the 20th, the Marshal opened a fierce cannonade on Carrickfergus, defended by Colonels McCarthy More and Cormac O'Neil, while the fleet bombarded it from sea. After eight days' incessant cannonade, the garrison surrendered on honourable terms, and Schomberg faced southward towards Dublin. Brave, and long experienced, the aged Duke moved according to the cautious maxims of the military school in which he had been educated. Had he advanced rapidly on the capital, James must have fallen back, as De Rosen advised, on the line of the Shannon; but O'Regan, at Charlemont, and Berwick, at Newry, seemed to him obstacles so serious, that nearly a month was wasted in advancing from Belfast to Dundalk, where he entrenched himself in September, and went into whiter quarters. Here a terrible dysentery broke out among his troops, said to have been introduced by some soldiers from Derry, and so destructive were its ravages, that there were hardly left healthy men enough to bury the dead. Several of the French Catholics under his command, also, deserted to James, who, from his head-quarters at Drogheda, offered every inducement to the deserters. Others discovered in the attempt were tried and hanged, and others, still suspected of similar designs, were marched down to Carlingford, and shipped for England. In November, James returned from Drogheda to Dublin, much elated that Duke Schomberg, whose fatal camp at Dundalk he had in vain attempted to raise, had shrunk from meeting him in the field.

CHAPTER VII.

THE REVOLUTIONARY WAR--CAMPAIGN OF 1690--BATTLE OF THE BOYNE--ITS CONSEQUENCES--THE SIEGES OF ATHLONE AND LIMERICK.

The armies now destined to combat for two kings on Irish soil were strongly marked by those distinctions of race and religion which add bitterness to struggles for power, while they present striking contrasts to the eye of the painter of military life and manners. King James's troops were chiefly Celtic and Catholic. There were four regiments commanded by O'Neils, two by O'Briens, two by O'Kellys, one each by McCarthy More, Maguire, O'More, O'Donnell, McMahon, and Magennis, principally recruited among their own clansmen. There were also the regiments of Sarsfield, Nugent, De Courcy, Fitzgerald, Grace, and Burke, chiefly Celts, in the rank and file. On the other hand, Schomberg led into the field the famous blue Dutch and white Dutch regiments; the Huguenot regiments of Schomberg, La Millinier, Du Cambon, and La Callimotte; the English regiments of Lords Devonshire, Delamere, Lovelace, Sir John Lanier, Colonels Langston, Villiers, and others; the Anglo-Irish regiments of Lords Meath, Roscommon, Kingston, and Drogheda; with the Ulstermen, under Brigadier Wolseley, Colonels Gustavus Hamilton, Mitchelburne, Loyd, White, St. Johns, and Tiffany. Some important changes had taken place on both sides during the winter months. D'Avaux and De Rosen had been recalled at James's request; Mountcashel, at the head of the first Franco-Irish brigade, had been exchanged for 6,000 French, under De Lauzan, who arrived the following March in the double character of general and ambassador. The report that William was to command in person in the next campaign, was, of itself, an indication pregnant with other changes to the minds of his adherents.

Their abundant supplies of military stores from England, wafted from every port upon the channel, where James had not a keel afloat, enabled the Williamite army to take the initiative in the campaign of 1690. At Cavan, Brigadier Wolseley repulsed the Duke of Berwick, with the loss of 200 men and some valuable officers. But the chief incident preceding William's arrival was the siege of Charlemont. This siege, which commenced apparently in the previous autumn, had continued during several months, till the garrison were literally starved out, in May. The famished survivors were kindly treated, by order of Schomberg, and their gallant and eccentric chief, O'Regan, was knighted by the King, for his persistent resistance. A month from the day on which Charlemont fell, (June 14th), William landed at Carrickfergus, accompanied by Prince George of Denmark, the Duke of Wurtemburg, the Prince of Hesse-Darmstadt, the second and last Duke of Ormond, Major-General Mackay, the Earls of Oxford, Portland, Scarborough, and Manchester, General Douglas, and other distinguished British and foreign officers. At Belfast, his first head-quarters, he ascertained the forces at his disposal to be upwards of 40,000 men, composed of "a strange medley of all nations"--Scandinavians, Swiss, Dutch, Prussians, Huguenot-French, English, Scotch, "Scotch-Irish," and Anglo-Irish. Perhaps the most extraordinary element in that strange medley was the Danish contingent of horse and foot. Irish tradition and Irish prophecy still teemed with tales of terror and predictions of evil at the hands of the Danes, while these hardy mercenaries observed, with grim satisfaction, that the memory of their fierce ancestors had not become extinct after the lapse of twenty generations. At the Boyne, and at Limerick, they could not conceal their exultation as they encamped on some of the very earthworks raised by men of their race seven centuries before, and it must be admitted they vindicated their descent, both by their courage and their cruelty.

On the 16th of June, James, informed of William's arrival, marched northward at the head of 20,000 men, French and Irish, to meet him. On the 22nd, James was at Dundalk and William at Newry; as the latter advanced, the Jacobites retired, and finally chose their ground at the Boyne, resolved to hazard a battle, for the preservation of Dublin, and the safety of the province of Leinster.

On the last day of June, the hostile forces confronted each other at the Boyne. The gentle, legendary river, wreathed in all the glory of its abundant foliage, was startled with the cannonade from the northern bank, which continued through the long summer's evening, and woke the early echoes of the morrow. William, strong in his veteran ranks, welcomed the battle; James, strong in his defensive position, and the goodness of his cause, awaited it with confidence. On the northern bank near to the ford of Oldbridge, William, with his chief officers, breakfasting on the turf, nearly lost his life from a sudden discharge of cannon; but he was quickly in the saddle, at all points reviewing his army. James, on the hill of Donore, looked down on his devoted defenders, through whose ranks rode Tyrconnell, lame and ill, the youthful Berwick, the adventurous Lauzan, and the beloved Sarsfield--everywhere received with cordial acclamations. The battle commenced at the ford of Oldbridge, between Sir Neil O'Neil, and the younger Schomberg; O'Neil fell mortally wounded, and the ford was forced. By this ford, William ordered his centre to advance under the elder Schomberg, as the hour of noon approached, while he himself moved with the left across the river, nearer to Drogheda. Lauzan, with Sarsfield's horse, dreading to be outflanked, had galloped to guard the bridge of Slane, five miles higher up the stream, where alone a flank movement was possible. The battle was now transferred from the gunners to the swordsmen and pikemen--from the banks to the fords and borders of the river, William, on the extreme left, swam his horse across, in imminent danger; Schomberg and Callimotte fell in the centre, mortally wounded. News was brought to William, that Dr. Walker--recently appointed to the See of Derry--had also fallen, "What brought him there?" was the natural comment of the soldier-prince. After seven hours' fighting the Irish fell back on Duleek, in good order. The assailants admitted five hundred killed, and as many wounded; the defenders were said to have lost from one thousand to fifteen hundred men--less than at Newtown-Butler. The carnage, compared with some great battles of that age, was inconsiderable, but the political consequences were momentous. The next day, the garrison of Drogheda, one thousand three hundred strong, surrendered; in another week, William was in Dublin, and James, terrified by the reports which had reached him, was *en route* for France. It is hardly an exaggeration to say, that the fate of Europe was decided by the result of the battle of the Boyne. At Paris, at the Hague, at Vienna, at Rome, at Madrid, nothing was talked of but the great victory of the Prince of Orange over Louis and James. It is one of the strangest complications of history that the vanquished Irish Catholics seem to have been never once thought of by Spain, Austria, or the Pope. In the greater issues of the European coalition against France, their interests, and their very existence, were for the moment forgotten.

The defeat at the Boyne, and the surrender of Dublin, uncovered the entire province of Leinster, Kilkenny, Wexford, Waterford, Duncannon, Clonmel, and other places of less importance, surrendered within six weeks. The line of the Shannon was fallen back upon by the Irish, and the points of attack and defence were now shifted to Athlone and Limerick. What Enniskillen and Derry had been, in the previous year, to the Williamite party in the north, cities of refuge, and strongholds of hope, these two towns upon the Shannon had now become, by the fortune of war, to King James's adherents.

On the 17th of July, General Douglas appeared before Athlone, and summoned it to surrender. The veteran commandant, Colonel Richard Grace, a Confederate of 1641, having destroyed the bridge, and the suburbs on the Leinster side of the Shannon, replied by discharging his pistol over the head of the drummer who delivered the message. Douglas attempted to cross the river at Lanesborough, but found the ford strongly guarded by one of Grace's outposts; after a week's ineffectual bombardment, he withdrew from before Athlone, and proceeded to Limerick, ravaging and slaying as he went.

Limerick had at first been abandoned by the French under Lauzan, as utterly indefensible. That gay intriguer desired nothing so much as to follow the King to France, while Tyrconnell, broken down with physical suffering and mental anxiety, feebly concurred in his opinion. They accordingly departed for Galway, leaving the city to its fate, and, happily for the national reputation, to bolder counsels than their own. De Boisseleau did not underrate the character of the Irish levies, who had retreated before twice their numbers at the Boyne; he declared himself willing to remain, and, sustained by Sarsfield, he was chosen as commandant. More than ten thousand foot had gathered "as if by instinct" to that city, and on the Clare side Sarsfield still kept together his cavalry, at whose head he rode to Galway and brought back. Tyrconnell. On the 9th of August, William, confident of an easy victory, appeared before the town, but more than twelve months were to elapse before all his power could reduce those mouldering walls, which the fugitive French ambassador had declared "might be taken with roasted apples."

An exploit, planned and executed by Sarsfield the day succeeding William's arrival, saved the city for another year, and raised that officer to the highest pitch of popularity. Along the Clare side of the Shannon, under cover of the night, he galloped as fast as horse could carry him, at the head of his dragoons, and crossed the river at Killaloe. One Manus O'Brien, a Protestant of Clare, who had encountered the flying horsemen, and learned enough to suspect their design, hastened to William's camp with the news, but he was at first laughed at for his pains. William, however, never despising any precaution in war, despatched Sir John Lanier with 500 horse to protect his siege-train, then seven miles in the rear, on the road between Limerick and Cashel. Sarsfield, however, was too quick for Sir John. The day after he had crossed at Killaloe he kept his men *perdu* in the hilly country, and the next night swooped down upon the convoy in charge of the siege-train, who were quietly sleeping round the ruined church of Ballanedy. The sentinels were sabred at their posts, the guards, half-dressed, fled in terror or were speedily killed. The gun-carriages were quickly yoked, and drawn together to a convenient place, where, planted in pits with ammunition, they were, with two exceptions, successfully blown to atoms. Lanier arrived within view of the terrific scene in time to feel its stunning effects. The ground for miles round shook as from an earthquake; the glare and roar of the explosion were felt in William's camp, and through the beleaguered city. On the morrow, all was known. Sarsfield was safely back in his old encampment, without the loss of a single man; Limerick was in an uproar of delight, while William's army, to the lowest rank, felt the depression of so unexpected a blow. A week later, however, the provident prince had a new siege-train of thirty-six guns and four mortars brought up from Waterford, pouring red-hot shot on the devoted city. Another week--on the 27th of August--a gap having been made in the walls near Saint John's gate, a storming party of the English guards, the Anglo-Irish, Prussians, and Danes, was launched into the breach. After an action of uncommon fierceness and determination on both sides, the besiegers retired with the loss of 30 officers, and 800 men killed, and 1,200 wounded. The besieged admitted 400 killed--their wounded were not counted. Four days later, William abandoned the siege, retreated to Waterford, and embarked for England, with Prince George of Denmark, the Dukes of Wurtemburg and Ormond, and others of his principal adherents. Tyrconnell, labouring with the illness of which he soon after died, took advantage of the honourable pause thus obtained, to proceed on his interrupted voyage to Prance, accompanied by the ambassador. Before leaving, however, the young

Duke of Berwick was named in his stead as Commander-in-Chief; Fitton, Nagle, and Plowden, as Lords Justices; sixteen "senators" were to form a sort of Cabinet, and Sarsfield to be second in military command. His enemies declared that Tyrconnell retired from the contest because his early spirit and courage had failed him; he himself asserted that his object was to procure sufficient succours from King Louis, to give a decisive issue to the war. His subsequent negotiations at Paris proved that though his bodily health might be wretched, his ingenuity and readiness of resource had not deserted him. He justified himself both with James and Louis, outwitted Lauzan, propitiated Louvois, disarmed the prejudices of the English Jacobites, and, in short, placed the military relations of France and Ireland on a footing they had never hitherto sustained. The expedition of the following spring, under command of Marshal Saint Ruth, was mainly procured by his able diplomacy, and though he returned to Ireland to survive but a few weeks the disastrous day of Aughrim, it is impossible from the Irish point of view, not to recall with admiration, mixed indeed with alloy, but still with largely prevailing admiration, the extraordinary energy, buoyancy and talents of Richard, Duke of Tyrconnell.

CHAPTER VIII.

THE WINTER OF 1690-91,

The Jacobite party in England were not slow to exaggerate the extent of William's losses before Athlone and Limerick. The national susceptibility was consoled by the ready reflection, that if the beaten troops were partly English, the commanders were mainly foreigners. A native hero was needed, and was found in the person of Marlborough, a captain, whose name was destined to eclipse every other English reputation of that age. At his suggestion an expedition was fitted out against Cork, Kinsale, and other ports of the south of Ireland, and the command, though not without some secret unwillingness on William's part, committed to him. On the 23rd of September, at the head of 8,000 fresh troops, amply supplied with all necessary munitions, Marlborough assaulted Cork. After five days' bombardment, in which the Duke of Grafton, and other officers and men were slain, the Governor, McEligot, capitulated on conditions, which, in spite of all Marlborough's exertions, were flagrantly violated. The old town of Kinsale was at once abandoned as untenable the same day, and the new fort, at the entrance to the harbour, was surrendered after a fortnight's cannonade. Covered with glory from a five weeks' campaign, Marlborough returned to England to receive the acclamations of the people and the most gracious compliments of the prince.

Berwick and Sarsfield on the one side and Ginkle and Lanier on the other, kept up the winter campaign till an advanced period, on both banks of the Shannon. About the middle of September, the former made a dash over the bridge of Banagher, against Birr, or Parsonstown, the family borough of the famous *Undertaker*. The English, in great force, under Lanier, Kirke, and Douglas, hastened to its relief, and the Irish fell back to Banagher. To destroy "that convenient pass" became now the object of one party, to protect it, of the other. After some skirmishing and manoeuvring on both sides, the disputed bridge was left in Irish possession, and the English fell back to the borough and castle of Sir Lawrence Parsons. During the siege of the new fort at Kinsale, Berwick and Sarsfield advanced as far as Kilmallock to its relief, but finding themselves so inferior in numbers to Marlborough, they were unwillingly compelled to leave its brave defenders to their fate,

Although the Duke of Berwick was the nominal Commander-in-Chief, his youth, and the distractions incident to youth, left the more mature and popular Sarsfield the possession of real power, both civil and military. Every fortunate accident had combined to elevate that gallant cavalry officer into the position of national leadership.

He was the son of a member of the Irish Commons, proscribed for his patriotism and religion in 1641, by Anna O'Moore, daughter of the organizer of the Catholic Confederation. He was a Catholic in religion, spoke Gaelic as easily as English, was brave, impulsive; handsome, and generous to a fault, like the men he led. In Tyrconnell's absence every sincere lover of the country came to him with intelligence, and looked to him for direction. Early in November he learned through his patriotic spies the intention of the Williamites to force the passage of the Shannon in the depth of winter. On the last day of December, accordingly, they marched in great force under Kirke and Lanier to Jonesboro', and under Douglas to Jamestown. At both points they found the indefatigable Sarsfield fully prepared for them, and after a fortnight's intense suffering from exposure to the weather, were glad to get back again to their snug quarters at Parsonstown.

Early in February Tyrconnell landed at Limerick with a French fleet, escorted by three vessels of war, and laden with provisions, but bringing few arms and no reinforcements. He had brought over, however, 14,000 golden louis, which were found of the utmost service in re-clothing the army, besides 10,000 more which he had deposited at Brest to purchase oatmeal for subsequent shipment. He also brought promises of military assistance on a scale far beyond anything France had yet afforded. It is almost needless to say he was received at Galway and Limerick with an enthusiasm which silenced, if it did not confute, his political enemies, both in Ireland and France.

During his absence intrigues and factions had been rifer than ever in the Jacobite ranks. Sarsfield had discovered that the English movement on the Shannon in December was partly hastened by foolish or treacherous correspondence among his own associates. Lord Riverston and his brother were removed from the Senate, or Council of Sixteen--four from each province--and Judge Daly, ancestor of the Dunsandle family, was placed under arrest at Galway. The youthful Berwick sometimes complained that he was tutored and overruled by Sarsfield; but though the impetuous soldier may occasionally have forgotten the lessons learned in courts, his activity seems to have been the greatest, his information the best, his advice the most disinterested, and his fortitude the highest of any member of the council. By the time of Tyrconnell's return he had grown to a height of popularity and power, which could not well brook a superior either in the cabinet or the camp.

On the arrival of the Lord Lieutenant, who was also Commander-in-Chief, the ambition of Sarsfield was gratified by the rank of Earl of Lucan, a title drawn from that pleasant hamlet, in the valley of the Liffey, where he had learned to lisp the catechism of a patriot at the knee of Anna O'Moore. But his real power was much diminished. Tyrconnell, Berwick, Sir Richard Nagle, who had succeeded the Earl of Melfort as chief secretary for King James, all ranked before him at the board, and when Saint Ruth arrived to take command-in-chief, he might fairly have complained that he was deprived of the chief reward to which he had looked forward.

The weary winter and the drenching spring months wore away, and the Williamite troops, sorely afflicted by disease, hugged their tents and huts. Some relief was sent by sea to the Jacobite garrison of Sligo, commanded by the stout old Sir Teague O'Regan, the former defender of Charlemont. Athlone, too, received some succours, and the line of the Shannon was still unbroken from Slieve-an-iron to the sea. But still the promised French assistance was delayed. Men were beginning to doubt both King Louis and King James, when, at length at the beginning of May, the French ships were signalled from the cliffs of Kerry. On the 8th, the Sieur de Saint Ruth, with Generals D'Usson and De Tesse, landed at Limerick, and assisted at a solemn *Te Deum* in St. Mary's Cathedral. They brought considerable supplies of clothes, provisions, and ammunitions, but neither veterans to swell the ranks, nor money to replenish the chest. Saint Ruth entered eagerly upon the discharge of his duties as generalissimo, while Sarsfield continued the nominal second in command.

CHAPTER IX.

THE REVOLUTIONARY WAR--CAMPAIGN OF 1691--BATTLE OF AUGHRIM--CAPITULATION OF LIMERICK.

S aint Ruth, with absolute powers, found himself placed at the head of from 20,000 to 25,000 men, in the field or in garrison, regular or irregular, but all, with hardly an exception, Irish. His and Tyrconnell's recent supplies had sufficed to renew the clothing and equipment of the greater part of the number, but the whole contents of the army chest, the golden hinge on which war moves, was estimated in the beginning of May to afford to each soldier only "a penny a day for three weeks." He had under him some of the best officers that France could spare, or Ireland produce, and he had with him the hearts of nine-tenths of the natives of the country.

A singular illustration of the popular feeling occurred the previous August. The Milesian Irish had cherished the belief ever since the disastrous day of Kinsale, that an O'Donnell from Spain, having on his shoulder a red mark (***ball derg***), would return to free them from the English yoke, in a great battle near Limerick. Accordingly, when a representative of the Spanish O'Donnells actually appeared at Limerick, bearing as we know many of his family have done, even to our day, the unmistakable red mark of the ancient Tyrconnell line, immense numbers of the country people who had held aloof from the Jacobite cause, obeyed the voice of prophecy, and flocked round the Celtic deliverer. From 7,000 to 8,000 recruits were soon at his disposal, and it was not without bitter indignation that the chief, so enthusiastically received, saw regiment after regiment drafted from among his followers, and transferred to other commanders. Bred up a Spanish subject--the third in descent from an Irish prince--it is not to be wondered at that he regarded the *Irish* cause as all in all, and the interests of King James as entirely secondary. He could hardly consider himself as bound in allegiance to that king; he was in no way indebted to him or his family, and if we learn that when the war grew desperate, but before it was ended, he had entered into a separate treaty for himself and his adherents, with William's generals, we must remember, before we condemn him, that we are speaking of an Hiberno-Spaniard, to whom the house of Stuart was no more sacred than the house of Orange.

The Williamite army rendezvoused at Mullingar towards the end of May, under Generals De Ginkle, Talmash and Mackay. On the 7th of June, they moved in the direction of Athlone, 18,000 strong, "the ranks one blaze of scarlet, and the artillery such as had never before been seen in Ireland." The capture of Ballymore Castle, in West-Meath, detained them ten days; on the 19th, joined by the Duke of Wurtemburg, the Prince of Hesse and the Count of Nassau, with 7,000 foreign mercenaries, the whole sat down before the English town of Athlone, which Saint Ruth, contrary to his Irish advisers, resolved to defend. In twenty-four hours those exposed outworks abandoned by the veteran Grace the previous year, fell, and the bombardment of the Irish town on the opposite or Connaught bank, commenced. For ten days--from the 20th to the 30th of June--that fearful cannonade continued. Storey, the Williamite chaplain, to whom we are indebted for many valuable particulars of this war, states that the besiegers fired above 12,000 cannon shot, 600 shells and many tons of stone, into the place. Fifty tons of powder were burned in the bombardment. The castle, an imposing but lofty and antique structure, windowed as much for a residence as a fortress, tumbled into ruins; the bridge was broken down and impassable; the town a heap of rubbish, where two men could no longer walk abreast. But the Shannon had diminished in volume as the summer advanced, and three Danes employed for that purpose found a ford above the bridge, and at six o'clock on the evening of the last day of June, 2,000 picked men, headed by Gustavus Hamilton's grenadiers, dashed into the ford at the stroke of a bell. At the same instant all the English batteries on the Leinster side opened on the Irish town, wrapping the river in smoke, and distracting the attention of the besiegers. Saint Ruth was, at this critical moment, at his camp two miles off, and D'Usson, the commandant, was also absent from his post. In half an hour the Williamites were masters of the heap of rubbish which had once been Athlone, with a loss of less than fifty men killed and wounded. For this bold and successful movement De Ginkle was created Earl of Athlone, and his chief officers were justly ennobled. Saint Ruth, over-confident, in a strange country, withdrew to Ballinasloe, behind the river Suck, and prepared to risk everything on the hazard of a pitched battle.

De Ginkle moved slowly from Athlone in pursuit of his enemy. On the morning of the 11th of July, as the early haze lifted itself in wreaths from the landscape, he found himself within range of the Irish, drawn up, north and south, on the upland of Kilcommodan hill, with a morass on either flank, through which ran two narrow causeways--on the right, "the pass of Urrachree," on the left, the causeway leading to the little village of Aughrim. Saint Ruth's force must have numbered from 15,000 to 20,000 men, with nine field-pieces; De Ginkle commanded from 25,000 to 30,000, with four batteries--two of which mounted six guns each. During the entire day, attack after attack, in the direction of Urrachree or of Aughrim was repulsed, and the assailants were about to retire in despair. As the sun sank low, a last desperate attempt was made with equal ill success. "Now, my children," cried the elated Saint Ruth, "the day is ours! Now I shall drive them back to the walls of Dublin!" At that moment he fell by a cannon shot to the earth, and stayed the advancing tide of victory. The enemy marked the check, halted, rallied and returned. Sarsfield, who had not been entrusted with his leader's plan of action, was unable to remedy the mischief which ensued. Victory arrested was converted into defeat. The sun went down on Aughrim, and the last great Irish battle between the Reformed and Roman religions. Four thousand of the Catholics were killed and wounded, and three thousand of the Protestants littered the field. Above five hundred prisoners, with thirty-two pairs of colours, eleven standards, and a large quantity of small arms, fell into the hands of the victors. One portion of the fugitive survivors fled to Galway, the larger part, including all the cavalry, to Limerick.

This double blow at Athlone and Aughrim shook to pieces the remaining Catholic power in Connaught. Galway surrendered ten days after the battle; Balldearg O'Donnell, after a vain attempt to throw himself into it in time, made terms with De Ginkle, and carried his two regiments into Flanders to fight on the side Spain and Rome had chosen to take in the European coalition. Sligo, the last western garrison, succumbed, and the brave Sir Teague O'Regan marched his 600 men, survivors, southward to Limerick.

Thus once more all eyes and all hearts in the British Islands were turned towards the well-known city of the lower Shannon. There, on the 14th of August, Tyrconnell expired, stricken down by apoplexy. On the 25th, De Ginkle, reinforced by all the troops he could gather in with safety, had invested the place on three sides. Sixty guns, none of less than 12 pounds calibre, opened their deadly fire against it. An English fleet ascended the river, hurling its missiles right and left. On the 9th of September the garrison made an unsuccessful sally, with heavy loss; on the 10th, a breach, forty yards wide, was made in the wall overhanging the river; on the night of the 15th, through the treachery or negligence of Brigadier Clifford, on guard at the Clare side of the river, a pontoon bridge was laid, and a strong English division crossed over in utter silence. The Irish horse, which had hitherto kept open communications with the country on that side, fell back to Six Mile Bridge. On the 24th, a truce of three days was agreed upon, and on the 3rd of October the memorable "Treaty of Limerick" was signed by the Williamite and Jacobite commissioners.

The *civil* articles of Limerick will be mentioned farther on; the ***military*** articles, twenty-nine in number, provided that all persons willing to expatriate themselves, as well officers and soldiers as rapparees and volunteers, should have free liberty to do so, to any place beyond seas, except England and Scotland; that they might depart in whole bodies, companies, or parties; that if plundered by the way, William's government should make good their loss; that fifty ships of 200 tons each should be provided for their transportation, besides two men-of-war for the principal officers; that the garrison of Limerick might march out with all their arms, guns and baggage, "colours flying, drums beating, and matches lighting!" It was also agreed, that those who so wished might enter the service of William, retaining their rank and pay; but though De Ginkle was most eager to secure for his master some of those stalwart battalions, only 1,000 out of the 13,000 that marched out of Limerick filed to the left at King's Island, Two thousand others accepted passes and protections; 4,500 sailed with Sarsfield from Cork, 4,700 with D'Usson and De Tesse, embarked in the Shannon on board a French fleet which arrived a week too late to prevent the capitulation; in English ships, 3,000 embarked with General Wauchop; all which, added to Mountcashel's brigade, over 5,000 strong, gave an Irish army of from 20,000 to 25,000 men to the service of King Louis.

As the ships from Ireland reached Brest and the ports of Brittany, James himself came down from Saint Germain to receive them. They were at once granted the rights of French citizenship without undergoing the forms of naturalization. Many of them rose to eminent positions in war and in diplomacy, became founders of distinguished families, or dying childless, left their hard-won gold to endow free bourses at Douay and Louvain, for poor Irish scholars destined for the service of the church, for which they had fought the good fight, in another sense, on the Shannon and the Boyne. The migration of ecclesiastics was almost as extensive as that of the military. They were shipped by dozens and by scores, from Dublin, Cork, and Galway. In seven years from the treaty, there remained but 400 secular and 800 regular clergy in the country. Nearly double that number, deported by threats or violence, were scattered over Europe, pensioners on the princes and bishops of their faith, or the institutions of their order. In Rome, 72,000 francs annually were allotted for the maintenance of the fugitive Irish clergy, and during the first three months of 1699, three remittances from the Holy Father, amounting to 90,000 livres, were placed in the hands of the Nuncio at Paris, for the temporary relief of the fugitives in France and Flanders. It may also be added here, that till the end of the eighteenth century, an annual charge of 1,000 Roman crowns was borne by the Papal treasury for the encouragement of Catholic Poor-schools in Ireland.

The revolutionary war, thus closed, had cost King William, or rather the people of England, at least 10,000,000 of pounds sterling, and with the other wars of that reign, laid the foundation of the English national debt. As to the loss of life, the Williamite chaplain, Storey, places it "at 100,000, young and old, besides treble the number that are ruined and undone." The chief consolation of the vanquished in that struggle was, that they had wrung even from their adversaries the reputation of being "one of the most warlike of nations"--that they "buried the synagogue with honour."

CHAPTER X.

REIGN OF KING WILLIAM.

From the date of the treaty of Limerick, William was acknowledged by all but the extreme Jacobites, at least *de facto*--King of Ireland. The prevailing party in Ulster had long recognized him, and the only expression of the national will then possible accepted his title, in the treaty signed at Limerick on the 3rd of October, 1691. For three years Ireland had resisted his power, for twelve years longer she was to bear the yoke of his government.

Though the history of William's twelve years' reign in Ireland is a history of proscription, the King himself is answerable only as a consenting party to such proscription. He was neither by temper nor policy a persecutor; his allies were Spain, Austria and Rome; he had thousands of Catholics in his own army, and he gave his confidence as freely to brave and capable men of one creed as of another. But the oligarchy, calling itself the "Protestant Ascendancy," which had grown so powerful under Cromwell and Charles II., backed as they once again were by all the religious intolerance of England, proved too strong for William's good intentions. He was, moreover, pre-occupied with the grand plans of the European coalition, in which Ireland, without an army, was no longer an element of calculation. He abandoned, therefore, not without an occasional grumbling protest, the vanquished Catholics to the mercy of that oligarchy, whose history, during the eighteenth century, forms so prominent a feature of the history of the kingdom.

The civil articles of Limerick, which Sarsfield vainly hoped might prove the *Magna Charta* of his co-religionists, were thirteen in number. Art. I. guaranteed to members of that denomination, remaining in the kingdom, "such privileges in the exercise of their religion as are consistent with the law of Ireland, or as they enjoyed in the reign of King Charles II.;" this article further provided, that "their majesties, as soon as their affairs will permit them to summon a Parliament in this kingdom, will endeavour to procure the said Roman Catholics such further security in that particular as may preserve them from any disturbance on account of their said religion." Art. II. guaranteed pardon and protection to all who had served King James, on taking the oath of allegiance prescribed in Art. IX., as follows:

"I, A. B., do solemnly promise and swear that I will be faithful and bear true allegiance to their majesties, King William and Queen Mary; so help me God."

Arts. III., IV., V. and VI. extended the provisions of Arts. I. and II. to merchants and other classes of men. Art. VII. permits "every nobleman and gentleman compromised in the said articles" to carry side arms and keep "a gun in their houses." Art. VIII. gives the right of removing goods and chattels without search. Art. IX. is as follows:

"The oath to be administered to such Roman Catholics as submit to their majesties' government *shall be the oath aforesaid, and no other*."

Art. X. guarantees that "no person or persons who shall at any time hereafter break these articles, or any of them, shall thereby make or cause any other person or persons to *forfeit or lose the benefit of them*." Arts. XI. and XII. relate to the ratification of the articles "within eight months or sooner." Art. XIII. refers to the debts of "Colonel John Brown, commissary of the Irish army, to several Protestants," and arranges for their satisfaction.

These articles were signed before Limerick, at the well known "Treaty Stone," on the Clare side of the Shannon, by Lord Scravenmore, Generals Mackay, Talmash, and De Ginkle, and the Lords Justices Porter and Coningsby, for King William, and by Sarsfield, Earl of Lucan, Viscount Galmoy, Sir Toby Butler, and Colonels Purcell, Cusack, Dillon, and Brown, for the Irish. On the 24th of February following, royal letters patent confirmatory of the treaty were issued from Westminster, in the name of the King and Queen, whereby they declared, that "we do for us, our heirs, and successors, as far as in us lies, ratify and confirm the same and every clause, matter, and thing therein contained. And as to such parts thereof, for which an act of Parliament shall be found to be necessary, we shall recommend the same to be made good by Parliament, and shall give our royal assent to any bill or bills that shall be passed by our two Houses of Parliament to that purpose. And whereas it appears unto us, that it was agreed between the parties to the said articles, that after the words Limerick, Clare, Kerry, Cork, Mayo, or any of them, in the second of the said articles; which words having been casually omitted by the writer of the articles, the words following, viz.: 'And all such as are under their protection in the said counties' should be inserted, and be part of the said omission, was not discovered till after the said articles were signed, but was taken notice of before the second town was surrendered, and that our said justices and generals, or one of them, did promise that the said clause should be made good, it being within the intention of the capitulation, and inserted in the foul draft thereof: Our further will and pleasure is, and we do hereby ratify and confirm the said omitted words, viz., 'And all such as are under their protection in the said counties,' hereby for us, our heirs and successors, ordaining and declaring that all and every person and persons therein concerned shall and may have, receive, and enjoy the benefit thereof, in such and the same manner as if the said words had been inserted in their proper place in the said second article, any omission, defect, or mistake in the said second article in any wise notwithstanding. Provided always, and our will and pleasure is, that these our letters patent shall be enrolled in our Court of Chancery, in our said kingdom of Ireland, within the space of one year next ensuing."

But the Ascendancy party were not to be restrained by the faith of treaties, or the obligations of the Sovereign. The Sunday following the return of the Lords Justices from Limerick, Dopping, Bishop of Meath, preached before them at Christ's church, on the crime of keeping faith with Papists. The grand jury of Cork, urged on by Cox, the Recorder of Kinsale, one of the historians of those times, returned in their inquest that the restoration of the Earl of Clancarty's estates "would be dangerous to the Protestant interest." Though both William and George I., interested themselves warmly for that noble family, the hatred of the new oligarchy proved too strong for the clemency of kings, and the broad acres of the disinherited McCarthys, remained to enrich an alien and bigoted aristocracy.

In 1692, when the Irish Parliament met, a few Catholic peers, and a very few Catholic commoners took their seats. One of the first acts of the victorious majority was to frame an oath in direct contravention to the oath prescribed by the ninth civil article of the treaty, to be taken by members of both Houses. This oath solemnly and explicitly denied "that in the sacrament of the Lord's supper there is any transubstantiation of the elements;" and as solemnly affirmed, "that the invocation or adoration of the Virgin Mary, or any other saint, and the sacrifice of the mass, as they are now used in the church of Rome, are damnable and idolatrous." As a matter of course, the Catholic peers and commoners retired from both Houses, rather than take any such oath, and thus the Irish Parliament assumed, in 1692, that exclusively Protestant character which it continued to maintain, till its extinction in 1800. The Lord Justice Sydney, acting in the spirit of his original instructions, made some show of resistance to the proscriptive spirit thus exhibited. But to teach him how they regarded his interference, a very small supply was voted, and the assertion of the absolute control of the Commons over all supplies--a sound doctrine when rightly interpreted--was vehemently asserted. Sydney had the satisfaction of proroguing and lecturing the House, but they had the satisfaction soon after of seeing him recalled through their influence in England, and a more congenial Viceroy in the person of Lord Capel sent over.

About the same time, that ancient engine of oppression, a Commission to inquire into estates forfeited, was established, and, in a short time, decreed that 1,060,792 acres were escheated to the crown. This was almost the last fragment of the patrimony of the Catholic inhabitants. When King William died, there did not remain in Catholic hands "one-sixth part" of what their grandfathers held, even after the passage of the Act of Settlement.

In 1695, Lord Capel opened the second Irish Parliament, summoned by King William, in a speech in which he assured his delighted auditors that the King was intent upon a firm settlement of Ireland upon a Protestant interest. Large supplies were at once voted to his majesty, and the House of Commons then proceeded to the appointment of a committee to consider what penal laws were already in force against the Catholics, not for the purpose of repealing them, but in order to add to their number. The principal penal laws then in existence were:

1. An act, subjecting all who upheld the jurisdiction of the See of Rome, to the penalties of a *premunire*; and ordering the oath of supremacy to be a qualification for office of every kind, for holy orders, and for a degree in the university.

2. An act for the uniformity of Common Prayer, imposing a fine of a shilling on all who should absent themselves from places of worship of the Established Church on Sundays.

3. An act, allowing the Chancellor to name a guardian to the child of a Catholic.

4. An act to prevent Catholics from becoming private tutors in families, without license from the ordinaries of their several parishes, and taking the oath of supremacy.

To these, the new Parliament added, 1. An act to deprive Catholics of the means of educating their children at home or abroad, and to render them incapable of being guardians of their own or any other person's children; 2. An act to disarm the Catholics; and, 3. Another to banish all the Catholic priests and prelates. Having thus violated the treaty, they gravely brought in a bill "to confirm the Articles of Limerick." "The very title of the bill," says Dr. Cooke Taylor, "contains evidence of its injustice." It is styled "A Bill for the Confirmation of Articles (not *the* articles) made at the Surrender of Limerick." And the preamble shows that the little word *the* was not accidentally omitted. It runs thus:--"That the said articles, or *so much of them as may consist with the safety and welfare of your majesty's subjects in these kingdoms*, may be confirmed," &c. The parts that appeared to these legislators inconsistent with "the safety and welfare of his majesty's subjects," were the first article, which provided for the security of the Catholics from all disturbances on account of their religion; those parts of the second article which confirmed the Catholic gentry of Limerick, Clare, Cork, Kerry, and Mayo, in the possession of their estates, and allowed all Catholics to exercise their trades and professions without obstruction; the fourth article, which extended the benefit of the peace to certain Irish officers then abroad; the seventh article, which allowed the Catholic gentry to ride armed; the ninth article, which provides that the oath of allegiance shall be the only oath required from Catholics; and one or two others of minor importance. All of these are omitted in the bill for "The confirmation of Articles made at the Surrender of Limerick."

The Commons passed the bill without much difficulty. The House of Lords, however, contained some few of the ancient nobility, and some prelates, who refused to acknowledge the dogma, "that no faith should be kept with Papists," as an article of their creed. The bill was strenuously resisted, and when it was at length carried, a strong protest against it was signed by Lords Londonderry, Tyrone, and Duncannon, the Barons of Ossory, Limerick, Killaloe, Kerry, Howth, Kingston, and

Strabane, and, to their eternal honour be it said, the Protestant bishops of Kildare, Elphin, Derry, Clonfert, and Killala!

The only other political incidents of this reign, important to Ireland, were the speech from the throne in answer to an address of the English Houses, in which William promised to discourage the woollen and encourage the linen manufacture in Ireland, and the publication of the famous argument for legislative independence, "The Case of Ireland Stated." The author of this tract, the bright precursor of the glorious succession of men, who, often defeated or abandoned by their colleagues, finally triumphed in 1782, was William Molyneux, member for the University of Dublin. Molyneux's book appeared in 1698, with a short, respectful, but manly dedication to King William. Speaking of his own motives in writing it, he says, "I am not at all concerned in wool or the wool trade. I am no ways interested in forfeitures or grants. I am not at all concerned whether the bishop or the society of Derry recover the lands they contest about." Such were the domestic politics of Ireland at that day; but Molyneux raised other and nobler issues when he advanced these six propositions, which lie supported with incontestible ability.

"1. How Ireland became a kingdom ***annexed*** to the crown of England. And here we shall at large give a faithful narrative of the first expedition of the Britons into this country, and King Henry II.'s arrival here, such as our best historians give us.

"2. We shall inquire whether this expedition and the English settlement that afterwards followed thereon, can properly be called a ***conquest***; or whether any victories obtained by the English in any succeeding ages in this kingdom, upon any rebellion, may be called a ***conquest*** thereof.

"3. Granting that it were a ***conquest***, we shall inquire what ***title*** a conquest gives.

"4. We shall inquire what ***concessions*** have been from time to time made to Ireland, to take off what even the most rigorous asserters of a conqueror's title do pretend to. And herein we shall show by what degrees the English form of government, and the English statute laws, came to be received among us; and this shall appear to be wholly by the ***consent*** of the people and the Parliament of Ireland.

"5. We shall inquire into the precedents and opinions of the learned in the laws relating to this matter, with observations thereon.

"6. We shall consider the reasons and arguments that may be further offered on one side and t'other; and we shall draw some general conclusions from the whole."

The English Parliament took alarm at these bold doctrines, seldom heard across the channel since the days of Patrick Darcy and the Catholic Confederacy. They ordered the book to be burned by the hands of the common hangman, as of "dangerous tendency to the crown and people of England, by denying the power of the King and Parliament of England to bind the kingdom and people of Ireland, and the subordination and dependence that Ireland had, and ought to have, upon England, as being united and annexed to the imperial crown of England." They voted an address to the King in the same tone, and received an answer from his majesty, assuring them that he would enforce the laws securing the dependence of Ireland on the imperial crown of Great Britain.

But William's days were already numbered. On the 8th of March, 1702, when little more than fifty years of age, he died from the effects of a fall from his horse. His reign over Ireland is synonymous to the minds of that people of disaster, proscription and spoliation; of violated faith and broken compacts; but these wrongs were done in his name rather than by his orders; often without his knowledge, and sometimes against his will. Rigid as that will was, it was forced to bend to the anti-Popery storm which swept over the British Islands after the abdication of King James; but the vices and follies of his times ought no more be laid to the personal account of William than of James or Louis, against whom he fought.

CHAPTER XI.

REIGN OF QUEEN ANNE.

The reign of Queen Anne occupies twelve years (1702 to 1714. The new sovereign, daughter of James by his first marriage, inherited the legacy of William's wars, arising out of the European coalition. Her diplomatists, and her troops, under the leadership of Marlborough, continued throughout her reign to combat against France, in Spain, Germany, and the Netherlands; the treaty of Utrecht being signed only the year before her majesty's decease. In domestic politics, the main occurrences were the struggle of the Whigs and Tories, immortalized for us in the pages of Swift, Steele, Addison, and Bolingbroke; the limitation of the succession to the descendants of the Electress Sophia, in the line of Hanover; and the abortive Jacobite movement on the Queen's death which drove Ormond and Atterbury into exile.

In Ireland, this is the reign, *par excellence*, of the penal code. From the very beginning of the Queen's reign, an insatiate spirit of proscription dictated the councils of the Irish oligarchy. On the arrival of the second and last Duke of Ormond, in 1703, as Lord-Lieutenant, the Commons waited on him in a body, with a bill "for discouraging the further growth of Popery," to which the duke having signified his entire concurrence, it was accordingly introduced, and became law. The following are among the most remarkable clauses of this act: The third clause provides, that if the son of an estated Papist shall conform to the established religion, the father shall be incapacitated from selling or mortgaging his estate, or disposing of any portion of it by will. The fourth clause prohibits a Papist from being the guardian of his own child; and orders, that if at any time the child, though ever so young, pretends to be a Protestant, it shall be taken from its own father, and placed under the guardianship of the nearest Protestant relation. The sixth clause renders Papists incapable of purchasing any manors, tenements, hereditaments, or any rents or profits arising out of the same, or of holding any lease of lives, or other lease whatever, for any term exceeding thirty-one years. And with respect even to such limited leases, it further enacts, that if a Papist should hold a farm producing a profit greater than one-third of the amount of the rent, his right to such should immediately cease, and pass over entirely to the first Protestant who should discover the rate of profit. The seventh clause prohibits Papists from succeeding to the properties or estates of their Protestant relations. By the tenth clause, the estate of a Papist, not having a Protestant heir, is ordered to be gavelled, or divided in equal shares between all his children. The sixteenth and twenty-fourth clauses impose the oath of abjuration, and the sacramental test, as a qualification for office, and for voting at elections. The twenty-third clause deprives the Catholics of Limerick and Galway of the protection secured to them by the articles of the treaty of Limerick. The twenty-fifth clause vests in her majesty all advowsons possessed by Papists.

Certain Catholic barristers, living under protection, not yet excluded from the practice of their profession, petitioned to be heard at the bar of the House of Commons. Accordingly, Mr. Malone, the ancestor of three generations of scholars and orators, Sir Stephen Rice, one of the most spotless characters of the age, formerly chief-justice under King James, and Sir Theobald Butler, were heard against the bill. The argument of Butler, who stood at the very head of his profession, remains to us almost in its entirety, and commands our admiration by its solidity and dignity. Never was national cause more worthily pleaded; never was the folly of religious persecution more forcibly exhibited. Alluding to the monstrous fourth clause of the bill, the great advocate exclaimed:--

"It is natural for the father to love the child; but we all know that children are but too apt and subject, without any such liberty as this bill gives, to slight and neglect their duty to their parents; and surely such an act as this will not be an instrument of restraint, but rather encourage them more to it.

"It is but too common with the son, who has a prospect of an estate, when once he arrives at the age of one and twenty, to think the old father too long in the way between him and it; and how much more will he be subject to it, when, by this act, he shall have liberty, before he comes to that age, to compel and force my estate from me, without asking my leave, or being liable to account with me for it, or out of his share thereof, to a moiety of the debts, portions, or other encumbrances, with which the estate might have been charged before the passing of this act!

"Is not this against the laws of God and man? Against the rules of reason and justice, by which all men ought to be governed? Is not this the only way in the world to make children become undutiful? and to bring the grey head of the parent to the grave with grief and tears?

"It would be hard from any man; but from a son, a child, the fruit of my body, whom I have nursed in my bosom, and tendered more dearly than my own life, to become my plunderer, to rob me of my estate, to cut my throat, and to take away my bread, is much more grievous than from any other, and enough to make the most flinty hearts to bleed to think on it. And yet this will be the case if this bill pass into a law; which I hope this honourable assembly will not think of, when they shall more seriously consider, and have weighed these matters.

"For God's sake, gentlemen, will you consider whether this is according to the golden rule, to do as you would be done unto? And if not, surely you will not, nay, you cannot, without being liable to be charged with the most manifest injustice imaginable, take from us our birthrights, and invest them in others, before our faces."

When Butler and Malone had closed, Sir Stephen Rice was heard, not in his character of council, but as one of the petitioners affected by the act. But neither the affecting position of that great jurist, who, from the rank of chief baron had descended to the outer bar, nor the purity of his life, nor the strength of his argument, had any effect upon the oligarchy who heard him. He was answered by quibbles and cavils, unworthy of record, and was finally informed that any rights which Papists "pretended to be taken from them by the Bill, was in their own power to remedy, by conforming, which in prudence they ought to do; and that they had none to blame but themselves." Next day the bill passed into law.

The remnant of the clergy were next attacked. On the 17th of March, 1705, the Irish Commons resolved, that "informing against Papists was an honourable service to the government," and that all magistrates and others who failed to put the penal laws into execution, "were betrayers of the liberties of the kingdom." But even these resolutions, rewards, and inducements were insufficient to satisfy the spirit of persecution.

A further act was passed, in 1709, imposing additional penalties. The first clause declares, that no Papist shall be capable of holding an annuity for life. The third provides, that the child of a Papist, on conforming, shall at once receive an annuity from his father; and that the Chancellor shall compel the father to discover, upon oath, the full value of his estate, real and personal, and thereupon make an order for the support of such conforming child or children, and for securing such a share of the property, after the father's death, as the court shall think fit. The fourteenth and fifteenth clauses secure jointures to Popish wives who shall conform. The sixteenth prohibits a Papist from teaching, even as assistant to a Protestant master. The eighteenth gives a salary of 30 pounds per annum to Popish priests who shall conform. The twentieth provides rewards for the discovery of Popish prelates, priests, and teachers, according to the following whimsical scale:--For discovering an archbishop, bishop, vicar-general, or other person, exercising any foreign ecclesiastical jurisdiction, 50 pounds; for discovering each regular clergyman, and each secular clergyman, not registered, 20 pounds; and for discovering each Popish schoolmaster or usher, 10 pounds. The twenty-first clause empowers two justices to summon before them any Papist over eighteen years of age, and interrogate him when and where he last heard mass said, and the names of the persons present, and likewise touching the residence of any Popish priest or schoolmaster; and if he refuse to give testimony, subjects him to a fine of 20 pounds, or imprisonment for twelve months.

Several other penal laws were enacted by the same Parliament, of which we can only notice one; it excluded Catholics from the office of sheriff, and from grand juries, and enacts, that, in trials upon any statute for strengthening the Protestant interest, the plaintiff might challenge a juror for being a Papist, which challenge the judge was to allow. By a royal proclamation of the same year, "all registered priests" were to take "the oath of abjuration before the 25th of March, 1710," under penalty of *premunire*. Under this proclamation and the tariff of rewards just cited, there grew up a class of men, infamous and detestable, known by the nickname of "priest hunters." One of the most successful of these traffickers in blood was a Portuguese Jew, named Garcia, settled at Dublin. He was very skilful at disguises. "He sometimes put on the mien of a priest, for he affected to be one, and thus worming himself into the good graces of some confiding Catholic got a clue to the whereabouts of the clergy." In 1718, Garcia succeeded in arresting seven unregistered priests, for whose detection he had a sum equal to two or three thousand dollars of American money. To such an excess was this trade carried, that a reaction set in, and a Catholic bishop of Ossory, who lived at the time these acts were still in force, records that "the priest-catchers' occupation became exceedingly odious both to Protestants and Catholics," and that himself had seen "ruffians of this calling assailed with a shower of stones, flung by both Catholics and Protestants." But this creditable reaction only became general under George II., twenty years after the passage of the act of Queen Anne. We shall have to mention some monstrous additions made to the code during the first George's reign, and some attempts to repair and perfect its diabolical machinery, even so late as George III.; but the great body of the penal law received its chief accessions from the oligarchical Irish Parliament, under Queen Anne. Hitherto, we have often had to point out, how with all its constitutional defects--with the law of Poynings, obliging heads of bills to be first sent to England--fettering its freedom of initiative;--how, notwithstanding all defects, the Irish Parliament had asserted, at many critical periods, its own and the people's rights, with an energy worthy of admiration. But the collective bigots of this reign were wholly unworthy of the name of a parliament. They permitted the woollen trade to be sacrificed without a struggle,--they allowed the bold propositions of Molyneux, one of their own number, to be condemned and reprobated without a protest. The knotted lash of Jonathan Swift was never more worthily applied, than to "the Legion Club," which he has consigned to such an unenviable immortality. Swift's inspiration may have been mingled with bitter disappointment and personal revenge; but, whatever motives animated him, his fearless use of his great abilities must always make him the first political, as he was certainly the first literary character of Ireland at that day. In a country so bare and naked as he found it; with a bigotry so rampant and united before him; it needed no ordinary courage and capacity to evoke anything like public opinion or public spirit. Let us be just to that most unhappy man of genius; let us proclaim that Irish nationality, bleeding at every pore, and in danger of perishing by the wayside, found shelter on the breast of Swift, and took new heart from the example of that bold churchman, before whom the Parliament, the bench of Bishops, and the Viceroy, trembled.

CHAPTER XII.

THE IRISH SOLDIERS ABROAD DURING THE REIGNS OF WILLIAM AND ANNE.

The close of the second reign from the siege of Limerick imposes the duty of casting our eyes over the map of Europe, in quest of those gallant exiles whom we have seen, in tens of thousands, submitting to the hard necessity of expatriation.

Many of the Meath and Leinster Irish, under their native commanders, the Kavanaghs and Nugents, carried their swords into the service of William's ally, the Emperor of Austria, and distinguished themselves in all the campaigns of Prince Eugene. Spain attracted to her standard the Irish of the north-west, the O'Donnells, the O'Reillys, and O'Garas, whose regiments, during more than one reign, continued to be known by flames of Ulster origin. In 1707, the great battle of Almanza, which decided the Spanish succession, was determined by O'Mahony's foot and Fitzjames's Irish horse. The next year Spain had five Irish regiments in her regular army, three of foot and two of dragoons, under the command of Lacy, Lawless, Wogan, O'Reilly, and O'Gara. But it was in France that the Irish served in the greatest number, and made the most impressive history for themselves and their descendants.

The recruiting agents of France had long been in the habit of crossing the narrow seas, and bringing back the stalwart sons of the western Island to serve their ambitious kings, in every corner of the continent. An Irish troop of horse served, in 1652, under Turenne, against the great Conde. In the campaigns of 1673, 1674 and 1675, under Turenne, two or three Irish regiments were in every engagement along the Rhine. At Altenheim, their commander, Count Hamilton, was created a major-general of France. In 1690, these old regiments, with the six new ones sent over by James, were formed into a brigade, and from 1690 to 1693, they went through the campaigns of Savoy and Italy, under Marshal Catinat, against Prince Eugene. Justin McCarthy, Lord Mountcashel, who commanded them, died at Bareges of wounds received at Staffardo. At Marsiglia, they routed, in 1693, the allies, killing Duke Schomberg, son to the Huguenot general who fell at the Boyne.

The "New" or Sarsfield's brigade was employed under Luxembourg, against King William, in Flanders, in 1692 and 1693. At Namur and Enghien, they were greatly distinguished, and William more than once sustained heavy loss at their hands. Sarsfield, their brigadier, for these services, was made mareschal-de-camp. At Landen, on the 29th of July, '93, France again triumphed to the cry, "Remember Limerick!" Sarsfield, leading on the fierce pursuers, fell, mortally wounded. Pressing his hand upon the wound, he took it away dripping with blood, and only said, "Oh, that this was for Ireland!"

In the war of the Spanish succession, the remnants of both brigades, consolidated into one, served under their favourite leader, the Marshal Duke of Berwick, through nearly all his campaigns in Belgium, Spain and Germany. The third Lord Clare, afterwards Field-Marshal Count Thomond, was by the Duke's side at Phillipsburg, in 1733, when he received his death-wound from the explosion of a mine. These exiled Clare O'Briens commanded for three generations their famous family regiment of dragoons. The first who followed King James abroad died of wounds received at the battle of Ramillies; the third, with better fortune, outlived for nearly thirty years the glorious day of Fontenoy. The Irish cavalry regiments in the service of France were Sheldon's, Galmoy's, Clare's, and Killmallock's; the infantry were known as the regiments of Dublin, Charlemont, Limerick, and Athlone. There were two other infantry regiments, known as Luttrel's and Dorrington's--and a regiment of Irish marines, of which the Grand Prior, Fitzjames, was colonel. During the latter years of Louis XIV., there could not have been less, at any one time, than from 20,000 to 30,000 Irish in his armies, and during the succeeding century, authentic documents exist to prove that 450,000 natives of Ireland died in the military service of France.

In the dreary reigns of William, Anne, and the two first Georges, the pride and courage of the disarmed and disinherited population abiding at home, drew new life and vigour from the exploits of their exiled brethren. The channel smuggler and the vagrant ballad-singer kept alive their fame for the lower class of the population, while the memoirs of Marlborough and Eugene, issuing from the Dublin press, communicated authentic accounts of their actions, to the more prejudiced, or better educated. The blows they struck at Landen, at Cremona, and at Almanza, were sensibly felt by every British statesman; when, in the bitterness of defeat, an English King cursed "the laws that deprived him of such subjects," the doom of the penal code was pronounced.

    The high character of the famous captains of these brigades was not confined to the field of battle. At Paris, Vienna, and Madrid, their wit and courtesy raised them to the favour of princes, over the jealousy of all their rivals. Important civil and diplomatic offices were entrusted to them--embassies of peace and war--the government of provinces, and the highest administrative offices of the state. While their kinsmen in Ireland were declared incapable of filling the humblest public employments, or of exercising the commonest franchise, they met British ambassadors abroad as equals, and checked or countermined the imperial policy of Great Britain. It was impossible that such a contrast of situations should not attract the attention of all thinking men! It was impossible that such reputations should shine before all Europe without reacting powerfully on the fallen fortunes of Ireland!

BOOK XI.
FROM THE ACCESSION OF GEORGE I. TO THE LEGISLATIVE UNION OF GREAT BRITAIN AND IRELAND.

CHAPTER I.

ACCESSION OF GEORGE I.--SWIFT'S LEADERSHIP.

The last years of Queen Anne had been years of intrigue and preparation with the Jacobite leaders throughout the three kingdoms. At their head stood Ormond, the second and last *Duke* of his name, and with him were associated at one stage or another of his design, Bolingbroke, Orrery, Bishop Atterbury, and other influential persons. It was thought that had this party acted promptly on the death of the Queen, and proclaimed James III. (or "the Pretender," as he was called by the partisans of the new dynasty), the Act of Succession might have remained a dead letter, and the Stuarts recovered their ancient sovereignty. But the partisans of the elector were the first in the field, and King George was accordingly proclaimed, on the 1st of August, at London, and on the 6th of August, at Dublin.

In Dublin, where serious apprehensions of a Jacobite rising were entertained, the proclamation was made by the glare of torches at the extraordinary hour of midnight. Two or three arrests of insignificant persons were made, and letters to Swift being found on one of them, the Dean was thought by his friends to be in some danger. But it was not correct to say, as many writers have done, that he found it necessary to retire from Dublin. The only inconvenience he suffered was from the hootings and revilings of the Protestant rabble in the street, and a brutal threat of personal violence from a young nobleman, upon whom he revenged himself in a characteristic petition to the House of Lords "for protection against the said lord." Pretending not to be quite sure of his assailant, he proceeds to explain: "Your petitioner is informed that the person who spoke the words above mentioned is of your Lordships' House, under the style and title of Lord Blaney; whom your petitioner remembers to have introduced to Mr. Secretary Addison, in the Earl of Wharton's government, and to have done him other good offices at that time, because he was represented as a young man of some hopes and a broken fortune." The entire document is a curious picture of the insolence of the ascendancy party of that day, even towards dignitaries of their own church who refused to go all lengths in the only politics they permitted or tolerated.

It was while smarting under these public indignities, and excluded from the society of the highest class in his own country, with two or three exceptions, that Swift laid the foundations of his own and his country's patriotism, among the educated middle class of the Irish capital. From the college and the clergy he drew Dr. Sheridan--ancestor of six generations of men and women of genius! Doctors Delaney, Jackson, Helsham, Walmsley, Stopford (afterwards Bishop of Cloyne), and the three reverend brothers Grattan. In the city he selected as his friends and companions four other Grattans, one of whom was Lord-Mayor, another physician to the castle, one a schoolmaster, the other a merchant. "Do you know the Grattans?" he wrote to the Lord-Lieutenant, Lord Carteret; "then pray obtain their acquaintance. The Grattans, my lord, can raise 10,000 men." Among the class represented by this admirable family of seven brothers, and in that of the tradesmen immediately below them, of which we may take his printers, Waters and Faulkner for types, Swift's haughty and indignant denunciations of the oligarchy of the hour produced striking effects. The humblest of the community began to raise their heads, and to fix their eyes steadily on public affairs and public characters. Questions of currency, of trade, of the administration of justice and of patronage, were earnestly discussed in the press and in society, and thus by slow but gradually ascending steps, a spirit of independence was promoted where hitherto only servility had reigned.

The obligations of his cotemporaries to Swift are not to be counted simply by what he was able to originate or to advocate in their behalf--for not much could be done in that way, in such times, and in such a position as his --but rather in regard to the enemies and maligners of that people, whom he exposed and punished. To understand the value of his example and inspiration, we must read over again his castigations of Wharton, of Burnet, of Boulter, of Whitshed, of Allan, and all the leaders of the oligarchy, in the Irish Parliament. When we have done so, we shall see at once how his imperial reputation, his personal position, and every faculty of his powerful mind were employed alike to combat injustice and proscription, to promote freedom of opinion and of trade, to punish the abuses of judicial power, and to cultivate and foster a spirit of self reliance and economy among all classes-- especially the humblest. In his times, and in his position, with a cassock "entangling his course," what more could have been expected of him?

The Irish Parliament met in 1715--elected, according to the then usage, for the lifetime of the King--commenced its career by an act of attainder against the Pretender, accompanied by a reward of 50,000 pounds for his apprehension. The Lords-Justices, the Duke of Grafton and the Earl of Galway, recommended in their speech to the Houses, that they should cultivate such unanimity among themselves as "at once to put an end to all other distinctions in Ireland, but that of Protestant and Papist." In the same speech, and in all the debates of that reign, the Catholics were spoken of as "the common enemy," and all who sympathized with them, as "enemies of the constitution." But far as this Parliament was from all our ideas of what a national legislature ought to be, it was precisely at this period, when the administration could not be worse, that the foundation was laid of the great contest for legislative independence, which was to continue through three generations, and to constitute the main staple of the Irish history of this century.

In the year 1717, the English House of Lords entertained and decided, as a court of last resort, an appeal from the Irish courts, already passed on by the Irish Lords, in the famous real-estate case of Annesley *versus* Sherlock. The proceeding was novel, and was protested against in the English House at the time by the Duke of Leeds, and in the Irish, by the majority of the whole House. But the British Parliament, not content with claiming the power, proceeded to establish the principle, by the declaratory act--6th George I.--for securing the dependence of Ireland on the crown of Great Britain. This statute, even more objectionable than the law of Poynings, continued unrepealed till 1782, notwithstanding all the arguments and all the protests of the Irish patriot party. The Lords of Ireland, unsupported by the bigoted and unprincipled oligarchy in the Commons, were shorn of their appellate jurisdiction, and their journals for many years contain few entries of business done, beyond servile addresses to successive Viceroys, and motions of adjournment.

In their session of 1723, the ascendancy party in the Commons proceeded to their last extreme of violence against the prostrate Catholics. An act was introduced founded on eight resolutions, "further to prevent the growth of Popery." One of these resolutions, regularly transmitted to England by the Viceroy-proposed that every priest, arrested within the realm, should suffer the penalty of *castration*! For the first time, a penal law was rejected with horror and indignation by the English Privy Council, and the whole elaborate edifice, overweighted with these last propositions, trembled to its base. But though badly shaken, it was yet far from coming down.

"Do not the corruptions and villainies of men," said Swift to his friend Delaney, "eat your flesh and exhaust your spirits?" They certainly gnawed at the heart of the courageous Dean, but at the same time, they excited rather than exhausted his spirits. In 1720 he resumed his pen, as a political writer, in his famous proposal "for the universal use of Irish manufactures." Waters, the printer of this piece, was indicted for a seditious libel, before Chief-Justice Whitshed, the immortal "*coram nobis*" of the Dean's political ballads. The jury were detained eleven hours, and sent out nine times, to compel them to agree on a verdict. They at length finally declared they could not agree, and a *nol. pros.* was soon after entered by the crown. This trial of Swift's printer in 1720, is the first of a long series of duels with the crown lawyers, which the Irish press has since maintained with as much firmness and self-sacrifice as any press ever exhibited. And it may be said that never, not even under martial law, was a conspicuous example of civic courage more necessary, or more dangerous. Browne, Bishop of Cork, had been in danger of deprivation for preaching a sermon against the well-known toast to the memory of King William; Swift was threatened, as we see, a few years earlier, with personal violence by a Whig lord, and pelted by a Protestant rabble, for his supposed Jacobitism; his friend, Dr. Sheridan, lost his Munster living for having accidentally chosen as his text, on the anniversary of King George's coronation, "sufficient for the day is the evil thereof." Such was the intolerance of the oligarchy towards their own clergy. What must it have been to others!

The attempt to establish a National Bank, and the introduction of a debased copper coinage, for which a patent had been, granted to one William Wood, next employed the untiring pen of Swift. The halfpenny controversy, was not, as is often said, a small matter; it was nearly as important as the bank project itself. Of the 100,000 pounds worth coined, the intrinsic value was shown to be not more than 6,000 pounds. Such was the storm excited against the patentee, that his Dublin agents were obliged to resign their connection with him, and the royal letters-patent were unwillingly cancelled. The bank project was also rejected by Parliament, adding another to the triumphs of the invincible Dean.

During the last years of this reign, Swift was the most powerful and popular person in Ireland, and perhaps in the empire. The freedom with which he advised Carteret the Viceroy, and remonstrated with Walpole, the Premier, on the misrule of his country, was worthy of the ascendancy of his genius. No man of letters, no churchman, no statesman of any country in any age, ever showed himself more thoroughly independent, in his intercourse with men of office, than Swift. The vice of Ireland was exactly the other way, so that in this respect also, the patriot was the liberator.

Rising with the rise of public spirit, the great churchman, in his fourth letter, in the assumed character of *M. B. Drapier*, confronted the question of legislative independence. Alluding to the pamphlet of Molyneux, published thirty years before, he pronounced its arguments invincible, and the contrary system "the very definition of slavery." "The remedy," he concludes, addressing the Irish people, "is wholly in your own hands, and therefore I have digressed a little, in order to refresh and continue that spirit so seasonably raised among you, and to let you see, that, by the laws of God, of nature, of nations, and of your country, *you are, and ought to be, as free a people as your brethren in England*." For this letter also, the printer, Harding, was indicted, but the Dublin grand jury, infected with the spirit of the times, unanimously ignored the bill. A reward of 300 pounds was then issued from the castle for the discovery of the author, but no informer could be found base enough to betray him. For a time, however, to escape the ovations he despised, and the excitement which tried his health, Swift retired to his friend Sheridan's cottage on the banks of Lough Ramor, in Cavan, and there recreated himself with long rides about the country, and the composition of the Travels of the immortal Gulliver.

Sir Robert Walpole, alarmed at the exhibition of popular intelligence and determination evoked by Swift, committed the government of Ireland to his rival, Lord Carteret--whom he was besides not sorry to remove to a distance--and appointed to the See of Armagh, which fell vacant about the time of the currency dispute, Dr. Hugh Boulter, Bishop of Bristol, one of his own creatures. This prelate, a politician by taste and inclination, modelled his policy on his patron's, as far as his more contracted sphere and inferior talents permitted. To buy members in market overt, with peerages, or secret service money, was his chief means of securing a Parliamentary majority. An Englishman by birth and education; the head of the Protestant establishment in Ireland, it was inevitable that his policy should be English and Protestant, in every particular. To resist, depress, disunite, and defeat the believers in the dangerous doctrines of Swift and Molyneux, was the sole rule of his nearly twenty years' political supremacy in Irish affairs. (1724-1742.) The master of a princely income, endowed with strong passions, unlimited patronage, and great activity, he may be said to have reigned rather than led, even when the nominal viceroyalty was in the hands of such able and accomplished men as Lords Carteret, Dorset and Devonshire. His failure in his first state trial, against Harding the printer, nothing discouraged him; he had come into Ireland to secure the English interest, by uprooting the last vestiges of Popery and independence, and he devoted himself to those objects with persevering determination. In 1727--the year of George the First's decease--he obtained the disfranchisement of Catholic electors by a clause quietly inserted without notice in a Bill regulating elections; and soon after he laid the foundations of those nurseries of proselytism, "the Charter Schools."

CHAPTER II.

REIGN OF GEORGE II.--GROWTH OF PUBLIC SPIRIT--THE "PATRIOT" PARTY--LORD CHESTERFIELD'S ADMINISTRATION.

The accession of King George II. in 1727, led to no considerable changes, either in England or Ireland. Sir Robert Walpole continued supreme in the one country, and Primate Boulter in the other. The Jacobites, disheartened by their ill success in 1715, and repelled rather than attracted by the austere character of him they called King James III., made no sign. The new King's first act was to make public the declaration he had addressed to the Privy Council, of his firm resolution to uphold the existing constitution "in church and state."

The Catholic population, beginning once more to raise their heads, thought this a suitable occasion to present a humble and loyal address of congratulation to the Lords Justices, in the absence of the Viceroy. Lord Delvin and several of their number accordingly appeared at the Castle, and delivered their address, which they begged might be forwarded to the foot of the throne. No notice whatever was taken of this document, either at Dublin or London, nor were the class who signed it permitted by law to "testify their allegiance" to the sovereign, for fifty years later--down to 1778.

The Duke of Dorset, who succeeded Lord Carteret as Viceroy in 1731, unlike his immediate predecessor, refrained from suggesting additional severities against the Catholics. His first term of office--two years--was almost entirely occupied with the fiercest controversy which had ever waged in Ireland between the Established Church and the Protestant Dissenters. The ground of the dispute was the sacramental test, imposed by law upon the members of both Houses, and all burgesses and councillors of corporate towns. By the operations of this law, when rigidly enforced,

Presbyterians and other dissenters were as effectually excluded from political and municipal offices as Catholics themselves. Against this exclusion it was natural that a body so numerous, and possessed of so much property, especially in Ulster, should make a vigorous resistance. Relying on the great share they had in the revolution, they endeavoured, though ineffectually, to obtain under King William the repeal of the Test Act of King Charles II. Under Queen Anne they were equally unsuccessful, as we may still read with interest in the pages of Swift, De Foe, Tennison, Boyse, and King. Swift, especially, brought to the controversy not only the zeal of a churchman, but the prejudices of an Anglo-Irishman, against the new-comers in the north. He upbraids them in 1708, as glad to leave then--barren hills of Lochaber for the fruitful vales of Down and Antrim, for their parsimony and their clannishness. He denied to them, with bitter scorn, the title they had assumed of "Brother Protestants," and as to the Papists, whom they affected to despise, they were, in his opinion, as much superior to the Dissenters, as a lion, though chained and clipped of its claws, is a stronger and nobler animal than an angry cat, at liberty to fly at the throats of true churchmen. The language of the Presbyterian champions was equally bold, denunciatory, and explicit. They broadly intimated, in a memorial to Parliament, that under the operation of the test, they would be unable to take up arms again, as they had done in 1688, for the maintenance of the Protestant succession; a covert menace of insurrection, which Swift and their other opponents did not fail to make the most of. Still farther to embarrass them, Swift got up a paper making out a much stronger case in favour of the Catholics than of "their brethren, the Dissenters," and the controversy closed, for that age, in the complete triumph of the established clergy.

This iniquitous deprivation of equal civil rights, accompanied with the onerous burthen of tithes falling heaviest on the cultivators of the soil, produced the first great Irish exodus to the North American colonies. The tithe of agistment or pasturage, lately abolished, had made the tithe of tillage more unjust and unequal. Outraged in their dearest civil and religious rights, thousands of the Scoto-Irish of Ulster, and the Milesian and Anglo-Irish of the other provinces, preferred to encounter the perils of an Atlantic flitting rather than abide under the yoke and lash of such an oligarchy. In the year 1729, five thousand six hundred Irish landed at the single port of Philadelphia; in the next ten years they furnished to the Carolinas and Georgia the majority of their immigrants; before the end of this reign, several thousands of heads of families, all bred and married in Ireland, were rearing up a free posterity along the slopes of the Blue Ridge in Virginia and Maryland, and even as far north as the valleys of the Hudson and the Merrimac. In the ranks of the thirteen United Colonies, the descendants of those Nonconformists were to repeat, for the benefit of George III., the lesson and example their ancestors had taught to James II. at Enniskillen and at Derry.

Swift, with all his services to his own order, disliked, and was disliked by them. Of the bishops he has recorded his utter contempt in some of the most cutting couplets that even he ever wrote. Boulter he detested; Narcissus Marsh he despised; with Dr. King of Dublin, Dr. Bolton of Cashel, and Dr. Horte of Tuam, he barely kept up appearances. Except Sterne, Bishop of Clogher, Berkely, Bishop of Cloyne, and Stopford, his successor, he entertained neither friendship nor respect for one of that order. And on their part, the right reverend prelates cordially reciprocated his antipathy. They resisted his being made a member of the Linen Board, a Justice of the Peace, or a Visitor of Trinity College. Had he appeared amongst them in Parliament as their peer, they would have been compelled to accept him as a master, or combine against him as an enemy. No wonder, then, that successive Viceroys shrank from nominating him to any of the mitres which death had emptied; "the original sin of his birth" was aggravated in their eyes by the actual sin of his patriotism. No wonder the sheets of paper that littered his desk, before he sunk into his last sad scene of dotage, were found scribbled all over with his favourite lines--

"Better we all were in our graves,   Than live in slavery to slaves."

But the seeds of manly thought he had so broadly sown, though for a season hidden even from the sight of the sower, were not dead, nor undergoing decay. With something of the prudence of the founder, "the Patriot party," as the opposition to the Castle party began to be called, occupied themselves at first with questions of taxation and expenditure. In 1729, the Castle attempted to make it appear that there was a deficit--that in short "the country owed the government"--the large sum of 274,000 pounds! The Patriots met this claim, by a motion for reducing the cost of all public establishments. This was the chosen ground of both parties, and a more popularly intelligible ground could not be taken. Between retrenchment and extravagance, between high taxes and low, even the least educated of the people could easily decide; and thenceforward for upwards of twenty years, no session was held without a spirited debate on the supplies, and the whole subject of the public expenditure.

The Duke of Devonshire, who succeeded the Duke of Dorset as Viceroy in 1737, contributed by his private munificence and lavish hospitalities to throw a factitious popularity round his administration. No Dublin tradesman could find it in his heart to vote against the nominee of so liberal a nobleman, and the public opinion of Dublin was as yet the public opinion of Ireland. But the Patriot party, though unable to stem successfully the tide of corruption and seduction thus let loose, held their difficult position in the legislature with great gallantry and ability. New men had arisen during the dotage of Swift, who revered his maxims, and imitated his prudence. Henry Boyle, speaker of the House of Commons, afterwards Earl of Shannon; Anthony Malone--son of the *confrere* of Sir Toby Butler, and afterwards Chancellor of the Exchequer, Sir Edward O'Brien, member for Clare, and his son, Sir Lucius, member for Ennis, were the pillars of the party. Out of doors, the most active spirit among the Patriots was Charles Lucas, a native of Clare, who, from his apothecary's shop in Dublin, attempted, not without both talents, zeal and energy, to play the part of Swift, at the press and among the people. His public writings, commenced in 1741, brought him at first persecution and exile, but they afterwards conducted him to the representation of the capital, and an honourable niche in his country's history.

The great event which may be said to divide into two epochs the reign of George II. was the daring invasion of Scotland in 1745, by "the young Pretender"--Charles Edward. This brave and unfortunate Prince, whose adventures will live for ever in Scottish song and romance, was accompanied from France by Sir Thomas Sheridan, Colonel O'Sullivan, and other Irish refugees, still fondly attached to the house of Stuart. It is not to be supposed that these gentlemen would be without correspondents in Ireland, nor that the state of that country could be a matter of indifference to the astute advisers of King George. In reality, Ireland was almost as much their difficulty as Scotland, and their choice of a Viceroy, at this critical moment, showed at once their estimate of the importance of the position, and the talents of the man.

Philip Dormer Stanhope, Earl of Chesterfield, a great name in the world of fashion, in letters, and in diplomacy, is especially memorable to us for his eight months' viceroyalty over Ireland. That office had been long the object of his ambition, and he could hardly have attained it at a time better calculated to draw out his eminent administrative abilities. By temper and conviction opposed to persecution, he connived at Catholic worship under the very walls of the Castle. The sour and jaundiced bigotry of the local oligarchy he encountered with **bon mots** and raillery. The only "dangerous Papist" he had seen in Ireland, he declared to the King on his return, was a celebrated beauty of that religion--Miss Palmer. Relying on the magical effect of doing justice to all classes, and seeing justice done, he was enabled to spare four regiments of troops for the war in Scotland, instead of demanding additions to the Irish garrisons. But whether to diminish the influence which his brilliant administration had created in England, or through the machinations of the oligarchy, still powerful at Dublin, within ten days from the decisive battle of Culloden, he was recalled. The fruits of his policy might be already observed, as he walked on foot, his countess on his arm, to the place of embarkation, amid the acclamations of all ranks and classes of the people, and their affectionate prayers for his speedy return.

CHAPTER III.

THE LAST JACOBITE MOVEMENT--THE IRISH SOLDIERS ABROAD--
FRENCH EXPEDITION UNDER THUROT, OR O'FARRELL.

The mention of the Scottish insurrection of 1745 brings naturally with it another reference to the history of the Irish soldiers in the military service of France. This year was in truth the most eventful in the annals of that celebrated legion, for while it was the year of Fontenoy and victory on the one hand, it was on the other the year of Culloden and defeat.

The decisive battle of Fontenoy, in which the Franco-Irish troops bore so decisive a part, was fought on the 11th of May, 1745. The French army, commanded by Saxe, and accompanied by King Louis, leaving 18,000 men to besiege Namur, and 6,000 to guard the Scheldt, took a position between that river and the allies, having their centre at the village of Fontenoy. The British and Dutch, under the King's favourite son, the Duke of Cumberland, were 55,000 strong; the French 45,000. After a hard day's fighting, victory seemed to declare so clearly against France, that King Louis, who was present, prepared for flight. At this moment Marshal Saxe ordered a final charge by the seven Irish regiments under Counts Dillon and Thomond. The tide was turned, beyond expectation, to the cry of "Remember Limerick!" France was delivered, England checked, and Holland reduced from a first to a second-rate power upon that memorable day. But the victory was dearly bought. One-fourth of all the Irish officers, including Count Dillon, were killed, and one-third of all the men. The whole number slain on the side of France was set down at 7,000 by English accounts, while they admitted for themselves alone, 4,000 British and 3,300 Hanoverians and Dutch. "Foremost of all," says the just-minded Lord Mahon, "were the gallant brigade of Irish exiles." It was this defeat of his favourite son which wrung from King George II. the oft-quoted malediction on the laws which deprived him of such subjects.

The expedition of Prince Charles Edward was undertaken and conducted by Irish aid, quite as much as by French or Scottish. The chief parties to it, besides the old Marquis of Tullibardine and the young Duke of Perth, were the Waterses, father and son, Irish bankers at Paris, who advanced one hundred and eighty thousand livres between them; Walsh, an Irish merchant at Nantz, who put a privateer of eighteen guns into the venture; Sir Thomas Geraldine, the Pretender's agent at Paris; Sir Thomas Sheridan, the prince's preceptor, who, with Colonels O'Sullivan and Lynch, Captain O'Neil, and other officers of the brigade, formed the staff, on which Sir John McDonald, a Scottish officer in the Spanish service, was also placed. Fathers Kelly and O'Brien volunteered in the expedition. On the 22nd of June, 1745, with seven friends, the prince embarked in Walsh's vessel, the Doutelle, at St. Nazaire, on the Loire, and on the 19th of July, landed on the northern coast of Scotland, near Moidart. The Scottish chiefs, little consulted or considered beforehand, came slowly and dubiously to the landing-place. Under their patriarchal control there were still in the kingdom about a hundred thousand men, and about one-twelfth of the Scottish population. Clanronald, Cameron of Lochiel, the Laird of McLeod, and a few others, having arrived, the royal standard was unfurled on the 19th of August at Glenfinin, where that evening twelve hundred men--the entire army so far-- were formed into camp, under the orders of O'Sullivan. From that day until the day of Culloden, O'Sullivan seems to have manoeuvred the prince's forces. At Perth, at Edinburgh, at Preston, at Manchester, at Culloden, he took command in the field, or in garrison; and even after the sad result, he adhered to his sovereign's son with an honourable fidelity which defied despair.

Charles, on his part, placed full confidence in his Irish officers. In his proclamation after the battle of Preston, he declared it was not his intention to enforce on the people of England, Scotland, or Ireland, "a religion they disliked." In a subsequent paper, he asks, "Have you found reason to love and cherish your governors as the fathers of the people of Great Britain and Ireland? Has a family upon whom a faction unlawfully bestowed the diadem of a rightful prince, retained a due sense of so great a trust and favour?" These and his other proclamations betrayed an Irish pen; probably Sir Thomas Sheridan's. One of Charles's English adherents, Lord Elcho, who kept a journal of the campaign, notes, complainingly, the Irish influence under which he acted. "The prince and his old governor, Sir Thomas Sheridan," are especially objected to, and the "Irish favourites" are censured in a body. While at Edinburgh, a French ship, containing some arms, supplies, and "Irish officers," arrived; at the same time efforts were made to recruit for the prince in Ireland; but the agents being taken in some cases, the channel narrowly watched, and the people not very eager to join the service, few recruits were obtained.

The Irish in France, as if to cover the inaction of their countrymen at home, strained every nerve. The Waterses and O'Brien of Paris were liberal bankers to the expedition. Into their hands James "exhausted his treasury" to support his gallant son. At Fontainebleau, on the 23rd of October, Colonel O'Brien, on the part of the prince, and the Marquis D'Argeusson for Louis XV., formed a treaty of "friendship and alliance," one of the clauses of which was, that certain Irish regiments, and other French troops, should be sent to sustain the expedition. Under Lord John Drummond a thousand men were shipped from Dunkirk, and arrived at Montrose in the Highlands about the time Charles had penetrated as far south as Manchester. The officers, with the prince, here refused to advance on London with so small a force; a retreat was decided on; the sturdy defence of Carlisle, and victory of Falkirk, checked the pursuit; but the overwhelming force of the Duke of Cumberland compelled them to evacuate Edinburgh, Perth, and Glasgow--operations which consumed February, March, and the first half of April, 1746.

The next plan of operations seems to have been to concentrate in the western Highlands, with Inverness for head-quarters. The town Charles easily got, but Fort-George, a powerful fortress, built upon the site of the castle where Macbeth was said to have murdered Duncan, commanded the Loch. Stapleton and his Irish, captured it, however, as well as the neighbouring Fort-Augustus. Joined by some Highlanders, they next attempted Fort-William, the last fortress of King George in the north, but on the 3rd of April were recalled to the main body.

To cover Inverness, his head-quarters, Charles resolved to give battle. The ground chosen, flanked by the river Nairn, was spotted with marsh and very irregular; it was called Culloden, and was selected by O'Sullivan. Brigadier Stapleton and Colonel Kerr reported against it as a field of battle; but Charles adopted O'Sullivan's opinion of its fitness for Highland warfare. When the preparations for battle began, "many voices exclaimed, 'We'll give Cumberland another Fontenoy!'" The Jacobites were placed in position by O'Sullivan, "at once their adjutant and quarter-master-general," and, as the burghers of Preston thought, "a very likely fellow." He formed two lines, the great clans being in the first, the Ogilvies, Gordons, and Murrays; the French and Irish in the second. Four pieces of cannon flanked each wing, and four occupied the centre. Lord George Murray commanded the right wing, Lord John Drummond the left, and Brigadier Stapleton the reserve. They mustered in all less than five thousand men. The British formed in three lines, ten thousand strong, with two guns between every second regiment of the first and second line. The action commenced about noon of April 16th, and before evening half the troops of Prince Charles lay dead on the field, and the rest were hopelessly broken. The retreat was pell-mell, except where "a troop of the Irish pickets, by a spirited fire, checked the pursuit, which a body of dragoons commenced after the Macdonalds, and Lord Lewis Gordon's regiments did similar service." Stapleton conducted the French and Irish remnant to Inverness, and obtained for them by capitulation "fair quarter and honourable treatment."

The unhappy prince remained on the field almost to the last. "It required," says Mr. Chambers, "all the eloquence, and, indeed, all the active exertion, of O'Sullivan to make Charles quit the field. A cornet in his service, when questioned on this subject at the point of death, declared he saw O'Sullivan, after using entreaties in vain, turn the head of the prince's horse and drag him away."

From that night forth, O'Sullivan, O'Neil, and a poor sedan carrier of Edinburgh, called Burke, accompanied him in all his wanderings and adventures among the Scottish islands. At Long Island they were obliged to part company, the prince proceeding alone with Miss Flora McDonald. He had not long left, when a French cutter hove in sight and took off O'Sullivan, intending to touch at another point, and take in the prince and O'Neil. The same night she was blown off the coast, and the prince, after many other adventures, was finally taken off at Badenoch, on the 15th of September, 1746, by the L'Heureux, a French armed vessel, in which Captain Sheridan (son of Sir Thomas), Mr. O'Beirne, a lieutenant in the French army, "and two other gentlemen," had adventured in search of him. Poor O'Neil, in seeking to rejoin his master, was taken prisoner, carried to London, and is lost from the record. O'Sullivan reached France safely, where, with Stapleton, Lynch, and the

Irish and Scotch officers, he was welcomed and honoured of all brave men.

Such was the last struggle of the Stuarts. For years after, the popular imagination in both countries clung fondly to Prince Charles. But the cause was dead. As if to bury it for ever, Charles, in despair, grew dissipated and desponding. In 1755, "the British Jacobites" sent Colonel McNamara, as their agent, to induce him to put away his mistress, Miss Walsingham, a demand with which he haughtily refused to comply. In 1766, when James III. died at Avignon, the French king and the Pope refused to acknowledge the prince by the title of Charles III. When the latter died, in 1788, at Rome, Cardinal York contented himself with having a medal struck, with the inscription "Henricus IX., Anglae Rex." He was the last of the Stuarts.

Notwithstanding the utter defeat of the Scottish expedition, and the scatterment of the surviving companies of the brigade on all sorts of service from Canada to India, there were many of the exiled Irish in France, who did not yet despair of a national insurrection against the house of Hanover. In the year 1759, an imposing expedition was fitted out at Brest under Admiral Conflaus, and another at Dunkirk, under Commodore Thurot, whose real name was O'Farrell. The former, soon after putting to sea, was encountered at Quiberon by the English under Hawke, and completely defeated; but the latter entered the British channel unopposed, and proceeded to the appointed *rendezvous*. While cruising in search of Conflaus, the autumnal equinox drove the intrepid Thurot into the Northern ocean, and compelled him to winter among the frozen friths of Norway and the Orkneys. One of his five frigates returned to France, another was never heard of, but with the remaining three he emerged from the Scottish Islands, and entered Lough Foyle early in 1760. He did not, however, attempt a landing at Derry, but appeared suddenly before Carrickfergus, on the 21st of February, and demanded its surrender. Placing himself at the head of his marines and sailors, he attacked the town, which, after a brave resistance by the commandant, Colonel Jennings, he took by assault. Here, for the first time, this earlier Paul Jones heard of the defeat of his admiral; after levying contributions on the rich burgesses and proprietors of Carrickfergus and Belfast, he again put to sea. His ships, battered by the wintry storms which they had undergone in northern latitudes, fell in near the Isle of Man with three English frigates, just out of port, under Commodore Elliott. A gallant action ensued, in which Thurot, or O'Farrell, and three hundred of his men were killed. The survivors struck to the victors, and the French ships were towed in a sinking state, into the port of Ramsey.

The life thus lost in the joint service of France and Ireland, was a life illustrative of the Irish refugee class among whom he became a leader. Left an orphan in childhood, O'Farrell, though of a good family, had been bred in France in so menial a condition that he first visited England as a domestic servant. From that condition he rose to be a dexterous and successful captain in the contraband trade, so extensive in those times. In this capacity he visited almost every port of either channel, acquiring that accurate knowledge which, added to his admitted bravery and capacity, placed him at length at the head of a French squadron. "Throughout the expedition," says Lord Mahon, "the honour and humanity of this brave adventurer are warmly acknowledged by his enemies." "He fought his ship," according to the same author, "until the hold was almost filled with water, and the deck covered with dead bodies."

CHAPTER IV.

REIGN OF GEORGE II. (CONCLUDED)--MALONE'S LEADERSHIP.

The Earl of Harrington, afterwards Duke of Devonshire, succeeded Lord Chesterfield in the government, in 1746. He was provided with a prime minister in the person of the new Archbishop of Armagh, Dr. George Stone, whose character, if he was not exceedingly calumniated by his cotemporaries, might be compared to that of the worst politicians of the worst ages of Europe. Originally, the son of the jailer of Winchester, he had risen by dint of talents, and audacity, to receive from the hands of his sovereign, the illustrious dignity of Primate of Ireland. But even in this exalted office, the abominable vices of his youth accompanied him. His house at Leixlip, was at once a tavern and a brothel, and crimes, which are nameless, were said to be habitual under his roof. "May the importation of Ganymedes into Ireland, be soon discontinued," was the public toast, which disguised under the transparent gauze of a mythological allusion, the infamies of which he was believed to be the patron. The prurient page of Churchill was not quite so scrupulous, and the readers of the satire entitled "The Times," will need no further key to the horrible charges commonly received on both sides of the channel, against Primate Stone.

The viceroyalty of Ireland, which had become an object of ambition to the first men in the empire, was warmly contested by the Earl of Harrington and the Duke of Dorset. The former, through his Stanhope influence and connections, prevailed over his rival, and arrived in Ireland, warmly recommended by the popular Chesterfield. During his administration, Primate Stone, proceeding from one extreme to another, first put forward the dangerous theory, that all surplus revenue belonged of right to the crown, and might be paid over by the Vice-Treasurers, to his majesty's order, without authority of Parliament. At this period, notwithstanding the vicious system of her land tenures, and her recent losses by emigration, Ireland found herself in possession of a considerable surplus revenue.

Like wounds and bruises in a healthy body, the sufferings and deprivations of the population rapidly disappeared under the appearance even of improvement in the government. The observant Chesterfield, who continued through life warmly attached to the country in which his name was remembered with so much affection, expresses to his friend, Chevenix, Bishop of Waterford, in 1751, his satisfaction at hearing "that Ireland improves daily, and that a spirit of industry spreads itself, to the great increase of trade and manufactures." This new-born prosperity the Primate and politicians of his school would have met by an annual depletion of the treasury, instead of assisting its march by the reduction of taxes, and the promotion of necessary public works. The surplus was naturally regarded, by the Patriot party, in the light of so much national capital; they looked upon it as an improvement fund, for the construction of canals, highways, and breakwaters, for the encouragement of the linen and other manufactures, and for the adornment of the capital with edifices worthy of the chief city of a flourishing kingdom.

The leader of the Patriot party, Anthony Malone, was compared at this period, by an excellent authority, to "a great sea in a calm." He was considered, even by the fastidious Lord Shelburne, the equal, in oratory, of Chatham and Mansfield. He seems to have at all times, however, sunk the mere orator in the statesman, and to have used his great powers of argument even more in Council than in the arena. His position at the bar, as Prime Sergeant, by which he took precedence even of the Attorney-General, gave great weight to his opinions on all questions of constitutional law. The roystering country gentlemen, who troubled their heads but little with anything besides dogs and horses, pistols and claret, felt secure in their new-fledged patriotism, under the broad aegis of the law extended over them by the most eminent lawyer of his age. The Speaker of the Commons, Henry Boyle, aided and assisted Malone, and when left free to combat on the floor, his high spirit and great fortune gave additional force to his example and confidence to his followers. Both were men too cautious to allow their adversaries any parliamentary advantage over them, but not so their intrepid coadjutor out of doors, Apothecary Lucas. He, like Swift, rising from local and municipal grievances to questions affecting the constitution of Parliament itself, was in 1749, against all the efforts of his friends in the House of Commons, declared by the majority of that House to be "an enemy to his country," and a reward was accordingly issued for his apprehension. For a time he was compelled to retire to England; but he returned, to celebrate in his Freeman's Journal the humiliation of the primate, and the defeat of the policy both of Lord Harrington, and his successor, the Duke of Dorset.

This nobleman, resolved to cast his predecessor into the shade by the brilliancy of his success, proceeded to take vigorous measures against the patriots. In his first speech to Parliament in 1751, he informed them his Majesty "consented" to the appropriation of the surplus revenue, by the House of Commons, and a clause was added to the annual supply bill in the English Council, containing the same obnoxious word, "consent." On this occasion, not feeling themselves strong enough to throw out the bill, and there being no alternative but rejection or acceptance, the Patriots permitted it to pass under protest. But the next session, when a similar addition was made, the Commons rejected the supply bill altogether, by a majority of 122 to 117. This was a measure of almost revolutionary consequence, since it left every branch of the public service unprovided for, for the ensuing twelve months.

Both the advisers of the King in England, and the Viceroy in Ireland, seemed by their insane conduct as if they desired to provoke such a collision. Malone's patent of precedence as Prime Sergeant was cancelled; the speaker was dismissed from the Privy Council, and the surplus revenue was withdrawn from the Vice-Treasurer, by a King's letter. The indignation of the Dubliners at these outrages rose to the utmost pitch. Stone, Healy, Hutchinson, and others of the Castle party, were waylaid and menaced in the streets, and the Viceroy himself hooted wherever he appeared. Had the popular leaders been men less cautious, or less influential, the year 1753 might have witnessed a violent revolutionary movement. But they planted themselves on the authority of the constitution, they united boldness with prudence, and they triumphed. The Primate and his creatures raised against them in vain the cuckoo cry of disloyalty, both in Dublin and London. The English Whigs, long engaged themselves in a similar struggle with the overgrown power of the crown, sympathized with the Irish opposition, and defended their motives both in society and in Parliament. The enemies of the Dorset family as naturally took their part, and the duke himself was obliged to go over to protect his interest at court, leaving the odious

Primate as one of the Lords-Justices. At his departure his guards were hardly able to protect him from the fury of the populace, to that waterside to which Chesterfield had walked on foot, seven years before, amid the benedictions of the same people.

The Patriots had at this crisis a great addition to their strength, in the accession of James, the twentieth Earl of Kildare, successively Marquis and Duke of Leinster. This nobleman, in the prime of life, married to the beautiful Emily Lennox, daughter of the Duke of Richmond, followed Dorset to England, and presented to the King, with his own hand, one of the boldest memorials ever addressed to a sovereign by a subject. After reciting the past services of his family in maintaining the imperial connection, he declared himself the organ of several thousands of his Majesty's liege subjects, "as well the nobles as the clergy, the gentry, and the commonalty of the kingdom." He dwells on the peculation and extravagance of the administration, under "the Duumvirate" of the Viceroy and the Primate, which he compares with the league of Strafford and Laud. He denounces more especially Lord George Sackville, son to Dorset, for his intermeddling in every branch of administration. He speaks of Dr. Stone as "a greedy churchman, who affects to be a second Wolsey in the senate." This high-toned memorial struck with astonishment the English ministers, who did not hesitate to hint, that, in a reign less merciful, it would not have passed with impunity. In Ireland it raised the hardy earl to the pinnacle of popular favour. A medal was struck in his honour, representing him guarding a heap of treasure with a drawn sword, and the motto--"Touch not, says Kildare." At the opening of the next Parliament, he was a full hour making his way among the enthusiastic crowd, from his house in Kildare street to College Green. In little more than a year, the Duke of Dorset, whom English ministers had in vain endeavoured to sustain, was removed, and the Primate, by his Majesty's orders, was struck from the list of privy counsellors.

Lord Harrington, now Duke of Devonshire, replaced the disgraced and defeated Dorset, and at once surrounded himself with advisers from the ranks of the opposition. The Earl of Kildare was his personal and political friend, and his first visit, on arriving, was paid at Carton. The Speaker, Mr. Boyle, the Earl of Bessborough, head of the popular family of the Ponsonbys, and Mr. Malone, were called to the Privy Council. Lucas, exalted rather than injured by years of exile, was elected one of the members for the city of Dublin, and the whole face of affairs promised a complete and salutary change of administration.

After a year in office, Devonshire returned to England in ill-health, leaving Lord Kildare as one of the Justices, an office which he continued to fill, till the arrival in September, 1756, of John, fourth Duke of Bedford, as Lord-Lieutenant, with Mr. Rigby, "a good four bottle man," as chief secretary.

The instructions of the Duke of Bedford, dictated by the genius and wisdom of Chatham, were, to employ "all softening and healing arts of government." His own desire, as a Whig, at the head of the Whig families of England, was to unite and consolidate the same party in Ireland, so as to make them a powerful auxiliary force to the English Whigs. Consistently with this design, lie wished well to the country he was sent to rule, and was sincerely desirous of promoting measures of toleration. But he found the Patriots distracted by success, and disorganized by the possession of power. The Speaker, who had struggled so successfully against his predecessors, was in the Upper House as Earl of Shannon, and the chair of the Commons was filled by John Ponsonby, of the Bessborough family. The Ponsonby following, and the Earl of Kildare's friends were at this period almost as much divided from each other in their views of public policy, as either were from the party of the Primate. The Ponsonby party, still directed by Malone, wished to follow up the recent victory on the money bills, by a measure of Catholic relief, a tax upon absentees, and a reduction of the pension list, shamelessly burthened beyond all former proportion. Lord Kildare and his friends were not then prepared to go such lengths, though that high spirited nobleman afterwards came into most of these measures. After endeavouring in vain to unite, these two interests, the Duke of Bedford found, or fancied himself compelled, in order to secure a parliamentary majority, to listen to the overtures of the, obsequious Primate, to restore him to the Council, and to leave him, together with his old enemy, Lord Shannon, in the situation of joint administrators, during his journey to England, in 1758. The Earl of Kildare, it should be remarked, firmly refused to be associated with Stone, on any terms, or for any time, long or short.

The closing of this important reign is notable for the first Catholic meeting held since the reign of Queen Anne. In the spring of 1757, four hundred respectable gentlemen attended by mutual agreement, at Dublin, among whom were Lords Devlin, Taafe, and Fingal, the antiquary, Charles O'Conor, of Balanagar, the historian of the *Civil Wars*, Dr. Curry, and Mr. Wyse, a merchant of Waterford, the ancestor of a still better known labourer in the same cause. The then recent persecution of Mr. Saul, a Dublin merchant, of their faith, for having harboured a young lady whose friends wished to coerce her into a change of religion, gave particular significance to this assembly. It is true the proceedings were characterized by caution amounting almost to timidity, but the unanimous declaration of their loyal attachment to the throne, at a moment when French invasion was imminent, produced the best effect, and greatly strengthened the hands of the Clanbrassils, Ponsonbys, Malones, Dalys, and other advocates of an enlarged toleration in both Houses. It is true no immediate legislation followed, but the way was prepared for future ameliorations by the discretion and tact of the Catholic delegates of 1757. They were thenceforth allowed at least the right of meeting and petitioning, of which they had long been deprived, and the restoration of which marks the first step in their gradual recovery of their civil liberties.

In 1759 a rumour broke out in Dublin that a legislative union was in contemplation by the Primate and his faction. On the 3rd of December, the citizens rose *en masse*, and surrounded the Houses of Parliament. They stopped the carriages of members, and obliged them to swear opposition to such a measure. Some of the Protestant bishops, and the Lord Chancellor were roughly handled; a privy counsellor was thrown into the river; the Attorney General was wounded and obliged to take refuge in the college; Lord Inchiquin was abused till he said his name was O'Brien, when the rage of the people "was turned into acclamations." The Speaker, Mr. Ponsonby, and the Chief Secretary, Mr. Rigby, had to appear in the porch of the House of Commons, solemnly to assure the citizens that no union was dreamed of, and if it was proposed, that they would be the first to resist it. Public spirit had evidently grown bold and confident, and we can well believe Secretary Rigby when he writes to the elder Pitt, that "the mob" declared, "since they have no chance of numbers in the House, they must have recourse to numbers out of doors."

CHAPTER V.

ACCESSION OF GEORGE III.--FLOOD'S LEADERSHIP-- OCTENNIAL PARLIAMENTS ESTABLISHED.

George III., grandson of the late king, commenced, in October, 1760, at the age of two and twenty, the longest reign in British history. Including the period of the regency, he reigned over his empire nearly sixty years --an extraordinary term of royal power, and quite as extraordinary for its events as for its extreme length.

The great movement of the Irish mind, at the beginning of this reign, was the limitation of the duration of Parliament, hitherto elected for the King's life. This reform, long advocated out of doors, and by the more progressive members within the House, was reserved for the new Parliament under the new reign. To this Parliament were returned several men of great promise, men of a new generation, nurtured in the school of Swift and Malone, but going even beyond their masters in their determination to liberate the legislature of their country from the undue influence of the crown and the castle. Among those new members were three destined to national celebrity, Dr. Lucas, Mr. Hussey Burgh, and Mr. Dennis Bowes Daly; and one destined to universal reputation--Henry Flood. This gentleman, the son of a former Chief Justice, intermarried into the powerful oligarchical family of the Beresfords, was only in his 28th year when first elected member for Kilkenny; but, in point of genius and acquirements, he was even then the first man in Ireland, and one of the first in the empire. For a session or two he silently observed the forms of the House, preparing himself for the great contest to come; but when at last he obtained the ear of his party he was heard to some purpose. Though far from advocating extreme measures, he had abundant boldness; he was not open to the objection levelled against the leader of the past generation, Mr. Malone, of whom Grattan said, "he was a colony-bred man, and he feared to bring down England upon Ireland."

The Duke of Bedford vacated the viceroyalty in 1761, and Lord Halifax took his place. In the first parliamentary session, Dr. Lucas introduced his resolutions limiting the duration of Parliament to seven years, a project which Flood afterwards adopted and mainly contributed to carry. The heads of the bill embodying these resolutions were transmitted to London by the Lord-Lieutenant, but never returned. In 1763, under the government of the Marquis of Hertford, similar resolutions were introduced and carried, but a similar fate awaited them. Again they were passed, and again rejected, the popular dissatisfaction rising higher and higher with every delay of the reform. At length, in the session of 1767, "the Septennial Bill," as it was called, was returned from England, changed to octennial, and with this alteration it passed into law, in February, 1768. A new Parliament the same year was elected under the new act, to which all the friends of the measure were triumphantly returned. The faithful Lucas, however, survived his success little better than two years; he died amid the very sincere regrets of all men who were not enemies of their country. At his funeral the pall was borne by the Marquis of Kildare, Lord Charlemont, Mr. Flood, Mr. Hussey Burgh, Sir Lucius O'Brien, and Mr. Ponsonby.

Lord Halifax, and his chief secretary, Mr. Hamilton (known to us as "the single-speech Hamilton," of literary history), received very graciously the loyal addresses presented by the Catholics, soon after his Majesty's accession. In a speech from the throne, the Viceroy proposed, but was obliged to abandon the proposition, to raise six regiments of Catholics, under their own officers, to be taken into the service of Portugal, the ally of Great Britain. His administration was otherwise remarkable neither for its length nor its importance; nor is there anything else of consequence to be mentioned of his lordship, except that his nephew, and chief secretary, had the honour to have Edmund Burke for his private secretary, and the misfortune to offend him.

During the government of the Marquis of Hertford, and his successor, Lord Townsend (appointed in 1768), the Patriot party contended on the ground of rendering the judges independent, diminishing the pension list, and modifying the law of Poynings, requiring heads of bills to be sent into England, and certified by both Privy Councils, before they could be passed upon by the legislature. The question of supply, and that of the duration of Parliament, being settled, these reforms were the next objects of exertion. When we know that the late King's mistresses, the Queen Dowager of Prussia, Prince Ferdinand, and other connections of the royal family, equally alien to the country, were pensioners to the amount of thousands of pounds annually on the Irish establishment, we can understand more clearly the bitterness of the battle Mr. Flood and his colleagues were called upon to fight in assailing the old system. But they fought it resolutely and perseveringly. Death had removed their most unscrupulous enemy, Primate Stone, during the Hertford administration, and the improved tone and temper of public opinion would not tolerate any attempt to raise up a successor of similar character. Lord Townsend, an old campaigner and *bon vivant*, was expressly chosen as most capable of restoring the old system of government by closeting and corruption, but he found the Ireland of his day very materially altered from the defenceless province, which Stone and Dorset had attempted to cajole or to coerce, twenty years before.

The Parliament of 1769--the first limited Parliament which Ireland had seen since the revolution--proved, in most respects, worthy of the expectations formed of it. John Ponsonby was chosen Speaker, and Flood regarded, around him, well-filled benches and cheering countenances. The usual supply bill was passed and sent up to the castle, but on its return from England was found to be altered--15,000 men, among other changes, being charged to the Irish military establishment, instead of 12,000, as formerly. The Commons, resolute to assert their rights, threw out the bill, as had been done in 1753, and the Lord Lieutenant, protesting in the House of Lords against their conduct, ordered them to be prorogued. Prorogation followed prorogation, till February, 1771, the interval being occupied in closeting and coquetting with members of the opposition, in the creation of new places, and the disposal of them to the relatives of those capable of being bought. No one was surprised, when the Houses reassembled, to find that a bare majority of the Commons voted a fulsome address of confidence to the Lord Lieutenant. But this address, Speaker Ponsonby indignantly refused to present. He preferred resignation to disgrace, and great was the amazement and indignation when his friend, Mr. Perry, elected by a bare majority, consented to take the post--no longer a post of honour.

In justice to Mr, Perry, however, it must be added, that in the chair as on the floor of Parliament, he still continued the patriot--that if he advanced his own fortunes, it was not at the expense of the country--that some of the best measures passed by this and the subsequent Parliament, owed their final success, if not their first suggestion, to his far-seeing sagacity.

The methods taken by Lord Townsend to effect his ends, not less than those ends themselves, aroused the spirit and combined the ranks of the Irish opposition. The press of Dublin teemed with philippics and satires, upon his creatures and himself. The wit, the scholarship, the elegant fancy, the irresistible torrent of eloquence, as well as the popular enthusiasm, were against him, and in 1772, borne down by these combined forces, he confessed his failure by resigning the sword of state into the hands of Lord Harcourt.

The new Viceroy, according to custom, began his reign by taking an exactly opposite course to his predecessor, and ended it by falling into nearly the same errors and abuses. He suggested an Absentee-tax, which was introduced by Flood, but rejected through the preponderating influence of the landed aristocracy. In preparing the tables of expenditure, he had caused arrears amounting to 265,000 pounds, and an annual increase of 100,000 pounds, to be added to the estimates. Moreover, his supply bill was discovered, at the second reading, to extend over *two years* instead of one--a discovery which occasioned the greatest indignation. Flood raised his powerful voice in warning, not unmingled with menace; Burgh declared, that if any member should again bring in such a bill, he would himself move his expulsion from the House; while George Ogle, member for Wexford, proposed that the bill itself should be burned before the porch, by the common hangman. He was reminded that the instrument bore the great seal; to which he boldly answered, that the seal would help to make it burn the better. It was not thought politic to take notice of this revolutionary retort.

CHAPTER VI.

FLOOD'S LEADERSHIP--STATE OF THE COUNTRY BETWEEN 1760 AND 1776.

England was engaged in two great wars during the period of Flood's supremacy in the Irish Parliament--the seven years' war, concluded by the peace of Paris in 1763, and the American war, concluded by the treaty of Versailles, in 1783. To each of these wars Ireland was the second largest contributor both as to men and money; and by both she was the severest sufferer, in her manufactures, her provision trade, and her general prosperity. While army contracts, and all sorts of military and naval expenditure in a variety of ways returned to the people of England the produce of their taxes, the Irish had no such compensation for the burdens imposed on their more limited resources. The natural result was, that that incipient prosperity which Chesterfield hailed with pleasure in 1751, was arrested in its growth, and fears began to be seriously entertained that the country would be driven back to the lamentable condition from which it had slowly and laboriously emerged during the reign of George II.

The absence of employment in the towns threw the labouring classes more and more upon the soil for sustenance, while the landlord legislation of the period threw them as helplessly back upon other pursuits than agriculture. Agrarian injustice was encountered by conspiracy, and for the first time in these pages, we have to record the introduction of the diabolical machinery of secret oath-bound associations among the Irish peasantry. Of the first of these combinations in the southern counties, a cotemporary writer gives the following account: "Some landlords in Munster," he says, "have let their lands to cotters far above their value, and, to lighten their burden, allowed commonange to their tenants by way of recompense:

afterwards, in despite of all equity, contrary to all compacts, the landlords enclosed these commons, and precluded their unhappy tenants from the only means of making their bargains tolerable." The peasantry of Waterford, Cork, and other southern counties met in tumultuous crowds, and demolished the new enclosures. The oligarchical majority took their usual cue on such occasions: they pronounced, at once, that the cause of the riots was "treason against the state;" they even obtained a select committee to "inquire into the cause and progress of the Popish insurrection in Munster." Although the London Gazette, on the authority of royal commissioners, declared that the rioters "consisted indiscriminately of persons of different persuasions," the Castle party would have it "another Popish plot." Even Dr. Lucas was carried away by the passions of the hour, and declaimed against all lenity, as cowardly and criminal.

A large military force, under the Marquis of Drogheda, was accordingly despatched to the south. The Marquis fixed his head-quarters at Clogheen, in Tipperary, the parish priest of which was the Rev. Nicholas Sheehy. The magistracy of the county, especially Sir Thomas Maude, William Bagnel, John Bagwell, Daniel Toler, and Parson Hewitson, were among the chief maintainers of the existence of a Popish plot, to bring in the French and the Pretender. Father Sheehy had long been fixed upon as their victim: largely connected with the minor gentry, educated in France, young, popular, eloquent and energetic, a stern denouncer of the licentious lives of the squires, and of the exacting tithes of the parsons, he was particularly obnoxious. In 1763 he was arrested on a charge of high treason, for drilling and enrolling Whiteboys, but was acquitted. Towards the close of that year, Bridge, one of the late witnesses against him, suddenly disappeared. A charge of murder was then laid against the priest of Clogheen, and a prostitute named Dunlea, a vagrant lad named Lonergan, and a convicted horse stealer called Toohey, were produced in evidence against him, after he had lain nearly a year in prison, heavily fettered. On the 12th of March, 1765, he was tried at Clonmel, on this evidence; and notwithstanding an *alibi* was proved, he was condemned, and beheaded on the third day afterwards. Beside the old ruined church of Shandraghan, his well-worn tomb remains till this day. He died in his thirty-eighth year. Two months later, Edward Sheehy, his cousin, and two respectable young farmers, named Buxton and Farrell, were executed under a similar charge, and upon the same testimony. All died with religious firmness and composure. The fate of their enemies is notorious; with a single exception, they met deaths violent, loathsome, and terrible. Maude died insane, Bagwell in idiocy, one of the jury committed suicide, another was found dead in a privy, a third was killed by his horse, a fourth was drowned, a fifth shot, and so through the entire list. Toohey was hanged for felony, the prostitute Dunlea fell into a cellar and was killed, and the lad Lonergan, after enlisting as a soldier, died of a loathsome disease in a Dublin infirmary.

In 1767, an attempt to revive the plot was made by the Munster oligarchy, without success. Dr. McKenna, Bishop of Cloyne, was arrested but enlarged; Mr. Nagle, of Garnavilla (a relative of Edmund Burke), Mr. Robert Keating, and several respectable Catholic gentlemen, were also arrested. It appears that Edmund Burke was charged by the ascendancy party with having "sent his brother Richard, recorder of Bristol, and Mr. Nagle, a relation, on a mission to Munster, to levy money on the Popish body for the use of the Whiteboys, who were exclusively Papists." The fact was, that Burke did originate a subscription for the defence of the second batch of victims, who, through his and other exertions, were fortunately saved from the fate of their predecessors.

Contemporaneous with the Whiteboys were the northern agrarians, called "Hearts of Steel," formed among the absentee Lord Downshire's tenants, in 1762; the "Oak Boys," so called from wearing oak leaves in their hats; and the "Peep o' Day Boys," the precursors of the Orange Association. The infection of conspiracy ran through all Ireland, and the disorder was neither short-lived nor trivial. Rightboys, Defenders, and a dozen other denominations descended from the same evil genius, whoever he was, that first introduced the system of signs, and passwords, and midnight meetings, among the peasantry of Ireland. The celebrated society of United Irishmen was the highest form which that principle, in our politics, ever reached. In its origin, it was mainly a Protestant organization.

From the first, the Catholic bishops and clergy strenuously opposed these secret societies. The Bishop of Cloyne issued a reprobatory pastoral; Father Arthur O'Leary employed his facile pen against them; the Bishop of Ossory anathematized them in his diocese. Priests in Kildare, Kilkenny, and Munster, were often in personal danger from these midnight legislators; their chapels had been frequently nailed up, and their bishops had been often obliged to remove them from one neighbourhood to another to prevent worse consequences. The infatuation was not to be stayed; the evil was engrafted on society, and many a long year, and woeful scene, and blighted life, and broken heart, was to signalize the perpetuation of secret societies among the population.

These startling symptoms of insubordination and lawlessness, while they furnished plausible pretexts to the advocates of repression, still further confirmed the Patriot party in their belief, that, nothing short of a free trade in exports and imports, and a thorough system of retrenchment in every branch of the public service, could save the nation from bankruptcy and ruin. This was Flood's opinion, and he had been long recognized as the leading spirit of the party. The aged Malone, true to his principles of conciliation and constitutionalism to the last, passed away from the scene, in the midst of the exciting events of 1776. For some years before his death, his former place had been filled by the younger and more vigorous member for Kilkenny, who, however, did not fail to consult him with all the deference due to his age, his services, and his wisdom. One of his last official acts was presiding over the committee of the whole House, which voted the American contingent, but rejected the admission of German troops to supply their place.

CHAPTER VII.

GRATTAN'S LEADERSHIP--"FREE TRADE," AND THE VOLUNTEERS.

The revolt of the American colonies against the oppressive legislation of the British Parliament, was the next circumstance that deeply affected the constitutional struggle, in which the Irish Parliament had so long been engaged. The similarity in the grievances of Ireland and the colonies, the close ties of kindred established between them, the extent of colonial commerce involved in the result, contributed to give the American Declaration of Independence more importance in men's eyes at Dublin, than anywhere else out of the colonies, except, perhaps, London.

The first mention made of American affairs to the Irish legislature, was in Lord Townsend's message in 1775, calling for the despatch of 4,000 men from the Irish establishment, to America, and offering to supply their place by as many foreign Protestant (German) troops. The demand was warmly debated. The proposition to receive the proffered foreign troops was rejected by a majority of thirty-eight, and the contingent for America passed on a division, upon Flood's plea that they would go out merely as "4,000 armed negotiators." This expression of the great parliamentary leader was often afterwards quoted to his prejudice, but we must remember, that, at the time it was employed, no one on either side of the contest had abandoned all hopes of accommodation, and that the significance of the phrase was rather pointed against Lord North than against the colonies. The 4,000 men went out, among them Lord Rawdon (afterwards Lord Moira), Lord Edward Fitzgerald, and many others, both officers and men, who were certainly no enemies of liberty, or the colonies.

Some slight relaxation of the commercial restrictions which operated so severely against Irish industry were made during the same year, but these were more than counterbalanced by the embargo on the export of provisions to America, imposed in February, 1776. This arbitrary measure--imposed by order in Council--was so near being censured by the Parliament then sitting, that the House was dissolved a month afterwards, and a new election ordered. To meet the new Parliament it was thought advisable to send over a new Viceroy, and accordingly Lord Buckinghamshire entered into office, with Sir Richard Heron as chief secretary.

In the last session of the late Parliament, a young *protege* of Lord Charlemont--he was only in his twenty-ninth year--had taken his seat for the borough of Charlemont. This was Henry Grattan, son of the Recorder of Dublin, and grandson of one of those Grattans who, according to Dean Swift, "could raise 10,000 men." The youth of Grattan had been neither joyous nor robust; in early manhood he had offended his father's conservatism; the profession of the law, to which he was bred, he found irksome and unsuited to his tastes; society, as then constituted, was repulsive to his over-sensitive spirit and high Spartan ideal of manly duty; no letters are sadder to read than the early correspondence of Grattan, till he had fairly found his inspiration in listening enraptured to the eloquent utterances of Chatham, or comparing political opinions with such a friend as Flood. At length he found a seat in the House of Commons, where, during his first session, he spoke on three or four occasions, briefly, modestly, and with good effect; there had been no sitting during 1776, nor before October of the following year; it was, therefore, in the sessions from '78 to '82 inclusive, that this young member raised himself to the head of the most eloquent men, in one of the most eloquent assemblies the world has ever seen.

The fact of Mr. Flood, after fourteen years of opposition, having accepted office under Lord Harcourt's administration, and defended the American expedition and the embargo, had greatly lessened the popularity of that eminent man. There was indeed, no lack of ability still left in the ranks of the opposition--for Burgh, Daly, and Yelverton were there; but for a supreme spirit like Grattan--whose burning tongue was ever fed from his heart of fire--there is always room in a free senate, how many soever able and accomplished men may surround him.

The fall of 1777 brought vital intelligence from America. General Burgoyne had surrendered at Saratoga, and France had decided to ally herself with the Americans.

The effect in England and in Ireland was immense. When the Irish Houses met, Mr. Grattan moved an address to the King in favour of retrenchment, and against the pension list, and Mr. Daly moved and carried an address deploring the continuance of the American war, with a governmental amendment assuring his Majesty that he might still rely on the services of his faithful Commons. The second Catholic relief bill, authorizing Papists to loan money on mortgage, to lease lands for any period not exceeding 999 years--to inherit and bequeath real property, so limited, passed, not without some difficulty, into law. The debate had been protracted, by adjournment after adjournment, over the greatest part of three months; the main motion had been further complicated by an amendment repealing the Test Act in favour of Dissenters, which was, fortunately, engrafted on the measure. The vote in the Commons, in favour of the bill so amended, was 127 *yeas* to 89 *nays*, and in the Lords, 44 **Contents** to 28 **Noncontents**.

In the English House of Commons, Lord Nugent moved, in April, a series of resolutions raising the embargo on the Irish provision trade; abolishing, so far as Ireland was concerned, the most restrictive clauses of the Navigation Act, both as to exports and imports, with the exception of the article of tobacco. Upon this the manufacturing and shipping interest of England, taking the alarm, raised such a storm in the towns and cities that the ministry of the day were compelled to resist the proposed changes, with a few trifling exceptions. But Grattan had caught up, in the other island, the cry of "free trade," and the people echoed it after their orator, until the whole empire shook with the popular demand.

But what gave pith and power to the Irish demands was the enrolment and arming of a numerous volunteer force, rendered absolutely necessary by the defenceless state of the kingdom. Mr. Flood had long before proposed a national militia, but being in opposition and in the minority, he had failed. To him and to Mr. Perry, as much as to Lord Charlemont and Mr. Grattan, the militia bill of 1778, and the noble army of volunteers equipped under its provisions, owed their origin. Whether this force was to be a regular militia, subject to martial law, or composed of independent companies, was for some months a subject of great anxiety at the castle; but necessity at length precipitated a decision in favour of volunteer companies, to be supplied with arms by the state, but drilled and clothed at their own expense, with power to elect their own officers. The official announcement of this decision once made, the organization spread rapidly over the whole kingdom. The Ulster corps, first organized, chose as their commander the Earl of Charlemont, while those of Leinster elected the Duke of Leinster. Simultaneously, resolutions against the purchase of English goods and wares were passed at public meetings, and by several of the corporate bodies. Lists of the importers of such goods were obtained at the custom houses, and printed in handbills, to the alarm of the importers. Swift's sardonic maxim, "to burn everything coming from England, *except the coals*," began to circulate as a toast in all societies, and the consternation of the Castle, at this resurrection of the redoubtable Dean, was almost equal to the apprehension entertained of him while living.

While the Castle was temporizing with both the military and the manufacture movement, in a vague expectation to defeat both, the press, as is usual in such national crises, teemed with publications of great fervour and ability. Dr. Jebb, Mr. (afterwards Judge) Johnson, Mr. Pollock, Mr. Charles Sheridan, Father Arthur O'Leary, and Mr. Dobbs, M.P., were the chief workers in this department of patriotic duty. Cheered, instructed, restrained within due bounds by these writings and the reported debates of Parliament, the independent companies proceeded with their organization. In July, 1779, after all the resources of prevarication had been exhausted, arms were issued to the several recognized corps, and the Irish volunteers became in reality a national army for domestic protection and defence.

When this point was reached, Mr. Grattan and his friends took anxious council as to their future movements. Parliament was to meet on the 12th of October, and in that sweet autumnal month, Grattan, Burgh, and Daly, met upon the sea-shore, near Bray, in view of one of the loveliest landscapes on earth, to form their plan for the session. They agreed on an amendment to the address in answer to the royal speech, demanding in explicit terms "free export and import" for Irish commerce. When Parliament met, and the address and amendment were moved, it was found that Flood, Burgh, Hutchinson, and Gardiner, though all holding offices of honour and emolument under government, would vote for it. Flood suggested to substitute the simple term "free trade," and with this and one other verbal alteration suggested by Burgh, the amendment passed with a single dissenting voice.

The next day the Speaker, Mr. Perry, who was all along in the confidence of the movers of the amendment, Daly, Grattan, Burgh, Flood, Hutchinson, Ponsonby,

Gardiner, and the whole House, went up with the amended address to the castle. The streets were lined with volunteers, commanded in person by the Duke of Leinster, who presented arms to the patriotic Commons as they passed. Most of the leading members wore the uniform of one or other of the national companies, and the people saw themselves at the same moment under the protection of a patriotic majority in the legislature, and a patriotic force in the field. No wonder their enthusiastic cheers rang through the corridors of the castle with a strangely jubilant and defiant emphasis. It was not simply the spectacle of a nation recovering its spirit, but recovering it with all military *eclat* and pageantry. It was the disarmed armed and triumphant--a revolution not only in national feeling, but in the external manifestation of that feeling. A change so profound stirred sentiments and purposes even deeper than itself, and suggested to the ardent imagination of Grattan the establishment of entire national independence, saving always the rights of the crown.

The next day, the Houses, not to be outdone in courtesy, voted their thanks to the volunteers for "their just and necessary exertions in defence of their country!"

CHAPTER VIII.

GRATTAN'S LEADERSHIP--LEGISLATIVE AND JUDICIAL INDEPENDENCE ESTABLISHED.

The task which Mr. Grattan felt called upon to undertake, was not *revolutionary*, in the usually accepted sense of the term. He was a Monarchist and a Whig in general politics; but he was an Irishman, proud and fond of his country, and a sincere lover of the largest religious liberty. With the independence of the judiciary and the legislature, with freedom of commerce and of conscience, he would be well content to stand by the British connection. "The sea," he said, in his lofty figurative language, "protests against union--the ocean against separation." But still, within certain legal limits, his task *was* revolutionary, and was undertaken under all the discouragements incident to the early stages of great constitutional reforms.

Without awaiting the action of the English Parliament, in relation to free trade, a public-spirited citizen of Dublin, Alderman James Horan, demanded an entry at the custom house, for some parcels of Irish woollens, which he proposed exporting to Rotterdam, contrary to the prohibitory enactment, the 10th and 11th of William III. The commissioners of customs applied for instructions to the Castle, and the Castle to the Secretary of State, Franklin's friend, Lord Hillsborough. For the moment a collision similar to that which had taken place at Boston, on a not dissimilar issue, seemed imminent. A frigate was stationed off Howth, with instructions, it was said, to intercept the prohibited woollens, but Alderman Horan, by the advice of his friends, allowed his application to remain on the custom house files. It had served its purpose of bringing home practically to the people, the value of the principle involved in the demand for freedom of exports and imports. At the same time that this practical argument was discussed in every circle, Mr. Grattan moved in the House of Commons, in amendment to the supply bill, that, "At this time it is inexpedient to grant new taxes." The government divided the House, but to their mortification found only 47 supporters; for Grattan's amendment there were 170. A subsequent amendment against granting duties for the support of the loan fund, was also carried by 138 to 100.

These adverse votes were communicated with great trepidation, by the Lord Lieutenant, to the British administration. At length Lord North thought it essential to make some concessions, and with this view he brought in resolutions, declaring the trade with the British colonies in America and Africa, and the free export of glass and woollens, open to the Irish merchant. A week later, similar resolutions were passed in the Irish Commons, and in February, 1780, "a free trade" in the sense in which it had been demanded, was established by law, placing Ireland in most respects, as to foreign and colonial commerce, on an equality with England.

In February, the Viceroy again alarmed the British administration, with the reported movement for the repeal of "Poyning's law,"--the statute which required heads of bills to be transmitted to, and approved in England, before they could be legislated upon. He received in reply, the royal commands to resist by every means in his power, any attempted "change in the constitution," and he succeeded in eliciting from the House of Lords, an address, strongly condemnatory of "the misguided men," who sought to raise such "groundless jealousies," between the two kingdoms. But the Patriot Commoners were not to be so deterred. They declared the repeal of Poyning's act, and the 6th of George I., to be their ultimatum, and notices of motion to that effect were immediately placed on the journals of the House of Commons.

In the early days of April, Grattan, who, more than any of our orators, except perhaps Burke, was sensitive to the aspects of external nature, and imbued with the poetry of her works, retired from the city, to his uncle Dean Marlay's house, Cellbridge Abbey, formerly the residence of Swift's ill-fated Vannessa. "Along the banks of that river," he said, many years afterwards, "amid the groves and bowers of Swift and Vannessa, I grew convinced that I was right; arguments, unanswerable, came to my mind, and what I then presaged, confirmed me in my determination to persevere." With an enthusiasm intensified and restrained--but wonderful in the fire and grandeur of its utterance--he rose in his place, on the 19th of the month, to move that "the King, Lords, and Commons of Ireland, are the only power competent to enact laws to bind Ireland." He was supported by Hussey Burgh, Yelverton, and Forbes; Flood favoured postponement, and laid the foundation of his future estrangement from Grattan; Daly was also for delay; Fitzgibbon, afterwards Lord Clare, Provost Hutchinson, and John Foster, afterwards Lord Oriel, resisted the motion. The Castle party moved in amendment that "there being an equivalent resolution already on the journals of the House"--alluding to one of the resolutions against Stafford's tyranny in 1641--a new resolution was unnecessary. This amendment was carried by 136 to 79, thus affirming the formula of independence adopted in 1641, but depriving Grattan of the honour of putting it, in his own words, on the record. The substantial result, however, was the same; the 19th of April was truly what Grattan described it, "a great day for Ireland." "It is with the utmost concern," writes the Viceroy next day to Lord Hillsborough, "I must acquaint your Lordship that although so many gentlemen expressed their concern that the subject had been introduced, the sense of the House *against* the obligation of *any statutes* of the Parliament of Great Britain, within this kingdom, is represented to me to have been almost unanimous."

Ten days later, a motion of Mr. Yelverton's to repeal Poyning's law, as far as related to the Irish privy council's supervision of heads of bills, was negatived by 130 to 105.

During the remainder of the session the battle of independence was fought on the Mutiny Bill. The Viceroy and the Chief Secretary, playing the game of power, were resolved that the influence of the crown should not be diminished, so far as the military establishments were concerned. Two justices of the peace in Sligo and Mayo, having issued writs of *habeas corpus* in favour of deserters from the army, on the ground that neither the British Mutiny Act, nor any other British statute, was binding on Ireland, unless confirmed by an act of its own legislature, brought up anew the whole question. Lord North, who, with all his proverbial tact and good humour, in the House of Commons, always pursued the most arbitrary policy throughout the empire, proposed a perpetual Mutiny Bill for Ireland, instead of the Annual Bill, in force in England. It was introduced in the Irish House of Commons by Mr. Gervase Parker Bushe, and, by a vote of two to one, postponed for a fortnight. During the interval, the British authorities remained obdurate to argument and remonstrance. In vain, the majority of the Irish privy counsellors advised concession; in vain, Flood, who was consulted, pointed out the futility of attempting to force such a measure; it was forced, and, under the cry of loyalty, a draft bill was carried through both Houses, and remitted to England in June. Early in August it was returned; on the 12th it was read a first time; on the 16th, a second; and it was carried through Committee by 114 to 62. It was at this emergency the Volunteers performed the second act of their great drama of Ireland's liberation. A series of reviews were held, and significant addresses presented to Lord Camden (then on a visit to the country), Lord Charlemont, Mr. Flood, and Mr. Grattan. On the reassembling of Parliament in August, when the bill was referred to, Mr. Grattan declared that he would resist it to the last; that if passed into law, he and his friends would *secede*, and would appeal to the people in "a formal instrument." A new series of corporation and county meetings was convened by the Patriot party, which warmly condemned the Perpetual Mutiny Act, and as warmly approved the repeal of Poyning's Act, and the 6th of George I.: questions which were all conceived to be intermixed together, and to flow from the assertion of a common principle. Parliament being prorogued in September, only threw the whole controversy back again into the furnace of popular agitation. The British Government tried a lavish distribution of titles and a change of Viceroys,--Lord Carlisle being substituted in December for Lord Buckingham--but the spirit abroad was too general and too earnest, to be quelled by the desertion of individuals, however numerous or influential. With Lord Carlisle, came, as Chief Secretary, Mr. Eden, afterwards Lord Auckland; he had been, with his chief, a peace commissioner to America, two years before, and had failed; he was an intriguing and accomplished man, but he proved himself as unequal as Heron or Rigby to combat the movement for Irish independence.

Parliament was not again called together till the month of October, 1781; the interval being busily occupied on both sides with endeavours to create and sustain a party. Soon after the meeting, Mr. Grattan, seconded by Mr. Flood, moved for a limitation of the Mutiny Bill, which was lost; a little later, Mr. Flood himself introduced a somewhat similar motion, which was also outvoted two to one; and again, during the session, Mr. Yelverton, having abandoned his promised motion against Poyning's law, on news of Lord Cornwallis's surrender reaching Dublin, Flood took it up, moved it, and was defeated. A further measure of relief for Roman Catholics, introduced by Mr. Gardiner, author of the act of 1778, and warmly supported by Grattan, was resisted by Flood in the one House, and Lord Charlemont in the other. It miscarried, and left another deposit of disagreement between the actual and the former leader of the Patriot party.

Still no open rupture had taken place between the two Patriot orators. When the convention of the volunteers was called at Dungannon for the 15th of February, 1782, they consulted at Charlemont House as to the resolutions to be passed. They were agreed on the constitutional question; Grattan, of his own generous free will, added the resolution in favour of emancipation. Two hundred and forty-two delegates, representing 143 corps, unanimously adopted the resolutions so drafted, as their own, and, from the old head-quarters of Hugh O'Neil, sent forth anew an unequivocal demand for civil and religious liberty. The example of Ulster soon spread through Ireland. A meeting of the Leinster volunteers, Mr. Flood in the chair, echoed it from Dublin; the Munster corps endorsed it unanimously at Cork; Lord Clanrickarde summoned together those of the western counties at Portumna--an historic spot, suggestive of striking associations. Strengthened by these demonstrations of public opinion, Mr. Grattan brought forward, on the 22nd of February, his motion declaratory of the rights of Ireland. An amendment in favour of a six months' postponement of the question was carried; but on the 16th of April, just two years from his first effort on the subject (the administration of Lord North having fallen in the meantime), the orator had the satisfaction of carrying his address declaratory of Irish legislative independence. It was on this occasion that he exclaimed: "I found Ireland on her knees; I watched over her with a paternal solicitude; I have traced her progress from injury to arms, and from arms to liberty. Spirit of Swift! Spirit of Molyneux! your genius has prevailed! Ireland is now a nation! in that new character I hail her! and bowing to her august presence, I say, ***Esto perpetua!***"

Never was a new nation more nobly heralded into existence! Never was an old nation more reverently and tenderly lifted up and restored! The Houses adjourned to give England time to consider Ireland's ***ultimatum***. Within a month it was accepted by the new British administration, and on the 27th of May, the new Whig Viceroy, the Duke of Portland, was authorized to announce from the throne the establishment of the judicial and legislative independence of Ireland.

CHAPTER IX.

THE ERA OF INDEPENDENCE--FIRST PERIOD.

The accession of the Rockingham administration to power, in 1782, was followed by the recall of Lord Carlisle, and the substitution, as Viceroy, of one of the leading Lords of the Whig party. The nobleman selected to this office was William Henry, third Duke of Portland, afterwards twice prime minister; then in the prime of life, possessed of a very ample fortune, and uniting in his own person the two great Whig families of Bentinck and Cavendish. The policy he was sent to represent at Dublin was undoubtedly an imperial policy; a policy which looked as anxiously to the integrity of the empire as any Tory cabinet could have desired; but it was, in most other respects, a policy of conciliation and concession, dictated by the enlarged wisdom of Burke, and adopted by the magnanimous candour of Fox. Yet by a generous people, who always find it more difficult to resist a liberal than an illiberal administration, it was, in reality, a policy more to be feared than welcomed; for its almost certain effects were to divide their ranks into two sections--a moderate and an extreme party--between whom the national cause, only half established, might run great danger of being lost, almost as soon as it was won.

With the Duke of Portland was associated, as Chief Secretary, Colonel Fitzpatrick, of the old Ossory family, one of those Irish wits and men of fashion, who form so striking a group in the middle and later years of King George III. As the personal and political friend of Flood, Charlemont, and Grattan, and the first Irish secretary for several administrations, he shared the brilliant ovation with which the Duke of Portland was received, on his arrival at Dublin; but for the reason already mentioned, the imperial, in so far as opposed to the national policy, found an additional advantage in the social successes and great personal popularity of the new secretary.

The critical months which decided the contest for independence--April and May--passed over fortunately for Ireland. The firmness of the leaders in both Houses, the energy especially of Grattan, whose cry was "No time, no time!" and the imposing attitude of the volunteers, carried the question. Lord Rockingham and Mr. Fox by letter, the new Viceroy and Secretary in person, had urged every argument for adjournment and delay, but Grattan's *ultimatum* was sent over to England, and finally and formally accepted. The demands were *five*. I. The repeal of the 6th of George I. II. The repeal of the Perpetual Mutiny Act. III. An Act to abolish the alteration or suppression of Bills. IV. An Act to establish the final jurisdiction of the Irish Courts and the Irish House of Lords. V. The repeal of Poyning's Law. This was the constitutional charter of 1782, which restored Ireland, for the first time in that century, to the rank and dignity of a free nation.

Concession once determined on, the necessary bills were introduced in both Parliaments simultaneously, and carried promptly into law. On the 27th of May, the Irish Houses were enabled to congratulate the Viceroy that "no constitutional question any longer existed between the two countries." In England it was proclaimed no less explicitly by Fox and his friends, that the independency of the two legislatures "was fixed and ascertained for ever." But there was, unfortunately, one ground for dispute still left, and on that ground Henry Flood and Henry Grattan parted, never to be reconciled.

The elder Patriot, whose conduct from the moment of his retirement from office, in consequence of his Free Trade vote and speech in '79, had been, with occasional exceptions, arising mostly from bodily infirmity, as energetic and consistent as that of Grattan himself, saw no sufficient constitutional guarantee in mere acts of Parliament repealing other acts. He demanded "express renunciation" of legislative supremacy on the part of England; while Grattan maintained the sufficiency of "simple repeal." It is possible even in such noble natures as these men had--so strangely are we constituted--that there was a latent sense of personal rivalry, which prompted them to grasp, each, at the larger share of patriotic honour. It is possible that there were other, and inferior men, who exasperated this latent personal rivalry. Flood had once reigned supreme, until Grattan eclipsed him in the sudden splendour of his career. In scholarship and in genius the elder Patriot was, taken all in all, the full peer of his successor; but Grattan had the national temperament, and he found his way more readily into the core of the national heart; he was the man of the later, the bolder, and the more liberal school; and such was the rapidity of his movements, that even Flood, from '79 to '82, seemed to be his follower, rather than his coadjutor. In the hopeful crisis of the struggle, the slower and more experienced statesman was for the moment lost sight of. The leading motions were all placed or left in the hands of Grattan by the consent of their leading friends; the bills repealing the Mutiny Act, the 6th George I., and Poyning's law, were entrusted to Burgh, Yelverton, and Forbes; the thanks of the House were voted to Grattan alone after the victory, with the substantial addition of 50,000 pounds to purchase for him an estate, which should become an enduring monument of the national gratitude.

The open rupture between the two great orators followed fast on the triumph of their common efforts. It was still the first month--the very honeymoon of independence. On the 13th of June, Mr. Grattan took occasion to notice in his place, that a late British act relating to the importation of sugars, was so generally worded as apparently to include Ireland; but this was explained to be a mere error of the clerk, the result of haste, and one which would be promptly corrected. Upon this Mr. Flood first took occasion to moot the insufficiency of "simple repeal," and the necessity of "express renunciation," on the part of England. On the 19th, he moved a formal resolution on the subject, which was superseded by the order of the day; but on the 19th of July, he again moved, at great length, and with great power of logical and historical argument, for leave to bring in an Irish Bill of Rights, declaring "the sole and exclusive right of the Irish Parliament to make laws in all cases whatsoever, *external and internal*." He was supported by Sir Simon Bradstreet, Mr. English, and Mr. Walshe, and opposed by Grattan, who, in one of his finest efforts, proposed a counter resolution, "that the legislature of Ireland is independent; and that any person who shall, by writing or otherwise, maintain that a right in any other country, to make laws for Ireland, *internally* or *externally*, exists or can be revived, *is inimical to the peace of both kingdoms*." This extreme proposition-- pointing out all who differed from himself as public enemies--the mover, however, withdrew, and substituted in its stead the milder formula, that leave was refused to bring in the bill, because the sole and exclusive right of legislation in the Irish Parliament in all cases, whether externally or internally, hath been already asserted by Ireland, and fully, finally, and irrevocably acknowledged by the British Parliament. Upon this motion Flood did not think it advisable to divide the House, so it passed without a division.

But the moot point thus voted down in Parliament disquieted and alarmed the minds of many out of doors. The volunteers as generally sided with Flood as the Parliament had sided with Grattan. The lawyer corps of the city of Dublin, containing all the great names of the legal profession, endorsed the constitutional law of the member for Kilkenny; the Belfast volunteers did likewise; and Grattan's own corps, in a respectful address, urged him to give his adherence to the views of "the best informed body of men in the kingdom,"--the lawyers' corps. Just at that moment Lord Abingdon, in the English House of Lords, gave notice of a mischievous motion to assert the external supremacy of the English Parliament; and Lord Mansfield, in the King's Bench, decided an Irish appeal case, notwithstanding the recent statute establishing the judicial independence of the Irish courts. It is true the case had been appealed before the statute was passed; and that Lord Abingdon withdrew his motion for want of a seconder; but the alarm was given, and the popular mind in Ireland, jealously watchful of its new-born liberties, saw in these attempts renewed cause for apprehension. In opposition to all this suddenly awakened suspicion and jealousy, Grattan, who naturally enough assumed his own interest in preserving the new constitution to be quite equal to those who cast doubts on its security, invariably held one language. The settlement already made, according to his view, was final; it was an international treaty; its maintenance must depend on the ability and disposition of the parties to uphold it, rather than on the multiplication of declaratory acts. Ireland had gone to England with a charter, not for a charter, and the nation which would insist upon the humiliation of another, was a foolish nation. This was the lofty light in which he viewed the whole transaction, and in this light, it must be added, he continued to view it till the last. Many of the chief English and Irish jurists of his time, Lord Camden, Lord Kenyon, Lord Erskine, Lord Kilwarden, Judges Chamberlain, Smith, and Kelly, Sir Samuel Rommilly, Sir Arthur Pigott, and several others, agreed fully in Grattan's doctrine, that the settlement of '82 was final and absolute, and "terminated all British jurisdiction over Ireland." But although these are all great names, the instinct of national self-preservation may be considered in such critical moments more than a counterpoise to the most matured opinions of the oracles of the law. Such must have been the conviction also of the English Parliament, for, immediately on their meeting in January, 1783, they passed the *Act of Renunciation* (23rd George III.), expressly declaring their admission of the "exclusive rights of the Parliament and Courts of Ireland in matters of legislature and judicature." This was Flood's greatest triumph. Six months before his doctrine obtained but three supporters in the Irish Commons; now, at his suggestion, and on his grounds, he saw it unanimously affirmed by the British Parliament.

On two other questions of the utmost importance these leading spirits also widely differed. Grattan was in favour of, and Flood opposed to, Catholic emancipation; while Flood was In favour of, and Grattan, at that moment, opposed to, a complete reform of parliamentary representation. The Catholic question had its next great triumph after Flood's death, as will be mentioned further on; but the history of the Irish reform movement of 1783, '84, and '85, may best be disposed of here.

The Reformers were a new party rising naturally out of the popular success of 1782. They were composed of all but a few of the more aristocratic corps of the volunteers, of the townsmen, especially in the seaports and manufacturing towns, of the admirers of American example, of the Catholics who had lately acquired property and recognition, but not the elective franchise, of the gentry of the second and third degree of wealth, overruled and overshadowed by the greater lords of the soil. The substantial grievance of which they complained was, that of the 300 members of the House of Commons, only 72 were returned by the people; 53 Peers having the power to nominate 123 and secure the election of 10 others; while 52 Commoners nominated 91 and controlled the choice of 4 others. The constitution of what ought to have been the people's house was, therefore, substantially in the hands of an oligarchy of about a hundred great proprietors, bound together by the spirit of their class, by intermarriage, and by the hereditary possession of power. To reduce this exorbitant influence within reasonable bounds, was the just and wise design to which Flood dedicated all his energies, after the passage of the *Act of Renunciation*, and the success of which would certainly have restored him to complete equality with Grattan.

In the beginning of 1783, the famous coalition ministry of Lord North and Mr. Pox was formed in England. They were at first represented at Dublin Castle, for a few months, by Lord Temple, who succeeded the Duke of Portland, and established the order of *Knights of Saint Patrick*; then by Lord Northington, who dissolved Parliament early in July. A general election followed, and the reform party made their influence felt in all directions. County meetings were held; conventions by districts and by provinces were called by the reforming Volunteers, in July, August, and September. The new Parliament was to be opened on the 14th of October, and the Volunteers resolved to call a convention of their whole body at Dublin, for the 10th of November.

The Parliament met according to summons, but though searching retrenchment was spoken of, no promise was held out of a constitutional reform; the limitation of the regular troops to a fixed number was declared advisable, and a vote of thanks to the Volunteers was passed without demur. But the proceedings of the Houses were soon eclipsed by the portentous presence of the Volunteer Convention. One hundred and sixty delegates of corps attended on the appointed day. The Royal Exchange was too small to accommodate them, so they adjourned to the Rotunda, accompanied by mounted guards of honour. The splendid and eccentric Bishop of Derry (Earl of Bristol), had his dragoon guards; the courtly but anxious Charlemont had his troop of horse; Flood, tall, emaciated, and solemn to sadness, was hailed with popular acclamations; there also marched the popular Mr. Day, afterwards Judge; Robert Stewart, father of Lord Castlereagh; Sir Richard Musgrave, a reformer also, in his youth, who lived to confound reform with rebellion in his old age. The Earl of Charlemont was elected president of this imposing body, and for an entire month Dublin was divided between the extraordinary spectacle of two legislatures--one sitting at the Rotunda, and the other at College Green, many members of each being members of the other; the uniform of the volunteer sparkling in the Houses, and the familiar voices of both Houses being heard deliberating and debating among the Volunteers.

At length, on the 29th of November, after three weeks' laborious gestation, Flood brought before Parliament the plan of reform agreed to by the Convention. It proposed to extend the franchise to every *Protestant* freeholder possessed of a lease worth forty shillings yearly; to extend restricted borough constituencies by annexing to them neighbouring populous parishes; that the voting should be held on one and the same day; that pensioners of the crown should be incapable of election; that members accepting office should be subject to re-election; that a stringent bribery oath should be administered to candidates returned; and, finally, that the duration of Parliament should be limited to three years. It was, indeed, an excellent Protestant Reform Bill, for though the Convention had received Father Arthur O'Leary with military honours, and contained many warm friends of Catholic rights, the majority were still intolerant of *religious* freedom. In this majority it is painful to have to record the names of Flood and Charlemont.

The debate which followed the introduction of this proposed change in the constitution was stormy beyond all precedent. Grattan, who just one month before (Oct. 28th) had that fierce vituperative contest with Flood familiar to every school-boy, in its worst and most exaggerated form, supported the proposal. The law officers of the crown, Fitzgibbon, Yelverton, Scott, denounced it as an audacious attempt of armed men to dictate to the House its own constitution. The cry of privilege and prerogative was raised, and the measure was rejected by 157 to 77. Flood, weary in mind and body, retired to his home; the Convention, which outsat the House, adjourned, amid the bitter indignation of some, and the scarcely concealed relief of others. Two days later they met and adopted a striking address to the throne, and adjourned *sine die*. This was, in fact, the last important day of the Volunteers as a political institution. An attempt a month later to re-assemble the Convention was dexterously defeated by the President, Lord Charlemont. The regular army was next session increased to 15,000 men; 20,000 pounds were voted to clothe and equip a rival force--"the Militia"--and the Parliament, which had three times voted them its thanks, now began to look with satisfaction on their rapid disorganization and disbandment.

This, perhaps, is the fittest place to notice the few remaining years of the public life of Henry Flood. After the session of 1785, in which he had been outvoted on every motion he proposed, he retired from the Irish Parliament, and allowed himself to be persuaded, at the age of fifty-three, to enter the English. He was elected for Winchester, and made his first essay on the new scene, on his favourite subject of representative reform. But his health was undermined; he failed, except on one or two occasions, to catch the ear of that fastidious assembly, and the figure he made there somewhat disappointed his friends. He returned to Kilkenny to die in 1791, bequeathing a large portion of his fortune to Trinity College, to enrich its MS.

library, and to found a permanent professorship of the Irish language. "He was an oak of the forest," said Grattan, "too old to be transplanted at fifty." "He was a man," said one who also knew him well, Sir Jonah Barrington, "of profound abilities, high manners, and great experience in the affairs of Ireland. He had deep information, an extensive capacity, and a solid judgment." In his own magnificent "Ode to Fame," he has pictured his ideal of the Patriot-orator, who finds some consolation amid the unequal struggle with the enemies of his country, foreign and domestic, in a prophetic vision of his own renown. Unhappily, the works of this great man come down to us in as fragmentary a state as those of Chatham; but enough remains to enable us to class him amongst the greatest masters of our speech, and, as far as the drawbacks allowed, among the foremost statesmen of his country.

It is painful to be left in doubt, as we are, whether he was ever reconciled to Grattan. The presumption, from the silence of their cotemporaries, is, that they never met again as friends. But it is consoling to remember that in his grave, the survivor rendered him that tribute of justice which almost takes the undying sting out of the philippic of 1783; it is well to know, also, that one of Grattan's latest wishes, thirty years after the death of Flood, when he felt his own last hours approaching, was, that it should be known that he "did not speak the vile abuse reported in the Debates" in relation to his illustrious rival. The best proof that what he did say was undeserved, is that that rival's reputation for integrity and public spirit has survived even his terrible onslaught.

CHAPTER X.

THE ERA OF INDEPENDENCE--SECOND PERIOD.

The second period of the era of independence may be said to embrace the nine years extending from the dissolution of the last Volunteer Convention, at the end of 1784, to the passage of the Catholic Relief Bill of 1793. They were years of continued interest and excitement, both in the popular and parliamentary affairs of the country; but the events are, with the exception of the last named, of a more secondary order than those of the previous period.

The session of 1785 was first occupied with debates relating to what might be called the cross-channel trade between England and Ireland. The question of trade brought with it, necessarily, the question of revenue; of the duties levied in both kingdoms; of the conflict of their commercial laws, and the necessity of their assimilation; of the appropriations to be borne by each, to the general expense of the army and navy; of the exclusive right of the English East India Company to the Indian trade;--in short, the whole of the fiscal and commercial relations of the two countries were now to be examined and adjusted, as their constitutional relations had been in previous years.

The first plan came from the Castle, through Mr. Thomas Orde, then Chief Secretary, afterwards Lord Bolton. It consisted of eleven propositions, embracing every division of the subject. They had been arrived at by consultation with Mr. Joshua Pim, a most worthy Quaker merchant, the founder of an equally worthy family; Mr. Grattan, Mr. Foster, and others. They were passed as resolutions in Ireland, and sent by Mr. Orde to England to see whether they would be adopted there also, the second Pitt, then Chancellor of the Exchequer, gave his concurrence, but when he introduced to the English Parliament *his* resolutions--twenty in number--it was found that in several important respects they differed from the Irish propositions. On being taken up and presented to the Irish Parliament, in August, the administration found they could command, in a full House, only a majority of sixteen for their introduction, and so the whole arrangement was abandoned. No definite commercial treaty between the two kingdoms was entered into until the Union, and there can be little doubt that the miscarriage of the Convention of 1785 was one of the determining causes of that Union.

The next session was chiefly remarkable for an unsuccessful attempt to reduce the Pension List. In this debate, Curran, who had entered the House in 1783, particularly distinguished himself. A fierce exchange of personalities with Mr. Fitzgibbon led to a duel between them, in which, fortunately, neither was wounded, but their public hostility was transferred to the arena of the courts, where some of the choicest *morceaux* of genuine Irish wit were uttered by Curran, at the expense of his rival, first as Attorney-General, and subsequently as Chancellor.

The session of 1787 was introduced by a speech from the throne, in which the usual paragraph in favour of the Protestant Charter Schools was followed by another advising the establishment of a general system of schools. This raised the entire question of education, one of the most difficult to deal with in the whole range of Irish politics. On the 10th of April, Mr. Orde--destined to be the author of just, but short-lived projects--introduced his plan of what might be called national education. He proposed to establish four great provincial academies, a second university in some north-western county, to reform the twenty-two diocesan schools, so richly endowed under the 28th Henry VIII., and to affiliate on Trinity College two principal preparatory schools, north and south. In 1784, and again in this very year, the humane John Howard had reported of the Irish Charter Schools, then half a century established, that they were "a disgrace to all society." Sir J. Fitzpatrick, the Inspector of Prisons, confirmed the general impression of Howard: he found the children in these schools "puny, filthy, ill clothed, without linen, indecent to look upon." A series of resolutions was introduced by Mr. Orde, as the basis of better legislation in the next session; but it is to be regretted that the proposed reform never went farther than the introduction and adoption of these resolutions.

The session of 1788 was signalized by a great domestic and a great imperial discussion--the Tithe question, and the Regency question.

The Tithe question had slumbered within the walls of Parliament since the days of Swift, though not in the lonely lodges of the secret agrarian societies. Very recent outbreaks of the old agrarian combinations against both excessive rents and excessive tithes, in the Leinster as well as in southern counties, had called general attention to the subject, when Grattan, in 1787, moved that, if it should appear, by the commencement of the following session, that tranquillity had been restored in the disturbed districts, the House would take into consideration the subject of tithes. Accordingly, very early in the next ensuing session, he moved for a committee on the subject, in a three hours' speech, which ranks among the very highest efforts of his own or any other age. He was seconded by Lord Kingsborough, one of the most liberal men of his order, and sustained by Curran and Brownlow; he was opposed by Attorney-General Fitzgibbon, and by Messrs. Hobart, Browne, and Parsons. The vote was, *for* the Committee of Inquiry, 49; **against** it, 121. A second attempt, a little later in the session, was equally unsuccessful, except for the moral effect produced out of doors by another of those speeches, which it is impossible to read even at this day, without falling into the attitude, and assuming the intonation, and feeling the heartfelt inspiration of the orator.

The Regency question was precipitated upon both Parliaments by the mental disorder, which, for the second or third time, attacked George III., in 1788. The question was, whether the Prince of Wales should reign with as full powers as if his father were actually deceased; whether there should be restrictions or no restrictions. Mr. Pitt and his colleagues contended successfully for restrictions in England, while Mr. Fox and the opposition took the contrary position. The English Houses and people went with Pitt, but the Irish Parliament went for an unconditional regency. They resolved to offer the crown of Ireland to him they considered *de* facto their Sovereign, as freely as they had rendered their allegiance to the incapable king; but the Lord Lieutenant--the Marquis of Buckingham--declined to transmit their over-zealous address, and by the time their joint delegation of both Houses reached London, George III. had recovered! They received the most gracious reception at Carlton House, but they incurred the implacable enmity of William Pitt, and created a second determining cause in his mind in favour of an early legislative union.

The prospect of the accession of the Prince to power, wrought a wonderful and a salutary change, though temporary, in the Irish Commons. In the session of 1789, Mr Grattan carried, by 105 to 85, a two months', in amendment to a twelve-months' supply bill. Before the two months expired he brought in his police bill, his pension bill, and his bill to prevent officers of the revenue from voting at elections, but ere these reforms could be passed into law, the old King recovered, the necessary majority was reversed, and the measures, of course, defeated or delayed till better times. The triumph of the oligarchy was in proportion to their fright. The House having passed a vote of censure on Lord Buckingham, the Viceroy, for refusing to transmit their address to the Regent, a threat was now held out that every one who had voted for the censure, holding an office of honour or emolument in Ireland, would be made "the victim of his vote." In reply to this threat, a "Round Robin" was signed by the Duke of Leinster, the Archbishop of Tuam, eighteen peers, all the leading Whig commoners--the Ponsonbys, Langrishes, Grattan, Connolly, Curran, O'Neil, Day, Charles Francis Sheridan, Bowes Daly, George Ogle, etc., etc.--declaring that they would regard any such proscription as an attack on the independence of Parliament, and would jointly oppose any administration who should resort to such proscription. But the bold and domineering spirit of Fitzgibbon--the leader of the Castle party, then, and long afterwards--did not shrink before even so formidable a phalanx. The Duke of Leinster was dismissed from the honorary office of Master of the Rolls; the Earl of Shannon, from the Vice-Treasurership; William Ponsonby from the office of Postmaster-General; Charles Francis Sheridan, from that of Secretary at War, and ten or twelve other prominent members of the *Irish* administration lost places and pensions to the value of 20,000 pounds a year, for their over-zeal for the Prince of Wales. At the same time, Mr. Fitzgibbon was appointed Lord Chancellor, a vacancy having opportunely occurred, by the death of Lord Lifford, in the very midst of the prescriptive crisis. This elevation transferred him to the Upper House, where, for the remaining years of the Parliament, he continued to dogmatize and domineer, as he had done in the Commons, often rebuked, but never abashed. Indeed, the milder manners of the patrician body were ill suited to resist this ermined demagogue, whose motto through life was ***audacity, again audacity, and always audacity***. The names of Wolfe, Toler, Corry, Coote, Beresford, and Cooke, are also found among the promotions to legal and administrative office; names familiar to the last generation as the pillars of the oligarchical faction, before and after the Union. To swamp the opposition peers, the Earls of Antrim, Tyrone, and Hillsborough were made Marquises of Antrim, Waterford, and Downshire; the Viscounts Glenawley, Enniskillen, Erne, and Carysfort, were created Earls of Annesley, Enniskillen, Erne, and Carysfort. Then Judge Scott became Viscount Clonmel; then the Lordships of Loftus, Londonderry, Kilmaine, Cloncurry, Mountjoy, Glentworth, and Caledon, were founded for as many convenient Commoners, who either paid for their patents, in boroughs, or in hard cash. It was the very reign and carnival of corruption, over which presided the invulnerable Chancellor--a true "King of Misrule." In reference to this appalling spectacle, well might Grattan exclaim--"In a free country the path of public treachery leads to the block; but in a nation governed like a province, to the helm!" But the thunders of the orator fell, and were quenched in the wide spreading waters of corruption.

The Whig Club--an out-of-door auxiliary of the opposition --was a creation of this year. It numbered the chief signers of the "Round Robin," and gained many adherents. It exercised very considerable influence in the general election of 1790, and for the few following years, until it fell to pieces in the presence of the more ardent politics which preceded the storm of 1798.

Backed though he was by Mr. Pitt, both as his relative and principal, the Marquis of Buckingham was compelled to resign the government, and to steal away from Dublin, under cover of night, like an absconding debtor. The Chancellor and the Speaker--Fitzgibbon and Foster, Irishmen at least by birth and name--were sworn in as Justices, until the arrival of the Earl of Westmoreland, in the ensuing January.

The last two Viceroys of the decade thus closed, form a marked contrast worthy of particular portraiture. The Duke of Rutland, a dashing profligate, was sent over, it was thought, to ruin public liberty by undermining private virtue, a task in which he found a willing helpmate in his beautiful but dissipated Duchess. During his three years' reign were sown the seeds of that reckless private expenditure, and general corruption of manners, which drove so many bankrupt lords and gentlemen into the market overt, where Lord Castlereagh and Secretary Cooke, a dozen years later, priced the value of their parliamentary cattle. Lord Rutland died of dissipation at little over thirty, and was succeeded by the Marquis of Buckingham (formerly Lord Temple), the founder of the Irish Order of Chivalry, a person of the greatest pretensions, as a reformer of abuses and an enemy of government by corruption. Yet with all his affected superiority to the base arts of his predecessor, the Marquis's system was still more opposite to every idea of just government than the Duke's. The one outraged public morals, the other pensioned and ennobled the betrayers of public trusts; the one naturalized the gaming-table and the keeping of mistresses as customs of Irish society; the other sold or allowed the highest offices and honours of the state--from a weighership in the butter market to an earl's coronet--to be put up at auction, and knocked down to the highest bidder. How cheering in contrast with the shameful honours, flaunted abroad in those shameful days, are even the negative virtues of the Whig patricians, and how splendid the heroic constancy of Charlemont, Grattan, Curran, and their devoted minority of honest legislators!

With Lord Westmoreland was associated, as Chief Secretary, Mr. Hobart, formerly in the army, a man of gay, convivial habits, very accomplished, and, politically, very unprincipled. These gentlemen, both favourites of Pitt, adopted the counsellors, and continued the policy of the late Viceroy. In pursuance of this policy, a dissolution took place, and the general election of 1790 was ordered. We have already exhibited the influences which controlled the choice of members of the House of Commons. Of the one hundred and five great proprietors, who owned two-thirds of the seats, perhaps a fourth might be found in the ranks of the Whig club. The only other hope for the national party was in the boroughs, which possessed a class of freemen, engaged in trade, too numerous to be bought, or too public spirited to be dictated to. Both influences combined might hope to return a powerful minority, and, on this occasion (1790) they certainly did so. Grattan and Lord Henry Fitzgerald were elected for Dublin, over the Lord Mayor and one of the Aldermen, backed by the whole power of the Castle; Curran, Ponsonby, Brownlow, Forbes, and nearly all "the victims of their vote" were re-elected. To these old familiar names were now added others destined to equal, if not still wider fame--Arthur Wellesley, member for Trim; Arthur O'Conor, member for Phillipstown; Jonah Barrington, member for Tuam; and Robert Stewart, one of the members for the County Down, then only in his twenty-second year, and, next to Lord Edward Fitzgerald, lately elected for Athy, the most extreme reformer among the new members. Arthur O'Conor, on the other hand, commenced his career with the Court by moving the address in answer to the speech from the throne!

The new Parliament, which met in July, 1790, unanimously re-elected Mr. Foster, Speaker; passed a very loyal address, and, after a fortnight's sitting, was prorogued till the following January. The session of '91 was marked by no event of importance, the highest opposition vote seems to have been from 80 to 90, and the ministerial majority never less than 50. The sale of Peerages, the East India trade, the Responsibility (for money warrants) Bill, the Barren Lands Bill, and the Pension Bill, were the chief topics. A committee to inquire into the best means of encouraging breweries, and discouraging the use of spirituous liquors, was also granted, and some curious facts elicited. Nothing memorable was done, but much that was memorable was said--for the great orator had still a free press, and a home audience to instruct and elevate. The truth is, the barrenness of these two sessions was due to the general prosperity of the country, more even than to the dexterous management of Major Hobart and the Cabinet balls of Lord Westmoreland. There was, moreover, hanging over the minds of men the electric pressure of the wonderful events with which France shook the Continent, and made the Islands tremble. There was hasty hope, or idle exultation, or pious fear, or panic terror, in the hearts of the leading spectators of that awful drama, according to the prejudices or principles they maintained. Over all the three kingdoms there was a preternatural calm, resembling that physical stillness which in other latitude precedes the eruption of volcanoes.

CHAPTER XI.

THE ERA OF INDEPENDENCE--THIRD PERIOD-- CATHOLIC RELIEF BILL OF 1793.

Before relating the consequences which attended the spread of French revolutionary opinions in Ireland, it is necessary to exhibit the new and very important position assumed by the Roman Catholic population at that period.

The relief bills in 1774 and 1778, by throwing open to Catholics the ordinary means of acquiring property, whether moveable or immoveable, had enabled many of them to acquire fortunes, both in land and in trade. Of this class were the most efficient leaders in the formation of the Catholic Committee of 1790--John Keogh, Edward Byrne, and Richard McCormick. They were all men who had acquired fortunes, and who felt and cherished the independence of self-made men. They were not simply Catholic agitators claiming an equality of civil and religious rights with their Protestant fellow-countrymen; they were nationalists, in the broadest and most generous meaning of the term. They had contributed to the ranks and expenses of the Volunteers; they had swelled the chorus of Grattan's triumph, and borne their share of the cost in many a popular contest. The new generation of Protestant patriots--such men as the Hon. Simon Butler, Wolfe Tone, and Thomas Addis Emmet, were their intimate associates, shared their opinions, and regarded their exclusion from the pale of the constitution as a public calamity.

There was another and a smaller, but not less important class--the remnant of the ancient Catholic peerage and landed gentry, who, through four generations, had preferred civil death to religious apostasy. It was impossible not to revere the heroic constancy of that class, and the personal virtues of many among them. But they were, perhaps, constitutionally, too timid and too punctilious to conduct a popular movement to a successful issue. They had, after much persuasion, lent their presence to the Committee, but on some alarm, which at that time seems to have been premature, of the introduction of French revolutionary principles among their associates, they seceded in a mass. A formal remonstrance against what remained, pretending to act for the Catholic body, was signed by Lord Kenmare and sixty-seven others, who withdrew. As a corrective, it was inadequate; as a preventive, useless. It no doubt hastened in the end the evil it deprecated in the beginning; it separated the Catholic gentry from the Catholic democracy, and thrust the latter more and more towards those liberal Protestants, mainly men of the middle class like themselves, who began about this time to club together at Belfast and Dublin, under the attractive title of "United Irishmen." Whatever they were individually, the union of so many hereditary Catholic names had been of very great service to the committee. So long as they stood aloof, the committee could not venture to speak for *all* the Catholics; it could only speak for a part, though that part might be nine-tenths of the whole: this gave for a time a doubtful and hesitating appearance to their proceedings. So low was their political influence, in 1791, that they could not get a single member of Parliament to present their annual petition. When at last it was presented, it was laid on the table and never noticed afterwards. To their further embarrassment, Mr. McKenna and some others formed "the Catholic Society," with the nominal object of spreading a knowledge of Catholic principles, through the press, but covertly, to raise up a rival organization, under the control of the seceders. At this period John Keogh's talents for negotiation and diplomacy saved the Catholic body from another term of anarchical imbecility.

A deputation of twelve having waited this year on the Chief Secretary with a list of the existing penal laws, found no intention, at the Castle, of further concession. They were "dismissed without an answer." Under these circumstances, the Committee met at Allen's Court. "It was their determination," says Keogh, "to give up the cause as desperate, lest a perseverance in what they considered an idle pursuit might not only prove ineffectual, but draw down a train of persecution on the body." Keogh endeavoured to rally them; proposed a delegation to London, to be sent at the expense of the Committee; offered, at last, to go at his own charge, if they authorized him. This proposal was accepted, and Keogh went. "I arrived in London," he adds, "without any introduction from this country, without any support, any assistance, any instructions." He remained three months, converted Mr. Dundas, brought back with him the son of Burke as Secretary, and a promise of four concessions: 1st. The magistracy. 2nd. The grand juries. 3rd. The sheriffs of counties. 4th. The bar. It was in this interview that Keogh, after obtaining Mr. Dundas's express permission and promise not to be offended, said to him, according to Charles Butler's account, "Since you give me this permission, and your deliberate promise not to be offended, I beg leave to repeat, that there *is* one thing which you ought to know, but which you don't suspect: you, Mr. Dundas, know nothing of Ireland." Mr. Dundas, as may be supposed, was greatly surprised; but, with perfect good humour, told Mr. Keogh that he believed this was not the case; it was true that he never had been in Ireland, but he had conversed with many Irishmen. "I have drunk," he said, "many a good bottle of wine with Lord Hillsborough, Lord Clare, and the Beresfords." "Yes, sir," said Mr. Keogh, "I believe you have; and that you drank many a good bottle of wine with them before you went to war with America."

On the return of Keogh to Dublin, a numerous meeting was held to hear his report. At this meeting, the fair promises of the English ministers were contrasted with the hostility of the Castle. The necessity of a strong organization, to overcome the one and hasten the other, was felt by all: it was then decided to form the Committee into a Convention. By this plan, the Catholics in each county and borough were called on to choose, in a private manner, certain electors, who were to elect two or more delegates, to represent the town or county in the general meeting at Dublin, on the 3rd day of December following. A circular, signed by Edward Byrne, Chairman, and Richard McCormick, Secretary, explaining the plan and the mode of election, was issued on the 14th of January, and the Catholics everywhere prepared to obey it.

The corporations of Dublin and other cities, the grand juries of Derry, Donegal, Leitrim, Roscommon, Limerick, Cork, and other counties, at once pronounced most strongly against the proposed Convention. They declared it "unconstitutional," "alarming," "most dangerous;" they denounced it as a copy of the National Assembly of France; they declared that they would "resist it to the utmost of their power;" they pledged "their lives and fortunes" to suppress it. The only answer of the Catholics was the legal opinion of Butler and Burton, two eminent lawyers, Protestants and King's counsellors, that the measure was entirely legal. They proceeded with their selection of delegates, and on the appointed day the Convention met. From the place of meeting', this Convention was popularly called "the Back Lane Parliament." Above 200 members were present.

The Convention proceeded (Mr. Byrne in the chair) to declare itself the only body competent to speak for the Catholics of Ireland. They next discussed the substance of the proposed petition to the King. The debate on this subject, full of life and colour, has been preserved for us in the memoirs of Tone, who, although a Protestant, had been elected Secretary to the Catholic Committee. Great firmness was exhibited by Teeling of Antrim, Bellew of Galway, McDermott of Sligo, Devereux of Wexford, Sir Thomas French, and John Keogh. These gentlemen contended, and finally carried, without a division, though not without a two-days' debate, a petition, asking complete and unrestricted emancipation. With the addition of the Chairman and Secretary, they were appointed as deputies to proceed to London, there to place the Catholic ultimatum in the hands of King George.

The deputies, whether by design or accident, took Belfast on their way to England. This great manufacturing town, at the head of the staple industry of the north, had been in succession the head-quarters of the Volunteers, the Northern Whigs, and the United Irishmen. Belfast had demanded in vain, for nearly a generation, that its 20,000 inhabitants should no longer be disfranchised, while a dozen burgesses--creatures of Lord Donegal--controlled the representation. Community of disfranchisement had made the Belfastians liberal; the Catholic deputies were publicly received with bonfires and ringing of bells, their expenses were paid by the citizens, and their carriage drawn along in triumph, on the road to Port-Patrick.

Arrived at London, after much negotiation and delay with ministers, a day was fixed for their introduction to the King. It was Wednesday, the 2nd of January, 1793; they were presented by Edmund Burke and the Home Secretary to George III., who "received them very graciously;" they placed in his hands the petition of their co-religionists, and, after some compliments, withdrew. In a few days, they were assured their case would be recommended to the attention of Parliament in the next royal speech, and so, leaving one of their number behind as "charge d'affaires," they returned to Dublin highly elated.

The Viceroy, on their return, was all attention to the Catholics; the Secretary, who, a year before, would not listen to a petition, now laboured to fix a limit to concession. The demand of complete emancipation, was not maintained in this negotiation as firmly as in the December debates of "the Back Lane Parliament." The shock of the execution of the King of France; the efforts of the secret committee of the House of Lords to inculpate certain Catholic leaders in the United-Irish system, and as patrons of the Defenders; the telling argument, that to press all was to risk all,--these causes combined to induce the sub-committee to consent to less than the Convention had decided to insist upon. Negotiation was the strong ground of the government, and they kept it. Finally, the bill was introduced by the Chief Secretary, and warmly supported by Grattan, Curran, Ponsonby, Forbes, and Hutchinson, Provost of Trinity College. It was resisted in the Lower House by Mr. Speaker Foster, Mr. Ogle, and Dr. Duigenan, an apostate, who exhibited all the bitterness of his class; and in the Upper House, by the Chancellor, the son of an apostate, and the majority of the lords spiritual. On the 9th day of April, 1793, it became the law of Ireland. "By one comprehensive clause," says Tone, "all penalties, forfeitures, disabilities, and incapacities are removed; the property of the Catholic is completely discharged from the restraints and limitations of the penal laws, and their liberty, in a great measure, restored, by the restoration of the right of elective franchise, so long withheld, so ardently pursued. The right of self-defence is established by the restoration of the privilege to carry arms, subject to a restraint, which does not seem unreasonable, as excluding none but the very lowest orders. The unjust and unreasonable distinctions affecting Catholics, as to service on grand and petty juries, are done away; the army, navy, and all other offices and places of trust are opened to them, subject to exceptions hereafter mentioned. Catholics may be masters or fellows of any college hereafter to be founded, subject to two conditions, that such college be a member of the University, and that it be not founded exclusively for the education of Catholics. They may be members of any lay body corporate, except Trinity College, any law, statute, or bye-law of such corporation to the contrary notwithstanding. They may obtain degrees in the University of Dublin. These, and some lesser immunities and privileges, constitute the grant of the bill, the value of which will be best ascertained by referring to the petition."

It is true, Catholics were still excluded from the high offices of Lord Lieutenant, Lord Deputy, and Lord Chancellor. What was much more important, they were excluded from sitting in Parliament--from exercising legislative and judicial functions, Still the franchise, the juries, the professions, and the University, were important concessions. Their first fruits were Daniel O'Connell and Thomas Moore!

The Committee having met to return thanks to the parliamentary supporters of the bill, their own future operations came also under debate. Some members advised that they should add reform to their programme, as the remnant of the penal laws were not sufficient to interest and attract the people. Some would have gone much further than reform; some were well content to rest on their laurels. There were ultras, moderate men, and conservatives, even in the twelve. The latter were more numerous than Wolfe Tone liked or expected. That ardent revolutionist had, indeed, at bottom, a strong dislike of the Catholic religion; he united himself with that body because he needed a party; he remained with them because it gave him importance; but he chiefly valued the position as it enabled him to further an ulterior design--an Irish revolution and a republic on the French plan. The example of France had, however, grown by this time rather a terror than an attraction to more cautious men than Tone. Edward Byrne, Sir Thomas French, and other leading Catholics, were openly hostile to any imitation of it, and the dinner at Daly's, to celebrate the passage of the act, was strongly anti-Gallican in spirit and sentiment. Keogh, McCormick, and McNevin, however, joined the United Irishmen, and the two latter were placed on the Directory. Keogh withdrew, when, in 1795, that organization became a secret society.

The Bishops, who had cheered on, rather than participated in the late struggle, were well satisfied with the new measure. They were, by education and conviction, conservatives. Dr. Plunkett of Meath, Dr. Egan of Waterford, Dr. Troy of Dublin, and Dr. Moylan of Cork, were the most remarkable for influence and ability at this period. Dr. Butler of Cashel, and his opponent, Dr. Burke of Ossory, the head of the resolute old ultramontane minority, were both recently deceased. With the exception of Dr. James Butler, Bishop of Cloyne and Ross, who deserted his faith and order on becoming unexpectedly heir to an earldom, the Irish prelates of the reign of George III. were a most zealous and devoted body. Lord Dunboyne's fall was the only cause of a reproach within their own ranks. That unhappy prelate made, many years afterwards, a death-bed repentance, was reconciled to his church, and bequeathed a large part of his inherited wealth to sustain the new national college, the founding of which, ever since the outbreak of the French revolution, the far-seeing Burke was urging upon Pitt and all his Irish correspondents.

In 1794, the Irish Bishops, having applied for a "royal license" to establish academies and seminaries, were graciously received, and Lord Fitzwilliam's government the next session brought in the Act of Incorporation. It became law on the 5th of June, 1795, and the college was opened the following October with fifty students. Dr Hussey, afterwards Bishop of Waterford, the friend of Burke, who stood by his deathbed, was first President; some refugee French divines were appointed to professorships; and the Irish Parliament voted the very handsome sum of 8,000 pounds a year to the new foundation. Maynooth, whatever its after lot, was the creation in the first instance of the Irish Parliament. We have thus, in the third century after the reformation, after three great religious wars, after four confiscations, after the most ingenious, cruel, and unchristian methods of oppression and proselytism, had been tried and had failed, the grand spectacle of the Catholics of Ireland restored, if not fully, yet to the most precious of the civil and religious liberties of a people! So powerless against conscience is and ever must be coercion!

CHAPTER XII.

THE ERA OF INDEPENDENCE--EFFECTS OF THE FRENCH REVOLUTION IN IRELAND--SECESSION OF GRATTAN, CURRAN, AND THEIR FRIENDS, FROM PARLIAMENT, IN 1797.

The era of independence which we have desired to mark distinctly to the reader's mind, may be said to terminate in 1797, with the hopeless secession of Grattan and his friends from Parliament. Did the events within and without the House justify that extreme measure? We shall proceed to describe them as they arose, leaving the decision of the question to the judgment of the reader.

The session of 1793, which extended into July, was, besides the Catholic Relief Bill, productive of other important results. Under the plea of the spread of French principles, and the widespread organization of seditious associations--a plea not wanting in evidence--an Arms Act was introduced and carried, prohibiting the importation of arms and gunpowder, and authorizing domiciliary visits, at any hour of the night or day, in search of such arms. Within a month from the passage of this bill, bravely but vainly opposed by Lord Edward Fitzgerald, and the opposition generally, the surviving Volunteer corps, in Dublin and its vicinity, were disbanded, their arms, artillery, and ammunition taken possession of either by force or negotiation, and the very wreck of that once powerful patriot army swept away. In its stead, by nearly the same majority, the militia were increased to 16,000 men, and the regulars from 12,000 to 17,000--thus placing at the absolute control of the Commander-in-Chief, and the chiefs of the oligarchy, a standing army of 33,000 men. At the same period, Lord Clare (he had been made an earl in 1792), introduced his Convention Act, against the assemblage in convention of delegates purporting to represent the people. With Grattan only 27 of the Commons divided against this measure, well characterized as "the boldest step that ever yet was made to introduce military government." "If this bill had been law," Grattan added, "the independence of the Irish Parliament, the emancipation of the Catholics, and even the English revolution of 1688, could never have taken place!" The teller in favour of the Convention Act was Major Wellesley, member for Trim, twenty years later--Duke of Wellington! It became and still remains the law of Ireland.

Against this reactionary legislation we must credit the session of '93, besides the Catholic Relief Bill and the East India Trade Bill, with Mr. Grattan's Barren Lands Bill, exempting all newly reclaimed lands from the payment of tithes for a period of seven years; Mr. Forbes's Pension Bill, limiting the pension list to 80,000 pounds sterling per annum, and fixing the permanent civil list at 250,000 pounds per annum; and the excellent measure of the same invaluable member, excluding from Parliament all persons holding offices of profit under the crown, except the usual ministerial officers, and those employed in the *revenue service*. This last salvo was forced into the bill by the oligarchical faction, for whose junior branches the revenue had long been a fruitful source of provision.

Parliament met next, on the 21st of January, '94, and held a short two-months' session. The most remarkable incidents of these two months were the rejection of Mr. George Ponsonby's annual motion for parliamentary reform, and the striking position taken by Grattan, Curran, and all but seven or eight of their friends, in favour of the war against the French republic. Mr. Ponsonby proposed, in the spirit of Flood's plan ten years earlier, to unite to the boroughs four miles square of the adjoining country, thus creating a counterpoise to the territorial aristocracy on the one hand, and the patrons of boroughs on the other; he also proposed to extend the suffrage to every tradesman who had served five years' apprenticeship, and gave each county *three* instead of two members, leaving intact, of course, the forty-shilling freehold franchise. Not more than 44 members, however, divided in favour of the new project, while 142 voted against it! Had it passed, the parliamentary history of the next six years could never have been written.

It was on this Reform bill, and on the debate on the address, that Grattan took occasion to declare his settled and unalterable hostility to those "French principles," then so fashionable with all who called themselves friends of freedom, in the three kingdoms. In the great social schism which had taken place in Europe, in consequence of the French revolution of 1789-'91, those kingdoms, the favourite seat of free inquiry and free discussion, could not hope to escape. The effects were visible in every circle, among every order of men; in all the churches, workshops, saloons, professions, into which men were divided. Among publicists, most of all, the shock was most severely felt; in England it separated Burke and Windham from Fox, Erskine, Sheridan, and Grey; in Ireland it separated Grattan and Curran from Lord Edward Fitzgerald, Arthur O'Conor, Addis Emmet, Wolfe Tone, and all those ardent, able, and honest men, who hailed the French, as the forerunner of a complete series of European republics, in which Ireland should shine out, among the brightest and the best.

Grattan, who agreed with and revered Burke, looked upon the "anti-Jacobin war," as a just and necessary war. It was not in his nature to do anything by halves, and he therefore cordially supported the paragraph in the address pledging Ireland's support to that war. He was a constitutionalist of the British, not of the French type. In the subsequent Reform debate he declared that he would always and ever resist those who sought to remodel the Irish constitution on a French original. He asserted, moreover, that great mischief had been already done by the advocates of such a design, "It"--this design--"has thrown back for the present the chance of any rational improvement in the representation of the people," he cried, "and has betrayed a good reform *to the hopes of a shabby insurrection*." Proceeding in his own condensed, crystalline antithesis, he thus enlarged on his own opinions: "There are two characters equally enemies to the reform of Parliament, and equally enemies to the government--the leveller of the constitution, and the friend of its abuses; they take different roads to arrive at the same end. The levellers propose to subvert the King and parliamentary constitution by a rank and unqualified democracy--the friends of its abuses propose to support the King and buy the Parliament, and in the end to overset both, by a rank and avowed corruption. They are both incendiaries; the one would destroy government to pay his court to liberty; the other would destroy liberty to pay his court to government; but the liberty of the one would be confusion, and the government of the other would be pollution."

We can well understand that this language pleased as little the United Irishmen as the Castle. It was known that in private he was accustomed to say, that, "the wonder was not that Mr. Sheares should die on the scaffold, but that Lord Clare was not there beside him." He stood in the midst of the ways, crying aloud, with the wisdom of his age and his genius, but there were few to heed his warnings. The sanguine innovator sneered or pitied; the truculent despot scowled or menaced; to the one his authority was an impediment, to the other his reputation was a reproach. It was a public situation as full of conflict as man ever occupied, and we are not astonished, on a nearer view, that it led, after three years hoping against hope, to the despairing secession of 1797.

A bright gleam of better things shot for an instant across the gloomy prospect, with which the year '94 closed for the country. Lord Westmoreland was recalled, and Lord Fitzwilliam, largely connected with Ireland by property, and one of the most just and liberal men in England, was to be his successor. The highest expectations were excited; the best men congratulated each other on the certain promise of better times close at hand; and the nation, ever ready to believe whatever it wished to believe, saw in prospect, the oligarchy restrained, the patriots triumphant, and the unfinished fabric of independence completed, and crowned with honour.

This new reign, though one of the shortest, was one of the most important Ireland ever saw. Lord Fitzwilliam, the nephew of Lord Rockingham, the first to acknowledge the constitution of 1782, had married a Ponsonby; he was a Burke whig--one of those who, with the Duke of Portland, Earl Spencer, and Mr. Windham, had followed the "great Edmund," in his secession from the Fox-and-Sheridan majority of that party, in 1791. Pitt, anxious to conciliate these new allies, had brought them all into office in 1794--Earl Fitzwilliam being placed in the dignified position of President of the Council. When spoken of for the Viceroyalty he wrote to Grattan, bespeaking his support, and that of "his friends, the Ponsonbys;" this letter and some others brought Grattan to London, where he had two or three interviews with Pitt, the Duke of Portland, and Lord Fitzwilliam. Better still, he made a pilgrimage to Beaconsfield, and had the benefit of the last advice of the aged Burke. With Pitt he was disappointed and dissatisfied, but he still hoped and expected great good from the appointment of Lord Fitzwilliam to the office of Viceroy. It seems to have been fully understood that the new Lord Lieutenant would have very full powers to complete the gracious work of Catholic emancipation: with this express understanding, Mr. Grattan was pressed to accept the Chancellorship of the Exchequer, but steadily declined; he upheld in that position Sir Henry Parnell, an old personal, rather than political friend, one of a family of whom Ireland has reason to retain a grateful recollection. He was, however, with Ponsonby, Curran, and others of his friends in both Houses, added to the Privy Council, where they were free to shape the measures of the new administration. At the King's levee, on the 10th of December, when Lord Fitzwilliam was sworn in, the aged Burke, in deep mourning for his idolized son, attended; Grattan was so much spoken to by the King as to draw towards him particular attention; Mr. Pitt, the Duke of Portland, and other ministers, were present. All took and held the tone that complete emancipation was a thing settled: Burke congratulated Grattan on the event, and the new Viceroy was as jubilant and as confident as anybody, that the great controversy was at length to be finally closed under his auspices.

On the 4th of January, Lord Fitzwilliam reached Dublin; and on the 25th of March he was recalled. The history of these three months--of this short-lived attempt to govern Ireland on the advice of Grattan--is full of instruction. The Viceroy had not for a moment concealed his intention of thoroughly reforming the Irish administration. On his arrival at the Castle, Mr. Cooke was removed from the Secretaryship, and Mr. Beresford from the Revenue Board. Great was the consternation, and unscrupulous the intrigues of the dismissed. When the Parliament met at the end of January, Grattan assumed the leadership of the House of Commons, and moved the address in answer to the speech from the throne. No opposition was offered--and it passed without a division. Immediately, a bill granting the Catholics complete emancipation--rendering them eligible even to the office of Chancellor, withheld in 1829--was introduced by Grattan. Then the oligarchy found their voices. The old cry of "the Church in danger" was raised, delegations proceeded to London, and every agency of influence was brought to bear on the King and the English cabinet. From the tenor of his letters, Lord Fitzwilliam felt compelled in honour to tell Mr. Pitt, that he might choose between him and the Beresfords. He did choose--but not till the Irish Parliament, in the exuberance of its confidence and gratitude, had voted the extraordinary subsidy of 20,000 men for the navy, and *a million, eight hundred thousand pounds, towards the expenses of the war with France!* Then, the popular Viceroy was recalled amid the universal regrets of the people. The day of his departure from Dublin was a day of general mourning, except with the oligarchical clique, whose leaders he had so resolutely thrust aside. To them it was a day of insolent and unconcealed rejoicing; and, what is not at all uncommon under such circumstances, the infatuated partisans of the French revolution, rejoiced hardly less than the extremest Tories, at the sudden collapse of a government equally opposed to the politics of both. Grattan, than whom no public man was ever more free from unjust suspicion of others, always remained under the conviction that Pitt had made merely a temporary use of Lord Fitzwilliam's popularity, in order to cheat the Irish out of the immense supplies they had voted; and all the documents of the day, which have since seen the light, accord well with that view of the transaction. Lord Fitzwilliam was immediately replaced by Lord Camden, whose Viceroyalty extended into the middle of the year 1798: a reign which embraced all that remains to us to narrate, of the Parliamentary politics of the era of Independence.

The sittings of Parliament were resumed during April, May, and June, but the complete emancipation bill was rejected three to one--155 to 55; the debates were now marked, on the part of Toler, Duigenan, Johnson, and others, with the most violent anti-Catholic spirit. All this tended to inflame still more the exasperated feeling which already prevailed in the country between Orangemen and Defenders. Thus it came, that the High Court of Parliament, which ought to have been the chief school of public wisdom--the calm correcting tribunal of public opinion--was made a principal engine in the dissemination of those prejudices and passions, which drove honest men to despair of constitutional redress, and swelled the ranks of the secret political societies, till they became co-extensive with the population.

The session of 1796 was even more hopeless than the immediately preceding one. A trade motion of Grattan's on the address commanded only 14 votes out of 140; in the next session his motion in favour of equal rights to persons of all religious creeds, obtained but 12 votes out of 160! From these figures it is clear that above a third of the members of the House no longer attended; that of those who did attend, the overwhelming and invariable majority--ten to one--were for all the measures of repression and coercion which marked these two sessions. The Insurrection Act, giving power to the magistrates of any county to proclaim martial law; the Indemnity Act, protecting magistrates from the consequences of exercising "a vigour beyond the law;" the Riot Act, giving authority to disperse any number of persons by force of arms without notice; the Suspension of the *habeas corpus* (against which only 7 members out of a House of 164 voted)--all were evidences to. Grattan, that the usefulness of the House of Commons, as then constituted, was, for the tune, lost or destroyed. It is quite clear that he came to this conviction slowly and reluctantly; that he struggled against it with manly fortitude through three sessions; that he yielded to it at length, when there was no longer a possibility of resistance,--when to move or to divide the House, had become a wretched farce, humiliating to the country, and unworthy of his own earnest and enthusiastic patriotism.

Under these circumstances, the powerless leader and his devoted staff resolved to withdraw, formally and openly, from further attendance on the House of Commons. The deplorable state of the country, delivered over to an irresponsible magistracy and all the horrors of martial law; the spread among the patriotic rising generation of French principles; the scarcely concealed design of the Castle to goad the people into insurrection, in order to deprive them of their liberties; all admonished the faithful few that the walls of Parliament were no longer their sphere of usefulness. One last trial was, however, made in May, 1797, for a reform of Parliament. Mr. George Ponsonby moved his usual motion, and Curran, Hardy, Sir Lawrence Parsons, Charles Kendall Bushe, and others, ably supported him. The division was 30 to 117. It was on this debate, that Grattan, whose mournful manner contrasted so strongly with his usual enthusiasm, concluded a solemn exposition of the evils the administration were bringing on the country, by these affecting words:--"We have offered you our measure--you will reject it; we deprecate yours--you will persevere; having no hopes left to persuade or to dissuade, and having discharged our duty, we shall trouble you no more, *and after this day shall not attend the House of Commons*." The secession thus announced was accomplished; at the general election, two months later, Grattan and his colleague, Lord Henry Fitzgerald, refused to stand again for Dublin; Curran, Lord Edward Fitzgerald, Arthur O'Conor, and others, followed his example. A few patriots, hoping against hope, were, however, returned, a sort of forlorn hope, to man the last redoubt of the Constitution. Of these was William Conyngham Plunkett, member for Charlemont, Grattan's old borough, a constitutionalist of the school of Edmund Burke, worthy to be named among the most illustrious of his disciples.

In the same July, on the 7th of the month, on which the Irish elections were held, that celebrated Anglo-Irish statesman expired at Beaconsfield, in the sixty-seventh year of his age. His last thoughts--his last wishes, like his first--were with his native land. His regards continued fixed on the state of Ireland, while vision and faculty remained. His last efforts in writing and conversation were to plead for toleration, concession and conciliation towards Ireland. The magisterial gravity of Burke was not calculated to permit him to be generally popular with an impulsive people, but as years roll on, and education extends its dominion, his reputation rises and brightens above every other reputation of his age, British or Irish. Of him no less truly than powerfully did Grattan say in the Imperial Parliament, in 1815: "He read everything, he saw everything, he foresaw everything. His knowledge of history amounted to a power of foretelling; and when he perceived the wild work that was doing in France, that great political physician, intelligent of symptoms, distinguished between the access of fever and the force of health; and what other men conceived to be the vigour of her constitution, he knew to be no more than the paroxysm of her madness; and then, prophet-like, he denounced the destinies of France, and in his prophetic fury, admonished nations."

CHAPTER XIII.

THE UNITED IRISHMEN.

Half measures of justice may satisfy the generation which achieves them, but their successors will look with other eyes, as well on what has been won as on that which is withheld. The part in possession will appear to their youthful sense of abstract right and wrong far less precious than the part in expectancy, for it is in the nature of the young to look forward, as it is of the old to turn their regards to the past. The very recollection of their fathers will stimulate the new generation to emulate their example, and will render them averse to being bound by former compromises. So necessary is it for statesmen, when they yield to a just demand long withheld, to yield gracefully and to yield all that is fairly due.

The celebrated group known to us as "the United Irishmen," were the birth of a new generation, entering together on the public stage. With few exceptions, the leading characters were all born within a few years of each other: Neilson in 1761, Tone, Arthur O'Conor and Lord Edward Fitzgerald in '62, McNevin in '63, Sampson and Thomas Addis Emmet in '64, and Russell in '67. They had emerged into manhood while the drums of the Volunteers were beating victorious marches, when the public hopes ran high, and the language of patriotism was the familiar speech of every-day life.

In a settled state of society it would have been natural for the first minds of the new generation to carry their talents, gratefully and dutifully, into the service of the first reputations of the old; but Irish society, in the last years of the last century, was not in a settled condition; the fascination of French example, and the goading sense of national wrongs only half-righted, inflamed the younger generation with a passionate thirst for speedy and summary justice on their oppressors. We must not look, therefore, to see the Tones and Emmets continuing in the constitutional line of public conduct marked out by Burke in the one kingdom, and Grattan in the other. The new age was revolutionary, and the new men were filled with the spirit of the age. Their actions stand apart; they form an episode in the history of the century to which there may be parallels, but a chapter in the history of their own country original and alone.

The United Irish Society sprung up at Belfast in October, 1791. In that month, Theobold Wolf Tone, then in his 28th year, a native of Kildare, a member of the bar, and an excellent popular pamphleteer, on a visit to his friend Thomas Russell, in the northern capital, was introduced to Samuel Neilson, proprietor of the **Northern Star** newspaper, and several other kindred spirits, all staunch reformers, or "something more." Twenty of these gentlemen meeting together, adopted a programme prepared by Tone, which contained these three simple propositions: that "English influence" was the great danger of Irish liberty; that a reform of Parliament could alone create a counterpoise to that influence; and that such a reform to be just should include Irishmen of all religious denominations. On Tone's return to Dublin, early in November, a branch society was formed on the Belfast basis. The Hon. Simon Butler, a leading barrister, was chosen Chairman, and Mr. Napper Tandy, an active middle-aged merchant, with strong republican principles, was Secretary. The solemn declaration or oath, binding every member "to forward a brotherhood of affection, an identity of interests, a communion of rights, and a union of power among Irishmen of all religious persuasions," was drawn up by the Dublin club, and became the universal bond of organization. Though the Belfast leaders had been long in the habit of meeting in "secret committee," to direct and control the popular movements in their vicinage, the new society was not, in its inception, nor for three years afterwards, a secret society. When that radical change was proposed, we find it resisted by a considerable minority, who felt themselves at length compelled to retire from an association, the proceedings of which they could no longer approve. In justice to those who remained, adopting secrecy as their only shield, it must be said, that the freedom of the press and of public discussion had been repeatedly and frequently violated before they abandoned the original maxims and tactics of their body, which were all open, and above-board.

In 1792, Simon Butler, and Oliver Bond--a prosperous Dublin merchant of northern origin--was summoned to the bar of the House of Lords, condemned to six months' imprisonment, and a fine of 500 pounds each, for having acted as Chairman and Secretary of one of the meetings, at which an address to the people, strongly reflecting on the corrupt constitution of Parliament, was adopted. In '94, Archibald Hamilton Rowan, one of the purest and most chivalrous characters of any age, was convicted, by a packed jury, of circulating the famous "Universal Emancipation" address of his friend, Dr. William Drennan, the poet-politician of the party. He was defended by Curran, in the still more famous speech in which occurs his apostrophe to "the genius of Universal Emancipation;" but he atoned in the cells of Newgate, for circulating the dangerous doctrine which Drennan had broached, and Curran had immortalized.

The regular place of meeting of the Dublin society was the Tailors' Hall, in Back Lane, a spacious building, called, from the number of great popular gatherings held in it, "the Back Lane Parliament." Here Tandy, in the uniform of his new National Guard, whose standard bore the harp without the crown, addressed his passionate harangues to the applauding multitude; here Tone, whose *forte*, however, was not oratory, constantly attended; here, also, the leading Catholics, Keogh and McCormack, the "Gog" and "Magog," of Tone's extraordinary *Memoirs*, were occasionally present. And here, on the night of the 4th of May, 1794, the Dublin society found themselves suddenly assailed by the police, their papers seized, their officers who were present arrested, and their meeting dispersed. From that moment we may date the new and *secret* organization of the brotherhood, though it was not in general operation till the middle of the following year.

This new organization, besides its secrecy, had other revolutionary characteristics. For "reform of Parliament" was substituted in the test, or oath, representation "of all the people of Ireland," and for petitions and publications, the enrolment of men, by baronies and counties, and the appointment of officers, from the least to the highest in rank, as in a regular army. The unit was a lodge of twelve members, with a chairman and secretary, who were also their corporal and sergeant; five of these lodges formed a company, and the officers of five such companies a baronial committee, from which again, in like manner, the county committees were formed. Each of the provinces had its Directory, while in Dublin the supreme authority was established, in an "Executive Directory" of five members. The orders of the Executive were communicated to not more than one of the Provincial Directors, and by him to one of each County Committee, and so in a descending scale, till the rank and file were reached; an elaborate contrivance, but one which proved wholly insufficient to protect the secrets of the organization from the ubiquitous espionage of the government.

In May, 1795, the new organization lost the services of Wolfe Tone, who was compromised by a strange incident, to a very serious extent. The incident was the arrest and trial of the Rev. William Jackson, an Anglican clergyman, who had imbibed the opinions of Price and Priestley, and had been sent to Ireland by the French Republic, on a secret embassy. Betrayed by a friend and countryman, named Cockayne, the unhappy Jackson took poison in prison, and expired in the dock. Tone had been seen with Jackson, and through the influence of his friends, was alone protected from arrest. He was compelled, however, to quit the country, in order to preserve his personal liberty. He proceeded with his family to Belfast, where, before taking shipping for America, he renewed with his first associates, their vows and projects, on the summit of "the Cave Hill," which looks down upon the rich valley of the Laggan, and the noble town and port at its outlet. Before quitting Dublin, he had solemnly promised Emmet and Russell, in the first instance, as he did his Belfast friends in the second, that he would make the United States his *route* to France, where he would negotiate a formidable national alliance, for "the United Irishmen."

In the year in which Tone left the country, Lord Edward Fitzgerald, brother of the Duke of Leinster, and formerly a Major in the British Army, joined the society; in the next year--near its close--Thomas Addis Emmet, who had long been in the confidence of the promoters, joined, as did, about the same time, Arthur O'Conor, nephew of Lord Longueville, and ex-member for Phillipstown, and Dr. William James McNevin, a Connaught Catholic, educated in Austria, then practising his profession with eminent success in Dublin. These were felt to be important accessions, and all four were called upon to act on "the Executive Directory," from time to time, during 1796 and 1797.

The coercive legislation carried through Parliament, session after session--the Orange persecutions in Armagh and elsewhere--the domiciliary visits--the military outrages in town and country--the free quarters, whipping and tortures--the total suppression of the public press --the bitter disappointment of Lord Fitzwilliam's recall--the annual failure of Ponsonby's motion for reform--finally, the despairing secession of Grattan and his friends from Parliament--had all tended to expand the system, which six years before was confined to a few dozen enthusiasts of Belfast and Dublin, into the dimensions of a national confederacy. By the close of this year, 500,000 men had taken the test, in every part of the country, and nearly 300,000 were reported as armed, either with firelocks or pikes. Of this total, 110,000 alone were returned for Ulster; about 60,000 for Leinster, and the remainder from Connaught and Munster. A fund, ludicrously small, 1,400 pounds sterling, remained in the hands of the Executive, after all the outlay which had taken place, in procuring arms, in extending the union, and in defending prisoners arrested as members of the society. Lord Edward Fitzgerald was chosen Commander-in-Chief; but the main reliance, for munitions, artillery, and officers, was placed upon the French Republic.

CHAPTER XIV.

NEGOTIATIONS WITH FRANCE AND HOLLAND--THE THREE EXPEDITIONS NEGOTIATED BY TONE AND LEWINES.

The close of the year 1795 saw France under the government of the Directory, with Carnot in the cabinet, and Pichegru, Jourdain, Moreau, Hoche, and Buonaparte at the head of its armies. This government, with some change of persons, lasted from October, 1795, to November, '99, when it was supplanted by the Consular Revolution. Within the compass of those four years lie the negotiations which were carried on and the three great expeditions which were fitted out by France and Holland, at the instance of the United Irishmen.

On the 1st of February, 1796, Tone, who had sailed from Belfast the previous June, arrived at Havre from New York, possessed of a hundred guineas and some useful letters of introduction. One of these letters, written in cipher, was from the French Minister at Philadelphia to the Minister of Foreign Affairs, Charles Lacroix; another was to the American Minister in France, Mr. Monroe, afterwards President of the United States, by whom he was most kindly received, and wisely advised, on reaching Paris. Lacroix received him courteously, and referred him to a subordinate called Madgett, but after nearly three months wasted in interviews and explanations, Tone, by the advice of Monroe, presented himself at the Luxembourg Palace, and demanded audience of the "Organizer of Victory." Carnot also listened to him attentively, asked and obtained his true name, and gave him another *rendezvous*. He was next introduced to Clarke (afterwards Duc de Feltre), Secretary at War, the son of an Irishman, whom he found wholly ignorant of Ireland; and finally, on the 12th of July, General Hoche, in the most frank and winning manner, introduced himself. At first the Directory proposed sending to Ireland no more than 5,000 men, while Tone pleaded for 20,000; but when Hoche accepted the command, he assured Tone he would go "in sufficient force." The "pacificator of La Vendee," as the young general was called--he was only thirty-two,--won at once the heart of the enthusiastic founder of the United Irishmen, and the latter seems to have made an equally favourable impression. He was at once presented with the commission of a *chef de brigade* of infantry--a rank answering to that of colonel with us--and was placed as adjutant on the general's staff. Hoche was all ardour and anxiety; Carnot cheered him on by expressing his belief that it would be "a most brilliant operation;" and certainly Tone was not the man to damp such expectations, or allow them to evaporate in mere complimentary assurances.

During the autumn months the expedition was busily being fitted out at Brest, and the general head-quarters were at Rennes. The Directory, to satisfy themselves that all was as represented by Tone, had sent an agent of their own to Ireland, by whom a meeting was arranged on the Swiss frontier between Lord Edward Fitzgerald, Arthur O'Conor, Dr. McNevin, and Hoche. From this meeting--the secret of which he kept to himself--the young general returned in the highest spirits, and was kinder than ever to his adjutant. At length, early in December, all was ready, and on the 16th the Brest fleet stood out to sea; 17 sail of the line, 13 frigates, and 13 smaller ships, carrying 15,000 picked troops, the *elite* of "the Army of the Ocean," and abundance of artillery and munitions of war. Tone was in the *Indomptable*, 80 guns, commanded by a Canadian, named Bedout; Hoche and the Admiral in the frigate *Fraternite*; Grouchy, so memorable for the part he played then and afterwards, was second in command. On the third morning, after groping about and losing each other in Atlantic fog, one-half the fleet (with the fatal exception of the *Fraternite*) found themselves close in with the coast of Kerry. They entered Bantry Bay, and came to anchor, ten ships of war, and "a long line of dark hulls resting on the green water." Three or four days they lay dormant and idle, waiting for the General and Admiral; Bouvet, the Vice-Admiral, was opposed to moving in the absence of his chief; Grouchy was irresolute and nervous; but at length, on Christmas day, the council of war decided in favour of debarkation. The landing was to take place next morning; 6,500 veterans were prepared to step ashore at daylight, but without their artillery, their military chest, and their general. Two hours beyond midnight Tone was roused from sleep by the wind, which he found blowing half a gale. Pacing the gallery of the *Indomptable* till day dawned, he felt it rising louder and angrier, every hour. The next day it was almost a hurricane, and the Vice-Admiral's frigate, running under the quarter of the great 80-gun ship, ordered them to slip anchor and stand out to sea. The whole fleet was soon driven off the Irish coast; that part of it, in which Grouchy and Tone were embarked, made its entrance into Brest on New Year's day; the ship which carried Hoche and the Admiral, only arrived at La Rochelle on the 15th. The Directory and the General, so far from being discouraged by this failure, consoled themselves by the demonstration they had made, of the possibility of a great fleet passing to and fro, in British waters, for nearly a month, without encountering a single British vessel of war. Not so the Irish negotiator; on him, light-hearted and daring as he was, the disappointment fell with crushing weight; but he magnanimously carried Grouchy's report to Paris, and did his utmost to defend the unlucky general from a cabal which had been formed against him.

While Tone was reluctantly following his new chief to the Meuse and the Rhine--with a promise that the Irish expedition was delayed, not abandoned--another, and no less fortunate negotiator, was raising up a new ally for the same cause, in an unexpected quarter. The Batavian republic, which had risen in the steps of Pichegru's victorious army, in 1794, was now eager to imitate the example of France. With a powerful fleet, and an unemployed army, its chiefs were quite ready to listen to any proposal which would restore the maritime ascendancy of Holland, and bring back to the recollection of Europe the memory of the puissant Dutch republic. In this state of affairs, the new agent of the Irish Directory, Edward John Lewines, a Dublin attorney, a man of great ability and energy, addressed himself to the Batavian government. He had been sent abroad with very general powers, to treat with Holland, Spain, France, or any other government at war with England, for a loan of half a million sterling, and a sufficient auxiliary force to aid the insurrection. During two months' stay at Hamburg, the habitual route in those days from the British ports to the continent, he had placed himself in communication with the Spanish agent there, and had, in forty days, received an encouraging answer from Madrid. On his way, probably to Spain, to follow up that fair prospect, he reached the Netherlands, and rapidly discovering the state of feeling in the Dutch, or as it was then called, the *Batavian* republic, he addressed himself to the Directors, who consulted Hoche, by whom in turn Tone was consulted. Tone had a high opinion of Lewines, and at once proceeded with him to the Hague, where they were joined, according to agreement, by Hoche. The Dutch Committee of Foreign Affairs, the Commander-in-Chief, General Dandaels, and the Admiral, De Winter, entered heartily into the project. There were in the Texel 16 ships of the line and 10 frigates, victualled for three months, with 15,000 men and 80 field guns on board. The only serious difficulty in the way was removed by the disinterestedness of Hoche; the French Foreign Minister having demanded that 5,000 French troops should be of the expedition, and that Hoche should command in chief; the latter, to conciliate Dandaels and the Dutch, undertook to withdraw the proposal, and gracefully yielded his own pretensions. All then was settled: Tone was to accompany Dandaels with the same rank he had in the Brest expedition, and Lewines to return, and remain, as "Minister-resident" at Paris. On the 8th of July, Tone was on board the flagship, the *Vryheid*, 74 guns, in the Texel, and "only waiting for a wind," to lead another navy to the aid of his compatriots.

But the winds, "the only unsubsidized allies of England," were strangely adverse. A week, two, three, four, five, passed heavily away, without affording a single day in which that mighty fleet could make an offing. Sometimes for an hour or two it shifted to the desired point, the sails were unclewed and the anchors shortened, but then, as if to torture the impatient exiles on board, it veered back again and settled steadily in the fatal south-west. At length, at the end of August, the provisions being nearly consumed, and the weather still unfavourable, the Dutch Directory resolved to land the troops and postpone the expedition. De Winter, as is known, subsequently found an opportunity to work out, and attack Lord Duncan, by whom he was badly beaten. Thus ended Irish hopes of aid from Holland. The indomitable Tone rejoined his chief on the Rhine, where, to his infinite regret, Hoche died the following month--September 18th, 1797--of a rapid consumption, accelerated by cold and carelessness. "Hoche," said Napoleon to Barry O'Meara at Saint Helena, "was one of the first generals France ever produced. He was brave, intelligent, abounding in talent, decisive and penetrating. Had he landed in Ireland, he would have succeeded. He was accustomed to civil war, had pacified La Vendee, and was well adapted for Ireland. He had a fine, handsome figure, a good address, was prepossessing and intriguing." The loss of such a patron, who felt himself, according to Tone's account, especially bound to follow up the object of separating Ireland from

England, was a calamity greater and more irreparable than the detention of one fleet or the dispersion of the other.

The third expedition, in promoting which Tone and Lewines bore the principal part, was decided upon by the French Directory, immediately after the conclusion of peace with Austria, in October, 1797. The decree for the formation of "the Army of England," named Buonaparte Commander-in-Chief, with Desaix as his second. Buonaparte consulted Clarke as to who he most confided in among the numerous Irish refugees then in Paris--there were some twenty or thirty, all more or less known, and more or less in communication with the Directory--and Clarke answered at once, "Tone, of course." Tone, with Lewines, the one in a military, the other in an ambassadorial capacity, had frequent interviews with the young conqueror of Italy, whom they usually found silent and absorbed, always attentive, sometimes asking sudden questions betraying great want of knowledge of the British Islands, and occasionally, though rarely, breaking out into irresistible invectives against Jacobinism and the English system, both of which he so cordially detested. Every assurance was given by the General, by the Directors, by Merlin du Douai, Barras, and Talleyrand especially, that the expedition against England would never be abandoned. Tone, in high spirits as usual, joined the division under the command of his countryman, General Kilmaine, and took up his quarters at Havre, where he had landed without knowing a soul in France two years before.

The winter wore away in busy preparations at Havre, at Brest, and at La Rochelle,--and, which seemed mysterious to the Irish exiles--at Toulon. All the resources of France, now without an enemy on the Continent, were put forth in these preparations. But it soon appeared they were not put forth for Ireland. On the 20th of May, 1798--within three days of the outbreak in Dublin, Wexford, and Kildare--Buonaparte sailed with the *elite* of all that expedition for Alexandria, and "the Army of England" became, in reality, "the Army of Egypt."

The bitterness, the despondency, and desperation which seized on the Irish leaders in France, and on the rank and file of the United Irishmen at home, on receiving this intelligence are sufficiently illustrated in the subsequent attempts under Humbert and Bompart, and the partial, ineffectual risings in Leinster, Ulster, and Connaught, during the summer and autumn of 1798. After all their high hopes from France and her allies, this was what it had come to at last! A few frigates, with three or four thousand men, were all that could be spared for the succour of a kingdom more populous than Egypt and Syria combined; the granary of England, and the key of her Atlantic position. It might have been some comfort to the family of Tone to have read, thirty years afterwards, in their American asylum, or for the aged Lewines to have read in the Parisian retreat in which he died, the memorable confession of Napoleon at Saint Helena: "If instead of the expedition to Egypt, I had undertaken that to Ireland, what," he asked, "could England do now? On such chances," he mournfully added, "depend the destinies of empires!"

CHAPTER XV.

THE INSURRECTION OF 1798.

It is no longer matter of assertion merely, but simple matter of fact, that the English and Irish ministers of George III. regarded the insurrectionary movement of the United Irishmen as at once a pretext and a means for effecting a legislative union between the two countries. Lord Camden, the Viceroy who succeeded Lord Fitzwilliam in March, '95--with Mr. Pelham as his Chief Secretary, in a letter to his relative, the Hon. Robert Stewart, afterwards Lord Castlereagh, announced this policy, in unmistakable terms, so early as 1793; and all the official correspondence published of late years, concerning that period of British and Irish history, establishes the fact beyond the possibility of denial.

Such being the design, it was neither the wish nor the interest of the Government, that the insurrection should be suppressed, unless the Irish constitution could be extinguished with it. To that end they proceeded in the coercive legislation described in a previous chapter; to that end they armed with irresponsible power the military officers and the oligarchical magistracy; with that view they quartered those yeomanry regiments, which were known to be composed of Orangemen, on the wretched peasantry of the most Catholic counties, while the corps in which Catholics or United Irishmen were most numerous, were sent over to England, in exchange for Scotch fencibles and Welsh cavalry. The outrages committed by all these volunteer troops, but above all by the Orange yeomanry of the country, were so monstrous, that the gallant and humane Sir John Moore exclaimed, "If I were an Irishman, I would be a rebel!"

It was, indeed, impossible for any man, however obscure, or however eminent, to live longer in the country, without taking sides. Yet the choice was at best a hard and unhappy one. On the one side was the Castle, hardly concealing its intention of goading on the people, in order to rob them of their Parliament; on the other was the injured multitude, bound together by a secret system which proved in reality no safeguard against traitors in their own ranks, and which had been placed by its Protestant chiefs under the auspices of an infidel republic. Between the two courses men made election according to their bias or their necessities, or as they took local or general, political or theological views of the situation. Both Houses of the legislature unanimously, sustained the government against the insurrection; as did the judges, the bar, and the Anglican clergy and bishops. The Presbyterian body were in the beginning all but unanimous for a republican revolution and the French alliance; the great majority of the Catholic peasantry were, as the crisis increased, driven into the same position, while all their bishops and a majority of the Catholic aristocracy, adhered to that which they, with the natural tendency of their respective orders, considered the side of religion and authority. Thus was the nation sub-divided within itself; Protestant civilian from Protestant ecclesiastic, Catholic layman from Catholic priest, tenant from lord, neighbour from neighbour, father from son, and friend from friend.

During the whole of '97, the opposing parties were in a ferment of movement and apprehension. As the year wore on, the administration, both English and Irish, began to feel that the danger was more formidable than they had foreseen. The timely storm which had blown Grouchy out of Bantry Bay, the previous Christmas, could hardly be reckoned on again, though the settled hostility of the French government knew no change. Thoroughly well informed by their legion of spies both on the Continent and in Ireland, every possible military precaution was taken. The Lord Lieutenant's proclamation for disarming the people, issued in May, was rigorously enforced by General Johnstone in the South, General Hutchinson in the West, and Lord Lake in the North. Two hundred thousand pikes and pike-heads were said to have been discovered or surrendered during the year, and several thousand firelocks. The yeomanry, and English and Scotch corps amounted to 35,000 men, while the regular troops were increased to 50,000 and subsequently to 80,000, including three regiments of the Guards. The defensive works at Cork, and other vulnerable points were strengthened at an immense cost; the "Pigeon House" fort, near Dublin, was enlarged, for the city itself was pronounced by General Vallancy,

Colonel Packenham, and other engineer authorities dangerously weak, if not wholly untenable. A system of telegraphic signals was established from all points of the coast with the Capital, and every precaution taken against the surprise of another French invasion.

During the summer assize, almost every considerable town and circuit had its state trial. The sheriffs had been carefully selected beforehand by the Castle, and the juries were certain to be of "the right sort," under the auspices of such sheriffs. Immense sums in the aggregate were contributed by the United Irish for the defence of their associates; at the Down assizes alone, not less than seven hundred or eight hundred guineas were spent in fees and retainers; but at the close of the term, Mr. Beresford was able to boast to his friend Lord Auckland, that but one of all the accused had escaped the penalty of death or banishment! The military tribunals, however, did not wait for the idle formalities of the civil courts. Soldiers and civilians, yeomen and townsmen, against whom the informer pointed his finger, were taken out, and summarily executed. Ghastly forms hung upon the thick-set gibbets, not only in the market places of country towns, and before the public prisons, but on all the bridges of the metropolis. Many of the soldiers, in every military district were shot weekly and almost daily for real or alleged complicity with the rebels. The horrid torture of picketing, and the blood-stained lash, were constantly resorted to, to extort accusations or confessions. Over all these atrocities the furious and implacable spirit of Lord Clare presided in Council, and the equally furious and implacable Luttrel, Lord Carhampton, as Commander-in-Chief. All moderate councils were denounced as nothing short of treason, and even the elder Beresford, the Privy Counsellor, was compelled to complain of the violence of his noble associates, and his inability to restrain the ferocity of his own nearest relatives-- meaning probably his son John Claudius, and his son-in-law, Sir George Hill.

It was while this spirit was abroad, a spirit as destructive as ever animated the Councils of Sylla or Marius in Old Rome, or prompted the decrees of Robespierre or Marat in France, that the genius and courage of one man redeemed the lost reputation of the law, and upheld against all odds the sacred claims of personal liberty. This man was John Philpot Curran, the most dauntless of advocates, one of the truest and bravest of his race. Although a politician of the school of Grattan, and wholly untainted with French principles, he identified himself absolutely with his unhappy clients, "predoomed to death." The genius of patriotic resistance which seemed to have withdrawn from the Island with Grattan's secession from Parliament, now re-appeared in the last place where it might have been expected--in those courts of death, rather than of justice--before those predetermined juries, besides the hopeless inmates of the crowded dock, personified in the person of Curran. Often at midnight, amid the clash of arms, his wonderful pleadings were delivered; sometimes, as in Dublin, where the court rooms adjoined the prisons, the condemned, or the confined, could hear, in their cells, his piercing accents breaking the stillness of the early morning, pleading for justice and mercy--pleading always with superhuman perseverance, but almost always in vain. Neither menaces of arrest, nor threats of assassination, had power to intimidate that all-daring spirit; nor, it may be safely said, can the whole library of human history present us a form of heroism superior in kind or degree to that which this illustrious advocate exhibited during nearly two years, when he went forth daily, with his life in his hand, in the holy hope to snatch some human victim from the clutch of the destroyer thirsting for his blood.

In November, '97, some said from fear of personal consequences, some from official pressure in a high quarter, Lord Carhampton resigned the command of the forces, and Sir Ralph Abercromby was appointed in his stead. There could not be a more striking illustration of the system of terror patronized by government than was furnished in the case of Sir Ralph as Commander-in- Chief. That distinguished soldier, with his half century of services at his back, had not been a week in Dublin before he discovered the weakness of the Viceroy, and the violence of his principal advisers, the Chancellor, the Speaker, Lord Castlereagh and the Beresfords. Writing in confidence to his son, he says, "The abuses of all kinds I found here can scarcely be believed or enumerated." The instances he cites of such abuses are sufficiently horrible to justify the strong language which brought down on his head so much hostility, when he declared in his proclamation of February '98, that the Irish army was "formidable to every one but the enemy." These well-known opinions were so repugnant to the Castle policy, that that party held a caucus in the Speaker's Chambers, at which it was proposed to pass a vote of censure in Parliament on the General, whom they denounced as "a sulky mule," "a Scotch beast," and by other similar names. Though the Parliamentary censure dropped, they actually compelled Lord

Camden to call on him to retract his magnanimous order. To this humiliation the veteran stooped "for the sake of the King's service," but at the same time he proffered his resignation. After two months' correspondence, it was finally accepted, and the soldier who was found too jealous of the rights of the people to be a fit instrument of their destruction, escaped from his high position, not without a profound sentiment of relief. His verdict upon the barbarous policy pursued in his time was always expressed, frankly and decisively. His entire correspondence, private and public, bears one and the same burthen--the violence, cruelty, and tyranny of Lord Camden's chief advisers, and the pitiful weakness of the Viceroy himself. Against the infamous plan of letting loose a lustful and brutal soldiery to live at "free quarters" on a defenceless and disarmed people--an outrage against which Englishmen had taken perpetual security at *their* revolution, as may be seen in "the Bill of Rights," he struggled during his six months' command, but with no great success. The plan, with all its horrors, was upheld by the Lord-Lieutenant, and more than any other cause, precipitated the rebellion which exploded at last, just as Sir Ralph was allowed to retire from the country. His temporary successor, Lord Lake, was troubled with no such scruples as the gallant old Scotsman.

Events followed each other in the first months of 1798, fast and furiously. Towards the end of February, Arthur O'Conor, Father James Quigley, the brothers John and Benjamin Binns, were arrested at Margate on their way to France; on the 6th of March, the *Press* newspaper, the Dublin organ of the party, as the *Star* had been the Ulster organ, was seized by Government, Lord Edward Fitzgerald and William Sampson being at the time in the office. On the 12th of March, on the information of the traitor, Thomas Reynolds, the Leinster delegates were seized in conclave, with all their papers, at the house of Oliver Bond, in Bridge Street, Dublin. On the same information. Addis Emmet and Dr. McNevin were taken in their own houses, and Sampson in the north of England: of all the executive, Lord Edward alone escaping those sent in search of him. This was, as Tone notes in his journal, on the ill news reaching France, "a terrible blow." O'Conor's arrest in Kent, Sampson's in Carlisle, and the other arrests in Belfast and Dublin, proved too truly that treason was at work, and that the much-prized oath of secrecy was no protection whatever against the devices of the Castle and the depravity of its secret agents. The extent to which that treason extended, the number of associates who were in the pay of their deadly enemies, was never known to the United Irish leaders; time has, however, long since "revealed the secrets of the prison-house," and we know now, that men they trusted with all their plans and hopes, such as McNally and McGucken, were quite as deep in the conspiracy to destroy them as Mr. Reynolds and Captain Armstrong.

The most influential members of the Dublin Society remaining at large contrived to correspond with each other, or to meet by stealth after the arrest at Bond's. The vacancies in the Executive were filled up by the brothers John and Henry Sheares, both barristers, sons of a wealthy Cork banker, and former member of Parliament, and by Mr. Lawless, a surgeon. For two months longer these gentlemen continued to act in concert with Lord Edward, who remained undetected, notwithstanding all the efforts of Government, from the 12th of March till the 19th of May following. During those two months the new directors devoted themselves with the utmost energy to hurrying on the armament of the people, and especially to making proselytes among the militia, where the gain of one man armed and disciplined was justly accounted equal to the enlistment of three or four ordinary adherents. This part of their plan brought the brothers Sheares into contact, among others, with Captain John Warneford Armstrong, of the Queen's County Yeomanry, whom they supposed they had won over, but who was, in reality, a better-class spy, acting under Lord Castlereagh's instructions. Armstrong cultivated them sedulously, dined at their table, echoed their opinions, and led the credulous brothers on to their destruction. All at last was determined on; the day of the rising was fixed--the 23rd day of May--and the signal was to be the simultaneous stoppage of the mail coaches, which started nightly from the Dublin post-office, to every quarter of the kingdom. But the counterplot anticipated the plot. Lord Edward, betrayed by a person called Higgins, proprietor of the *Freeman's Journal*, was taken on the 19th of May, after a desperate struggle with Majors Swan and Sirr, and Captain Ryan, in his hiding-place in Thomas Street; the brothers Sheares were arrested in their own house on the morning of the 21st, while Surgeon Lawless escaped from the city, and finally from the country, to France. Thus, for the second time, was the insurrection left without a head; but the organization had proceeded too far to be any longer restrained, and the Castle, moreover, to use the expression of Lord Castlereagh, "took means to make it explode."

The first intelligence of the rebellion was received in Dublin on the morning of the 24th of May. At Rathfarnham, within three miles of the city, 500 insurgents attacked Lord Ely's yeomanry corps with some success, till Lord Roden's dragoons, hastily despatched from the city, compelled them to retreat, with the loss of some prisoners and two men killed, whom Mr. Beresford saw the next day, literally "*cut to pieces*--a horrid sight." At Dunboyne the insurgents piked an escort of the Reay Fencibles (Scotch) passing through their village, and carried off their baggage. At Naas, a large popular force attacked the garrison, consisting of regulars, Ancient Britons (Welsh), part of a regiment of dragoons, and the Armagh Militia; the attack was renewed three times with great bravery, but finally, discipline, as it always will, prevailed over mere numbers, and the assailants were repulsed with the loss of 140 of their comrades. At Prosperous, where they cut off to a man a strong garrison composed of North Cork Militia, under Captain Swayne, the rising was more successful. The commander in this exploit was Dr. Esmonde, brother of the Wexford baronet, who, being betrayed by one of his own subalterns, was the next morning arrested at breakfast in the neighbourhood, and suffered death at Dublin on the 14th of the following month.

There could hardly be found a more unfavourable field for a peasant war than the generally level and easily accessible county of Kildare, every parish of which is within a day's march of Dublin. From having been the residence of Lord Edward, it was, perhaps, one of the most highly organized parts of Leinster, but as it had the misfortune to be represented by Thomas Reynolds, as county delegate, it laboured under the disadvantage of having its organization better known to the government than any other. We need hardly be surprised, therefore, to find that the military operations in this county were all over in ten days or a fortnight; when those who had neither surrendered nor fallen, fell back into Meath or Connaught, or effected a junction with the Wicklow rebels in their mountain fastnesses. Their struggle, though so brief, had been creditable for personal bravery. Attacked by a numerous cavalry and militia under General Wilford, by 2,500 men, chiefly regulars, under General Dundas, and by 800 regulars brought up by forced marches from Limerick, under Sir James Duff, they showed qualities, which, if well directed, would have established for their possessors a high military reputation. At Monastereven they were repulsed with loss, the defenders of the town being in part Catholic loyalists, under Captain Cassidy; at Rathangan, they were more successful, taking and holding the town for several days; at Clane, the captors of Prosperous were repulsed; while at Old Killcullen, their associates drove back General Dundas' advance, with the loss of 22 regulars and Captain Erskine killed. Sir James Duff's wanton cruelty in sabring and shooting down an unarmed multitude on the Curragh, won him the warm approval of the extermination party in the Capital, while Generals Wilford and Dundas narrowly escaped being reprimanded for granting a truce to the insurgents under Aylmer, and accepting of the surrender of that leader and his companions. By the beginning of June the six Kildare encampments of insurgents were totally dispersed, and their most active officers in prison or fugitives west or south.

By a preconcerted arrangement, the local chiefs of the insurrection in Dublin and Meath, gathered with their men on the third day after the outbreak, at the historic hill of Tara. Here they expected to be joined by the men of Cavan, Longford, Louth and Monaghan; but before the northerners reached the trysting place, three companies of the Reay Fencibles, under Captain McClean, the Kells and Navan Yeomanry, under Captain Preston, (afterwards Lord Tara,) and a troop of cavalry under Lord Fingal, surrounded the royal hill. The insurgents, commanded by Gilshine and other leaders, intrenched themselves in the graveyard which occupies the summit of Tara, and stoutly defended their position. Twenty-six of the Highlanders and six of the Yeomanry fell in the assault, but the bullet reached farther than the pike, and the defenders were driven, after a sharp action, over the brow of the eminence, and many of them shot or sabred down as they fled.

Southward from the Capital the long pent-up flame of disaffection broke out on the same memorable day, May 23rd. At Dunlavin, an abortive attempt on the barrack revealed the fact that many of the Yeomanry were thoroughly with the insurgents. Hardly had the danger from without passed over, when a military inquiry was improvised. By this tribunal, nineteen Wexford, and nine Kildare Yeomanry, were ordered to be shot, and the execution of the sentence followed immediately on its rending. At Blessington, the town was seized, but a nocturnal attack on Carlow was repulsed with great loss. In this last affair, the rebels had ***rendezvoused*** in the domain of Sir Edward Crosbie, within two miles of the town. Here arms were distributed and orders given by their leader, named Roche. Silently and quickly they reached the town they hoped to surprise. But the regular troops, of which the garrison was chiefly composed, were on the alert, though their preparations were made full as silently. When the peasantry emerged from Tullow Street, into an exposed space, a deadly fire was opened upon them from the houses on all sides. The regulars, in perfect security themselves, and abundantly supplied with ammunition, shot them down with deadly unerring aim. The people soon found there was nothing for it but retreat, and carrying off as best they could their killed and wounded, they retired sorely discomfited. For alleged complicity in this attack, Sir Edward Crosbie was shortly afterward arrested, tried and executed. There was not a shadow of proof against him; but he was known to sympathize with the sufferings of his countrymen, to have condemned in strong language the policy of provocation, and that was sufficient. He paid with the penalty of his head for the kindness and generosity of his heart.

CHAPTER XVI.

THE INSURRECTION OF 1798--THE WEXFORD INSURRECTION.

The most formidable insurrection, indeed the only really formidable one, broke out in the county of Wexford, a county in which it was stated there were not 200 sworn United Irishmen, and which Lord Edward Fitzgerald had altogether omitted from his official list of counties organized in the month of February. In that brief interval, the Government policy of provocation had the desired effect, though the explosion was of a nature to startle those who occasioned it.

Wexford, geographically, is a peculiar county, and its people are a peculiar people. The county fills up the south-eastern corner of the island, with the sea south-east, the river Barrow to the west, and the woods and mountains of Carlow and Wicklow to the north. It is about forty miles long by twenty-four broad; the surface undulating and rising into numerous groups of detached hills, two or more of which are generally visible from each conspicuous summit. Almost in the midst flows the river Slaney, springing from a lofty Wicklow peak, which sends down on its northern slope the better known river Liffey. On the estuary of the Slaney, some seventy miles south of Dublin, stands the county town, the traveller journeying to which by the usual route then taken, passed in succession through Arklow, Gorey, Ferns, Enniscorthy, and other places of less consequence, though familiar enough in the fiery records of 1798. North-westward, the only road in those days from Carlow and Kilkenny, crossed the Blackstairs at Scollagh-gap, entering the county at Newtownbarry, the ancient Bunclody; westward, some twenty miles, on the river Barrow, stands New Ross, often mentioned in this history, the road from which to the county town passes through Scullabogue and Taghmon (*Ta'mun*), the former at the foot of Carrickbyrne rock, the latter at the base of what is rather hyperbolically called "the *mountain* of Forth." South and west of the town, towards the estuary of Waterford, lie the baronies of Forth and Bargy, a great part of the population of which, even within our own time, spoke the language Chaucer and Spenser wrote, and retained many of the characteristics of their Saxon, Flemish, and Cambrian ancestors. Through this singular district lay the road towards Duncannon fort, on Waterford harbour, with branches running off to Bannow, Ballyhack, and Dunbrody. We shall, therefore, speak of all the localities we may have occasion to mention as on or near one of the four main roads of the county, the Dublin, Carlow, Ross, and Waterford roads.

The population of this territory was variously estimated in 1798, at 150,000, 180,000, and 200,000. They were, generally speaking, a comfortable and contented peasantry, for the Wexford landlords were seldom absentees, and the farmers held under them by long leases and reasonable rents. There were in the country few great lords, but there was little poverty and no pauperism. In such a soil, the secret societies were almost certain to fail, and if it had not been for the diabolical experiments of Lord Kingsborough's North Cork Militia, it is very probable that that orderly and thrifty population would have seen the eventful year we are describing pass over their homes without experiencing any of the terrible trials which accompanied it. But it was impossible for human nature to endure the provocations inflicted upon this patient and prosperous people. The pitch-cap and the triangle were resorted to on the slightest and most frivolous pretexts. "A sergeant of the North Cork Militia," says Mr. Hay, the county historian, "nicknamed, **Tom the Devil**, was most ingenious in devising new modes of torture. Moistened gunpowder was frequently rubbed into the hair cut close and then set on fire; some, while shearing for this purpose, had the tips of their ears snipt off; sometimes an entire ear, and often both ears were completely cut off; and many lost part of their noses during the like preparation. But, strange to tell," adds Mr. Hay, "these atrocities were publicly practised without the least reserve in open day, and no magistrate or officer ever interfered, but shamefully connived at this extraordinary mode of quieting the people! Some of the miserable sufferers on these shocking occasions, or some of their relations or friends, actuated by a principle of retaliation, if not of revenge, cut short the hair of several persons whom they either considered as enemies or suspected of having pointed them out as objects for such desperate treatment. This was done with a view that those active citizens should fall in for a little experience of the like discipline, or to make the fashion of short hair so general that it might no longer be a mark of party distinction." This was the origin of the nickname "Croppy," by which, during the remainder of the insurrection, it was customary to designate all who were suspected or proved to be hostile to, the government.

Among the magistracy of the county were several persons who, whatever might have been their conduct in ordinary times, now showed themselves utterly unfit to be entrusted with those large discretionary powers which Parliament had recently conferred upon all justices of the peace. One of these magistrates, surrounded by his troops, perambulated the county with an executioner, armed with all the equipments of his office; another carried away the lopped hands and fingers of his victims, with which he stirred his punch in the carousals that followed every expedition. At Carnew, midway between the Dublin and Carlow roads, on the second day of the insurrection, twenty-eight prisoners were brought out to be shot at as targets in the public ball alley; on the same day Enniscorthy witnessed its first execution for treason, and the neighbourhood of Ballaghkeen was harried by Mr. Jacob, one of the magistrates whose method of preserving the peace of the county has been just referred to. The majority of the bench, either weakly or willingly, sanctioned these atrocities, but some others, among them a few of the first men in the county, did not hesitate to resist and condemn them. Among these were Mr. Beauchamp Bagenal Harvey of Bargy Castle, Mr. Fitzgerald of Newpark, and Mr. John Henry Colclough of Tintern Abbey; but all these gentlemen were arrested on Saturday, the 26th of May--the same day, or more strictly speaking, the eve of the day on which the Wexford outbreak occurred.

On the day succeeding these arrests, being Whitsunday, Father John Murphy, parish priest of Kilcormick, the son of a small farmer of the neighbourhood, educated in Spain, on coming to his little wayside chapel, found it laid in ashes. To his flock, as they surrounded him in the open air, he boldly preached that it would be much better for them to die in a fair field than to await the tortures inflicted by such magistrates as Archibald Jacob, Hunter Gowan, and Hawtrey White. He declared his readiness to share their fate, whatever it might be, and in response, about 2,000 of the country people gathered in a few hours upon Oulart Hill, situated about half-way between Enniscorthy and the sea, and eleven miles north of Wexford. Here they were attacked on the afternoon of the same day by the North Cork Militia, Colonel Foote, the Shilmalier Yeoman cavalry, Colonel Le Hunte, and the Wexford cavalry. The rebels, strong in their position, and more generally accustomed to the use of arms than persons in their condition in other parts of the country, made a brave and successful stand. Major Lambert, the Hon. Captain De Courcy (brother of Lord Kinsale), and some other officers, fell before the long-shore guns of the Shilmalier fowlers; of the North Cork detachment, only the colonel, a sergeant, and two or three privates escaped; the cavalry, at the top of their speed, galloped back to the county town.

The people were soon thoroughly aroused. Another popular priest of the diocese, Michael Murphy, on reaching Gorey, finding his chapel also rifled, and the altar desecrated, turned his horse's head and joined the insurgents, who had gathered on Kilthomas hill, near Carnew. Signal fires burned that night on all the eminences of the county, which seemed as if they had been designed for so many watch-towers; horns resounded; horsemen galloped far and near; on the morrow of Whitsunday all Wexford arose, animated with the passions and purposes of civil war.

On the 28th, Ferns, Camolin, and Enniscorthy were taken by the insurgents; the latter, after an action of four hours, in which a captain, two lieutenants, and eighty of the local yeomanry fell. The survivors fled to Wexford, which was as rapidly as possible placed in a state of defence. The old walls and gates were still in good repair, and 300 North Cork, 200 Donegal, and 700 local militia ought to have formed a strong garrison within such ramparts, against a mere tumultuous peasantry. The yeomen, however, thought otherwise, and two of the three imprisoned popular magistrates were sent to Enniscorthy to exhort and endeavour to disperse the insurgents. One of them only returned, the other, Mr. Fitzgerald, joined the rebels, who, continuing their march, were allowed to take possession of the county town without striking a blow. Mr. Bagenal Harvey, the magistrate still in prison, they insisted on making their Commander-in-Chief; a gentleman of considerable property, by no means destitute of courage, but in every other respect quite unequal to the task imposed upon him. After a trial of his generalship at the battle of Ross, he was transferred to the more pacific office of President of the Council, which continued to sit and direct operations from Wexford, with the co-operation of a sub-committee at Enniscorthy. Captain Matthew Keogh, a retired officer of the regular army, aged but active, was made governor of the town, in which a couple of hundred armed men were left as his guards. An attempt to relieve the place from Duncannon had utterly failed. General Fawcett, commanding that important fortress, set out on his march with this object on the 30th of May--his advanced guard of 70 Meathian yeomanry, having in charge three howitzers, whose slower movements it was expected the main force would overtake long before reaching the neighbourhood of danger. At Taghmon this force was joined by Captain Adams with his command, and thus reinforced they continued their march to Wexford. Within three miles of the town the road wound round the base of the "three rock" mountain; evening fell as the royalists approached this neighbourhood, where the victors of Oulart, Enniscorthy, and Wexford had just improvised a new camp. A sharp volley from the long-shore-men's guns, and a furious onslaught of pikes threw the royal detachment into the utmost disorder. Three officers of the Meathian cavalry, and nearly one hundred men were placed *hors de combat*; the three howitzers, eleven gunners, and several prisoners taken; making the third considerable success of the insurgents within a week.

Wexford county now became the theatre of operations, on which all eyes were fixed. The populace gathered as if by instinct into three great encampments, on Vinegar Hill, above Enniscorthy; on Carrickbyrne, on the road leading to Ross, and on the hill of Corrigrua, seven miles from Gorey. The principal leaders of the first division were Fathers Kearns and Clinch, and Messrs. Fitzgerald, Doyle, and Redmond; of the second, Bagenal Harvey, and Father Philip Roche; of the last, Anthony Perry of Inch, Esmond Kyan, and the two Fathers Murphy, Michael, and John. The general plan of operations was that the third division should move by way of Arklow and Wicklow on the Capital; the second to open communication with Carlow, Kilkenny, and Kildare by Newtownbarry and Scollagh-gap; while the first was to attack New Ross, and endeavour to hasten the rising in Munster.

On the 1st of June, the advance of the northern division marching upon Gorey, then occupied in force by General Loftus, were encountered four miles from the town, and driven back with the loss of about a hundred killed and wounded. On the 4th of June, Loftus, at the instance of Colonel Walpole, aid-de-camp to the Lord Lieutenant, who had lately joined him with considerable reinforcements, resolved to beat up the rebel quarters at Corrigrua. It was to be a combined movement; Lord Ancram, posted with his militia and dragoons at the bridge of Scaramalsh, where the poetic Banna joins the Slaney, was to prevent the arrival of succours from Vinegar Hill; Captain McManus, with a couple of companies of yeomanry, stationed at another exposed point from which intelligence could be obtained and communicated; while the General and Colonel Walpole, marched to the attack by roads some distance apart, which ran into one within two miles of Corrigrua camp. The main body of the King's troops were committed to the lead of Walpole, who had also two six-pounders and a howitzer. After an hour-and-a-half's march he found the country changed its character near the village of Clogh (*clo'*), where the road descending from the level arable land, dips suddenly into the narrow and winding pass of Tubberneering. The sides of the pass were lined with a bushy shrubbery, and the roadway at the bottom embanked with ditch and dike. On came the confident Walpole, never dreaming that these silent thickets were so soon to re-echo the cries of the onslaught. The 4th dragoon guards, the Ancient Britons, under Sir Watkyn Wynne, the Antrim militia, under Colonel Cope, had all entered the defile before the ambuscade was discovered. Then, at the first volley, Walpole fell, with several of those immediately about Ms person; out from the shrubbery rushed the pikemen, clearing ditch and dike at a bound; dragoons and fencibles went down like the sward before the scythe of the mower; the three guns were captured, and turned on the flying survivors; the regimental flags taken, with all the other spoils pertaining to such a retreat. It was, in truth, an immense victory for a mob of peasants, marshalled by men who that day saw their first, or, at most, their second action. Before forty-eight hours they were masters of Gorey, and talked of nothing less than the capture of Dublin within another week or fortnight!

From Vinegar Hill the concerted movement was made against Newtonbarry, on the 2nd of June, the rebels advancing by both banks of the Slaney, under cover of a six-pounder-- the only gun they had with them. The detachment in command of the beautiful little town, half hidden in its leafy valley, was from 600 to 800 strong, with a troop of dragoons, and two battalion guns, under command of Colonel L'Estrange; these, after a sharp fusilade on both sides, were driven out, but the assailants, instead of following up the blow, dispersed for plunder or refreshment, were attacked in turn, and compelled to retreat, with a reported loss of 400 killed.

Three days later, however, a still more important action, and a yet more disastrous repulse from the self-same cause, took place at New Ross, on the Barrow.

The garrison of Ross, on the morning of the 5th of June, when General Harvey appeared before it, consisted of 1,400 men--Dublin, Meath, Donegal, and Clare militia, Mid-Lothian fencibles, and English artillery. General Johnson, a veteran soldier, was in command, and the place, strong in its well preserved old walls, had not heard a shot fired in anger since the time of Cromwell. Harvey was reported to have with him 20,000 men; but if we allow for the exaggeration of numbers common to all such movements, we may, perhaps, deduct one-half, and still leave him at the head of a formidable force--10,000 men, with three field-pieces. Mr. Furlong, a favourite officer, being sent forward to summon the town, was shot down by a sentinel, and the attack began. The main point of assault was the gate known as "three bullet gate," and the hour, five o'clock of the lovely summer's morning. The obstinacy with which the town was contested, may be judged from the fact, that the fighting continued for nearly ten hours, with the interruption of an hour or two at noon. This was the fatal interruption for the rebels. They had, at a heavy cost, driven out the royalists, with the loss of a colonel (Lord Mountjoy), three captains, and above 200 men killed: but of their friends and comrades treble the number had fallen. Still the town, an object of the first importance, was theirs, when worn out with heat, fatigue, and fasting since sunrise, they indulged themselves in the luxury of a deep unmeasured carouse. The fugitive garrison finding themselves unpursued, halted to breathe on the Kilkenny bank of the river, were rallied by the veteran Johnson, and led back again across the bridge, taking the surprised revellers completely unprepared. A cry was raised that this was a fresh force from Waterford; the disorganised multitude endeavoured to rally in turn, but before the leaders could collect their men, the town was once more in possession of the Bang's troops. The rebels, in their turn, unpursued by their exhausted enemies, fell back upon their camping ground of the night before, at Corbet hill and Slieve-kielter. At the latter, Father Philip Roche, dissatisfied with Harvey's management, established a separate command, which he transferred to a layman of his own name, Edward Roche, with whom he continued to act and advise during the remainder of this memorable month.

The summer of 1798 was, for an Irish summer, remarkably dry and warm. The heavy Atlantic rains which at all seasons are poured out upon that soil, seemed suspended in favour of the insurgent multitudes, amounting to 30,000, or 40,000 at the highest, who, on the different hill summits, posted their nightly sentinels, and threw themselves down on turf and heather to snatch a short repose. The kindling of a beacon, the lowing of cattle, or the hurried arrival of scout or messenger, hardly interfered with slumbers which the fatigues of the day, and, unhappily also, the potations of the night rendered doubly deep. An early morning mass mustered all the Catholics, unless the very depraved, to the chaplain's tent--for several of the officers, and the chaplains always were supplied with tents; and then a hasty meal was snatched before the sun was fairly above the horizon, and the day's work commenced. The endurance exhibited by the rebels, their personal strength, swiftness and agility; their tenacity of life, and the ease with which their worst wounds were healed, excited the astonishment of the surgeons and officers of the regular army. The truth is, that the virtuous lives led by that peaceful peasantry before the outbreak, enabled them to withstand privations and hardships under which the better fed and better clad Irish yeomen and English guardsmen would have sunk prostrate in a week.

Several signs now marked the turning of the tide against the men of Wexford. Waterford did not rise after the battle of Ross; while Munster, generally, was left to undecided councils, or held back in hopes of another French expedition. The first week of June had passed over, and neither northward nor westward was there any movement formidable enough to draw off from the devoted county the combined armies which were now directed against its camps. A gunboat fleet lined the coast from Bannow round to Wicklow, which soon after appeared off Wexford bar, and forced an entrance into the harbour. A few days earlier, General Needham marched from Dublin, and took up his position at Arklow, at the head of a force variously stated at 1,500 to 2,000 men, composed of 120 cavalry under Sir Watkyn Wynne, two brigades of militia under Colonels Cope and Maxwell, and a brigade of English and Scotch fencibles under Colonel Skerrett. There were also at Arklow about 300 of the Wexford and Wicklow mounted yeomanry raised by Lord Wicklow, Lord Mountnorris, and other gentlemen of the neighbourhood. Early on the morning of the 9th of June the northern division of the rebels left Gorey in two columns, in order if possible to drive this force from Arklow. One body proceeding by the coast road hoped to turn the English position by way of the strand, the other taking the inner line of the Dublin road, was to assail the town at its upper or inland suburb. But General Needham had made the most of his two days' possession; barricades were erected across the road, and at the entrance to the main street; the graveyard and bridge commanding the approach by the shore road were mounted with ordnance; the cavalry were posted where they could best operate, near the strand; the barrack wall was lined with a *banquette* or stage, from which the musketeers could pour their fire with the greatest advantage, and every other precaution taken to give the rebels a warm reception. The action commenced early in the afternoon, and lasted till eight in the evening--five or six hours. The inland column suffered most severely from the marksmen on the *banquette*, and the gallant Father Michael Murphy, whom his followers believed to be invulnerable, fell leading them on to the charge for the third time. On the side of the sea, Esmond Kyan was badly wounded in the arm, which he was subsequently obliged to have amputated, and though the fearless Shilmaliers drove the cavalry into and over the Avoca, discipline and ordnance prevailed once again over numbers and courage. As night fell, the assailants retired slowly towards Coolgreney, carrying off nine carloads of their wounded, and leaving, perhaps, as many more on the field; their loss was variously reported from 700 to 1,000, and even 1,500. The opposite force returned less than 100 killed, including Captain Knox, and about as many wounded. The repulse was even more than that at Ross, dispiriting to the rebels, who, as a last resort, now decided to concentrate all their strength on the favourite position at Vinegar Hill.

Against this encampment, therefore, the entire available force of regulars and militia within fifty miles of the spot were concentrated by orders of Lord Lake, the Commander-in-Chief. General Dundas from Wicklow was to join General Loftus at Carnew on the 18th; General Needham was to advance simultaneously to Gorey; General Sir Henry Johnson to unite at Old Ross with Sir James Duff from Carlow; Sir Charles Asgill was to occupy Gore's bridge and Borris; Sir John Moore was to land at Ballyhack ferry, march to Foulke's Mill, and united with Johnson and Duff, to assail the rebel camp on Carrickbyrne. These various movements ordered on the 16th, were to be completed by the 20th, on which day, from their various new positions, the entire force, led by these six general officers, was to surround Vinegar Hill, and make a simultaneous attack upon the last stronghold of the Wexford rebellion.

This elaborate plan failed of complete execution in two points. *First*, the camp on Carrickbyrne, instead of waiting the attack, sent down its fighting men to Foulke's Mill, where, in the afternoon of the 20th they beat up Sir John Moore's quarters, and maintained from 3 o'clock till dark, what that officer calls "a pretty sharp action." Several tunes they were repulsed and again formed behind the ditches and renewed the conflict; but the arrival of two fresh regiments, under Lord Dalhousie, taught them that there was no farther chance of victory. By this affair, however, though at a heavy cost, they had prevented the junction of all the troops, and, not without satisfaction, they now followed the two Roches, the priest and the layman, to the original position of the mountain of Forth; Sir John Moore, on his part, taking the same direction, until he halted within sight of the walls of Wexford. The other departure from Lord Lake's plan was on the side of General Needham, who was ordered to approach the point of attack by the circuitous route of Oulart, but who did not come up in time to complete the investment of the hill.

On the morning of the appointed day, about 13,000 royal troops were in movement against the 20,000 rebels whom they intended to dislodge. Sir James Duff obtained possession of an eminence which commanded the lower line of the rebel encampment, and from this point a brisk cannonade was opened against the opposite force; at the same time the columns of Lake, Wilford, Dundas, and Johnson, pushed up the south-eastern, northern and western sides of the eminence, partially covered by the fire of these guns, so advantageously placed. After an hour and a half's desperate fighting, the rebels broke and fled by the unguarded side of the hill. Their rout was complete, and many were cut down by the cavalry, as they pressed in dense masses on each other, over the level fields and out on the open highways. Still this action was far from being one of the most fatal as to loss of life, fought in that county; the rebel dead were numbered only at 400, and the royalists killed and wounded at less than half that number.

It was the last considerable action of the Wexford rising, and all the consequences which followed being attributed arbitrarily to this cause, helped to invest it with a disproportionate importance. The only leader lost on the rebel side was Father Clinch of Enniscorthy, who encountered Lord Roden hand to hand in the retreat, but who, while engaged with his lordship whom he wounded, was shot down by a trooper. The disorganization, however, which followed on the dispersion, was irreparable. One column had taken the road by Gorey to the mountains of Wicklow--another to Wexford, where they split into two parts, a portion crossing the Slaney into the sea-coast parishes, and facing northward by the shore road, the other falling back on "the three rocks" encampment, where the Messrs. Roche held together a fragment of their former command. Wexford town, on the 22nd, was abandoned to Lord Lake, who established himself in the house of Governor Keogh, the owner being lodged in the common jail. Within the week, Bagenal Harvey, Father Philip Roche, and Kelly of Killane, had surrendered in despair, while Messrs. Grogan and Colclough, who had secreted themselves in a cave in the great Saltee Island, were discovered, and conducted to the same prison. Notwithstanding the capitulation agreed to by Lord Kingsborough, the execution and decapitation of all these gentlemen speedily followed, and their ghastly faces looked down for many a day from the iron spikes above the entrance of Wexford Court House. Mr. Esmond Kyan, the popular hero of the district, as merciful as brave, was discovered some time subsequently paying a stealthy visit to his family; he was put to death on the spot, and his body, weighted with heavy stones, thrown into the harbour. A few mornings afterwards the incoming tide deposited it close by the dwelling of his father-in-law, and the rites of Christian burial, so dear to all his race, were hurriedly rendered to the beloved remains.

The insurrection in this county, while it abounded in instances of individual and general heroism, was stained also, on both sides, by many acts of diabolical cruelty. The aggressors, both in time and in crime were the yeomanry and military; but the popular movement dragged wretches to the surface who delighted in repaying torture with torture, and death with death. The butcheries of Dunlavin and Carnew were repaid by the massacres at Scullabogue and Wexford bridge, in the former of which 110, and in the latter 35 or 40 persons were put to death in cold blood, by the monsters who absented themselves from the battles of Ross and Vinegar Hill. The executions at Wexford bridge would probably have been swelled to double the number, had not Father Corrin, one of the priests of the town, rushing in between his Protestant neighbours and the ferocious Captain Dixon, and summoning all present to pray, invoked the Almighty "to show them the same mercy" they showed their prisoners. This awful supplication calmed even that savage rabble, and no further execution took place. Nearly forty years afterwards, Captain Kellet, of Clonard, ancestor of the Arctic discoverer, and others whom he had rescued from the very grasp of the executioner, followed to the grave that revered and devoted minister of mercy!

It would be a profitless task to draw out a parallel of the crimes committed on both sides. Two facts only need be recorded: that although from 1798 to 1800, not less than ***sixty-five*** places of Catholic worship were demolished or burned in Leinster, (twenty-two of which were in Wexford county), only **one** Protestant Church, that of Old Ross, was destroyed in retaliation; and that although towards men, especially men in arms, the rebels acted on the fierce Mosaic maxim of "an eye for an eye and a tooth for a tooth," no outrage upon women is laid to their charge, even by their most exasperated enemies.

CHAPTER XVII.

THE INSURRECTION ELSEWHERE--FATE OF THE LEADING UNITED IRISHMEN.

On the 21st of June, the Marquis Cornwallis, whose name is so familiar in American and East Indian history, arrived in Dublin, to assume the supreme power, both civil and military. As his Chief Secretary, he recommended Lord Castlereagh, who had acted in that capacity during the latter part of Lord Camden's administration in consequence of Mr Pelham's illness; and the Pitt-Portland administration appointed his lordship accordingly, because, among other good and sufficient reasons, "he was so unlike an Irishman."

While the new Viceroy came to Ireland still more resolute than his predecessor to bring about the long-desired legislative union, it is but justice to his memory to say, that he as resolutely resisted the policy of torture and provocation pursued under Lord Camden. That policy had, indeed, served its pernicious purpose, and it was now possible for a new ruler to turn a new leaf; this Lord Cornwallis did from the hour of his arrival, not without incurring the ill-concealed displeasures of the Castle cabal. But his position gave him means of protection which Sir Ralph Abercromby had not; he was known to enjoy the personal confidence of the King; and those who did not hesitate three months before to assail by every abusive epithet the humane Scottish Baronet, hesitated long before criticising with equal freedom the all-powerful Viceroy.

The sequel of the insurrection may be briefly related: next to Wexford, the adjoining county of Wicklow, famous throughout the world for its lakes and glens, maintained the chief brunt of the Leinster battle. The brothers Byrne, of Ballymanus, with Holt, Hackett, and other local leaders, were for months, from the difficult nature of the country, enabled to defy those combined movements by which, as in a huge net, Lord Lake had swept up the camps of Wexford. At Hacketstown, on the 25th of June, the Byrnes were repulsed with considerable loss, but at Ballyellis, on the 30th, fortune and skill gave them and their Wexford comrades a victory, resembling in many respects that of Clough. General Needham, who had again established his head-quarters at Gorey, detached Colonel Preston, with some troops of Ancient Britons, the 4th and 5th dragoons, and three yeomanry corps, to attack the insurgents who were observed in force in the neighbourhood of Monaseed. Aware of this movement, the Byrnes prepared in the ravine of Ballyellis a well-laid ambuscade, barricading with carts and trees the farther end of the pass. Attacked by the royalists they retreated towards this pass, were hotly pursued, and then turned on their pursuers. Two officers and sixty men were killed in the trap, while the terrified rear-rank fled for their lives to the shelter of their head-quarters. At Ballyraheene, on the 2nd of July, the King's troops sustained another check in which they lost two officers and ten men, but at Ballygullen, on the 4th, the insurgents were surrounded between the forces of General Needham, Sir James Duff, and the Marquis of Huntley. This was the last considerable action in which the Wicklow and Wexford men were unitedly engaged. In the dispersion which followed, "Billy Byrne of Ballymanus," the hero of his county, paid the forfeit of his life; while his brother, Garrett, subsequently surrendered, and was included in the Banishment Act.

Anthony Perry of Inch, and Father Kearns, leading a much diminished band into Kildare, formed a junction with Aylmer and Reynolds of that county, and marched into Meath, with a view of reaching and surprising Athlone. The plan was boldly and well conceived, but their means of execution were deplorably deficient. At Clonard they were repulsed by a handful of troops well armed and posted; a combined movement always possible in Meath, drove them from side to side during the midweek of July, until at length, hunted down as they were, they broke up in twos and threes to seek any means of escape. Father Kearns and Mr. Perry were, however, arrested, and executed by martial law at Edenderry. Both died bravely; the priest sustaining and exhorting his companion to the last.

Still another band of the Wexford men, under Father John Murphy and Walter Devereux, crossed the Barrow at Gore's bridge, and marched upon Kilkenny. At

Lowgrange they surprised an outpost; at Castlecomer, after a sharp action, they took the town, which Sir Charles Asgill endeavoured, but without success, to relieve. Thence they continued their march towards Athy in Kildare, but being caught between two or rather three fires, that of Major Mathews, from Maryboro', General Dunne, from Athy, and Sir Charles Asgill, they retreated on old Leighlin, as if seeking the shelter of the Carlow mountains. At Killcomney Hill, however, they were forced into action under most unfavourable circumstances, and utterly routed. One, Father Murphy, fell in the engagement, the other, the precursor of the insurrection, was captured three days afterward, and conveyed a prisoner to General Duff's headquarters at Tullow. Here he was put on his trial before a Military Commission composed of Sir James Duff, Lord Roden, Colonels Eden and Foster, and Major Hall. Hall had the meanness to put to him, prisoner as he was, several insulting questions, which at length the high-spirited rebel answered with a blow. The Commission thought him highly dangerous, and instantly ordered him to execution. His body was burned, his head spiked on the market-house of Tullow, and his memory gibbeted in all the loyal publications of the period. On his person, before execution, were found a crucifix, a pix, and letters from many Protestants, asking his protection; as to his reputation, the priest who girded on the sword only when he found his altar overthrown and his flock devoured by wolves, need not fear to look posterity in the face.

Of the other Leinster leaders, Walter Devereux, the last colleague of Father Murphy, was arrested at Cork, on the eve of sailing for America, tried and executed; Fitzgerald and Aylmer were spared on condition of expatriation; months afterwards, Holt surrendered, was transported, and returned after several years, to end his days where he began his career; Dwyer alone maintained the life of a Rapparee for five long years among the hills of Wicklow, where his adventures were often of such a nature as to throw all fictitious conceptions of an outlaw's life into commonplace by comparison. Except in the fastnesses frequented by this extraordinary man, and in the wood of Killaughram, in Wexford, where the outlaws, with the last stroke of national humour, assumed the name of *The Babes in the Wood*, the Leinster insurrection was utterly trodden out within two months from its first beginning, on the 23rd of May. So weak against discipline, arms, munitions and money, are all that mere naked valour and devotion can accomplish!

In Ulster, on the organization of which so much time and labour had been expended for four or five years preceding, the rising was not more general than in Leinster, and the actual struggle lasted only a week. The two counties which moved *en masse* were Down and Antrim, the original chiefs of which, such as Thomas Russell and Samuel Neilson, were unfortunately in prison. The next leader on whom the men of Antrim relied, resigned his command on the very eve of the appointed day; this disappointment and the arrest of the Rev. Steele Dickson in Down, compelled a full fortnight's delay. On the 7th of June, however, the more determined spirits resolved on action, and the first movement was to seize the town of Antrim, which, if they could have held it, would have given them command of the communications with Donegal and Down, from both of which they might have expected important additions to their ranks. The leader of this enterprise was Henry John McCracken, a cotton manufacturer of Belfast, thirty two years of age, well educated, accomplished and resolute, with whom was associated a brother of William Orr, the proto-martyr of the Ulster Union. The town of Antrim was occupied by the 22nd light dragoons, Colonel Lumley, and the local yeomanry under Lord O'Neil. In the first assault the insurgents were successful, Lord O'Neil, five officers, forty-seven rank and file having fallen, and two guns being captured; but Lumley's dragoons had hardly vanished out of sight, when a strong reinforcement from Blaris camp arrived and renewed the action, changing premature exultation into panic and confusion. Between two and three hundred of the rebels fell, and McCracken and his staff, deserted by their hasty levies, were arrested, wearied and hopeless, about a month later, wandering among the Antrim hills. The leaders were tried at Belfast and executed.

In Down two actions were fought, one at Saintfield on the 7th of June, under Dr. Jackson--where Colonel Stapleton was severely handled--and another and more important one at Ballynahinch, under Henry Munro, on the 13th, where Nugent, the district General, commanded in person. Here, after a gallant defence, the men of Down were utterly routed; their leader, alone and on foot, was captured some five or six miles from the field, and executed two days afterwards before his own door at Lisburn. He died with the utmost composure; his wife and mother looking down, on the awful scene from the windows of his own house.

In Munster, with the exception of a trifling skirmish between the West-Meath yeomanry under Sir Hugh O'Reilly, with whom were the Caithness legion, under Major Innes, and a body of 300 or 400 ill-armed peasants, who attacked them on the 19th of June, on the road from Clonakilty to Bandon, there was no notable attempt at insurrection. But in Connaught, very unexpectedly, as late as the end of August, the flame extinguished in blood in Leinster and Ulster, again blazed up for some days with portentous brightness. The counties of Mayo, Sligo, Roscommon and Galway had been partially organized by those fugitives from Orange oppression in the North, who, in the years '95, '96, and '97, had been compelled to flee for their lives into Connaught, to the number of several thousands. They brought with the tale of their sufferings the secret of Defenderism; they first taught the peasantry of the West, who, safe in their isolated situation and their overwhelming numbers, were more familiar with poverty than with persecution, what manner of men then held sway over all the rest of the country, and how easily it would be for Irishmen once united and backed by France, to establish under their own green flag, both religious and civil liberty.

When, therefore, three French frigates cast anchor in Killalla Bay, on the 22nd of August, they did not find the country wholly unprepared, though far from being as ripe for revolt as they expected. These ships had on board 1,000 men, with arms for 1,000 more, under command of General Humbert, who had taken on himself, in the state of anarchy which then prevailed in France, to sail from La Rochelle with this handful of men, in aid of the insurrection. With Humbert were Mathew Tone and Bartholmew Teeling; and immediately on his arrival he was joined by Messrs. McDonnell, Moore, Bellew, Barrett, O'Dowd, and O'Donnell of Mayo, Blake of Galway, Plunkett of Roscommon, and a few other influential gentlemen of that Province-- almost all Catholics. Three days were spent at Killalla, which was easily taken, in landing stores, enrolling recruits, and sending out parties of observation. On the 4th, (Sunday,) Humbert entered Ballina without resistance, and on the same night set out for Castlebar, the county town. By this time intelligence of his landing was spread over the whole country, and both Lord Lake and General Hutchinson had advanced to Castlebar, where they had from 2,000 to 3,000 men under their command. The place could be reached only by two routes from the north-west, by the Foxford road, or a long deserted mountain road which led over the pass of Barnagee, within sight of the town. Humbert, accustomed to the long marches and difficult country of La Vendee, chose the unfrequented and therefore unguarded route, and, to the consternation of the British generals, descended through the pass of Barnagee, soon after sunrise, on the morning of Monday, August 27th. His force consisted of 900 French bayonets, and between 2,000 and 3,000 new recruits. The action, which commenced at 7 o'clock, was short, sharp, and decisive; the yeomanry and regulars broke and fled, some of them never drawing rein till they reached Tuam, while others carried their fears and their falsehoods as far inland as Athlone--more than sixty miles from the scene of action. In this engagement, still remembered as "the races," the royalists confessed to the loss, killed, wounded, or prisoners, of 18 officers, and about 350 men, while the French commander estimated the killed alone at 600. Fourteen British guns and five stand of colours were also taken. A hot pursuit was continued for some distance by the native troops under Mathew Tone, Teeling, and the Mayo officers; but Lord Roden's famous corps of "Fox hunters" covered the retreat and checked the pursuers at French Hill. Immediately after the battle a Provisional Government was established at Castlebar, with Mr. Moore of Moore Hall, as President; proclamations addressed to the inhabitants at large, commissions to raise men, and *assignats* payable by the future Irish Republic, were issued in its name.

Meanwhile the whole of the royalist forces were now in movement toward the capital of Mayo, as they had been toward Vinegar Hill two months before. Sir John Moore and General Hunter marched from Wexford toward the Shannon. General Taylor, with 2,500 men, advanced from Sligo towards Castlebar; Colonel Maxwell was ordered from Enniskillen to assume command at Sligo; General Nugent from Lisburn occupied Enniskillen, and the Viceroy, leaving Dublin in person, advanced rapidly through the midland counties to Kilbeggan, and ordered Lord Lake and General Hutchinson, with such of their command as could be depended on, to assume the aggressive from the direction of Tuam. Thus Humbert and his allies found themselves surrounded on all sides--their retreat cut off by sea, for their frigates had returned to France immediately on their landing; three thousand men against not less than thirty thousand, with at least as many more in reserve, ready to be called into action at a day's notice.

The French general determined if possible to reach the mountains of Leitrim, and open communications with Ulster, and the northern coast, upon which he hoped soon to see succour arrive from France. With this object he marched from Castlebar to Cooloney (35 miles), in one day; here he sustained a check from Colonel Vereker's militia, which necessitated a change of route; turning aside, he passed rapidly through Dromahaine, Manor-Hamilton, and Ballintra, making for Granard, from which accounts of a formidable popular outbreak had just reached him. In three days and a half he had marched 110 miles, flinging half his guns into the rivers that he crossed, lest they should fall into the hands of his pursuers. At Ballinamuck, county Longford, on the borders of Leitrim, he found himself fairly surrounded, on the morning of the 8th of September; and here he prepared to make a last desperate stand. The end could not be doubtful, the numbers against him being ten to one; after an action of half an hour's duration, two hundred of the French having thrown down their arms, the remainder surrendered, as prisoners of war. For the rebels no terms were thought of, and the full vengeance of the victors was reserved for them. Mr. Blake, who had formerly been a British officer, was executed on the field; Mathew Tone and Teeling were executed within the week in Dublin; Mr. Moore, President of the Provisional Government, was sentenced to banishment by the clemency of Lord Cornwallis, but died on shipboard; ninety of the Longford and Kilkenny militia who had joined the French were hanged, and the country generally given up to pillage and massacre. As an evidence of the excessive thirst for blood, it may be mentioned that at the re-capture of Killalla a few days later, four hundred persons were killed, of whom fully one-half were non-combatants.

The disorganization of all government in France in the latter half of '98, was illustrated not only by Humbert's unauthorized adventure, but by a still weaker demonstration under General Reay and Napper Tandy, about the same time. With a single armed brig these daring allies made a descent, on the 17th of September, on Rathlin Island, well equipped with eloquent proclamations, bearing the date "first year of Irish liberty." From the postmaster of the island they ascertained Humbert's fate, and immediately turned the prow of their solitary ship in the opposite direction; Reay, to rise in after times to honour and power; Tandy, to continue in old age the dashing career of his manhood, and to expiate in exile the crime of preferring the country of his birth to the general centralizing policy of the empire with which he was united. Twelve days after the combat at Ballinamuck, while Humbert and his men were on their way through England to France, a new French fleet, under

Admiral Bompart, consisting of one 74-gun ship, "the Hoche," eight frigates, and two smaller vessels, sailed from Brest. On board this fleet were embarked 3,000 men under General Hardi, the remnant of the army once menacing England. In this fleet sailed Theobold Wolfe Tone, true to his motto, ***nil desperandum***, with two or three other refugees of less celebrity. The troops of General Hardi, however, were destined never to land. On the 12th of October, after tossing about for nearly a month in the German ocean and the North Atlantic, they appeared off the coast of Donegal, and stood in for Lough Swilly. But another fleet also was on the horizon. Admiral Sir John Borlase Warren, with an equal number of ships, but a much heavier armament, had been cruising on the track of the French during the whole time they were at sea. After many disappointments, the flag-ship and three of the frigates were at last within range and the action began. Six hours' fighting laid the Hoche a helpless log upon the water; nothing was left her but surrender; two of the frigates shared the same fate on the same day; another was captured on the 14th, and yet another on the 17th. The remainder of the fleet escaped back to France.

The French officers landed in Donegal were received with courtesy by the neighbouring gentry, among whom was the Earl of Cavan, who entertained them at dinner. Here it was that Sir George Hill, son-in-law to Commissioner Beresford, an old college friend of Tone's, identified the founder of the United Irishmen under the uniform of a French Adjutant-General. Stepping up to his old schoolmate he addressed him by name, which Tone instantly acknowledged, inquiring politely for Lady Hill, and other members of Sir George's family. He was instantly arrested, ironed, and conveyed to Dublin under a strong guard. On the 10th of November he was tried by court-martial and sentenced to be hanged: he begged only for a soldier's death--"to be shot by a platoon of grenadiers." This favour was denied him, and the next morning he attempted to commit suicide. The attempt did not immediately succeed; but one week later--on the 19th of November--he died from the results of his self-inflicted wound, with a compliment to the attendant physician upon his lips. Truth compels us to say he died the death of a Pagan; but it was a Pagan of the noblest and freest type of Grecian and Roman times. Had it occurred in ancient days, beyond the Christian era, it would have been a death every way admirable; as it was, that fatal final act must always stand between Wolfe Tone and the Christian people for whom he suffered, sternly forbidding them to invoke him in their prayers, or to uphold him as an example to the young men of their country. So closed the memorable year 1798, on the baffled and dispersed United Irishmen. Of the chiefs imprisoned in March and May, Lord Edward had died of his wounds and vexation; Oliver Bond of apoplexy; the brothers Sheares, Father Quigley, and William Michael Byrne on the gibbet. In July, on Samuel Nelson's motion, the remaining prisoners in Newgate, Bridewell, and Kilmainham, agreed, in order to stop the effusion of blood, to expatriate themselves to any country not at war with England, and to reveal the general secrets of their system, without inculpating individuals. These terms were accepted, as the Castle party needed their evidence to enable them to promote the cherished scheme of legislative Union. But that evidence delivered before the Committees of Parliament by Emmet, McNevin, and O'Conor, did not altogether serve the purposes of government. The patriotic prisoners made it at once a protest against, and an exposition of, the despotic policy under which their country had been goaded into rebellion. For their firmness they were punished by three years' confinement in Fort George, in the Scottish Highlands, where, however, a gallant old soldier, Colonel Stuart, endeavoured to soften the hard realities of a prison by all the kind attentions his instructions permitted him to show these unfortunate gentlemen. At the peace of Amiens, (1802), they were at last allowed the melancholy privilege of expatriation. Russell and Dowdall were permitted to return to Ireland, where they shared the fate of Robert Emmet in 1803; O'Conor, Corbet, Allen, Ware, and others, cast their lot in France, where they all rose to distinction; Emmet, McNevin, Sampson, and the family of Tone were reunited in New York, where the many changes and distractions of a great metropolitan community have not even yet obliterated the memories of their virtues, their talents, and their accomplishments.

It is impossible to dismiss this celebrated group of men, whose principles and conduct so greatly influenced their country's destiny, without bearing explicit testimony to their heroic qualities as a class. If ever a body of public men deserved the character of a brotherhood of heroes, so far as disinterestedness, courage, self-denial, truthfulness and glowing love of country constitute heroism, these men deserved that character. The wisdom of their conduct, and the intrinsic merit of their plans, are other questions. As between their political system and that of Burke, Grattan and O'Connell, there always will be, probably, among their countrymen, very decided differences of opinion. That is but natural: but as to the personal and political virtues of the United Irishmen there can be no difference; the world has never seen a more sincere or more self-sacrificing generation.

CHAPTER XVIII.

ADMINISTRATION OF LORD CORNWALLIS--BEFORE THE UNION.

Nothing strengthens a dynasty," said the first Napoleon, "more than an unsuccessful rebellion." The partial uprising; of the Irish people in 1798 was a rebellion of this class, and the use of such a failure to an able and unscrupulous administration, was illustrated in the extinction of the ancient legislature of the kingdom, before the recurrence of the third, anniversary of the insurrection.

This project, the favourite and long-cherished design of Mr. Pitt, was cordially approved by his principal colleagues, the Duke of Portland, Lord Grenville, and Mr. Dundas; indeed, it may be questioned whether it was not as much Lord Grenville's design as Pitt's, and as much George the Third's personal project as that of any of his ministers. The old King's Irish policy was always of the most narrow and illiberal description. In his memorandum on the recall of Lord Fitzwilliam, he explains his views with the business-like brevity which characterized all his communications with his ministers while he retained possession of his faculties; he was totally opposed to Lord Fitzwilliam's emancipation policy, which he thought adopted "in implicit obedience to the heated imagination of Mr. Burke." To Lord Camden his instructions were, "to support the old English interest as well as the Protestant religion," and to Lord Cornwallis, that no further "indulgence could be granted to Catholics," but that he should steadily pursue the object of effecting the union of Ireland and England.

The new Viceroy entered heartily into the views of his Sovereign. Though unwilling to exchange his English position as a Cabinet Minister and Master-General of Ordnance for the troubled life of a Lord-Lieutenant of Ireland, he at length allowed himself to be persuaded into the acceptance of that office, with a view mainly to carrying the Union. He was ambitious to connect his name with that great imperial measure, so often projected, but never formally proposed. If he could only succeed in incorporating the Irish with the British legislature, he declared he would feel satisfied to retire from all other public employments; that he would look on his day as finished, and his evening of ease and dignity fully earned. He was not wholly unacquainted with the kingdom against which he cherished these ulterior views; for he had been, nearly thirty years before, when he fell under the lash of *Junius*, one of the Vice-Treasurers of Ireland. For the rest he was a man of great information, tact, and firmness; indefatigable in business; tolerant by temperament and conviction; but both as a general and a politician it was his lot to be identified in India and in Ireland with successes which might better have been failures, and in America, with failures which were much more beneficial to mankind than his successes.

In his new sphere of action his two principal agents were Lord Clare and Lord Castlereagh, both Irishmen; the Chancellor, the son of what in that country is called a "spoiled priest," and the Secretary, the son of an ex-volunteer, and member of Flood's Reform Convention. It is not possible to regard the conduct of these high officials in undermining and destroying the ancient national legislature of their own country, in the same light as that of Lord Cornwallis, or Mr. Pitt, or Lord Grenville. It was but natural, that as Englishmen, these ministers should consider the empire in the first place; that they should desire to centralize all the resources and all the authority of both Islands in London; that to them the existence of an independent Parliament at Dublin, with its ample control over the courts, the revenues, the defences, and the trade of that kingdom, should appear an obstacle and a hindrance to the unity of the imperial system. From their point of view they were quite right, and had they pursued their end, complete centralization, by honourable means, no stigma could attach to them even in the eyes of Irishmen; but with Lords Clare and Castlereagh the case was wholly different. Born in the land, deriving income as well as existence from the soil, elected to its Parliament by the confidence of their countrymen, attaining to posts of honour in consequence of such election, that they should voluntarily offer their services to establish an alien and a hostile policy on the ruins of their own national constitution, which, with all its defects, was national, and was corrigible; this betrayal of their own, at the dictate of another

State, will always place the names of Clare and Castlereagh on the detested list of public traitors. Yet though in such treason, united and identified, no two men could be more unlike in all other respects. Lord Clare was fiery, dogmatic, and uncompromising to the last degree; while Lord Castlereagh was stealthy, imperturbable, insidious, bland, and adroit. The Chancellor endeavoured to carry everything with a high hand, with a bold, defiant, confident swagger; the Secretary, on the contrary, trusted to management, expediency, and silent tenacity of purpose. The one had faith in violence, the other in corruption; they were no inapt personifications of the two chief agencies by which the union was effected--Force and Fraud.

The Irish Parliament, which had been of necessity adjourned during the greater part of the time the insurrection lasted, assembled within a week of Lord Cornwallis' arrival. Both Houses voted highly loyal addresses to the King and Lord-Lieutenant, the latter seconded in the Commons by Charles Kendal Bushe, the college companion of Wolfe Tone! A vote of 100,000 pounds to indemnify those who had suffered from the rebels--subsequently increased to above 1,000,000 pounds--was passed *una voce*; another, placing on the Irish establishment certain English militia regiments, passed with equal promptitude. In July, five consecutive acts--a complete code of penalties and proscription--were introduced, and, after various debates and delays, received the royal sanction on the 6th of October, the last day of the session of 1798. These acts were: 1. The Amnesty Act, the exceptions to which were so numerous "that few of those who took any active part in the rebellion," were, according to the Cornwallis' correspondence, "benefited by it." 2. An Act of Indemnity, by which all magistrates who had "exercised a vigour beyond the law" against the rebels, were protected from the legal consequences of such acts. 3. An act for attainting Lord Edward Fitzgerald, Mr. Harvey, and Mr. Grogan, against which Curran, taking "his instructions from the grave," pleaded at the bar of the House of Lords, but pleaded in vain. (This act was finally reversed by the Imperial Parliament in 1819.) 4. An act forbidding communication between persons in Ireland and those enumerated in the Banishment Act, and making the return to Ireland, after sentence of banishment by a court-martial, a transportable felony. 5. An act to compel fifty-one persons therein named to surrender before 1st of December, 1798, under pain of high treason. Among the fifty-one were the principal refugees at Paris and Hamburg-Tone, Lewines, Tandy, Deane Swift, Major Plunkett, Anthony McCann, Harvey Morres, etc. On the same day in which the session terminated, and the royal sanction was given to these acts, the name of Henry Grattan was, a significant coincidence, formally struck, by the King's commands, from the roll of the Irish Privy Council!

This legislation of the session of 1798, was fatal to the Irish Parliament. The partisans of the Union, who had used the rebellion to discredit the constitution, now used the Parliament to discredit itself. Under the influence of a fierce reactionary spirit, when all merciful and moderate councils were denounced as treasonable, it was not difficult to procure the passage of sweeping measures of proscription. But with their passage vanished the former popularity of the domestic legislature. And what followed? The constitution of '82 could only be upheld in the hearts of the people; and, with all its defects, it had been popular before the sudden spread of French revolutionary notions distracted and dissipated the public opinion which had grown up within the era of independence. To make the once cherished authority, which liberated trade in '79, and half emancipated the Catholics in '93, the last executioner of the vengeance of the Castle against the people, was to place a gulf between it and the affections of that people in the day of trial. To make the anti-unionists in Parliament, such as the Speaker, Sir Lawrence Parsons, Plunkett, Ponsonby and Bushe, personally responsible for this vindictive code, was to disarm them of the power, and almost of the right, to call on the people whom they turned over, bound hand and foot, to the mercy of the minister in '98, to aid them against the machinations of that same minister in '99. The last months of the year were marked besides by events already referred to, and by negotiations incessantly carried on, both in England and Ireland, in favour of the Union. Members of both Houses were personally courted and canvassed by the Prime Minister, the Secretaries of State, the Viceroy and the Irish Secretary. Titles, pensions and offices were freely promised. Vast sums of secret service money, afterwards added as a charge to the public debt of Ireland, were remitted from Whitehall. An army of pamphleteers, marshalled by Under-Secretary Cooke, and confidentially directed by the able but anti-national Bishop of Meath, (Dr. O'Beirne,) and by Lord Castlereagh personally, plied their pens in favour of "the consolidation of the empire." The Lord Chancellor, the Chief Secretary and Mr. Beresford, made journeys to England, to assist the Prime Minister with their local information, and to receive his imperial confidence in return. The Orangemen were neutralized by securing a majority of their leaders; the Catholics, by the establishment of familiar communication with the bishops. The Viceroy complimented Dr. Troy at Dublin; the Duke of Portland lavished personal attentions on Dr. Moylan, in England. The Protestant clergy were satisfied with the assurance that the maintenance of their establishment would be made a fundamental article of the Union, while the Catholic bishops were given to understand that complete Emancipation would be one of the first measures submitted to the Imperial Parliament. The oligarchy were to be indemnified for their boroughs, while the advocates of Reform were shown how hopeless it was to expect a House constituted of *their* nominees, ever to enlarge or amend its own exclusive constitution. Thus for every description of people a particular set of appeals and arguments was found, and for those who discarded the affectation of reasoning on the surrender of their national existence, there were the more convincing arguments of titles, employments, and direct pecuniary purchase. At the close of the year of the rebellion, Lord Cornwallis was able to report to Mr. Pitt that the prospects of carrying the measure were better than could have been expected, and on this report he was authorized to open the matter formally to Parliament in his speech at the opening of the following session.

On the 22nd of January, 1799, the Irish legislature met under circumstances of great interest and excitement. The city of Dublin, always keenly alive to its metropolitan interests, sent its eager thousands by every avenue towards College Green. The Viceroy went down to the Houses with a more than ordinary guard, and being seated on the throne in the House of Lords, the Commons were summoned to the bar. The House was considered a full one, 217 members being present. The viceregal speech congratulated both Houses on the suppression of the late rebellion, on the defeat of Bompart's squadron, and the recent French victories of Lord Nelson; then came, amid profound expectation, this concluding sentence:--"The unremitting industry," said the Viceroy, "with which our enemies persevere in their avowed design of endeavouring to effect a separation of this kingdom from Great Britain, must have engaged your attention, and his Majesty commands me to express his anxious hope that this consideration, joined to the sentiment of mutual affection and common interest, may dispose the Parliaments in both kingdoms to provide the most effectual means of maintaining and improving a connection essential to their common security, and of consolidating, as far as possible, into one firm and lasting fabric, the strength, the power, and the resources of the British empire." On the paragraph of the address, re-echoing this sentiment, which was carried by a large majority in the Lords, a debate ensued in the Commons, which lasted till one o'clock of the following day, above twenty consecutive hours. Against the suggestion of a Union spoke Ponsonby, Parsons, Fitzgerald, Barrington, Plunkett, Lee, O'Donnell and Bushe; in its favour, Lord Castlereagh, the Knight of Kerry, Corry, Fox, Osborne, Duigenan, and some other members little known. The galleries and lobbies were crowded all night by the first people of the city, of both sexes, and when the division was being taken, the most intense anxiety was manifested, within doors and without. At length the tellers made their report to the Speaker, himself an ardent anti-Unionist, and it was announced that the numbers were--"for the address 105, for the amendment 106," so the paragraph in favour of "consolidating the empire" was lost by one vote! The remainder of the address, tainted with the association of the expunged paragraph, was barely carried by 107 to 105. Mr. Ponsonby had attempted to follow his victory by a solemn pledge binding the majority never again to entertain the question, but to this several members objected, and the motion was withdrawn. The ministry found some consolation in this withdrawal, which they characterized as "a retreat after a victory," but to the public at large, unused to place much stress on the minor tactics of debate, nothing appeared but the broad, general fact, that the first overture for a Union had been rejected. It was a day of immense rejoicing in Dublin; the leading anti-Unionists were escorted in triumph to their homes, while the Unionists were protected by strong military escorts from the popular indignation. At night the city was illuminated, and the patrols were doubled as a protection to the obnoxious minority.

Mr. Ponsonby's amendment, affirmed by the House of Commons, was in these words:--"That the House would be ready to enter into any measure short of surrendering their free, resident and independent legislature as established in 1782." This was the *ultimatum* of the great party which rallied in January, 1799, to the defence of the established constitution of their country. The arguments with which they sustained their position were few, bold, and intelligible to every capacity. There was the argument from Ireland's geographical situation, and the policy incident to it; the historical argument; the argument for a resident gentry occupied and retained in the country by their public duties; the commercial argument; the revenue argument; but above all, the argument of the incompetency of Parliament to put an end to its own existence. "Yourselves," exclaimed the eloquent Plunkett, "you may extinguish, but Parliament you cannot extinguish. It is enthroned in the hearts of the people--it is enshrined in the sanctuary of the constitution--it is as immortal as the island that protects it. As well might the frantic suicide imagine that the act which destroys his miserable body should also extinguish his eternal soul. Again, therefore, I warn you. Do not dare to lay your hands on the Constitution--it is above your powers!"

These arguments were combated on the grounds that the islands were already united under one crown--that that species of union was uncertain and precarious--that the Irish Parliament was never in reality a national legislature; that it existed only as an instrument of class legislation; that the Union would benefit Ireland materially as it had benefited Scotland; that she would come in for a full share of imperial honours, expenditure and trade; that such a Union would discourage all future hostile attempts by France or any other foreign power against the connection, and other similar arguments. But the division which followed the first introduction of the subject showed clearly to the Unionists that they could not hope to succeed with the House of Commons as then constituted; that more time and more preparation were necessary. Accordingly, Lord Castlereagh was authorized in March, to state formally in his place, that it was not the intention of the government to bring up the question again during that session; an announcement which was hailed with a new outburst of rejoicing in the city.

But those who imagined the measure was abandoned were sadly deceived. Steps were immediately taken by the Castle to deplete the House of its majority, and to supply their places before another session with forty or fifty new members, who would be entirely at the beck of the Chief Secretary. With this view, thirty-two new county judgeships were created; a great number of additional inspectorships and commissioners were also placed at the Minister's disposal; thirteen members had peerages for themselves or for their wives, with remainder to their children, and nineteen others were presented to various lucrative offices. The "Escheatorship of Munster"--a sort of Chiltern Hundreds office--was accepted by those who agreed to withdraw from opposition, for such considerations, but who could not be got to reverse their votes. By these means, and a lavish expenditure of secret service money, it was hoped that Mr. Pitt's stipulated majority of "not less than fifty" could be secured during the year.

The other events of the session of '99, though interesting in themselves, are of little importance compared to the union debates. In the English Parliament, which met on the same day as the Irish, a paragraph identical with that employed by Lord Cornwallis in introducing the subject of the Union, was inserted in the King's speech. To this paragraph, repeated in the address, an amendment was moved by the celebrated Richard Brinsley Sheridan, and resisted with an eloquence scarcely inferior to his own, by his former *protege* and countryman, George Canning. Canning, like Sheridan, had sprung from a line of Irish literateurs and actors; he had much of the wit and genius of his illustrious friend, with more worldly wisdom, and a higher sentiment of personal pride. In very early life, distinguished by great oratorical talents, he had deliberately attached himself to Mr. Pitt, while Sheridan remained steadfast to the last, in the ranks of the Whig or liberal party. For the land of their ancestors both had, at bottom, very warm, good wishes; but Canning looked down upon her politics from the heights of empire, while Sheridan felt for her honour and her interests with the affection of an expatriated son. We can well credit his statement to Grattan, years afterwards, when referring to his persistent opposition to the Union, he said, he would "have waded in blood to his knees," to preserve the Constitution of Ireland. In taking this course he had with him a few eminent friends: General Fitzpatrick, the former Irish Secretary, Mr. Tierney, Mr. Hobhouse, Dr. Lawrence, the executor of Edmund Burke, and Mr., afterwards Earl Grey. Throughout the entire discussion these just minded Englishmen stood boldly forward for the rights of Ireland, and this highly honourable conduct was long remembered as one of Ireland's real obligations to the Whig party.

The resolutions intended to serve as "the basis of union," were introduced by Mr. Pitt, on the 21st of January, and after another powerful speech in opposition, from Mr. Grey, who was ably sustained by Mr. Sheridan, Dr. Lawrence, and some twenty others, were put and carried. The following are the resolutions:--

1st. "In order to promote and secure the essential interests of Great Britain and Ireland, and to consolidate the strength, power, and resources of the British empire, it will be advisable to concur in such measures as may tend to unite the two kingdoms of Great Britain and Ireland into one kingdom, in such manner, and in such terms and conditions as may be established by acts of the respective Parliaments of his Majesty's said kingdoms.

2nd. "It would be fit to propose as the first article, to serve as a basis of the said union, that the said kingdoms of Great Britain and Ireland shall, on a day to be agreed upon, be united into one kingdom, by the name of the United Kingdom of Great Britain and Ireland.

3rd. "For the same purpose it would be fit to propose, that the succession to the monarchy and the imperial crown of the said United Kingdom, shall continue limited and settled, in the same manner as the imperial crown of the said Great Britain and Ireland now stands limited and settled, according to the existing law, and to the terms of the union between England and Scotland.

4th. "For the same purpose it would be fit to propose that the said United Kingdom be represented in one and the same Parliament, to be styled the Parliament of the United Kingdom of Great Britain and Ireland; and that such a number of Lords, spiritual and temporal, and such a number of members of the House of Commons, as shall be hereafter agreed upon by the acts of the respective Parliaments as aforesaid, shall sit and vote in the said Parliament on the part of Ireland, and shall be summoned, chosen, and returned, in such manner as shall be fixed by an act of the Parliament of Ireland previous to the said union; and that every member hereafter to sit and vote in the said Parliament of the United Kingdom shall, until the said Parliament shall otherwise provide, take, and subscribe the said oaths, and make the same declarations as are required by law to be taken, subscribed, and made by the members of the Parliaments of Great Britain and Ireland.

5th. "For the same purpose it would be fit to propose, that the Churches of England and Ireland, and the doctrine, worship, discipline, and government thereof, shall be preserved as now by law established.

6th. "For the same purpose it would be fit to propose, that his Majesty's subjects in Ireland shall at all times be entitled to the same privileges, and be on the same footing in respect of trade and navigation in all ports and places belonging to Great Britain, and in all cases with respect to which treaties shall be made by his Majesty, his heirs, or successors, with any foreign power, as his Majesty's subjects in Great Britain; that no duty shall be imposed on the import or export between Great

Britain and Ireland, of any articles now duty free, and that on other articles there shall be established, for a time to be limited, such a moderate rate of equal duties as shall, previous to the Union, be agreed upon and approved by the respective Parliaments, subject, after the expiration of such limited time, to be diminished equally with respect to both kingdoms, but in no case to be increased; that all articles which may at any time hereafter be imported into Great Britain from foreign parts shall be importable through either kingdom into the other, subject to the like duties and regulations, as if the same were imported directly from foreign parts: that where any articles, the growth, produce, or manufacture of either kingdom, are subject to an internal duty in one kingdom, such counter-vailing duties (over and above any duties on import to be fixed as aforesaid) shall be imposed as shall be necessary to prevent any inequality in that respect; and that all matters of trade and commerce, other than the foregoing, and than such others as may before the Union be specially agreed upon for the due encouragement of the agriculture and manufactures of the respective kingdoms, shall remain to be regulated from time to time by the United Parliament.

7th. "For the like purpose it would be fit to propose, that the charge arising from the payment of the interests or sinking fund for the reduction of the principal of the debt incurred in either kingdom before the Union, shall continue to be separately defrayed by Great Britain and Ireland respectively; that, for a number of years to be limited, the future ordinary expenses of the United Kingdom, in peace or war, shall be defrayed by Great Britain and Ireland jointly, according to such proportions as shall be established by the respective Parliaments previous to the Union; and that, after the expiration of the time to be so limited, the proportion shall not be liable to be varied, except according to such rates and principles, as shall be in like manner agreed upon previous to the Union.

8th. "For the like purpose, that all laws in force at the time of the Union, and all the courts of civil or ecclesiastical jurisdiction within the respective kingdoms, shall remain as now by law established within the same, subject only to such alterations or regulations as may from time to time as circumstances may appear to the Parliament of the United Kingdom to require."

Mr. Pitt, on the passage of these resolutions, proposed an address stating that the Commons had proceeded with the utmost attention to the consideration of the important objects recommended in the royal message, that they entertained a firm persuasion of the probable benefits of a complete and entire Union between Great Britain and Ireland, founded on equal and liberal principles; that they were therefore induced to lay before his Majesty such propositions as appeared to them to be best calculated to form the basis of such a settlement, leaving it to his wisdom in due time and in proper manner, to communicate them to the Lords and Commons of Ireland, with whom they would be at all times ready to concur in all such measures as might be found most conducive to the accomplishment of that great and salutary work.

On the 19th of March, Lord Grenville introduced the same resolutions in the Lords, where they were passed after a spirited opposition speech from Lord Holland, and the basis, so far as the King, Lords, and Commons of England were concerned, was laid. In proroguing the Irish Houses on the 1st of June, Lord Cornwallis alluded to these resolutions, and the anxiety of the King, as the common father of his people, to see both kingdoms united in the enjoyment of the blessings of a free constitution.

This prorogation was originally till August, but in August it was extended till January, 1800. In this long interval of eight months, the two great parties, the Unionists and the anti-Unionists were incessantly employed, through the press, in social intercourse, in the grand jury room, in county and city meetings, by correspondence, petitions, addresses, each pushing forward its own views with all the zeal and warmth of men who felt that on one side they were labouring for the country, on the other for the empire. Two incidents of this interval were deeply felt in the patriot ranks, the death at an advanced age of the venerable Charlemont, the best member of his order Ireland had ever known, and the return to the kingdom and to public life of Lord Charlemont's early friend and *protege*, Henry Grattan. He had spent above a year in England, chiefly in Wales and the Isle of Wight. His health all this time had been wretched; his spirits low and despondent, and serious fears were at some moments entertained for his life. He had been forbidden to read or write, or to hear the exciting news of the day. Soothed and cheered by that admirable woman, whom Providence had given him, he passed the crisis, but he returned to breathe his native air, greatly enfeebled in body, and sorely afflicted in mind. The charge of theatrical affectation of illness has been brought against Grattan by the Unionists,--against Grattan who, as to his personal habits, was simplicity itself! It is a charge undeserving of serious contradiction.

CHAPTER XIX.

LAST SESSION OF THE IRISH PARLIAMENT--THE LEGISLATIVE UNION OF GREAT BRITAIN AND IRELAND.

When the Irish Parliament met for the last time, on the 15th of January, 1800, the position of the Union question stood thus: 27 new Peers had been added to the House of Lords, where the Castle might therefore reckon with safety on a majority of three to one. Of the Lords spiritual, only Dr. Marlay of Waterford, and Dr. Dixon of Down and Conor, had the courage to side with their country against their order. In the Commons there was an infusion of some 50 new borough members, many of them general officers, such as Needham, and Pakenham, all of them nominees of the Castle, except Mr. Saurin, returned for Blessington, and Mr. Grattan, at the last moment, for Wicklow. The great constitutional body of the bar had, at a general meeting, the previous December, declared against the measure by 162 to 33. Another powerful body, the bankers, had petitioned against it, in the interest of the public credit. The Catholic bishops, in their annual meeting, had taken up a position of neutrality as a body, but under the artful management of Lord Castlereagh, the Archbishops of Dublin and Tuam, with the Bishop of Cork, and some others, were actively employed in counteracting anti-Union movements among the people. Although the vast majority of that people had too much reason to be disgusted and discontented with the legislation of the previous three years, above 700,000 of them petitioned against the measure, while all the signatures which could be obtained in its favour, by the use of every means at the command of the Castle, did not much exceed 7,000.

The Houses were opened on the 15th of January. The Viceroy not going down, his message was read in the Lords, by the Chancellor, and in the Commons, by the

Chief Secretary. It did not directly refer to the basis laid down in England, nor to the subject matter itself; but the leaders of the Castle party in both Houses, took care to supply the deficiency. In the Lords, proxies included, Lord Clare had 75 to 26 for his Union address: in the Commons, Lord Castlereagh congratulated the country on the improvement which had taken place in public opinion, since the former session. He briefly sketched his plan of Union, which, while embracing the main propositions of Mr. Pitt, secured the Church establishment, bid high for the commercial interests, hinted darkly of emancipation to the Catholics, and gave the proprietors of boroughs to understand that their interest in those convenient constituencies would be capitalized, and a good round sum given to buy out their perpetual patronage. In amendment to the address, Sir Lawrence Parsons moved, seconded by Mr. Savage of Down, that the House would maintain *intact* the Constitution of '82, and the debate proceeded on this motion. Ponsonby replied to Castlereagh; Plunkett and Bushe were answered by the future judges, St. George Daly and Luke Fox; Toler contributed his farce, and Dr. Duigenan his fanaticism. Through the long hours of the winter's night the eloquent war was vigorously maintained. One who was himself a distinguished actor in the struggle, (Sir Jonah Barrington,) has thus described it: "Every mind," he says, "was at its stretch, every talent was in its vigour: it was a momentous trial; and never was so general and so deep a sensation felt in any country. Numerous British noblemen and commoners were present at that and the succeeding debate, and they expressed opinions of Irish eloquence which they had never before conceived, nor ever after had an opportunity of appreciating. Every man on that night seemed to be inspired by the subject. Speeches more replete with talent and energy, on both sides, never were heard in the Irish Senate; it was a vital subject. The sublime, the eloquent, the figurative orator, the plain, the connected, the metaphysical reasoner, the classical, the learned, and the solemn declaimer, in a succession of speeches so full of energy and enthusiasm, so interesting in their nature, so important in their consequence, created a variety of sensations even in the bosom of a stranger, and could scarcely fail of exciting some sympathy with a nation which was doomed to close for ever that school of eloquence which had so long given character and celebrity to Irish talent."

At the early dawn, a special messenger from Wicklow, just arrived in town, roused Henry Grattan from his bed. He had been elected the previous night for the borough of Wicklow, (which cost him 2,400 pounds sterling), and this was the bearer of the returning officer's certificate. His friends, weak and feeble as he was, wished him to go down to the House, and his heroic wife seconded their appeals. It was seven o'clock in the morning of the 16th when he reached College Green, the scene of his first triumphs twenty years before. Mr. Egan, one of the staunchest anti-Unionists, was at the moment, on some rumour, probably, of his approach, apostrophising warmly the father of the Constitution of '82, when that striking apparition appeared at the bar. Worn and emaciated beyond description, he appeared leaning on two of his friends, Arthur Moore and W. B. Ponsonby. He wore his volunteer uniform, blue with red facings, and advanced to the table, where he removed his cocked hat, bowed to the Speaker, and took the oaths. After Mr. Egan had concluded, he begged permission from his seat beside Plunkett, to address the House sitting, which was granted, and then in a discourse of two hours' duration, full of his ancient fire and vigour, he asserted once again, by the divine right of intellect, his title to be considered the first Commoner of Ireland. Gifted men were not rare in that assembly; but the inspiration of the heart, the uncontrollable utterance of a supreme spirit, not less than the extraordinary faculty of condensation, in which, perhaps, he has never had a superior in our language, gave the Grattan of 1800 the same pre-eminence among his cotemporaries, that was conceded to the Grattan of 1782. After eighteen hours' discussion the division was taken, when the result of the long recess was clearly seen; for the amendment there appeared 96, for the address 138 members. The Union majority, therefore, was 42. It was apparent from that moment that the representation of the people in Parliament had been effectually corrupted; that that assembly was no longer the safeguard of the liberties of the people. Other ministerial majorities confirmed this impression. A measure to enable 10,000 of the Irish militia to enter the regular army, and to substitute English militia in their stead, followed; an inquiry into outrages committed by the sheriff and military in King's county, was voted down; a similar motion somewhat later, in relation to officials in Tipperary met the same fate. On the 5th of February, a formal message proposing a basis of Union was received from his Excellency, and debated for twenty consecutive hours--from 4 o'clock of one day, till 12 of the next. Grattan, Plunkett, Parnell, Ponsonby, Saurin, were, as always, eloquent and able, but again the division told for the minister, 160 to 117--majority 43. On the 17th of February, the House went into Committee on the proposed articles of Union, and the Speaker (John Foster) being now on the floor, addressed the House with great ability in review of Mr. Pitt's recent Union speech, which he designated "a paltry production." But again, a majority mustered, at the nod of the minister, 161 to 140--a few not fully committed showing some last faint spark of independence. It was on this occasion that Mr. Corry, Chancellor of the Exchequer, member for Newry, made for the third or fourth time that session, an attack on Grattan, which brought out, on the instant, that famous "philippic against Corry," unequalled in our language, for its well-suppressed passion, and finely condensed denunciation. A duel followed, as soon as there was sufficient light; the Chancellor was wounded, after which the Castlereagh tactics of "fighting down the opposition," received an immediate and lasting check.

Throughout the months of February and March, with an occasional adjournment, the Constitutional battle was fought on every point permitted by the forms of the House. On the 25th of March, the Committee, after another powerful speech from the Speaker, finally reported the resolutions which were passed by 154 to 107--a majority of 47. The Houses then adjourned for six weeks, to allow time for corresponding action to be taken in England. There was little difficulty in carrying the measure. In the Upper House, Lords Derby, Holland, and King only opposed it; in the Lower, Sheridan, Tierney, Grey, and Lawrence mustered on a division, 30 votes against Pitt's 206. On the 21st of May, in the Irish Commons, Lord Castlereagh obtained leave to bring in the Union Bill by 160 to 100; on the 7th of June the final passage of the measure was effected. That closing scene has been often described, but never so graphically, as by the diamond pen of Jonah Barrington.

"The galleries were full, but the change was lamentable. They were no longer crowded with those who had been accustomed to witness the eloquence and to animate the debates of that devoted assembly. A monotonous and melancholy murmur ran through the benches; scarcely a word was exchanged amongst the members; nobody seemed at ease; no cheerfulness was apparent; and the ordinary business, for a short time, proceeded in the usual manner.

"At length, the expected moment arrived: the order of the day for the third reading of the bill for a 'legislative union between Great Britain and Ireland' was moved by Lord Castlereagh. Unvaried, tame, cold-blooded, the words seemed frozen as they issued from his lips; and, as if a simple citizen of the world, he seemed to have no sensation on the subject.

"At that moment he had no country, no God, but his ambition. He made his motion, and resumed his seat, with the utmost composure and indifference.

"Confused murmurs again ran through the House. It was visibly affected. Every character, in a moment, seemed involuntarily rushing to its index--some pale, some flushed, some agitated--there were few countenances to which the heart did not despatch some messenger. Several members withdrew before the question could be repeated, and an awful, momentary silence succeeded their departure. The Speaker rose slowly from that chair which had been the proud source of his honours and of his high character. For a moment he resumed his seat, but the strength of his mind sustained him in his duty, though his struggle was apparent. With that dignity which never failed to signalize his official actions, he held up the bill for a moment in silence. He looked steadily around him on the last agony of the expiring Parliament. He at length repeated, in an emphatic tone, 'As many as are of opinion that THIS BILL do pass, say *ay*! The affirmative was languid, but indisputable. Another momentary pause ensued. Again his lips seemed to decline their office. At length, with an eye averted from the object he hated, he proclaimed, with a subdued voice, '*The, AYES have it*.' The fatal sentence was now pronounced. For an instant he stood statue-like; then indignantly, and with disgust, flung the bill upon the table, and sank into his chair with an exhausted spirit. An independent country was thus degraded into a province. Ireland, as a nation, was extinguished."

The final division in the Commons was 153 to 88, nearly 60 members absenting themselves, and in the Lords, 76 to 17. In England all the stages were passed in July, and on the 2nd of August, the anniversary of the King's accession, the royal assent was given to the twofold legislation, which declared the kingdoms of Great Britain and Ireland one and inseparable!

By the provisions of this statute, compact, or treaty, the Sovereignty of the United Kingdom was to follow the order of the Act of Succession; the Irish peerage was to be reduced by the filling of one vacancy for every three deaths, to the number of one hundred; from among these, twenty-eight representative Peers were to be elected for life, and four spiritual Lords to sit in succession. The number of Irish representatives in the Imperial Parliament was fixed at one hundred (increased to one hundred and five); the churches of England and Ireland were united like the kingdoms, and declared to be one in doctrine and discipline. The debt of Ireland, which was less than 4,000,000 pounds in 1797, increased to 14,000,000 pounds in '99, and had risen to nearly 17,000,000 pounds in 1801, was to be alone chargeable to Ireland, whose proportionate share of general taxation was then estimated at 2-17ths of that of the United Kingdom. The Courts of Law, the Privy Council, and the Viceroyalty, were to remain at Dublin, the cenotaph and the shadows of departed nationality.

On the 1st day of January, 1801, in accordance with this great Constitutional change, a new imperial standard was run up on London Tower, Edinburgh Castle, and Dublin Castle. It was formed of the three crosses of St. Patrick, Saint Andrew, and Saint George, and is that popularly known to us as "the Union Jack." The *fleur de lis*, and the word "France," were struck from the royal title, which was settled, by proclamation, to consist henceforth of the words **Dei Gratia, Britanniarum Rex, Fidei Defensor**.

The foul means by which this counter revolution was accomplished, have, perhaps, been already sufficiently indicated. It may be necessary, however, in order to account for the continued hostility of the Irish people to the measure, after more than sixty years' experience of its results, to recapitulate them very briefly. Of all who voted for the Union, in both Houses, it was said that only six or seven were known to have done so on conviction. Great borough proprietors, like Lord Ely and Lord Shannon, received as much as 45,000 pounds sterling in "compensation" for their loss of patronage; while proprietors of single seats received 15,000 pounds. That the majority was avowedly purchased, in both Houses, is no longer matter of inference, nay, that some of them were purchased twice over is now well known. Lord Carysfort, an active partisan of the measure, writing in February, 1800, to his friend the Marquis of Buckingham, frankly says: "The majority, which has been bought at an enormous price, must be bought over again, perhaps more than once, before all the details can be gone through." His lordship himself, and the order to which he belonged, and those who aspired to enter it, were, it must be added, among the most insatiable of these purchased supporters. The Dublin *Gazette* for July, 1800, announced not less than sixteen new peerages, and the same publication for the last week of the year, contained a fresh list of twenty-six others. Forty-two creations in six months was a stretch of prerogative far beyond the most arbitrary of the Stuarts or Tudors, and forms one, not of the least unanswerable evidences, of the utterly corrupt considerations which secured the support of the Irish majority in both Houses.

It was impossible that a people like the Irish, disinterested and unselfish to a fault, should ever come to respect a compact brought about by such means and influences as these. Had, however, the Union, vile as were the means by which it was accomplished, proved to the real benefit of the country--had equal civil and religious rights been freely and at once extended to the people of the lesser kingdom--there is no reason to doubt that the measure would have become popular in time, and the vices of the old system be better remembered than its benefits, real or imaginary. But the Union was never utilized for Ireland; it proved in reality what Samuel Johnson had predicted, when spoken of in his day: "Do not unite with us, sir," said the gruff old moralist to an Irish acquaintance; "it would be the union of the shark with his prey; we should unite with you only to destroy you."

In glancing backward over the long political connexion of Ireland and England, we mark four great epochs. The Anglo-Norman invasion in 1169; the statute of Kilkenny decreeing eternal separation between the races, "the English pale" and "the Irish enemy," 1367; the Union of the Crowns, in 1541, and the Legislative Union, in 1801. One more cardinal event remains to be recorded--the Emancipation of the Catholics, in 1829.

BOOK XII.
FROM THE UNION OF GREAT BRITAIN AND IRELAND TO THE EMANCIPATION OF THE CATHOLICS.

CHAPTER I.

AFTER THE UNION--DEATH OF LORD CLARE-- ROBERT EMMET'S EMEUTE.

The plan of this brief compendium of Irish history obliges us to sketch for some years farther on, the political and religious annals of the Irish people. Having described in what manner their distinctive political nationality was at length lost, it only remains to show how their religious liberties were finally recovered.

The first striking effect of the Union was to introduce Catholic Emancipation into the category of imperial difficulties, and to assign it the very first place on the list. By a singular retribution, the Pitt administration with its 200 of a House of Commons majority, its absolute control of the Lords, and its seventeen years' prescription in its favour, fell upon this very question, after they had used it to carry the Union, within a few weeks of the consummation of that Union. The cause of this crisis was the invincible obstinacy of the King, who had taken into his head, at the time of Lord Fitzwilliam's recall from Ireland, that his coronation oath bound him in conscience to resist the Catholic claims. The suggestion of this obstacle was originally Lord Clare's; and though Lord Kenyon and Lord Stowell had declared it unfounded in law, Lord Loughborough and Lord Eldon were unfortunately of a different opinion. With George III. the idea became a monomaniac certainty, and there is no reason to doubt that he would have preferred abdication to its abandonment.

The King was not for several months aware how far his Prune Minister had gone on the Catholic question in Ireland. But those who were weary of Pitt's ascendancy, were, of course, interested in giving him this important information. The minister himself, wrapped in his austere self-reliance, did not volunteer explanations even to his Sovereign, and the King broke silence very unexpectedly, a few days after the first meeting of the Imperial Parliament (January 22nd, 1801). Stepping up to Mr. Dundas at the levee, he began in his usual manner, "What's this? what's this? this, that this young Lord (Castlereagh) has brought over from Ireland to throw at my head? The most Jacobinical thing I ever heard of! Any man who proposes such a thing is my personal enemy." Mr. Dundas replied respectfully but firmly, and immediately communicated the conversation to Mr. Pitt. The King's remarks had been overheard by the bystanders, so that either the minister or the Sovereign had now to give way. Pitt, at first, was resolute; the King then offered to impose silence on himself as regarded the whole subject, provided Mr. Pitt would agree to do likewise, but the haughty minister refused, and tendered his resignation. On the 5th of February, within five weeks of the consummation of the Union, this tender was most reluctantly and regretfully accepted. Lord Grenville, Mr. Dundas, and others of his principal colleagues went out of office with him; Lord Cornwallis and Lord Castlereagh following their example. Of the new Cabinet, Addington, the Speaker, was Premier, with Lord Hardwicke as Lord-Lieutenant of Ireland. By the enemies of Pitt this was looked upon as a mere administration ***ad interim***; as a concerted arrangement to enable him to evade an unfavourable peace--that of Amiens--which he saw coming; but it is only fair to say, that the private letters of the period, since published, do not sanction any such imputation. It is, however, to be observed, ***per contra***, that three weeks after his formal resignation, he had no hesitation in assuring the King, who had just recovered from one of his attacks brought on by this crisis, that he would never again urge the Catholic claims on his Majesty's notice. On this understanding he returned to office in the spring of 1804; to this compact he adhered till his death, in January, 1806.

In Ireland, the events immediately consequent upon the Union, were such as might have been expected. Many of those who had been instrumental in carrying it, were disappointed and discontented with their new situation in the empire. Of these, the most conspicuous and the least to be pitied, was Lord Clare. That haughty, domineering spirit, accustomed to dictate with almost absolute power to the Privy Counsellors and peerage of Ireland, experienced nothing but mortification in the Imperial House of Lords. The part he hoped to play on that wider stage he found impossible to assume; he confronted there in the aged Thurlow and the astute Loughborough, law lords as absolute as himself, who soon made him conscious that, though a main agent of the Union, he was only a stranger in the united legislature. The Duke of Bedford reminded him that "the Union had not transferred his dictatorial powers to the Imperial Parliament;" other noble Lords were hardly less severe. Pitt was cold, and Grenville ceremonious; and in the arrangements of the Addington ministry he was not even consulted. He returned to Ireland before the first year of the Union closed, in a state of mind and temper which preyed upon his health. Before the second session of the Imperial Parliament assembled, he had been borne to the grave amid the revilings and hootings of the multitude. Dublin, true to its ancient disposition, which led the townsfolk of the twelfth century to bury the ancestor of Dermid McMurrogh with the carcass of a dog, filled the grave of the once splendid Lord Chancellor with every description of garbage.

On the other hand, Lord Castlereagh, younger, suppler, and more accommodating to English prejudices, rose from one Cabinet office to another, until at length, in fifteen years from the Union, he directed the destinies of the Empire, as absolutely, as he had moulded the fate of Ireland. To Castlereagh and the Wellesley family, the Union was in truth, an era of honour and advancement. The sons of the spendthrift amateur, Lord Mornington, were reserved to rule India, and lead the armies of Europe; while the son of Flood's colleague in the Reform convention of 1783, was destined to give law to Christendom, at the Congress of Vienna.

A career very different in all respects from those just mentioned, closed in the second year of Dublin's widowhood as a metropolis. It was the career of a young man of four-and-twenty, who snatched at immortal fame and obtained it, in the very agony of a public, but not for him, a shameful death. This was Robert, youngest brother of Thomas Addis Emmet, whose *emeute* of 1803 would long since have sunk to the level of other city riots, but for the matchless dying speech of which it was the prelude and the occasion. This young gentleman was in his 20th year when expelled with nineteen others from Trinity College, in 1798, by order of the visitors, Lord Clare and Dr. Duigenan. His reputation as a scholar and debater was already established within the college walls, and the highest expectations were naturally entertained of him, by his friends. One of his early college companions --Thomas Moore--who lived to know all the leading men of his age, declares that of all he had ever known, he would place among "the highest of the few" who combined in "the greatest degree pure moral worth with intellectual power"--Robert Emmet. After the expatriation of his brother, young Emmet visited him at Fort-George, and proceeded from thence to the Continent. During the year the Union was consummated he visited Spain, and travelled through Holland, France, and Switzerland, till the peace of Amiens. Subsequently he joined his brother's family in Paris, and was taken into the full confidence of the exiles, then in direct communication with Buonaparte and Talleyrand. It was not concealed from the Irish by either the First Consul, or his minister, that the peace with England was likely to have a speedy termination; and, accordingly, they were not unprepared for the new declaration of war between the two countries, which was officially made at London and Paris, in May, 1803--little more than twelve months after the proclamation of the peace of Amiens.

It was in expectation of this rupture, and a consequent invasion of Ireland, that Robert Emmet returned to Dublin, in October, 1802, to endeavour to re-establish in some degree the old organization of the United Irishmen. In the same expectation, McNevin, Corbet, and others of the Irish in France, formed themselves, by permission of the First Consul, into a legion, under command of Tone's trusty aid-de-camp, McSheehey; while Thomas Addis Emmet and Arthur O'Conor remained at Paris, the plenipotentiaries of their countrymen. On the rupture with England Buonaparte took up the Irish negotiation with much earnestness; he even suggested to the exiles the colours and the motto under which they were to fight, when once landed on their own soil. The flag on a tricolour ground, was to have a green centre, bearing the letters ***R.I.--Republique Irlandaise***. The legend at large was to be: ***L'independence de l'Irlande--Liberte de Conscience***; a motto which certainly told the whole story. The First Consul also suggested the formation of an Irish Committee at Paris, and the preparation of statements of Irish grievances for the *Moniteur*, and the semi-official papers.

Robert Emmet seems to have been confidently of opinion soon after his return to Dublin, that nineteen out of the thirty-two counties would rise; and, perhaps, if a sufficient French force had landed, his opinion might have been justified by the fact. So did not think, however, John Keogh, Valentine Lawless (Lord Cloncurry), and other close observers of the state of the country. But Emmet was enthusiastic, and he inspired his own spirit into many. Mr. Long, a merchant, placed 1,400 pounds sterling at his disposal; he had himself, in consequence of the recent death of his father, stock to the amount of 1,500 pounds converted into cash, and with these funds he entered actively on his preliminary preparations. His chief confidants and assistants were Thomas Russell and Mathew Dowdall, formerly prisoners at Fort-George, but now permitted to return; William Putnam McCabe, the most adventurous of all the party, a perfect Proteus in disguise; Gray, a Wexford attorney; Colonel Lumm of Kildare, an old friend of Lord Edward Fitzgerald; Mr. Long, before mentioned; Hamilton, an Enniskillen barrister, married to Russell's niece; James Hope of Templepatrick, and Michael Dwyer, the Wicklow outlaw, who had remained since '98 uncaptured in the mountains.

In the month of March, when the renewal of hostilities with France was decided on in England, the preparations of the conspirators were pushed forward with redoubled energy. The still wilder conspiracy headed by Colonel Despard in London, the previous winter, the secret and the fate of which was well known to the Dublin leaders --Dowdall being Despard's agent--did not in the least intimidate Emmet or his friends. Despard suffered death in February, with nine of his followers, but his Irish confederates only went on with their arrangements with a more reckless resolution. Their plan was the plan of O'Moore and McGuire, to surprise the Castle, seize the authorities and secure the capital; but the Dublin of 1803 was in many respects very different from the Dublin of 1641. The discontent, however, arising from the recent loss of the Parliament might have turned the city scale in Emmet's favour, had its first stroke been successful. The emissaries at work in the Leinster and Ulster counties gave besides sanguine reports of success, so that, judging by the information in his possession, an older and cooler head than Robert Emmet's might well have been misled into the expectation of nineteen counties rising if the signal could only be given from Dublin Castle. If the blow could be withheld till August, there was every reason to expect a French invasion of England, which would drain away all the regular army, and leave the people merely the militia and the volunteers to contend against. But all the Dublin arrangements exploded in the melancholy *emeute* of the 23rd of July, 1803, in which the Chief-Justice, Lord Kilwarden, passing through the disturbed quarter of the city at the time, was cruelly murdered; for which, and for his cause, Emmet suffered death on the same spot on the 20th of September following. For the same cause, the equally pure-minded and chivalrous Thomas Russell was executed at Downpatrick; Kearney, Roche, Redmond and Howley also suffered death at Dublin; Alien, Putnam, McCabe, and Dowdall escaped to France, where the former became an officer of rank in the army of Napoleon; Michael Dwyer, who Lad surrendered on condition of being allowed to emigrate to' North America, died in exile in Australia, in 1825. Others of Emmet's known or suspected friends, after undergoing two, three, and even four years' imprisonment, were finally discharged without trial. Mr. Long, his generous banker, and James Hope, his faithful emissary, were both permitted to end; their days in Ireland.

The trial of Robert Emmet, from the wonderful death-speech delivered at it, is perfectly well known. But in justice to a man of genius equal if not superior to his own--an Irishman, whose memory is national property, as well as Emmet's, it must here be observed, that the latter never delivered, and had no justification to deliver the vulgar diatribe against Plunkett, his prosecutor, now constantly printed in the common and incorrect versions of that speech. Plunkett, as Attorney-General, in 1803, had no option but to prosecute for the crown; he was a politician of a totally different school from that of Emmet; he shared all Burke and Grattan's horror of French revolutionary principles. In the fervour of his accusatory oration he may have gone too far; he may have, and in reading it now, it is clear to us that he did press too hard upon the prisoner in the dock. He might have performed his awful office with more sorrow and less vehemence, for there was no doubt about Ms jury. But withal, he gave no fair grounds for any such retort as is falsely attributed to Emmet, the very style of which proves its falsity. It is now well known that the apostrophe in the death-speech, commencing "you viper," alleged to have been addressed to Plunkett, was the interpolation many years afterwards of that literary Ishmaelite--Walter Cox of the *Hibernian Magazine*,--who through such base means endeavoured to aim a blow at Plunkett's reputation. The personal reputation of the younger Emmet, the least known to his countrymen of all the United Irish leaders, except by the crowning act of his death, is safe beyond the reach of calumny, or party zeal, or time's changes. It is embalmed in the verse of Moore and Southey, and the precious prose of Washington Irvine. Men of genius in England and America have done honour to his memory; in the annals of his own country his name deserves to stand with those youthful chiefs, equally renowned, and equally ready to seal their patriotism with their blood--Sir Cahir O'Doherty and Hugh Roe O'Donnell.

CHAPTER II.

ADMINISTRATION OF LORD HARDWICKE (1801 TO 1806), AND OF THE DUKE OF BEDFORD (1806 TO 1808).

During the five years in which Lord Hardwicke was Viceroy of Ireland, the *habeas corpus* remained suspended, and the Insurrection Act continued in force. These were the years in which the power of Napoleon made the most astonishing strides; the years in which he remodelled the German Empire, placed on his head the iron crown of Lombardy, on his sister's that of Etruria, and on his brother's that of Holland; when the Consulate gave place to the Empire, and Dukedoms and Principalities were freely distributed among the marshals of the Grand Army. During all these years, Napoleon harassed England with menaces of invasion, and excited Ireland with corresponding hopes of intervention. The more far-seeing United Irishmen, however, had so little faith in these demonstrations that Emmet and McNevin emigrated to the United States, leaving behind them in the ranks of the French Army, those of their compatriots who, either from habit or preference, had become attached to a military life. It must however be borne in mind, for it is essential to the understanding of England's policy towards Ireland, in the first twelve or fourteen years after the Union, that the wild hope of a French invasion never forsook the hearts of a large portion of the Irish people, so long as Napoleon Buonaparte continued at the head of the government of France. During the whole of that period the British government were kept in constant apprehension for Ireland; under this feeling they kept up and increased the local militia; strengthened garrisons, and replenished magazines; constructed a chain of Martello towers round the entire coast, and maintained in full rigour the Insurrection Act. They refused, indeed, to the Munster magistrates in 1803, and subsequently, the power of summary convictions which they possessed in '98; but they sent special Commissions of their own into the suspected counties, who sentenced to death with as little remorse as if they had been so many hydrophobic dogs. Ten, twelve, and even twenty capital executions was no uncommon result of a single sitting of one of those murderous commissions, over which Lord Norbury presided; but it must be added that there were other judges, who observed not only the decencies of everyday life, but who interpreted the law in mercy as well as in justice. They were a minority, it is true, but there were some such, nevertheless.

The session of the Imperial Parliament of 1803-'4, was chiefly remarkable for its war speeches and war budget. In Ireland 50,000 men of the regular militia were under arms and under pay; 70,000 volunteers were enrolled, battalioned, and ready to be called out in case of emergency, to which it was proposed to add 25,000 sea-fencibles. General Fox, who it was alleged had neglected taking proper precaution at the time of Robert Emmet's *emeute*, was replaced by Lord Cathcart, as Commander-in-Chief. The *public* reports at least of this officer, were highly laudatory of the discipline and conduct of the Irish militia.

In May, 1804, Mr. Pitt returned to power, as Chancellor of the Exchequer and Prime Minister, when the whole Pitt policy towards Ireland, France, and America, was of course resumed; a policy which continued to be acted on during the short remainder of the life of its celebrated author.

The year 1805 may be called the first year of the revival of public spirit and public opinion after the Union. In that year Grattan had allowed himself to be persuaded by Fox, into entering the Imperial Parliament, and his old friend Lord Fitzwilliam found a constituency for him, in his Yorkshire borough of Malton. About the same time, Pitt, or his colleagues, induced Plunkett to enter the same great assembly, providing him with a constituency at Midhurst, in Sussex. But they did not succeed--if they ever attempted--to match Plunkett with Grattan. Those great men were warm and close friends in the Imperial as they had been in the Irish Parliament; very dissimilar in their genius, they were both decided anti-Jacobins; both strenuous advocates of the Catholic claims, and both proud and fond of their original country. Grattan had more poetry, and Plunkett more science; but the heart of the man of colder exterior opened and swelled out, in one of the noblest tributes ever paid by one great orator to another, when Plunkett introduced in 1821, in the

Imperial Parliament, his allusion to his illustrious friend, then recently deceased.

Preparatory to the meeting of Parliament in 1805, the members of the old Catholic Committee, who had not met for any such purpose for several years, assembled in Dublin, and prepared a petition which they authorized their chairman, Lord Fingall, to place in such hands as he might choose, for presentation in both Houses. His lordship on reaching London waited on Mr. Pitt, and entreated him to take charge of the petition; but he found that the Prime Minister had promised the King one thing and the Catholics another, and, therefore, declined acceding to his request. He then gave the petition into the charge of Lord Grenville and Mr. Fox, and by them the subject was brought accordingly before the Lords and Commons. This debate in the Commons was remarkable in many respects, but most of all for Grattan's *debut*. A lively curiosity to hear one of whom so much had been said in his own country, pervaded the whole House, as Grattan rose. His grotesque little figure, his eccentric action, and his strangely cadenced sentences rather surprised than attracted attention, but as he warmed with the march of ideas, men of both parties warmed to the genial and enlarged philosophy, embodied in the interfused rhetoric and logic of the orator; Pitt was seen to beat time with his hand to every curiously proportioned period, and at length both sides of the House broke into hearty acknowledgments of the genius of the new member for Malton. But as yet their cheers were not followed by their votes; the division against going into Committee was 336 to 124.

In sustaining Fox's motion, Sir John Cox Hippesley had suggested "the Veto" as a safeguard against the encroachments of Rome, which the Irish bishops would not be disposed to refuse. Archbishop Troy, and Dr. Moylan, Bishop of Cork, gave considerable praise to this speech, and partly at their request it was published in pamphlet form. This brought up directly a discussion among the Catholics, which lasted until 1810, was renewed in 1813, and not finally set at rest till the passage of the bill of 1829, without any such safeguard. Sir John C. Hippesley had modelled his proposal, he said, on the liberties of the Gallican Church. "Her privileges," he added, "depended on two prominent maxims: 1st. That the Pope had no authority to order or interfere in anything in which the civil rights of the kingdom were concerned. 2nd. That notwithstanding the Pope's supremacy was acknowledged in cases purely spiritual, yet, in other respects, his power was limited by the decrees of the ancient councils of the realm." The Irish Church, therefore, was to be similarly administered, to obviate the objections of the opponents of complete civil emancipation.

In February, 1806, on the death of Pitt, Mr. Fox came into power, with an uncertain majority and a powerful opposition. In April, the Duke of Bedford arrived, as Viceroy, at Dublin, and the Catholics presented, through Mr. Keogh, a mild address, expressive of their hopes that "the glorious development" of their emancipation would be reserved for the new government. The Duke returned an evasive answer in public, but privately, both at Dublin and London, the Catholics were assured that, as soon as the new Premier could convert the King--as soon as he was in a position to act--he would make their cause his own. No doubt Fox, who had great nobleness of soul, intended to do so; but on the 13th of September of the same year, he followed his great rival, Pitt, to the vaults of Westminster Abbey. A few months only had intervened between the death of the rivals.

Lords Grey and Grenville, during the next recess, having formed a new administration, instructed their Irish Secretary, Mr. Elliot, to put himself in communication with the Catholics, in relation to a measure making them eligible to naval and military offices. The Catholics accepted this proposal with pleasure, but at the opening of the session of 1807, in a deputation to the Irish government, again urged the question of complete emancipation. The bill in relation to the army and navy had, originally, the King's acquiescence; but early in March, after it had passed the Commons, George III. changed his mind--if the expression may be used of him --at that time. He declared he had not considered it at first so important as he afterwards found it; he intimated that it could not receive his sanction; he went farther --he required a written pledge from Lords Grey and Grenville never again to bring forward such a measure, "nor ever to propose anything connected with the Catholic question." This unconstitutional pledge they refused to give, hurried the bill into law, and resigned. Mr. Spencer Perceval was then sent for, and what was called "the No-Popery Cabinet," in which Mr. Canning and Lord Castlereagh were the principal Secretaries of State, was formed. Thus, for the second time in six years, had the Catholic question made and unmade cabinets.

The Catholics were a good deal dispirited in 1805, by the overwhelming majority by which their petition of that year was refused to be referred to a committee.

In 1806, they contented themselves with simply addressing the Duke of Bedford, on his arrival at Dublin. In 1807, the "No-Popery Cabinet," by the result of the elections, was placed in possession of an immense majority--a fact which excluded all prospects of another change of government. But the Committee were too long accustomed to disappointments to despair even under these reverses. Early in the next session their petition was presented by Mr. Grattan in the Commons, and Lord Donoughmore in the Lords. The majority against going into committee was, in the Commons, 153; in the Lords, 87. Similar motions in the session of 1808, made by the same parties, were rejected by majorities somewhat reduced, and the question, on the whole, might be said to have recovered some of its former vantage ground, in despite of the bitter, pertinacious resistance of Mr. Perceval, in the one House, and the Duke of Portland, in the other.

The short-lived administration of Mr. Fox, though it was said to include "all the talents," had been full of nothing but disappointment to his Irish supporters. The Duke of Bedford was, indeed, a great improvement on Lord Hardwicke, and Mr. Ponsonby on Lord Redesdale, as Chancellor, and the liberation of the political prisoners confined since 1803 did honour to the new administration. But there the measures of justice so credulously expected, both as to persons and interests, ended. Curran, whose professional claims to advancement were far beyond those of dozens of men who had been, during the past ten years, lifted over his head, was neglected, and very naturally dissatisfied; Grattan, never well adapted for a courtier, could not obtain even minor appointments for his oldest and staunchest adherents; while the Catholics found their Whig friends, now that they were in office, as anxious to exact the hard conditions of the Veto as Castlereagh himself.

In truth, the Catholic body at this period, and for a few years subsequently, was deplorably disorganized. The young generation of Catholic lawyers who had grown up since the Relief Act of '93 threw the profession open to them, were men of another stamp from the old generation of Catholic merchants, who had grown up under the Relief Act of 1778. In the ten years before the Union, the Catholic middle class was headed by men of business; in the period we have now reached, their principal spokesmen came from "the Four Courts." John Keogh, the ablest, wisest and firmest of the former generation, was now passing into the decline of life, was frequently absent from the Committee, and when present, frequently overruled by younger and more ardent men. In 1808, his absence, from illness, was regretted by Mr. O'Connell in an eloquent speech addressed to the Committee on the necessity of united action and incessant petitions. "Had he been present," said the young barrister, "his powers of reasoning would have frightened away the captious objections" to that course, "and the Catholics of Ireland would again have to thank their old and useful servant for the preservation of their honour and the support of their interests." It was a strange anomaly, and one which continued for some years longer, that the statesmen of the Catholic body should be all Protestants. A more generous or tolerant spirit than Grattan's never existed; a clearer or more fearless intellect than Plunkett's was not to be found; nobler and more disinterested friends than Ponsonby, Curran, Burroughs and Wallace, no people ever had; but still they were friends from without; men of another religion, or of no particular religion, advising and guiding an eminently religious people in their struggle for religious liberty. This could not always last; it was not natural, it was not desirable that it should last, though some years more were to pass away before Catholic Emancipation was to be accomplished by the union, the energy and the strategy of the Catholics themselves.

CHAPTER III.

ADMINISTRATION OF THE DUKE OF RICHMOND (1807 TO 1813).

Charles, fourth Duke of Richmond, succeeded the Duke of Bedford, as Viceroy, in April, 1807, with Lord Manners as Lord Chancellor, John Foster, Chancellor of the Exchequer--for the separate exchequer of Ireland continued to exist till 1820--and Sir Arthur Wellesley as Chief Secretary. Of these names, the two last were already familiar to their countrymen, in connection with the history of their own Parliament; but the new Chief Secretary had lately returned home covered with Indian laurels, and full of the promise of other honours and victories to come.

The spirit of this administration was repressive, anti-Catholic and high Tory. To maintain and strengthen British power, to keep the Catholics quiet, to get possession of the Irish representation and convert it into a means of support for the Tory party in England, these were the leading objects of the seven years' administration of the Duke of Richmond. Long afterwards, when the Chief Secretary of 1807 had become "the most high, mighty and noble prince," whom all England and nearly all Europe delighted to honour, he defended the Irish administration of which he had formed a part, for its habitual use of corrupt means and influence, in arguments which do more credit to his frankness than his morality. He had "to turn the moral weakness of individuals to good account," such was his argument. He stoutly denied that "the whole nation is, or ever was corrupt;" but as "almost every man of mark has his price," the Chief Secretary was obliged to use corrupt influences "to command a majority in favour of order;" however the particular kinds of influence employed might go against his grain, he had, as he contended, no other alternative but to employ them.

With the exception of a two months' campaign in Denmark --July to September, 1807--Sir Arthur Wellesley continued to fill the office of Chief Secretary, until his departure for the Peninsula, in July, 1808. Even then he was expressly requested to retain the nominal office, with power to appoint a deputy, and receive meanwhile the very handsome salary of 8,000 pounds sterling a year. In the wonderful military events, in which during the next seven years Sir Arthur was to play a leading part, the comparatively unimportant particulars of his Irish Secretariate have been long since forgotten. We have already described the general spirit of that administration: it is only just to add, that the dispassionate and resolute secretary, though he never shrank from his share of the jobbery done daily at the Castle, repressed with as much firmness the over-zeal of those he calls "red-hot Protestants," as he showed in resisting, at that period, what he considered the unconstitutional pretensions of the Catholics. An instance of the impartiality to which he was capable of rising, when influenced by partisans or religious prejudices, is afforded by his letter dissuading the Wexford yeomanry from celebrating the anniversary of the battle of Vinegar Hill. He regarded such a celebration as certain "to exasperate party spirit," and "to hurt the feelings of others;" he, therefore, in the name of the Lord-Lieutenant, strongly discouraged it, and the intention was accordingly abandoned. It is to be regretted that the same judicious rule was not at the same tune enforced by government as to the celebration of the much more obsolete and much more invidious anniversaries of Aughrim and the Boyne.

The general election which followed the death of Fox, in November, 1806, was the first great trial of political strength under the Union. As was right and proper, Mr. Grattan, no longer indebted for a seat to an English patron, however liberal, was returned at the head of the poll for the city of Dublin. His associate, however, the banker, La Touche, was defeated; the second member elect being Mr. Robert Shaw, the Orange candidate. The Catholic electors to a man, under the vigorous prompting of John Keogh and his friends, polled their votes for their Protestant advocate; they did more, they subscribed the sum of 4,000 pounds sterling to pay the expenses of the contest, but this sum Mrs. Grattan induced the treasurer to return to the subscribers. Ever watchful for her husband's honour, that admirable woman, as ardent a patriot as himself, refused the generous tender of the Catholics of Dublin. Although his several elections had cost Mr. Grattan above 54,000 pounds--more than the whole national grant of 1782--she would not, in this case, that any one else should bear the cost of his last triumph in the widowed capital of his own country.

The great issue tried in this election of 1807, in those of 1812, 1818, and 1826, was still the Catholic question. All other Irish, and most other imperial domestic questions were subordinate to this. In one shape or another, it came up in every session of Parliament. It entered into the calculations of every statesman of every party; it continued to make and unmake cabinets; in the press and in every society, it was the principal topic of discussion. While tracing, therefore, its progress, from year to year, we do but follow the main stream of national history; all other branches come back again to this centre, or exhaust themselves in secondary and forgotten results.

The Catholics themselves, deprived in Ireland of a Parliament on which they could act directly, were driven more and more Into permanent association, as the only means of operating a change in the Imperial legislature. The value of a legal, popular, systematic, and continuous combination of "the people" acting within the law, by means of meetings, resolutions, correspondence, and petitions, was not made suddenly, nor by all the party interested, at one and the same time. On the minds of the more sagacious, however, an impression, favourable to such organized action, grew deeper year by year, and at last settled into a certainty which was justified by success.

In May, 1809, the Catholic Committee had been reconstructed, and its numbers enlarged. In a series of resolutions it was agreed that the Catholic lords, the surviving delegates of 1793, the committee which managed the petitions of 1805 and 1807, and such persons "as shall distinctly appear to them to possess the confidence of the Catholic body," do form henceforth the General Committee. It was proposed by O'Connell, to avoid "the Convention Act," "that the noblemen and gentlemen aforesaid are not representatives of the Catholic body, or any portion thereof." The Committee were authorized to collect funds for defraying expenses; a Treasurer was chosen, and a permanent Secretary, Mr. Edward Hay, the historian of the Wexford rebellion--an active and intelligent officer. The new Committee acted with great judgment in 1810, but in 1811 Lord Fingal and his friends projected a General Assembly of the leading Catholics, contrary to the Convention Act, and to the resolution just cited. O'Connell was opposed to this proposition; yet the assembly met, and were dispersed by the authorities. The Chairman, Lord Fingal, and Drs. Sheridan and Kirwan, Secretaries, were arrested. Lord Fingal, however, was not prosecuted, but the Secretaries were, and one of them expiated by two years' imprisonment his violation of the act. To get rid of the very pretext of illegality, the Catholic Committee dissolved, but only to reappear under a less vulnerable form, as "the Catholic Board."

It is from the year 1810 that we must date the rise, among the Catholics themselves, of a distinctive line of policy, suited to the circumstances of the present century, and the first appearance of a group of public men, capable of maintaining and enforcing that policy. Not that the ancient leaders of that body were found deficient, in former times, either in foresight or determination; but new times called for new men; the Irish Catholics were now to seek their emancipation from the imperial government; new tactics and new combinations were necessary to success; and, in brief, instead of being liberated from their bonds at the good will and pleasure of benevolent Protestants, it was now to be tested whether they were capable of contributing to their own emancipation,--whether they were willing and able to assist their friends and to punish their enemies.

Though the Irish Catholics could not legally meet in convention any more than their Protestant fellow-countrymen, there was nothing to prevent them assembling voluntarily, from every part of the kingdom, without claim to delegation. With whom the happy idea of "the aggregate meetings" originated is not certainly known, but to O'Connell and the younger set of leading spirits this was a machinery capable of being worked with good effect. No longer confined to a select Committee, composed mainly of a few aged and cautious, though distinguished persons, the fearless "agitators," as they now began to be called, stood face to face with the body of the people themselves. The disused theatre in Fishamble Street was their habitual place of meeting in Dublin, and there, in 1811 and 1812, the orators met to criticise the conduct of the Duke of Richmond--to denounce Mr. Wellesley Pole--to attack Secretaries of State and Prime Ministers--to return thanks to Lords Grey and Grenville for refusing to give the unconstitutional anti-Catholic pledge required by the King, and to memorial the Prince Regent. From those meetings, especially in the year 1812, the leadership of O'Connell must be dated. After seven years of wearisome probation, after enduring seven years the envy and the calumny of many who, as they were his fellow-labourers, should have been his friends; after demonstrating for seven years that his judgment and his courage were equal to his eloquence, the successful Kerry barrister, then in his thirty-seventh year, was at length generally recognized as "the counsellor" of his co-religionists --as the veritable "Man of the People." Dangers, delays and difficulties lay thick and dark in the future, but from the year, when in Dublin, Cork and Limerick, the voice of the famous advocate was recognized as the voice of the Catholics of Ireland, their cause was taken out of the category of merely ministerial measures, and exhibited in its true light as a great national contest, entered into by the people themselves for complete civil and religious freedom.

Sir Arthur Wellesley had been succeeded in 1810 in the Secretaryship by his brother, Mr. Wellesley Pole, who chiefly signalized his administration by a circular against conventions, and the prosecution of Sheridan and Kirwan, in 1811. He was in turn succeeded by a much more able and memorable person--*Mr*., afterwards Sir Robert Peel. The names of Peel and Wellington come thus into juxtaposition in Irish politics in 1812, as they will be found hi juxtaposition on the same subject twenty and thirty years later.

Early in the session of 1812, Mr. Perceval, the Premier, had been assassinated in the lobby of the House of Commons, by Bellingham, and a new political crisis was precipitated on the country. In the government which followed, Lord Liverpool became the chief, with Castlereagh and Canning as members of his administration. In the general election which followed, Mr. Grattan was again returned for Dublin, and Mr. Plunkett was elected for Trinity College, but Mr. Curran was defeated at Newry, and Mr. Christopher Hely Hutchinson, the liberal candidate, at Cork. Upon the whole, however, the result was favourable to the Catholic cause, and the question was certain to have several additional Irish supporters in the new House of Commons.

In the administrative changes that followed, Mr. Peel, though only in his twenty-fourth year, was appointed to the important post of Chief Secretary, The son of the first baronet of the name--this youthful statesman had first been elected for Cashel, almost as soon as he came of age, in 1809. He continued Chief Secretary for six years, from the twenty-fourth to the thirtieth year of his age. He distinguished himself in the House of Commons almost as soon as he entered it, and the predictions of his future premiership were not, even then, confined to members of his own family. No English statesman, since the death of William Pitt, has wielded so great a power in Irish affairs as Sir Robert Peel, and it is, therefore, important to consider, under what influence, and by what maxims he regulated his public conduct during the time he filled the most important administrative office in that country.

Sir Robert Peel brought to the Irish government, notwithstanding his Oxford education and the advantages of foreign travel which he had enjoyed, prejudices the most illiberal, on the subject of all others on which a statesman should be most free from prejudice--religion. An anti-Catholic of the school of Mr. Perceval and Lord Eldon, he at once constituted himself the principal opponent of Grattan's annual motion in favour of Catholic Emancipation. That older men, born in the evil time, should be bigots and defenders of the Penal Code, was hardly wonderful, but a young statesman, exhibiting at that late day, such studied and active hostility to so large a body of his fellow subjects, naturally drew upon his head the execrations of all those whose enfranchisement he so stubbornly resisted. Even his great abilities were most absurdly denied, under this passionate feeling of wrong and injustice. His Constabulary and his Stipendiary Magistracy were resisted, ridiculed, and denounced, as outrages on the liberty of the subject, and assaults on the independence of the bench. The term *Peeler* became synonymous with spy, informer, and traitor, and the Chief Secretary was detested not only for the illiberal sentiments he had expressed, but for the machinery of order he had established. After half a century's experience, we may safely say, that the Irish Constabulary have shown themselves to be a most valuable police, and as little deserving of popular ill-will as any such body can ever expect to be, but they were judged very differently during the Secretaryship of their founder; for, at that time, being new and intrusive, they may, no doubt, have deserved many of the hard and bitter things which were generally said of them.

The first session of the new Parliament in the year 1813-- the last of the Duke of Richmond's Viceroyalty--was remarkable for the most important debate which had yet arisen on the Catholic question. In the previous year, a motion of Canning's, in favour of "a final and conciliatory adjustment," which was carried by an unexpected majority of 235 to 106, encouraged Grattan to prepare a detailed Emancipation Bill, instead of making his usual annual motion of referring the Catholic petitions to the consideration of the Committee. This bill recited the establishment of the Protestant succession to the crown, and the establishment of the Protestant religion in the State. It then proceeded to provide that Roman Catholics might sit and vote in Parliament; might hold all offices, civil and military, except the offices of Chancellor or Keeper of the Great Seal in England, or Lord-Lieutenant, Lord Deputy, or Chancellor of Ireland; another section threw open to Roman Catholics all lay corporations, while a proviso excluded them either from holding or bestowing benefices in the Established Church. Such was the Emancipation Act of 1813, proposed by Grattan; an act far less comprehensive than that introduced by the same statesman in 1795, into the Parliament of Ireland, but still, in many of its provisions, a long stride in advance.

Restricted and conditioned as this measure was, it still did not meet the objections of the opponents of the question, in giving the crown a Veto in the appointment of the bishops. Sir John Hippesley's pernicious suggestion--reviving a very old traditional policy--was embodied by Canning in one set of amendments, and by Castlereagh in another. Canning's amendments, as summarised by the eminent Catholic jurist, Charles Butler, were to this effect:--

"He first appointed a certain number of Commissioners, who were to profess the Catholic religion, and to be lay peers of Great Britain or Scotland, possessing a freehold estate of one thousand pounds a year; to be filled up, from time to time, by his Majesty, his heirs, or successors. The Commissioners were to take an oath for the faithful discharge of their office, and the observance of secrecy in all matters not thereby required to be disclosed, with power to appoint a Secretary with salary (proposed to be five hundred pounds a year), payable out of the consolidated fund. The Secretary was to take an oath similar to that of the Commissioners.

"It was then provided, that every person elected to the discharge of Roman Catholic episcopal functions in Great Britain or Scotland should, previously to the discharge of his office, notify his then election to the Secretary; that the Secretary should notify it to the Commissioners, and they to the Privy Council, with a certificate 'that they did not know or believe anything of the person nominated, which tended to impeach his loyalty or peaceable conduct;' unless they had knowledge of the contrary, in which case they should refuse their certificate. Persons obtaining such a certificate were rendered capable of exercising episcopal functions within the United Kingdom; if they exercised them without a certificate, they were to be considered guilty of a misdemeanor, and liable to be sent out of the kingdom.

"Similar provisions respecting Ireland were then introduced."

"The second set of clauses," says Mr. Butler, "was suggested by Lord Castlereagh, and provided that the Commissioners under the preceding clauses--with the addition, as to Great Britain, of the Lord Chancellor, or Lord Keeper, or first Commissioner of the Great Seal for the time being, and of one of his Majesty's principal Secretaries of State, being a Protestant, or such other Protestant member of his Privy Council as his Majesty should appoint--and with a similar addition in respect to Ireland--and with the further addition, as to Great Britain, of the person then exercising episcopal functions among the Catholics in London--and, in respect to Ireland, of the titular Roman Catholic Archbishops of Armagh and Dublin,--should be Commissioners for the purposes thereinafter mentioned.

"The Commissioners thus appointed were to take an oath for the discharge of their office, and observance of secrecy, similar to the former, and employ the same Secretary, and three of them were to form a quorum.

"The bill then provided, that subjects of his Majesty, receiving any bull, dispensation, or other instrument, from the See of Rome, or any person in foreign parts, acting under the authority of that See, should, within six weeks, send a copy of it, signed with his name, to the Secretary of the Commissioners, who should transmit the same to them.

"But with a proviso, that if the person receiving the same should deliver to the Secretary of the Commission, within the time before prescribed, a writing under his hand, certifying the fact of his having received such a bull, dispensation, or other instrument, and accompanying his certificate with an oath, declaring that 'it related, wholly and exclusively, to spiritual concerns, and that it did not contain, or refer to, any matter or thing which did or could, directly or indirectly, affect or interfere with the duty and allegiance which he owed to his Majesty's sacred person and government, or with the temporal, civil, or social rights, properties, or duties of any other of his Majesty's subjects, then the Commissioners were, in their discretion, to receive such certificate and oath, in lieu of the copy of the bull, dispensation, or other instrument.

"Persons conforming to these provisions were to be exempted from all pains and penalties, to which they would be liable under the existing statutes; otherwise, they were to be deemed guilty of a high misdemeanor; and in lieu of the pains and penalties, under the former statutes, be liable to be sent out of the kingdom.

"The third set of clauses provided that, within a time to be specified, the Commissioners were to meet and appoint their Secretary, and give notice of it to his Majesty's principal Secretaries of State in Great Britain and Ireland; and the provisions of the act were to be in force from that time."

On the second reading, in May, the Committee of Parliament, on motion of the Speaker, then on the floor, struck out the clause enabling Catholics "to sit and vote in either House of Parliament," by a majority of four votes: 251 against 247. Mr. Ponsonby immediately rose, and, observing that, as "the bill without the clause," was unworthy both of the Catholics and its authors, he moved the chairman do leave the chair. The committee rose, without a division, and the Emancipation Bill of 1813 was abandoned.

Unhappily, the contest in relation to the Veto, which had originated in the House of Commons, was extended to the Catholic body at large. Several of the noblemen, members of the board, were not averse to granting some such power as was claimed to the crown; some of the professional class, more anxious to be emancipated than particular as to the means, favoured the same view. The bishops at the time of the Union, were known to have entertained the idea, and Sir John Hippesley had published their letters, which certainly did not discourage his proposal. But the second order of the clergy, the immense majority of the laity, and all the new prelates, called to preside over vacant sees, in the first decade of the century, were strongly opposed to any such connexion with the head of the State. Of this party, Mr. O'Connell was the uncompromising organ, and, perhaps, it was his course on this very subject of the Veto, more than anything else, which established his pretensions to be considered the leader of the Catholic body. Under the prompting of the majority, the Catholic prelates met and passed a resolution declaring that they could not accept the bill of 1813 as a satisfactory settlement. This resolution they formally communicated to the Catholic Board, who voted them, on O'Connell's motion, enthusiastic thanks. The minority of the Board were silent rather than satisfied, and their dissatisfaction was shown rather by their absence from the Board meetings than by open opposition.

Mr. O'Connell's position, from this period forward, may be best understood from the tone in which he was spoken of in the debates of Parliament. At the beginning of the session of 1815, we find the Chief Secretary (Mr. Peel) stating that he "possesses more influence than any other person" with the Irish Catholics, and that no meeting of that body was considered complete unless a vote of thanks to Mr. O'Connell was among the resolutions.

CHAPTER IV.

O'CONNELL'S LEADERSHIP--1813 TO 1821.

While the Veto controversy was carried into the press and the Parliamentary debates, the extraordinary events of the last years of Napoleon's reign became of such extreme interest as to cast into the shade all questions of domestic policy. The Parliamentary fortunes of the Catholic question varied with the fortunes of the war, and the remoteness of external danger. Thus, in 1815, Sir Henry Parnell's motion for a committee was rejected by a majority of 228 to 147; in 1816, on Mr. Grattan's similar motion, the vote was 172 to 141; in 1817, Mr. Grattan was again defeated by 245 to 221; in this session an act exempting officers in the army and navy from forswearing Transubstantiation passed and became law. The internal condition of the Catholic body, both in England and Ireland, during all those years, was far from enviable. In England there were Cisalpine and Ultramontane factions; in Ireland, Vetoists and anti-Vetoists. The learned and amiable Charles Butler--among jurists, the ornament of his order, was fiercely opposed to the no less learned Dr. Milner, author of "The End of Controversy," and "Letters to a Prebendary." In Ireland, a very young barrister, who had hardly seen the second anniversary of his majority, electrified the aggregate meetings with a new Franco-Irish order of eloquence, naturally enough employed in the maintenance of Gallican ideas of church government. This was Richard Lalor Shiel, the author of two or three successful tragedies, and the man, next to O'Connell, who wielded the largest tribunitian power over the Irish populace during the whole of the subsequent agitation. Educated at Stoneyhurst, he imbibed from refugee professors French idioms and a French standard of taste, while, strangely enough, O'Connell, to whom he was at first opposed, and of whom he became afterwards the first lieutenant, educated in France by British refugees, acquired the cumbrous English style of the Douay Bible and the Rheims Testament. The contrast between the two men was every way extreme; physically, mentally, and politically; but it is pleasant to know that their differences never degenerated into distrust, envy or malice; that, in fact, Daniel O'Connell had throughout all his after life no more steadfast personal friend than Richard Lalor Shiel.

In the progress of the Catholic agitation, the next memorable incident was O'Connell's direct attack on the Prince Regent. That powerful personage, the *de facto* Sovereign of the realm, had long amused the Irish Catholics with promises and pledges of being favourable to their cause. At an aggregate meeting, in June, 1812, Mr. O'Connell maintained that there were four distinct pledges of this description in existence: 1. One given in 1806, through the Duke of Bedford, then Lord-Lieutenant, to induce the Catholics to withhold their petitions for a time. 2. Another given the same year in the Prince's name by Mr. Ponsonby, then Chancellor. 3. A pledge given to Lord Kenmare, *in writing*, when at Cheltenham. 4. A verbal pledge given to Lord Fingal, in the presence of Lords Clifford and Petre, and reduced to writing and signed by these three noblemen, soon after quitting the Prince's presence. Over the meeting at which this indictment was preferred, Lord Fingal presided, and the celebrated "witchery" resolutions, referring to the influence then exercised on the Prince by Lady Hertford, were proposed by his lordship's son, Lord Killeen. It may, therefore, be fairly assumed, that the existence of the fourth pledge was proved, the first and second were never denied, and as to the third--that given to Lord Kenmare--the only correction ever made was, that the Prince's message was delivered verbally, by his Private Secretary, Colonel McMahon, and not in writing. Lord Kenmare, who died in the autumn of 1812, could not be induced, from a motive of delicacy, to reduce his recollection of this message to writing, but he never denied that he had received it, and O'Connell, therefore, during the following years, always held the Prince accountable for this, as for his other promises. Much difference of opinion arose as to the wisdom of attacking a person in the position of the Prince; but O'Connell, fully persuaded of the utter worthlessness of the declarations made in that quarter, decided for himself that the bold course was the wise course. The effect already was various. The English Whigs, the Prince's early and constant friends, who had followed him to lengths that honour could hardly sanction, and who had experienced his hollow-heartedness when lately called to govern during his father's illness; they, of course, were not sorry to see him held up to odium in Ireland, as a dishonoured gentleman and a false friend. The Irish Whigs, of whom Lord Moira and Mr. Ponsonby were the leaders, and to whom Mr. Grattan might be said to be attached rather than to belong, saw the rupture with regret, but considered it inevitable. Among "the Prince's friends" the attacks upon him in the Dublin meetings were regarded as little short of treason; while by himself, it is well known the "witchery" resolutions of 1812 were neither forgotten nor forgiven.

The political position of the Holy See, at this period, was such as to induce and enable an indirect English influence to be exercised, through that channel, upon the Irish Catholic movement. Pope Pius VII., a prisoner in France, had delegated to several persons at Rome certain vicarious powers, to be exercised in his name, in case of necessity; of these, more than one had followed him into exile, so that the position of his representative devolved at length upon Monsignor Quarrantotti, who, early in 1814, addressed a rescript to Dr. Poynter, vicar-apostolic of the London district, commendatory of the Bill of 1813, including the Veto, and the Ecclesiastical Commission proposed by Canning and Castlereagh. Against these dangerous concessions, as they considered them, the Irish Catholics despatched their remonstrances to Rome, through the agency of the celebrated Wexford Franciscan, Father Richard Hayes; but this clergyman, having spoken with too great freedom, was arrested, and suffered several months' confinement in the Eternal City. A subsequent embassy of Dr. Murray, coadjutor to the Archbishop of Dublin, on behalf of his brother prelates, was attended with no greater advantage, though the envoy himself was more properly treated. On his return to Ireland, at a meeting held to hear his report, several strong resolutions were unanimously adopted, of which the spirit may be judged from the following--the concluding one of the series--"Though we sincerely venerate the supreme Pontiff as visible head of the Church, we do not conceive that our apprehensions for the safety of the Roman Catholic Church in Ireland can or ought to be removed by any determination of His Holiness, adopted or intended to be adopted, not only without our concurrence, but in direct opposition to our repeated resolutions and the very energetic memorial presented on our behalf, and so ably supported by our Deputy, the Most Reverend Dr. Murray; who, in that quality, was more competent to inform His Holiness of the real state and interests of the Roman Catholic Church in Ireland than any other with whom he is said to have consulted."

The resolutions were transmitted to Rome, signed by the two Archbishops present, by Dr. Everard, the coadjutor of the Archbishop of Cashel, by Dr. Murray, the coadjutor of the Archbishop of Dublin, by the Bishops of Meath, Cloyne, Clonfert, Kerry, Waterford, Derry, Achonry, Killala, Killaloe, Kilmore, Ferns, Limerick, Elphin, Cork, Down and Conor, Ossory, Raphoe, Clogher, Dromore, Kildare and Leighlin, Ardagh, and the Warden of Galway. Dr. Murray, and Dr. Murphy, Bishop of Cork, were commissioned to carry this new remonstrance to Rome, and the greatest anxiety was felt for the result of their mission.

A strange result of this new *embroglio* in the Catholic cause was, that it put the people on the defensive for their religious liberties, not so much against England as against Home. The unlucky Italian Monsignor who had volunteered his sanction of the Veto, fared scarcely better at the popular gatherings than Lord Castlereagh, or Mr. Peel. "Monsieur Forty-eight," as he was nicknamed, in reference to some strange story of his ancestor taking his name from a lucky lottery ticket of that number, was declared to be no better than a common Orangeman, and if the bitter denunciations uttered against him, on the Liffey and the Shannon, had only been translated into Italian, the courtly Prelate must have been exceedingly amazed at the democratic fury of a Catholic population, as orthodox as himself, but much more jealous of State interference with things spiritual. The second order of the clergy were hardly behind the laity, in the fervour of their opposition to the rescript of 1814. Then--entire body, secular and regular, residing in and about Dublin, published a very strong protest against it, headed by Dr. Blake, afterwards Bishop of Dromore, in which it was denounced as "pregnant with mischief" and entirely "non-obligatory upon the Catholic Church in Ireland." The several ecclesiastical provinces followed up these declarations with a surprising unanimity, and although a Vetoistical address to His Holiness was despatched by the Cisalpine club in England, the Irish ideas of Church government triumphed at Rome. Drs. Murray and Milner were received with his habitual kindness by Pius VII.; the illustrious Cardinal Gonsalvi was appointed by the Pope to draw up an explanatory rescript, and Monsignor Quarrantotti was removed from his official position. The firmness manifested at that critical period by the Irish church has since been acknowledged with many encomiums by all the successors of Pope Pius VII.

The Irish government under the new Viceroy, Lord Whitworth (the former ambassador to Napoleon), conceiving that the time had come, in the summer of 1814, to suppress the Catholic Board, a proclamation forbidding his Majesty's subjects to attend future meetings of that body issued from Dublin Castle, on the 3rd of June. The leaders of the body, after consultation at Mr. O'Connell's residence, decided to bow to this proclamation and to meet no more as a Board; but this did not prevent them, in the following winter, from holding a new series of Aggregate meetings, far more formidable, in some respects, than the deliberative meetings which had been suppressed. In the vigorous and somewhat aggressive tone taken at these meetings, Lord Fingal, the chief of the Catholic peerage, did not concur, and he accordingly withdrew for some years from the agitation, Mr. Shiel, the Bellews, Mr. Ball, Mr. Wyse of Waterford, and a few others, following his example. With O'Connell remained the O'Conor Don, Messrs. Finlay and Lidwell (Protestants), Purcell O'Gorman, and other popular persons. But the cause sustained a heavy blow in the temporary retirement of Lord Fingal and his friends, and an attempt to form a "Catholic Association," in 1815, without their co-operation, signally failed.

During the next five years, the fortunes of the great Irish question fluctuated with the exigencies of Imperial parties. The second American war had closed, if not gloriously, at least without considerable loss to England; Napoleon had exchanged Elba for St. Helena: Wellington was the Achilles of the Empire, and Castlereagh its Ulysses. Yet it was not in the nature of those free Islanders, the danger and pressure of foreign war removed, to remain always indifferent to the two great questions of domestic policy--Catholic Emancipation and Parliamentary Reform. In the session of 1816, a motion of Sir John Newport's to inquire into the state of Ireland, was successfully resisted by Sir Robert Peel, but the condition and state of public feeling in England could not be as well ignored by a Parliament sitting in London. In returning from the opening of the Houses in January, 1817, the Regent was hooted in the street, and his carriage riddled with stones. A reward of 1,000 pounds, issued for the apprehension of the ringleaders, only gave additional *eclat* to the fact, without leading to the apprehension of the assailants.

The personal unpopularity of the Regent seems to have increased, in proportion as death removed from him all those who stood nearest to the throne. In November, 1817, his oldest child, the Princess Charlotte, married to Leopold, since King of Belgium, died in childbed; in 1818, the aged Queen Charlotte died; in January, 1820, the old King, in the eighty-second year of his age, departed this life. Immediately afterwards the former Princess of Wales, long separated from her profligate husband, returned from the Continent to claim her rightful position as Queen Consort. The disgraceful accusations brought against her, the trial before the House of Lords which followed, the courage and eloquence of her counsel, Brougham and Denman, the eagerness with which the people made her cause their own, are all well remembered events, and all beside the purpose of this history. The unfortunate lady died after a short illness, on the 7th of August, 1821; the same month in which Ms Majesty--George IV. --departed on that Irish journey, so satirized in the undying verse of Moore and Byron.

Two other deaths, far more affecting than any among the mortalities of royalty, marked the period at which we have arrived. These were the death of Curran in 1817, and the death of Grattan, in 1820.

Curran, after his failure to be returned for Newry, in 1812, had never again attempted public life. He remained in his office of Master of the Rolls, but his health began to fail sensibly. During the summers of 1816 and '17, he sought for recreation in Scotland, England and France, but the charm which travel could not give--the charm of a cheerful spirit--was wanting. In October, 1817, his friend, Charles Phillips, was suddenly called to his bed-side at Brompton, near London, and found him with one side of his face and body paralyzed cold. "And this was all," says his friend, "that remained of Curran--the light of society--the glory of the forum-- the Fabricius of the senate--the idol of his country." Yes! even to less than this, was he soon to sink. On the evening of the 14th of October, he expired, in the 68th year of his age, leaving a public reputation as free from blemish as ever did any man who had acted a leading part, in times like those through which he had passed. He was interred in London, but twenty years afterwards, the committee of the Glasnevin Cemetery, near Dublin, obtained permission of his representatives to remove his ashes to their grounds, where they now finally repose. A tomb modelled from the tomb of Scipio covers the grave, bearing the simple but sufficient inscription--CURRAN. Thus was fulfilled the words he had uttered long before--"The last duties will be paid by that country on which they are devolved; nor will it be for charity that a little earth will be given to my bones. Tenderly will those duties be paid, as the debt of well-earned affection, and of gratitude not ashamed of her tears."

Grattan's last days were characteristic of his whole life. As the session of 1820 progressed, though suffering from his last struggle with disease, he was stirred by an irresistible desire to make his way to London, and present once more the petition of the Catholics. Since the defeat of his Relief Bill of 1813, there had been some estrangement between him and the more advanced section of the agitators, headed by O'Connell. This he was anxious, perhaps, to heal or to overcome. He thought, moreover, that even if he should die in the effort, it would be, as he said himself, "a good end." Amid--

"The trees which a nation had given, and which bowed   As if each brought a new civic crown to his head,"

he consulted with the Catholic delegates early in May. O'Connell was the spokesman, and the scene may yet be rendered immortal by some great national artist. All present felt that the aged patriot was dying, but still he would go once more to London, to fall, as he said, "at his post." In leaving Ireland he gave to his oldest friends directions for his funeral--that he might be buried in the little churchyard of Moyanna, on the estate the people gave him in 1782! He reached London, by slow stages, at the end of May, and proposed to be in his place in the House on the 4th of June. But this gratification was not permitted him: on the morning of the 4th, at six o'clock, he called his son to his bed-side, and ordered him to bring him a paper containing his last political opinions. "Add to it," he said, with all his old love of antithesis, "that I die with a love of liberty in my heart, and this declaration in favour of my country, in my hand."

So worthily ended the mortal career of Henry Grattan. He was interred by the side of his old friend, Charles James Pox, in Westminster Abbey; the mourners included the highest imperial statesmen, and the Catholic orphan children; his eulogium was pronounced in the House of Commons by William Conyngham Plunkett, and in the Irish capital by Daniel O'Connell.

CHAPTER V.

RETROSPECT OF THE STATE OF RELIGION AND LEARNING DURING THE REIGN OF GEORGE III.

Before relating the decisive events in the contest for Catholic Emancipation, which marked the reign of George IV. we may be permitted to cast a glance backward over the religious and secular state of Ireland, during the sixty years' reign of George III.

The relative position of the great religious denominations underwent a slow but important revolution during this long reign. In the last days of George II., a Chief-Justice was bold enough to declare that "the laws did not presume a Papist to exist in the kingdom;" but under the sway of his successor, though much against that successor's will, they advanced from one constitutional victory to another, till they stood, in the person of the Earl Marshal, on the very steps of the throne. In the towns and cities, the Catholic laity, once admitted to commerce and the professions, rose rapidly to wealth and honour. A Dublin Papist was at the head of the wine trade; another was the wealthiest grazier in the kingdom; a third, at Cork, was the largest provision merchant. With wealth came social ambition, and the heirs of these enfranchised merchants were by a natural consequence the judges and legislators of the next generation.

The ecclesiastical organization of Ireland, as described in 1800 by the bishops in answer to queries of the Chief Secretary, was simple and inexpensive. The four archbishops and twenty bishops, were sustained by having certain parishes attached to their cathedrals, ***in commendam***: other ***Cathedraticum*** there seems to have been none. Armagh had then 350 parish priests, Tuam 206, Cashel 314, and Dublin 156: in all 1126. The number of curates or coadjutors was at least equal to that of the parish priests; while of regulars then returned the number did not exceed 450. This large body of religious--24 prelates, nearly 3,000 clergy--exclusive of female religious--were then, and have ever since been, sustained by the voluntary contributions of the laity, paid chiefly at the two great festivals of Christmas and Easter, or by customary offerings made at the close of the ceremonies of marriages, baptisms, and death. Though the income of some of the churches was considerable, in the great majority of cases the amount received barely sufficed to fulfil the injunction of St. Patrick to his disciples, that "the lamp should take but that wherewith it was fed."

The Presbyterian clergy, though in some respects more dependent on their congregations than the Catholics were, did not always, nor in all cases, depend on the voluntary principle for their maintenance. The Irish Supply Bill contained an annual item before the Union of 7,700 pounds for the Antrim Synod, and some other dissenting bodies. The ***Regium Donum*** was not, indeed, general; but that it might be made so, was one of the inducements held out to many of that clergy to secure their countenance for the Legislative Union.

The Established Church continued, of course, to monopolize University honours, and to enjoy its princely revenues and all political advantages. Trinity College continued annually to farm its 200,000 acres at a rental averaging 100,000 pounds sterling. Its wealth, and the uses to which it is put, are thus described by a recent writer: "Some of Trinity's senior fellows enjoy higher incomes than Cabinet ministers; many of her tutors have revenues above those of cardinals; and junior fellows, of a few days' standing, frequently decline some of her thirty-one church livings with benefices which would shame the poverty of scores of continental, not to say Irish, Catholic archbishops. Even eminent judges hold her professorships; some of her chairs are vacated for the Episcopal bench only; and majors and field officers would acquire increased pay by being promoted to the rank of head porter, first menial, in Trinity College. Apart from her princely fellowships and professorships, her seventy Foundation, and sixteen non-Foundation Scholarships, her thirty Sizarships, and her fourteen valuable Studentships, she has at her disposal an aggregate, by bequests, benefactions, and various endowments, of 117 permanent exhibitions, amounting to upwards of 2,000 pounds per annum." The splendour of the highest Protestant dignitaries may be inferred from what has been said formerly of the Bishop of Derry, of the Era of Independence. The state maintained by the chief bishop--Primate Robinson, who ruled Armagh from 1765 to 1795--is thus described by Mr. Cumberland in his *Memoirs*. "I accompanied him," says Cumberland, "on Sunday forenoon to his cathedral. We went in his chariot of six horses attended by three footmen behind, whilst my wife and daughters, with Sir William Robinson, the primate's elder brother, followed in my father's coach, which he lent me for the journey. At our approach the great western door was thrown open, and my friend (in person one of the finest men that could be seen) entered, like another Archbishop Laud, in high prelatical state, preceded by his officers and ministers of the church, conducting him in files to the robing chamber, and back again to the throne. It may well be conceived with what invidious eyes the barely tolerated Papists of the city of Saint Patrick must have looked on all this pageantry, and their feelings were no doubt those in some degree of all their co-religionists throughout the kingdom."

The Irish Establishment, during the reign of George III., numbered among its prelates and clergy many able and amiable men. At the period of the Union, the two most distinguished were Dr. O'Beirne, Bishop of Meath, an ex-priest, and Dr. Young, Bishop of Clonfert, a former fellow of Trinity College. As a Bible scholar, Dr. Young ranked deservedly high, but as a variously accomplished writer, Dr. O'Beirne was the first man of his order. His political papers, though occasionally disfigured with the bigotry natural to an apostate, are full of a vigorous sagacity; his contributions to general literature, such as his paper on *Tanistry*, in Vallency's *Collectanea*, show how much greater things still he was capable of. It is not a little striking that the most eminent bishop, as well as the most celebrated Anglican preacher of that age, in Ireland (Dean Kirwan), should both have been ordained as Catholic priests.

The national literature which we have noted a century earlier, as changing gradually its tongue, was now mainly, indeed we might almost say solely, expressed in English. It is true the songs of "Carolan the Blind," were sung in Gaelic by the Longford firesides, where the author of "the Deserted Village" listened to their exquisite melody, moulding his young ear to a sense of harmony full as exquisite; but the glory of the Gaelic muse was past. He, too, unpromising as was his exterior, was to be one of the bright harbingers of another great era of Hiberno-English literature. When, within two generations, out of the same exceedingly restricted class of educated Irishmen and women, we count the names of Goldsmith, Samuel Madden, Arthur Murphy, Henry Brooke, Charles Macklin, Sheridan, Burke, Edmund Malone, Maria Edgeworth, Lady Morgan, "Psyche" Tighe, and Thomas Moore, it is impossible not to entertain a very high opinion of the mental resources of that population, if only they were fairly wrought and kindly valued by the world.

One memorable incident of literary history--the Ossianic outbreak of 1760--aided powerfully though indirectly in the revival of the study of the ancient Celtic history of Scotland and Ireland. Something was done then, by the Royal Irish Academy, to meet that storm of Anglo-Norman incredulity and indignation; much more has been done since, to place the original records of the Three Kingdoms on a sound critical basis. The dogmatism of the unbelievers in the existence of a genuine body of ancient Celtic literature has been rebuked; and the folly of the theorists who, upon imaginary grounds, constructed pretentious systems, has been exposed. The exact originals of MacPherson's odes have not been found, after a century of research, and may be given up, as non-existent; but the better opinion seems now to be, by those who have studied the fragments of undoubted antiquity attributed to the son of the warrior Fion, that whatever the modern translator may have invented, he certainly did not invent Ossian.

To the stage, within the same range of time, Ireland gave some celebrated names: Quinn, Barry, Sheridan, Mrs. Woffington, Mrs. Jordan, and Miss O'Neill; and to painting, one pre-eminent name--the eccentric, honest, and original, James Barry.

But of all the arts, that in which the Irish of the Georgian era won the highest and most various triumphs was the art of Oratory, What is now usually spoken of as "the Irish School of Eloquence," may be considered to have taken its rise from the growth of the Patriot party in Parliament, in the last years of George II. Every contemporary account agrees in placing its first great name--Anthony Malone--on the same level with Chatham and Mansfield. There were great men before Malone, as before Agamemnon; such as Sir Toby Butler, Baron Rice, and Patrick Darcy; but he was the first of our later succession of masters. After him came Flood and John Hely Hutchinson; then Grattan and Curran; then Plunkett and Bushe; then O'Connell and Shiel. In England, at the same time, Burke, Barre, Sheridan, and Sir Phillip Francis, upheld the reputation of Irish oratory; a reputation generously acknowledged by all parties, as it was illustrated in the ranks of all. The Tories, within our own recollection, applauded as heartily the Irish wit and fervour of Canning, Croker, and North, as the Whigs did the exhibition of similar qualities in their Emancipation allies.

Nothing can be less correct, than to pronounce judgment on the Irish School, either of praise or blame, in sweeping general terms. Though a certain family resemblance may be traced among its great masters, no two of them will be found nearly alike. There are no echoes, no servile imitators, among them. In vigorous argumentation and severe simplicity, Plunkett resembled Flood, but the temperament of the two men--and Oratory is nearly as much a matter of temperament as of intellect--was widely different. Flood's movement was dramatic, while Plunkett's was mathematical. In structural arrangement, Shiel, occasionally--very occasionally--reminds us of Grattan; but if he has not the wonderful condensation of thought, neither has he the frequent antithetical abuses of that great orator. Burke and Sheridan are as distinguishable as any other two of their contemporaries; Curran stands alone; O'Connell never had a model, and never had an imitator who rose above mimicry. Every combination of powers, every description of excellence, and every variety of style and character, may be found among the masterpieces of this great school. Of their works many will live for ever. Most of Burke's, many of Grattan's, and one or two of Curran's have reached us in such preservation as promises immortality. Selections from Flood, Sheridan, Canning, Plunkett and O'Connell will survive; Shiel will be more fortunate for he was more artistic, and more watchful of his own fame. His exquisite finish will do, for him, what the higher efforts of men, more indifferent to the audience of posterity, will have forfeited for them.

It is to be observed, farther, that the inspiration of all these men was drawn from the very hearts of the people among whom they grew. With one or two exceptions, sons of humble peasants, of actors, of at most middle class men, they were true, through every change of personal position, to the general interests of the people--to the common weal. From generous thoughts and a lofty scorn of falsehood, fanaticism and tyranny, they took their inspiration; and as they were true to human nature, so will mankind, through successive ages, dwell fondly on their works and guard lovingly their tombs.

CHAPTER VI.

THE IRISH ABROAD, DURING THE REIGN OF GEORGE III.

The fond tenacity with which the large numbers of the Irish people who have established themselves in foreign states have always clung to their native country; the active sympathy they have personally shown for their relatives at home; the repeated efforts they have made to assist the Irish in Ireland, in all their public undertakings, requires that, as an element in O'Connell's final and successful struggle for Catholic Emancipation, we should take a summary view of the position of "the Irish abroad."

While the emigrants of that country to America naturally pursued the paths of peace, those who, from choice or necessity, found their way to the European Continent, were, with few exceptions, employed mainly in two departments--war and diplomacy. An Irish Abbe, liked the celebrated preacher, McCarthy--or an Irish merchant firm, such as the house of the same name at Bordeaux, might be met with, but most of those who attained any distinction did so by the sword or the pen, in the field or the cabinet.

In France, under the revolutionary governments from '91 to '99, the Irish were, with their old-world notions of God and the Devil, wholly out of place; but under the Consulate and the Empire, they rose to many employments of the second class, and a few of the very first. From the ranks of the expatriated of '98, Buonaparte promoted Arthur O'Conor and William Corbet to the rank of General; Ware, Alien, Byrne, the younger Tone, and Keating, to that of Colonel. As individuals, the Emperor was certainly a benefactor to many Irishmen; but, as a nation, it was one of then: most foolish delusions, to expect in him a deliverer. On the restoration of the Bourbons, the Irish officers who had acquired distinction under Napoleon adhered generally to his fortunes, and tendered their resignations; in their place, a new group of Franco-Irish descendants of the old Brigades-men, began to show themselves in the *salons* of Paris, and the Bureaus of the Ministers. The last swords drawn for "the legitimate branch" in '91, was by Count Dillon and his friend Count Wall; their last defender, in 1830, was General Wall, of the same family.

Though the Irish in France, especially those resident at Paris, exercised the greatest influence in favour of their original country--an influence which met all travelled Englishmen, wherever the French language was understood--their compatriots in Spain and Austria had also contributed their share to range Continental opinion on the side of Ireland. Three times, during the century, Spain was represented at London by men of Irish birth, or Irish origin. The British merchant who found Alexander O'Reilly Governor of Cadiz, or the diplomatist who met him as Spanish ambassador, at the Court of Louis XVI., could hardly look with uninstructed eyes, upon the lot of his humblest namesake in Cavan. This family, indeed, produced a succession of eminent men, both in Spain and Austria. "It is strange," observed Napoleon to those around him, on his second entry into Vienna, in 1809, "that on each occasion--in November, 1805, as this day --on arriving in the Austrian capital, I find myself in treaty and in intercourse with the respectable Count O'Reilly." Napoleon had other reasons for remembering this officer; it was his dragoon regiment which saved the remnant of the Austrians, at Austerlitz. In the Austrian army list at that period, when she was the ally of England, there were above forty Irish names, from the grading of Colonel up to that of Field-Marshal. In almost every field of the Peninsula, Wellington and Anglesea learned the value of George the Second's imprecation on the Penal Code, which deprived him of such soldiers as conquered at Fontenoy. It cannot be doubted that even the constant repetition of the names of the Blakes, O'Donnells, and Sarsfields, in the bulletins sent home to England, tended to enforce reflections of that description on the statesmen and the nation, and to inspirit and sustain the struggling Catholics. A powerful argument for throwing open the British army and navy to men of all religions, was drawn from these foreign experiences; and, if such men were worthy to hold military commissions, why not also to sit in Parliament, and on the Bench?

The fortunes of the Irish in America, though less brilliant for the few, were more advantageous as to the many. They were, during the war of the revolution, and the war of 1812, a very considerable element in the American republic. It was a violent exaggeration to say, as Lord Mountjoy did in moving for the repeal of the Penal laws, "that England lost America by Ireland;" but it is very certain that Washington placed great weight on the active aid of the gallant Pennsylvania, Maryland, and Southern Irish troops, and the sturdy Scotch-Irish of New Hampshire. Franklin, in his visit to Ireland, before the rupture, and Jefferson in his correspondence, always enumerates the Irish, as one element of reliance, in the contest between the Colonies and the Empire.

In the immediate cause of the war of 1812, this people were peculiarly interested. If the doctrines of "the right of search" and "once a subject always a subject," were to prevail, no Irish emigrant could hope to become --or having become, could hope to enjoy the protection of--an American citizen. It was, therefore, natural that men of that origin should take a deep interest in the war, and it seems something more than a fortuitous circumstance, when we find in the chairman of the Senatorial Committee of 1812, which authorized the President to raise the necessary levies--an Irish emigrant, John Smilie, and in the Secretary-at-war, who acted under the powers thus granted, the son of an Irish emigrant, John Caldwell Calhoun. On the Canadian frontier, during the war which followed, we find in posts of importance, Brady, Mullany, McComb, Croghan and Reilly; on the lakes, Commodore McDonough, and on the ocean, Commodores Shaw and Stewart--all Irish. On the Mississippi, another son of Irish emigrant parents, with his favourite lieutenants, Carroll, Coffee, and Butler, brought the war to a close by their brilliant defence of New Orleans. The moral of that victory was not lost upon England; the life of Andrew Jackson, with a dedication "to the People of Ireland" was published at London and Dublin, by the most generally popular writer of that day--William Cobbett.

In the cause of South American independence, the Irish under O'Higgins and McKenna in Chili, and under Bolivar and San Martin in Colombia and Peru, were largely engaged, and honourably distinguished. Colonel O'Conor, nephew to Arthur, was San Martin's chief of the staff; General Devereux, with his Irish legion, rendered distinguished services to Bolivar and Don Bernardo. O'Higgins was hailed as the Liberator of Chili. During that long ten years' struggle, which ended with the evacuation of Carraccas in 1823, Irish names are conspicuous on almost every field of action. Bolivar's generous heart was warmly attached to persons of that nation. "The doctor who constantly attends him," says the English General, Miller, "is Dr. Moore, an Irishman, who had followed the Liberator from Venezuela to Peru. He is a man of great skill in his profession, and devotedly attached to the person of the Liberator. Bolivar's first aide-de-camp, Colonel O'Leary, is a nephew of the celebrated Father O'Leary. In 1818, he embarked, at the age of seventeen, in the cause of South American independence, in which he has served with high distinction, having been present at almost every general action fought in Colombia, and has received several wounds. He has been often employed on diplomatic missions, and in charges of great responsibility, in which he has always acquitted himself with great ability."

That these achievements of the Irish abroad produced a favourable influence on the situation of the Irish at home, we know from many collateral sources; we know it also from the fact, that when O'Connell succeeded in founding a really national organization, subscriptions and words of encouragement poured in on him, not only from France, Spain, and Austria, but from North and South America, not only from the Irish residents in those countries, but from their native inhabitants--soldiers and statesmen--of the first consideration. The services and virtues of her distinguished children in foreign climes, stood to the mother country instead of treaties and alliances.

CHAPTER VII.

O'CONNELL'S LEADERSHIP--THE CATHOLIC ASSOCIATION-- 1821 TO 1826.

At the beginning of the year 1821, O'Connell, during the intervals of Ms laborious occupations in court and on circuit, addressed a series of stirring letters to "the People of Ireland," remarkable as containing some of the best and most trenchant of his political writings. His object was to induce the postponement of the annual petition for Emancipation, and the substitution instead of a general agitation for Parliamentary reform, in conjunction with the English reformers. Against this conclusion--which he ridiculed "as the fashion for January, 1821"--Mr. Shiel published a bitter, clever, rhetorical reply, to which O'Connell at once sent forth a severe and rather contemptuous rejoinder. Shiel was quite content to have Mr. Plunkett continue Grattan's annual motion, with all its "conditions" and "securities." O'Connell declared he had no hope in petitions except from a reformed Parliament, and he, therefore, was opposed to such motions altogether, especially as put by Mr. Plunkett, and the other advocates of a Veto. Another session was lost in this controversy, and when Parliament rose, it was announced that George IV. was coming to Ireland "on a mission of Conciliation."

On this announcement, Mr. O'Connell advised that the Catholics should take advantage of his Majesty's presence to assemble and consider the state of their affairs; but a protest against "connecting in any manner the King's visit with Catholic affairs," was circulated by Lords Fingal, Netterville, Gormanstown, and Killeen, Messrs. Baggott, Shiel, Wyse, and other Commoners. O'Connell yielded, as he often did, for the sake of unanimity. The King's visit led to many meetings and arrangements, in some of which his advice was taken, while in others he was outvoted or overruled. Nothing could exceed the patience he exhibited at this period of his life, when his natural impetuous temperament was still far from being subdued by the frosts of age.

Many liberal Protestants at this period--the King's brief visit--were so moved with admiration of the judicious and proper conduct of the Catholic leaders, that a new but short-lived organization, called "the Conciliation Committee," was formed. The ultra Orange zealots, however, were not to be restrained even by the presence of the Sovereign for whom they professed so much devotion. In the midst of the preparations for his landing, they celebrated, with all its offensive accompaniments, the 12th of July, and at the Dublin dinner to the King--though after he had left the room--they gave their charter toast of "the glorious, pious, and immortal memory." The Committee of Conciliation soon dwindled away, and, like the visit of George IV., left no good result behind.

The year 1822 was most remarkable, at its commencement, for the arrival of the Marquis of Wellesley, as Lord-Lieutenant, and at its close, for the assault committed on him in the theatre by the Dublin Orangemen. Though the Marquis had declined to interfere in preventing the annual Orange celebration, he was well known to be friendly to the Catholics; their advocate, Mr. Plunkett, was his Attorney General; and many of their leaders were cordially welcomed at the Castle. These proofs were sufficient for the secret tribunals which sat upon his conduct, and when his Lordship presented himself, on the night of the 14th of December, at the theatre, he was assailed by an organized mob, one of whom flung a heavy piece of wood, and another a quart bottle, towards the state box. Three Orangemen, mechanics, were arrested and tried for the offence, but acquitted on a technical defect of evidence; a general feeling of indignation was excited among all classes in consequence, and it is questionable if Orangeism, in Dublin, ever recovered the disgust occasioned by that dastardly outrage.

The great and fortunate event, however, for the Catholics, was the foundation of their new Association, which was finally resolved upon at an Aggregate Meeting held in "Townsend Street Chapel," on the 10th of May, 1823. This meeting had been called by an imposing requisition signed with singular unanimity by all the principal Catholic gentlemen. Lord Killeen presided. Mr. O'Connell moved the formation of the Association; Sir Thomas Esmonde seconded the motion; Mr. Shiel-

-lately and sincerely reconciled to O'Connell--sustained it. The plan was simple and popular. The Association was to consist of members paying a guinea a year, and associates paying a shilling; a standing committee was to form the government; the regular meetings were to be weekly--every Saturday; and the business to consist of organization, correspondence, public discussions, and petitions. It was, in effect, to be a sort of extern and unauthorized Parliament, acting always within the Constitution, with a view to the modification of the existing laws, by means not prohibited in those laws themselves. It was a design, subtle in conception, but simple in form; a natural design for a lawyer-liberator to form; and for a people strongly prepossessed in his favour to adopt; but one, at the same time, which would require a rare combination of circumstances to sustain for any great length of time, under a leader less expert, inventive, and resolute.

The Parliamentary position of the Catholic question, at the moment of the formation of the Association, had undergone another strange alteration. Lord Castlereagh, having attained the highest honours of the empire, died by his own hand the previous year. Lord Liverpool remained Premier, Lord Eldon Chancellor, Mr. Canning became Foreign Secretary, with Mr. Peel, Home Secretary, the Duke of Wellington continuing Master-General of the Ordnance. To this cabinet, so largely anti-Catholic, the chosen organ of the Irish Catholics, Mr. Plunkett, was necessarily associated as Irish Attorney General. His situation, therefore, was in the session of 1823 one of great difficulty; this Sir Francis Burdett and the radical reformers at once perceived, and in the debates which followed, pressed him unmercifully. They quoted against him his own language denouncing cabinet compromises on so vital a question, in 1813, and to show their indignation, when he rose to reply, they left the House in a body. His speech, as always, was most able, but the House, when he sat down, broke into an uproar of confusion. Party spirit ran exceedingly high; the possibility of advancing the question during the session was doubtful, and a motion to adjourn prevailed. A fortnight later, at the first meeting of the Catholic Association, a very cordial vote of thanks to Plunkett was carried by acclamation.

The new Catholic organization was labouring hard to merit popular favour. Within the year of its organization we find the Saturday meetings engaged with such questions as church rates; secret societies; correspondence with members of both Houses; voting public thanks to Mr. Brougham; the penal laws relating to the rights of sepulture; the purchase of a Catholic cemetery near Dublin; the commutation of tithes; the admission of Catholic freemen into corporations; the extension of the Association into every county in Ireland, and other more incidental subjects. The business-like air of the weekly meetings, at this early period, is remarkable: they were certainly anything but mere occasions for rhetorical display. But though little could be objected against, and so much might be said in favour of the labours of the Association, it was not till nearly twelve months after its organization, when O'Connell proposed and carried his system of monthly penny subscriptions to the "Catholic Rent," that it took a firm and far-reaching hold on the common people, and began to excite the serious apprehensions of the oligarchical factions in Ireland and England.

This bold, and at this time much ridiculed step, infused new life and a system hitherto unknown into the Catholic population. The parish collectors, corresponding directly with Dublin, established a local agency, co-extensive with the kingdom; the smallest contributor felt himself personally embarked in the contest; and the movement became, in consequence, what it had not been before, an eminently popular one. During the next six months the receipts from penny subscriptions exceeded 100 pounds sterling per month, representing 24,000 subscribers; during the next year they averaged above 500 pounds a week, representing nearly half a million enrolled Associates!

With the additional means at the disposal of the Finance Committee of the Association, its power rose rapidly. A morning and an evening journal were at its command in Dublin; many thousands of pounds were expended in defending the people in the courts, and prosecuting their Orange and other enemies. Annual subsidies, of 5,000 pounds each, were voted for the Catholic Poor schools, and the education of missionary priests for America; the expenses of Parliamentary and electioneering agents were also heavy. But for all these purposes "the Catholic Rent," of a penny per month from each associate, was found amply sufficient.

At the close of 1824, the government, really alarmed at the formidable proportions assumed by the agitation, caused criminal informations to be filed against Mr. O'Connell, for an alleged seditious allusion to the example of Bolivar, the liberator of South America; but the Dublin grand jury ignored the bills of indictment founded on these informations. Early in the following session, however, a bill to suppress

"Unlawful Associations in Ireland," was introduced by Mr. Goulburn, who had succeeded Sir Robert Peel as Chief Secretary, and was supported by Plunkett--a confirmed enemy of all extra-legal combinations. It was aimed directly at the Catholic Association, and passed both Houses; but O'Connell found means "to drive," as he said, "a coach and six through it." The existing Association dissolved on the passage of the act; another, called "the *New* Catholic Association," was formed for "charitable and other purposes," and the agitators proceeded with their organization, with one word added to then--title, and immensely additional *eclat* and success.

In Parliament, the measure thus defeated was followed by another, the long-promised Relief Bill. It passed in the Commons in May, accompanied by two clauses, or as they were called, "wings," most unsatisfactory to the Catholic body. One clause disfranchised the whole class of electors known as the "forty-shilling freeholders;" the other provided a scale of state maintenance for the Catholic clergy. A bishop was to have 1,000 pounds per annum; a dean 300 pounds; a parish priest 200 pounds; a curate 60 pounds. This measure was thrown out by the House of Lords, greatly to the satisfaction, at least, of the Irish Catholics. It was during this debate in the Upper House that the Duke of York, presumptive heir to the throne, made what was called his "ether speech"--from his habit of dosing himself with that stimulant on trying occasions. In this speech he declared, that so "help him God," he would never, never consent to acknowledge the claims put forward by the Catholics. Before two years were over, death had removed him to the presence of that Awful Being whose name he had so rashly invoked, and his brother, the Duke of Clarence, assumed his position, as next in succession to the throne.

The Catholic delegates, Lord Killeen, Sir Thomas Esmonde, Lawless, and Shiel, were in London at the time the Duke of York made his memorable declaration. If, on the one hand, they were regarded with dislike amounting to hatred, on the other, they were welcomed with cordiality by all the leaders of the liberal party. The venerable Earl Fitzwilliam emerged from his retirement to do them honour; the gifted and energetic Brougham entertained them with all hospitality; at Norfolk House they were banqueted in the room in which George III. was born: the millionaire-demagogue Burdett, the courtly, liberal Lord Grey, and the flower of the Catholic nobility, were invited to meet them. The delegates were naturally cheered and gratified; they felt, they must have felt, that their cause had a grasp upon Imperial attention, which nothing but concession could ever loosen.

Committees of both Houses, to inquire into the state of Ireland, had sat during a great part of this Session, and among the witnesses were the principal delegates, with Drs. Murray, Curtis, Kelly, and Doyle. The evidence of the latter--the eminent Prelate of Kildare and Leighlin--attracted most attention. His readiness of resource, clearness of statement, and wide range of information, inspired many of his questioners with a feeling of respect, such as they had never before entertained for any of his order. His writings had already made him honourably distinguished among literary men; his examination before the Committees made him equally so among statesmen. From that period he could reckon the Marquises of Anglesea and Wellesley, Lord Lansdowne and Mr. Brougham, among his correspondents and friends, and, what he valued even more, among the friends of his cause. Mr. O'Connell, on the other hand, certainly lost ground in Ireland by his London journey. He had, unquestionably, given his assent to both "wings," in 1825, as he did to the remaining one in 1828, and thereby greatly injured his own popularity. His frank and full recantation of his error, on his return, soon restored him to the favour of the multitude, and enabled him to employ, with the best effect, the enormous influence which he showed he possessed at the general elections of 1826. By him mainly the Beresfords were beaten in Waterford, the Fosters in Louth, and the Leslies in Monaghan. The independence of Limerick city, of Tipperary, Cork, Kilkenny, Longford, and other important constituencies, was secured. The parish machinery of the Association was found invaluable for the purpose of bringing up the electors, and the people's treasury was fortunately able to protect to some extent the fearless voter, who, in despite of his landlord, voted according to the dictates of his own heart.

The effect of these elections on the empire at large was very great. When, early in the following spring, Lord Liverpool, after fifteen years' possession of power, died unexpectedly, George IV. sent for Canning and gave him *carte blanche* to form a cabinet without excepting the question of Emancipation. That high spirited and really liberal statesman associated with himself a ministry, three-fourths of whom were in favour of granting the Catholic claims. This was in the month of April; but to the consternation of those whose hopes were now so justly raised, the gifted Premier held office only four months; his lamented death causing another "crisis," and one more postponement of "the Catholic question."

CHAPTER VIII.

O'CONNELL'S LEADERSHIP--THE CLARE ELECTION--EMANCIPATION OF THE CATHOLICS.

A very little reflection will enable us to judge, even at this day, the magnitude of the contest in which O'Connell was the great popular leader, during the reign of George IV. In Great Britain, a very considerable section of the ancient peerage and gentry, with the Earl Marshal at their head, were to be restored to political existence, by the act of Emancipation; a missionary, and barely tolerated clergy were to be clothed, in their own country, with the commonest rights of British subjects --protection to life and property. In Ireland, seven-eighths of the people, one-third of the gentry, the whole of the Catholic clergy, the numerous and distinguished array of the Catholic bar, and all the Catholic townsmen, taxed but unrepresented in the corporate bodies, were to enter on a new civil and social condition, on the passage of the act. In the colonies, except Canada, where that church was protected by treaty, the change of Imperial policy towards Catholics was to be felt in every relation of life, civil, military, and ecclesiastical, by all persons professing that religion. Some years ago, a bishop of Southern Africa declared, that, until O'Connell's time, it was impossible for Catholics to obtain any consideration from the officials at the Cape of Good Hope. Could there be a more striking illustration of the magnitude of the movement, which, rising in the latitude of Ireland, flung its outermost wave of influence on the shores of the Indian ocean?

The adverse hosts to be encountered in this great contest, included a large majority of the rank and wealth of both kingdoms. The King, who had been a Whig in his youth, had grown into a Tory in his old age; the House of Lords were strongly hostile to the measure, as were also the universities, both in England and Ireland; the Tory party, in and out of Parliament; the Orange organization in Ireland; the civil and military authorities generally, with the great bulk of the rural magistracy and the municipal authorities. The power to overcome this power should be indeed formidable, well organized and wisely directed.

The Lord Lieutenant selected by Mr. Canning, was the Marquis of Anglesea, a frank soldier, as little accustomed to play the politician as any man of his order and distinction could be. He came to Ireland, in many respects the very opposite of Lord Wellesley; no orator certainly, and so far as he had spoken formerly, an enemy rather than a friend to the Catholics. But he had not been three months in office when he began to modify his views; he was the first to prohibit, in Dublin, the annual Orange outrage on the 12th of July, and by subsequent, though slow degrees, he became fully convinced that the Catholic claims could be settled only by Concession. Lord Francis Leveson Gower, afterwards Earl of Ellesmere, accompanied the Marquis as Chief Secretary.

The accession to office of a prime minister friendly to the Catholics, was the signal for a new attempt to raise that "No-Popery" cry which had already given twenty years of political supremacy to Mr. Perceval and Lord Liverpool. In Ireland, this feeling appeared under the guise of what was called "the New Reformation," which, during the summer of 1827, raged with all the proverbial violence of the *odium theologicum* from Cork to Derry. Priests and parsons, laymen and lawyers, took part in this general politico-religious controversy, in which every possible subject of difference between Catholic and Protestant was publicly discussed. Archbishop Magee of Dublin, the Rev. Sir Harcourt Lees, son of a former English placeman at the Castle, and the Rev. Mr. Pope, were the clerical leaders in this crusade; Exeter-Hall sent over to assist them the Honourable and Reverend Baptist Noel, Mr. Wolff, and Captain Gordon, a descendant of the hero of the London riot of 1798. At Derry, Dublin, Carlow, and Cork, the challenged agreed to defend their doctrines. Father Maginn, Maguire, Maher, McSweeney, and some others accepted these challenges; Messrs. O'Connell, Shiel, and other laymen, assisted, and the oral discussion of theological and historical questions became as common as town talk in every Irish community. Whether, in any case, these debates conduced to conversion is doubtful; but they certainly supplied the Catholic laity with a body of facts and arguments very necessary at that time, and which hardly any other occasion could have presented. The Right Rev. Dr. Doyle, however, considered them far from beneficial to the cause of true religion; and though he tolerated a first discussion in his diocese, he positively forbade a second. The Archbishop of Armagh and other prelates issued their mandates to the clergy to refrain from these oral disputes, and the practice fell into disuse.

The notoriety of "the Second Reformation" was chiefly due to the ostentatious patronage of it by the lay chiefs of the Irish oligarchy. Mr. Synge, in Clare, Lord Lorton, and Mr. McClintock at Dundalk, were indefatigable in their evangelizing exertions. The Earl of Roden--to show his entire dependence on the translated Bible--threw all his other books into a fish pond on his estate. Lord Farnham was even more conspicuous in the revival; he spared neither patronage nor writs of ejectment to convert his tenantry. The reports of conversions upon his lordship's estates, and throughout his county, attracted so much notice, that Drs. Curtis, Crolly, Magauran, O'Reilly, and McHale, met on the 9th of December, 1826, at Cavan, to inquire into the facts. They found, while there had been much exaggeration on the part of the reformers, that some hundreds of the peasantry had, by various powerful temptations, been led to change their former religion. The bishops received back some of the converts, and a jubilee established among them completed their reconversion. The Hon. Mr. Noel and Captain Gordon posted to Cavan, with a challenge to discussion for their lordships; of course, their challenge was not accepted. Thomas Moore's inimitable satire was the most effective weapon against such fanatics.

The energetic literature of the Catholic agitation attracted much more attention than its oral polemics. Joined to a bright army of Catholic writers, including Dr. Doyle, Thomas Moore, Thomas Furlong, and Charles Butler, there was the powerful phalanx of the *Edinburgh Review* led by Jeffrey and Sidney Smith, and the English liberal press, headed by William Cobbett. Thomas Campbell, the Poet of Hope, always and everywhere the friend of freedom, threw open his *New Monthly*, to Shiel, and William Henry Curran, whose sketches of the Irish Bar and Bench, of Dublin politics, and the county elections of 1826, will live as long as any periodical papers of the day. The indefatigable Shiel, writing French as fluently as English, contributed besides to the *Gazette de France* a series of papers, which were read with great interest on the Continent. These articles were the precursors of many others, which made the Catholic question at length an European question. An incident quite unimportant in itself, gave additional zest to these French articles. The Duke de Montebello, with two of his friends, Messrs. Duvergier and Thayer, visited Ireland in 1826. Duvergier wrote a series of very interesting letters on the "State of Ireland," which, at the time, went through several editions. At a Catholic meeting at Ballinasloe, the Duke had some compliments paid him, which he gracefully acknowledged, expressing his wishes for the success of their cause. This simple act excited a great deal of criticism in England. The Paris press was roused in consequence, and the French Catholics, becoming more and more interested, voted an address and subscription to the Catholic Association. The Bavarian Catholics followed their example, and similar communications were received from Spain and Italy.

But the movement abroad did not end in Europe. An address from British India contained a contribution of three thousand pounds sterling. From the West Indies and Canada, generous assistance was rendered.

In the United States sympathetic feeling was most active. New York felt almost as much interested in the cause as Dublin. In 1826 and 1827, associations of "Friends of Ireland" were formed at New York, Boston, Washington, Norfolk, Charleston, Augusta, Louisville, and Bardstown. Addresses in English and French were prepared for these societies, chiefly by Dr. McNevin, at New York, and Bishop England, at Charleston. The American, like the French press, became interested in the subject, and eloquent allusions were made to it in Congress. On the 20th of January, 1828, the veteran McNevin wrote to Mr. O'Connell--"Public opinion in America is deep, and strong, and universal, in your behalf. This predilection prevails over the broad bosom of our extensive continent. Associations similar to ours are everywhere starting into existence--in our largest and wealthiest cities--in our hamlets and our villages--in our most remote sections; and at this moment, the propriety of convening, at Washington, delegates of the friends of Ireland, of all the states, is under serious deliberation. A fund will erelong be derived from American patriotism in the United States, which will astonish your haughtiest opponents."

The Parliamentary fortunes of the great question were at the same time brightening. The elections of 1826, had, upon the whole, given a large increase of strength to its advocates. In England and Scotland, under the influence of the "No-Popery" cry, they had lost some ground, but in Ireland they had had an immense triumph. The death of the generous-hearted Canning, hastened as it was by anti-Catholic intrigues, gave a momentary check to the progress of liberal ideas; but they were retarded only to acquire a fresh impulse destined to bear them, in the next few years, farther than they had before advanced in an entire century.

The *ad interim* administration of Lord Goderich gave way, by its own internal discords, in January, 1828, to the Wellington and Peel administration. The Duke was Premier, the Baronet leader of the House of Commons; with Mr. Huskisson, Lord Palmerston, in the cabinet; Lord Anglesea remained as Lord Lieutenant. But this coalition with the friends of Canning was not destined to outlive the session of 1828; the lieutenants of the late Premier were doomed, for some time longer, to suffer for their devotion to his principles.

This session of 1828, is--in the history of religious liberty--the most important and interesting in the annals of the British Parliament. Almost at its opening, the extraordinary spectacle was exhibited of a petition signed by 800,000 Irish Catholics, praying for the repeal of "the Corporation and Test Acts," enacted on the restoration of Charles II., against the non-Conformists. Monster petitions, both for and against the repeal of these acts, as well as for and against Catholic emancipation, soon became of common occurrence. Protestants of all sects petitioned for, but still more petitioned against equal rights for Catholics; while Catholics petitioned for the rights of Protestant dissenters. It is a spectacle to look back upon with admiration and instruction; exhibiting as it does, so much of a truly tolerant spirit in Christians of all creeds, worthy of all honour and imitation.

In April, "the Corporation and Test Acts" were repealed; in May, the Canningites seceded from the Duke's government, and one of the gentlemen brought in to fill a vacant seat in the Cabinet--Mr. Vesey Fitzgerald, member for Clare-- issued his address to his electors, asking a renewal of their confidence. Out of this event grew another, which finally and successfully brought to an issue the century-old Catholic question.

The Catholic Association, on the accession of the Wellington-Peel Cabinet, had publicly pledged itself to oppose every man who would accept office under these statesmen. The memory of both as ex-secretaries--but especially Peel's--was odious in Ireland. When, however, the Duke had sustained, and ensured thereby the passage of the repeal of "the Corporation and Test Acts," Mr. O'Connell, at the suggestion of Lord John Russell the mover of the repeal, endeavoured to get his angry and uncompromising resolution against the Duke's government rescinded. Powerful as he was, however, the Association refused to go with him, and the resolution remained. So it happened that when Mr. Fitzgerald presented himself to the electors of Clare, as the colleague of Peel and Wellington, the Association at once endeavoured to bring out an opposition candidate. They pitched with this view on Major McNamara, a liberal Protestant of the county, at the head of one of its oldest families, and personally popular; but this gentleman, after keeping them several days in suspense, till the time of nomination was close at hand, positively declined to stand against his friend, Mr. Fitzgerald, to the great dismay of the associated Catholics.

In their emergency, an idea, so bold and original, that it was at first received with general incredulity by the external public, was started. It was remembered by Sir David De Roose, a personal friend of O'Connell's, that the late sagacious John Keogh had often declared the Emancipation question would never be brought to an issue till some Catholic member elect stood at the bar of the House of Commons demanding his seat. A trusted few were at first consulted on the daring proposition, that O'Connell himself, in despite of the legal exclusion of all men of his religion, should come forward for Clare. Many were the consultations, and diverse the judgments delivered on this proposal, but at length, on the reception of information from the county itself, which gave strong assurance of success, the hero of the adventure decided for himself. The bold course was again selected as the wise course, and the spirit-stirring address of "the arch-Agitator" to the electors, was at once issued from Dublin. "Your county," he began by saying, "wants a representative. I respectfully solicit your suffrages, to raise me to that station.

"Of my qualification to fill that station, I leave you to judge. The habits of public speaking, and many, many years of public business, render me, perhaps, equally suited with most men to attend to the interests of Ireland in Parliament.

"You will be told I am not qualified to be elected; the assertion, my friends, is untrue. I am qualified to be elected, and to be your representative. It is true that as a Catholic I cannot, and of course never will, take the oaths at present prescribed to members of Parliament; but the authority which created these oaths (the Parliament), can abrogate them: and I entertain a confident hope that, if you elect me, the most bigoted of our enemies will see the necessity of removing from the chosen representative of the people an obstacle which would prevent him from doing his duty to his king and to his country."

This address was followed instantly by the departure of all the most effective agitators to the scene of the great contest. Shiel went down as conducting agent for the candidate; Lawless left his Belfast newspaper, and Father Maguire his Leitrim flock; Messrs. Steele and O'Gorman Mahon, both proprietors in the county, were already in the field, and O'Connell himself soon followed. On the other hand, the leading county families, the O'Briens, McNamaras, Vandeleurs, Fitzgeralds and others, declared for their old favourite, Mr. Fitzgerald. He was personally much liked in the county; the son of a venerable anti-Unionist, the well-remembered Prime Sergeant, and a man besides of superior abilities. The county itself was no easy one to contest; its immense constituency (the 40-shilling freeholders had not yet been abolished), were scattered over a mountain and valley region, more than fifty miles long by above thirty wide. They were almost everywhere to be addressed in both languages--English and Irish--and when the canvass was over, they were still to be brought under the very eyes of the landlords, upon the breath of whose lips their subsistence depended, to vote the overthrow and conquest of those absolute masters. The little county town of Ennis, situated on the river Fergus, about 110 miles south-west of Dublin, was the centre of attraction or of apprehension, and the hills that rise on either side of the little prosaic river soon swarmed with an unwonted population, who had resolved, subsist how they might, to see the election out. It is hardly an exaggeration to say that the eyes of the empire were turned, during those days of June, on the ancient patrimony of King Brian. "I fear the Clare election will end ill," wrote the Viceroy to the leader of the House of Commons. "This business," wrote the Lord Chancellor (Eldon), "must bring the Roman Catholic question to a crisis and a conclusion." "May the God of truth and justice protect and prosper you," was the public invocation for O'Connell's success, by the bishop of Kildare and Leighlin. "It was foreseen," said Sir Robert Peel, long afterwards, "that the Clare election would be the turning point of the Catholic question." In all its aspects, and to all sorts of men, this, then, was no ordinary election, but a national event of the utmost religious and political consequence. Thirty thousand people welcomed O'Connell into Ennis, and universal sobriety and order characterized the proceedings. The troops called out to overawe the peasantry, infected by the prevailing good humour, joined in their cheers. The nomination, the polling, and the declaration, have been described by the graphic pen of Shiel. At the close of the poll the numbers were--O'Connell, 2,057; Fitzgerald, 1,075; so Daniel O'Connell was declared duly elected, amidst the most extraordinary manifestations of popular enthusiasm. Mr. Fitzgerald, who gracefully bowed to the popular verdict, sat down, and wrote his famous despatch to Sir Robert Peel: "All the great interests," he said, "my dear Peel, broke down, and the desertion has been universal. Such a scene as we have had! Such a tremendous prospect as is open before us!"

This "tremendous prospect," disclosed at the hustings of Ennis, was followed up by demonstrations which bore a strongly revolutionary character. Mr. O'Connell, on his return to Dublin, was accompanied by a *levee en masse*, all along the route, of a highly imposing description. Mr. Lawless, on his return to Belfast, was escorted through Meath and Monaghan by a multitude estimated at 100,000 men, whom only the most powerful persuasions of the Catholic clergy, and the appeals of the well-known liberal commander of the district, General Thornton, induced to disperse. Troops from England were ordered over in considerable numbers, but whole companies, composed of Irish Catholics, signalized their landing at Waterford and Dublin by cheers for O'Connell. Reports of the continued hostility of the government suggested desperate councils. Mr. Ford, a Catholic solicitor, openly proposed, in the Association, exclusive dealing and a run on the banks for specie, while Mr. John Claudius Beresford, and other leading Orangemen, publicly predicted a revival of the scenes and results of 1798.

The Clare election was, indeed, decisive; Lord Anglesea, who landed fully resolved to make no terms with those he had regarded from a distance as no better than rebels, became now one of their warmest partisans. His favourite counsellor was Lord Cloncurry, the early friend of Emmet and O'Conor; the true friend to the last of every national interest. For a public letter to Bishop Curtis, towards the close of 1828, in which he advises the Catholics to stand firm, he was immediately recalled from the government; but his former and his actual chief, within three months from the date of his recall, was equally obliged to surrender to the Association. The great duke was, or affected to be, really alarmed for the integrity of the empire, from the menacing aspect of events in Ireland. A call of Parliament was accordingly made for an early day, and, on the 5th of March, Mr. Peel moved a committee of the whole House, to go into a "consideration of the civil disabilities of his Majesty's Roman Catholic subjects." This motion, after two days' debate, was carried by a majority of 188. On the 10th of March the Relief Bill was read for the first time, and passed without opposition, such being the arrangement entered into while in committee. But in five days all the bigotry of the land had been aroused; nine hundred and fifty-seven petitions had already been presented against it; that from the city of London was signed by more than "an hundred thousand freeholders." On the 17th of March it passed to a second reading, and on the 30th to a third, with large majorities in each stage of debate. Out of 320 members who voted on the final reading, 178 were in its favour. On the 31st of March it was carried to the Lords by Mr. Peel, and read a first time; two days later, on the 2nd of April, it was read a second time, on motion of the Duke of Wellington; a bitterly contested debate of three days followed; on the 10th, it was read a third time, and passed by a majority of 104. Three days later the bill received the royal assent, and became law.

The only drawbacks on this--great measure of long-withheld justice, were, that it disfranchised the "forty-shilling freeholders" throughout Ireland, and condemned Mr. O'Connell, by the insertion of the single word "hereafter," to go back to Clare for re-election. In this there was little difficulty for him, but much petty spleen in the framers of the measure.

While the Relief Bill was still under discussion, Mr. O'Connell presented himself, with his counsel, at the bar of the House of Commons, to claim his seat as member for Clare. The pleadings in the case were adjourned from day to day, during the months of March, April, and May. A committee of the House, of which Lord John Russell was Chairman, having been appointed in the meantime to consider the petition of Thomas Mahon and others, against the validity of the election, reported that Mr. O'Connell had been duly elected. On the 15th of May, introduced by Lords Ebrington and Duncannon, the new member entered the House, and advanced to the table to be sworn by the Clerk. On the oath of abjuration being tendered to him, he read over audibly these words--"that the sacrifice of the mass, and the invocation of the blessed Virgin Mary, and other saints, as now practised in the Church of Rome, are impious and idolatrous:" at the subsequent passage, relative to the falsely imputed Catholic "doctrine of the dispensing power" of the Pope, he again read aloud, and paused. Then slightly raising his voice, he bowed, and added, "I decline, Mr. Clerk, to take this oath. Part of it I know to be false; another part I do not believe to be true."

He was subsequently heard at the bar, in his own person, in explanation of his refusal to take the oath, and, according to custom, withdrew. The House then entered into a very animated discussion on the Solicitor General's motion "that Mr. O'Connell, having been returned a member of this House before the passing of the Act for the Relief of the Roman Catholics, he is not entitled to sit or vote in this House unless he first takes the oath of supremacy." For this motion the vote on a division was 190 against 116: majority, 74. So Mr. O'Connell had again to seek the suffrages of the electors of Clare.

A strange, but well authenticated incident, struck with a somewhat superstitious awe both Protestants and Catholics, in a corner of Ireland the most remote from Clare, but not the least interested in the result of its memorable election. A lofty column on the walls of Deny bore the effigy of Bishop Walker, who fell at the Boyne, armed with a sword, typical of his martial inclinations, rather than of his religious calling. Many long years, by day and night, had his sword, sacred to liberty or ascendancy, according to the eyes with which the spectator regarded it, turned its steadfast point to the broad estuary of Lough Foyle. Neither wintry storms nor summer rains had loosened it in the grasp of the warlike churchman's effigy, until, on the 13th day of April, 1829--the day the royal signature was given to the Act of Emancipation --the sword of Walker fell with a prophetic crash upon the ramparts of Derry, and was shattered to pieces. So, we may now say, without bitterness and almost without reproach, so may fall and shiver to pieces, every code, in every land beneath the sun, which impiously attempts to shackle conscience, or endows an exclusive caste with the rights and franchises which belong to an entire People!

End of Volume 2 of 2.

www.bookjungle.com email: sales@bookjungle.com fax: 630-214-0564 mail: Book Jungle PO Box 2226 Champaign, IL 61825

The Codes Of Hammurabi And Moses
W. W. Davies

QTY

The discovery of the Hammurabi Code is one of the greatest achievements of archaeology, and is of paramount interest, not only to the student of the Bible, but also to all those interested in ancient history...

Religion   **ISBN:** *1-59462-338-4*   Pages:132
MSRP $12.95

The Theory of Moral Sentiments
Adam Smith

QTY

This work from 1749. contains original theories of conscience amd moral judgment and it is the foundation for systemof morals.

Philosophy   **ISBN:** *1-59462-777-0*   Pages:536
MSRP $19.95

Jessica's First Prayer
Hesba Stretton

QTY

In a screened and secluded corner of one of the many railway-bridges which span the streets of London there could be seen a few years ago, from five o'clock every morning until half past eight, a tidily set-out coffee-stall, consisting of a trestle and board, upon which stood two large tin cans, with a small fire of charcoal burning under each so as to keep the coffee boiling during the early hours of the morning when the work-people were thronging into the city on their way to their daily toil...

Childrens   **ISBN:** *1-59462-373-2*   Pages:84
MSRP $9.95

My Life and Work
Henry Ford

QTY

Henry Ford revolutionized the world with his implementation of mass production for the Model T automobile. Gain valuable business insight into his life and work with his own auto-biography... "We have only started on our development of our country we have not as yet, with all our talk of wonderful progress, done more than scratch the surface. The progress has been wonderful enough but..."

Biographies/   **ISBN:** *1-59462-198-5*   Pages:300
MSRP $21.95

www.bookjungle.com *email:* sales@bookjungle.com *fax:* 630-214-0564 *mail: Book Jungle PO Box 2226 Champaign, IL 61825*

The Art of Cross-Examination
Francis Wellman

I presume it is the experience of every author, after his first book is published upon an important subject, to be almost overwhelmed with a wealth of ideas and illustrations which could readily have been included in his book, and which to his own mind, at least, seem to make a second edition inevitable. Such certainly was the case with me; and when the first edition had reached its sixth impression in five months, I rejoiced to learn that it seemed to my publishers that the book had met with a sufficiently favorable reception to justify a second and considerably enlarged edition. ..

Reference   ISBN: *1-59462-647-2*   Pages:412   MSRP *$19.95*   QTY

On the Duty of Civil Disobedience
Henry David Thoreau

Thoreau wrote his famous essay, On the Duty of Civil Disobedience, as a protest against an unjust but popular war and the immoral but popular institution of slave-owning. He did more than write—he declined to pay his taxes, and was hauled off to gaol in consequence. Who can say how much this refusal of his hastened the end of the war and of slavery ?

Law   ISBN: *1-59462-747-9*   Pages:48   MSRP *$7.45*   QTY

Dream Psychology Psychoanalysis for Beginners
Sigmund Freud

Sigmund Freud, born Sigismund Schlomo Freud (May 6, 1856 - September 23, 1939), was a Jewish-Austrian neurologist and psychiatrist who co-founded the psychoanalytic school of psychology. Freud is best known for his theories of the unconscious mind, especially involving the mechanism of repression; his redefinition of sexual desire as mobile and directed towards a wide variety of objects; and his therapeutic techniques, especially his understanding of transference in the therapeutic relationship and the presumed value of dreams as sources of insight into unconscious desires.

Psychology   ISBN: *1-59462-905-6*   Pages:196   MSRP *$15.45*   QTY

The Miracle of Right Thought
Orison Swett Marden

Believe with all of your heart that you will do what you were made to do. When the mind has once formed the habit of holding cheerful, happy, prosperous pictures, it will not be easy to form the opposite habit. It does not matter how improbable or how far away this realization may see, or how dark the prospects may be, if we visualize them as best we can, as vividly as possible, hold tenaciously to them and vigorously struggle to attain them, they will gradually become actualized, realized in the life. But a desire, a longing without endeavor, a yearning abandoned or held indifferently will vanish without realization.

Self Help   ISBN: *1-59462-644-8*   Pages:360   MSRP *$25.45*   QTY

www.bookjungle.com email: sales@bookjungle.com fax: 630-214-0564 mail: Book Jungle PO Box 2226 Champaign, IL 61825

QTY

	Title	ISBN	Price
☐	**The Rosicrucian Cosmo-Conception Mystic Christianity** by *Max Heindel*	ISBN: 1-59462-188-8	$38.95
	The Rosicrucian Cosmo-conception is not dogmatic, neither does it appeal to any other authority than the reason of the student. It is: not controversial, but is: sent forth in the, hope that it may help to clear...		New Age/Religion Pages 646
☐	**Abandonment To Divine Providence** by *Jean-Pierre de Caussade*	ISBN: 1-59462-228-0	$25.95
	"The Rev. Jean Pierre de Caussade was one of the most remarkable spiritual writers of the Society of Jesus in France in the 18th Century. His death took place at Toulouse in 1751. His works have gone through many editions and have been republished...		Inspirational/Religion Pages 400
☐	**Mental Chemistry** by *Charles Haanel*	ISBN: 1-59462-192-6	$23.95
	Mental Chemistry allows the change of material conditions by combining and appropriately utilizing the power of the mind. Much like applied chemistry creates something new and unique out of careful combinations of chemicals the mastery of mental chemistry...		New Age Pages 354
☐	**The Letters of Robert Browning and Elizabeth Barret Barrett 1845-1846 vol II** by *Robert Browning* and *Elizabeth Barrett*	ISBN: 1-59462-193-4	$35.95
			Biographies Pages 596
☐	**Gleanings In Genesis (volume I)** by *Arthur W. Pink*	ISBN: 1-59462-130-6	$27.45
	Appropriately has Genesis been termed "the seed plot of the Bible" for in it we have, in germ form, almost all of the great doctrines which are afterwards fully developed in the books of Scripture which follow...		Religion/Inspirational Pages 420
☐	**The Master Key** by *L. W. de Laurence*	ISBN: 1-59462-001-6	$30.95
	In no branch of human knowledge has there been a more lively increase of the spirit of research during the past few years than in the study of Psychology, Concentration and Mental Discipline. The requests for authentic lessons in Thought Control, Mental Discipline and...		New Age/Business Pages 422
☐	**The Lesser Key Of Solomon Goetia** by *L. W. de Laurence*	ISBN: 1-59462-092-X	$9.95
	This translation of the first book of the "Lernegton" which is now for the first time made accessible to students of Talismanic Magic was done, after careful collation and edition, from numerous Ancient Manuscripts in Hebrew, Latin, and French...		New Age/Occult Pages 92
☐	**Rubaiyat Of Omar Khayyam** by *Edward Fitzgerald*	ISBN: 1-59462-332-5	$13.95
	Edward Fitzgerald, whom the world has already learned, in spite of his own efforts to remain within the shadow of anonymity, to look upon as one of the rarest poets of the century, was born at Bredfield, in Suffolk, on the 31st of March, 1809. He was the third son of John Purcell...		Music Pages 172
☐	**Ancient Law** by *Henry Maine*	ISBN: 1-59462-128-4	$29.95
	The chief object of the following pages is to indicate some of the earliest ideas of mankind, as they are reflected in Ancient Law, and to point out the relation of those ideas to modern thought.		Religiom/History Pages 452
☐	**Far-Away Stories** by *William J. Locke*	ISBN: 1-59462-129-2	$19.45
	"Good wine needs no bush, but a collection of mixed vintages does. And this book is just such a collection. Some of the stories I do not want to remain buried for ever in the museum files of dead magazine-numbers an author's not unpardonable vanity..."		Fiction Pages 272
☐	**Life of David Crockett** by *David Crockett*	ISBN: 1-59462-250-7	$27.45
	"Colonel David Crockett was one of the most remarkable men of the times in which he lived. Born in humble life, but gifted with a strong will, an indomitable courage, and unremitting perseverance...		Biographies/New Age Pages 424
☐	**Lip-Reading** by *Edward Nitchie*	ISBN: 1-59462-206-X	$25.95
	Edward B. Nitchie, founder of the New York School for the Hard of Hearing, now the Nitchie School of Lip-Reading, Inc, wrote "LIP-READING Principles and Practice". The development and perfecting of this meritorious work on lip-reading was an undertaking...		How-to Pages 400
☐	**A Handbook of Suggestive Therapeutics, Applied Hypnotism, Psychic Science** by *Henry Munro*	ISBN: 1-59462-214-0	$24.95
			Health/New Age/Health/Self-help Pages 376
☐	**A Doll's House: and Two Other Plays** by *Henrik Ibsen*	ISBN: 1-59462-112-8	$19.95
	Henrik Ibsen created this classic when in revolutionary 1848 Rome. Introducing some striking concepts in playwriting for the realist genre, this play has been studied the world over.		Fiction/Classics/Plays 308
☐	**The Light of Asia** by *sir Edwin Arnold*	ISBN: 1-59462-204-3	$13.95
	In this poetic masterpiece, Edwin Arnold describes the life and teachings of Buddha. The man who was to become known as Buddha to the world was born as Prince Gautama of India but he rejected the worldly riches and abandoned the reigns of power when...		Religion/History/Biographies Pages 170
☐	**The Complete Works of Guy de Maupassant** by *Guy de Maupassant*	ISBN: 1-59462-157-8	$16.95
	"For days and days, nights and nights, I had dreamed of that first kiss which was to consecrate our engagement, and I knew not on what spot I should put my lips..."		Fiction/Classics Pages 240
☐	**The Art of Cross-Examination** by *Francis L. Wellman*	ISBN: 1-59462-309-0	$26.95
	Written by a renowned trial lawyer, Wellman imparts his experience and uses case studies to explain how to use psychology to extract desired information through questioning.		How-to/Science/Reference Pages 408
☐	**Answered or Unanswered?** by *Louisa Vaughan*	ISBN: 1-59462-248-5	$10.95
	Miracles of Faith in China		Religion Pages 112
☐	**The Edinburgh Lectures on Mental Science (1909)** by *Thomas*	ISBN: 1-59462-008-3	$11.95
	This book contains the substance of a course of lectures recently given by the writer in the Queen Street Hall, Edinburgh. Its purpose is to indicate the Natural Principles governing the relation between Mental Action and Material Conditions...		New Age/Psychology Pages 148
☐	**Ayesha** by *H. Rider Haggard*	ISBN: 1-59462-301-5	$24.95
	Verily and indeed it is the unexpected that happens! Probably if there was one person upon the earth from whom the Editor of this, and of a certain previous history, did not expect to hear again...		Classics Pages 380
☐	**Ayala's Angel** by *Anthony Trollope*	ISBN: 1-59462-352-X	$29.95
	The two girls were both pretty, but Lucy who was twenty-one who supposed to be simple and comparatively unattractive, whereas Ayala was credited, as her Bombwhat romantic name might show, with poetic charm and a taste for romance. Ayala when her father died was nineteen...		Fiction Pages 484
☐	**The American Commonwealth** by *James Bryce*	ISBN: 1-59462-286-8	$34.45
	An interpretation of American democratic political theory. It examines political mechanics and society from the perspective of Scotsman James Bryce		Politics Pages 572
☐	**Stories of the Pilgrims** by *Margaret P. Pumphrey*	ISBN: 1-59462-116-0	$17.95
	This book explores pilgrims religious oppression in England as well as their escape to Holland and eventual crossing to America on the Mayflower, and their early days in New England...		History Pages 268

www.bookjungle.com *email: sales@bookjungle.com fax: 630-214-0564 mail: Book Jungle PO Box 2226 Champaign, IL 61825*

QTY

The Fasting Cure *by Sinclair Upton* ISBN: *1-59462-222-1* $13.95
In the Cosmopolitan Magazine for May, 1910, and in the Contemporary Review (London) for April, 1910, I published an article dealing with my experiences in fasting. I have written a great many magazine articles, but never one which attracted so much attention... New Age/Self Help/Health Pages 164

Hebrew Astrology *by Sepharial* ISBN: *1-59462-308-2* $13.45
In these days of advanced thinking it is a matter of common observation that we have left many of the old landmarks behind and that we are now pressing forward to greater heights and to a wider horizon than that which represented the mind-content of our progenitors... Astrology Pages 144

Thought Vibration or The Law of Attraction in the Thought World ISBN: *1-59462-127-6* $12.95
by William Walker Atkinson Psychology/Religion Pages 144

Optimism *by Helen Keller* ISBN: *1-59462-108-X* $15.95
Helen Keller was blind, deaf, and mute since 19 months old, yet famously learned how to overcome these handicaps, communicate with the world, and spread her lectures promoting optimism. An inspiring read for everyone... Biographies/Inspirational Pages 84

Sara Crewe *by Frances Burnett* ISBN: *1-59462-360-0* $9.45
In the first place, Miss Minchin lived in London. Her home was a large, dull, tall one, in a large, dull square, where all the houses were alike, and all the sparrows were alike, and where all the door-knockers made the same heavy sound... Childrens/Classic Pages 88

The Autobiography of Benjamin Franklin *by Benjamin Franklin* ISBN: *1-59462-135-7* $24.95
The Autobiography of Benjamin Franklin has probably been more extensively read than any other American historical work, and no other book of its kind has had such ups and downs of fortune. Franklin lived for many years in England, where he was agent... Biographies/History Pages 332

Name	
Email	
Telephone	
Address	
City, State ZIP	

☐ Credit Card   ☐ Check / Money Order

Credit Card Number	
Expiration Date	
Signature	

Please Mail to: Book Jungle
PO Box 2226
Champaign, IL 61825
or Fax to: 630-214-0564

ORDERING INFORMATION

web: *www.bookjungle.com*
email: *sales@bookjungle.com*
fax: *630-214-0564*
mail: *Book Jungle PO Box 2226 Champaign, IL 61825*
or PayPal *to sales@bookjungle.com*

Please contact us for bulk discounts

DIRECT-ORDER TERMS

20% Discount if You Order Two or More Books
Free Domestic Shipping!
Accepted: Master Card, Visa, Discover, American Express

www.ingramcontent.com/pod-product-compliance
Lightning Source LLC
Chambersburg PA
CBHW081935170426
43202CB00018B/2925